Truckers'
Handbook

Everything a truck driver needs while out on the road

Published in association with **SCANIA** and **TRUCKING** magazine

Contents

How to use this guide

This handbook is the ultimate companion for truck and coach drivers or anyone who lives life on the road.

The first part of the book provides invaluable information for new and experienced drivers alike. It advises on everything from how to operate your vehicle and its equipment to personal driver health and laws applicable to truckers, all presented with clear colour photographs and diagrams. There is also a glossary of slang and technical terms, lists of contact details useful to the driver, dealership addresses and a dictionary in six languages.

The second part of the book reviews in detail the most popular truckers' haunts, truck-friendly filling stations and fuel bunkers in the UK and Ireland. These are shown in an easy-to-read symbol format. Information provided in this section covers everything from canopy height, showers and fuel cards accepted to the price of a cup of tea. All entries can be located on the colour maps at the back of the book, using the site identity code.

Your comments

Extensive research was carried out when compiling information for all the sites listed. However, please be aware that some site details and prices pay have changed since publication. If you have any comments or observations about any site, we'd greatly appreciate it if you could go to www.truckershandbook.co.uk, where you can enter details which will then be noted for the next reprint of the book.

Crawley Crossing Bunker Stop

C H Jones Ltd, Bedford Road
Husbourne Crawley, Bedfordshire MK43 0UT
T 01908 281084

OFF THE A507 From the M1, exit at junction 13 and head south on the A507 towards Woburn. Crawley Crossing is half a mile along on the right.

CREDIT/DEBIT CARDS

FUEL CARDS (see key on page 6)

TRUCK FACILITIES
P *with voucher* £6.00
Voucher value £1.00
Coach parking available, shared with LGV
Quiet area. Fridge lorry area
Ample room for manoeuvring

DRIVER FACILITIES
Showers – 1 unisex (free), washroom, TV
Euros changed/accepted
Truckers' accessories, CB repairs/sales
Takeaway food

SITE COMMENTS/INFORMATION
This site is number 180 in the keyfuels book

Truckers' shop 08:30-17:00 Mon-Thurs, 08:00-15:00 Fri. Café 07:00-22:00 Mon-Thurs, 07:00-08:00 Fri
Bunker fuel, showers and other on-site facilities 24 hours

T482

---

1. Full name and address of site

2. Comprehensive directions

3. Easy-to-understand symbols for popular services and facilities – see opposite for full details

4. Site opening times

5. List of credit/debit cards accepted by site

6. List of fuel cards accepted by site – see panel opposite for full details

7. Listings of additional services and facilities

8. Identity code – cross-referenced on maps at back of book

KEY TO SYMBOLS

 LGV canopy height, shown in metres. If the box is not highlighted it means there is no LGV canopy

 Fuel available. May also list fuel supplier and number of pumps

 Red Diesel available (known as Green Diesel in Ireland)

 Card-operated automatic fuel bunker

 Air available for LGVs

 Forecourt water available for LGVs

 Oil available

 Parking details

 Site/parking accessible for abnormal loads (when phone symbol appears, drivers must telephone in advance)

 Standpipe

 A symbol that is faded out, as here, indicates that the facility is not available at this site

 Secure site

 Toilets

 Cashpoint machine (* = charge for use)

 Cashback facility

 Payphone

 Hot flask water available

 Shop

 Sandwiches, cold snacks available (price indicates average cost for sandwich)

 Tea, coffee, hot drinks available (price indicates average cost)

 Café, restaurant, hot food available (price indicates average cost for breakfast)

 Bar, pub, licensed to sell alcohol

KEY TO FUEL CARDS

1 Diesel Direct/Keyfuels/CH Jones
2 Securicor/Fuelserve
3 UK Fuels/Fastfuels
4 Overdrive/Allstar/Dial/PHH
5 BP
6 Routex
7 ESSO
8 Shell
9 Texaco
10 IDS
11 Moran
12 Harpur
13 Petrolplus/Routemate
14 MOL/DKV

15 Conoco Phillilps
16 Brobot
17 CSC Greencard
18 CSC Goldcard
19 Total Euro Traffic
20 EMO
21 DCI
22 UTA
23 RIX
24 Statoil
25 Dieseline
26 Maxol
27 CPL Petroleum
28 Nicholls
29 Stafford Oil
30 Total Butler

31 Silveys
32 Fuelwise
33 Top Oil
34 TDCS
35 BP Plus
36 BP Agency
37 BP Supercharge
38 Shell Gold
39 Shell Agency
40 Euro Shell
41 Esso Euro
42 Q8 cards
43 Murco
44 Jet
45 Gulf
46 Total Fina Elf Power

YOU AND THE LAW

THE MANAGEMENT OF HEALTH AND SAFETY AT WORK REGULATIONS 1999

This is an enormous act and too large to print in this book. The main act pertaining to general employment and self-employment can be accessed free via the Internet at www.legislation.hmso.gov.uk, or is available in book form from any HMSO bookstore.

MANUAL HANDLING

Manual handling isn't just about lifting and carrying. It also applies to lowering, pushing, pulling, moving, holding and restraining an object, animal or person, and covers the use of force to operate levers and handle power tools. Here is a list of the types of manual handling most likely to cause injury:
• Work that involves too much bending, reaching or twisting.
• Work that involves sudden, jerky, or hard to control movements.
• Work that involves long periods of time spent holding the same position.
• Work that is fast and repetitive.
• Work that involves the regular handling of heavy weights.
• Work where force is needed to carry out a task.
   So as you can see, that covers pretty much everything a lorry driver does. But there are steps you can take to avoid injury. Where provided,

use mechanical devices (cages, trolleys, wheels, sack trucks or pallet trucks) as often as possible. If something looks heavy, ask for assistance to move it – don't do it alone out of bravado and regret it later. And of course, always use correct manual handling techniques at all times.
   Remember, it's your responsibility to yourself to lift things safely, and it's your employer's responsibility to provide you with help (mechanical or otherwise) to enable you to do this. Below I've provided some diagrams depicting manual handling. For more information go to www.hse.gov.uk and select 'Manual Handling Operations Regulations 1992'.

SEAT BELTS

If your vehicle is fitted with seat belts, they must be worn by both driver and passenger. If they're not working, don't use the vehicle. Don't risk being fined up to £500. Remember that seat belts are there for a reason. They may be uncomfortable, but they could save your life in the event of an accident.

THE WORKING TIME DIRECTIVE

Introduction
Working time legislation in the road transport sector originates from three EU directives:
• **Main Directive** – introduced in the UK in 1998, but at the time the transport sector was temporarily excluded from the rules
• **Horizontal Amending Directive (HAD)** – introduced in 2003 and amended the Main

TO CORRECTLY LIFT A LOAD, YOU SHOULD FOLLOW THESE STEPS:

Assess the load. If you believe it will be too heavy for you to lift on your own, get help.

STEP ONE

Place your feet shoulder-width apart (one slightly in front of the other) and bend your knees until you're at the level where you can grip the load from the base and about two-thirds of the way in from the edge nearest to you. Then raise your head and prepare to lift.

STEP TWO

Directive by removing the exemption for the transport sector. It applied the full rules of the Main Directive to non-mobile workers and some of the rules to mobile workers.
• **Road Transport Directive (RTD)** – introduced in 2005, applied specific rules to mobile workers in the road transport sector (drivers and crew of vehicles subject to EU drivers' hours rules).
See the diagram below for details on which rules apply to which workers.

'Mobile Worker' is defined by HAD as any worker employed as a member of travelling personnel by a company that operates transport services for passengers or goods by road. This covers drivers and crew, apprentices and trainees of goods vehicles and includes own account operations.

Are you a 'Mobile Worker'?

Yes → No

Yes branch:

Is the journey subject to EU Hours Rule? — No → HAD applies. (48-hour week, health assessments, statutory leave, adequate rest)

Yes ↓

HAD applies (Health assessments, statutory leave)

Do you work only occasionally under EU Hours Rule? (See "occasional Drivers) — Yes → RTD does not apply

— No → Road Transport Directive applies

No branch:

HAD applies the full provisions of the Main Directive

Lift the load with your back straight. Straighten your knees slowly and pull the load towards you.

STEP THREE

Hold the load close to your body as you carry it.

STEP FOUR

RTD (Road Transport Directive)

- The Working Week starts at 00:00 hours on Monday and ends at 24:00 hours on Sunday. This is known as the 'fixed week'.
- The Maximum Average Working Week is 48 hours. This average is worked out over a period of 17–18 weeks (known as a 'Reference Period'). This Reference Period can be extended to a maximum of 26 weeks and set by calendar by individual companies with the consent of their workforce under what is known as a 'Collective or Workforce Agreement'. This means that different companies may all end up working to different Reference Periods. If you work for an agency *their* Reference Period will apply to you, not the Reference Period of the company you have been hired to work for.
- There is a Maximum Weekly Working Time of 60 hours. Remember that if you work 60 hours one week, some of your other working weeks within that Reference Period will have to consist of fewer than 48 hours in order to bring your Average Working Week back down to 48 hours.
- 'Working Time' does not include Breaks, Daily or Weekly Rest Periods, Periods of Availability (POA), voluntary or unpaid work (such as for charities) or evening classes or day release courses. Neither does it include work undertaken for the Territorial Army, Retained Fire-fighters or Special Constables. However, your company may request that you do inform them of any work undertaken for any of these latter three services. 'Working Time' does however include: Work meetings, training that is part of normal work and is part of the commercial operation, overtime and any other paid work undertaken for any other road transport employer. The latter must be declared by the driver and included in the calculation of working time.
- If time spent DRIVING on your shift does not amount to that which legally requires you to take a 'Tachograph Break' the RTD requires you to take a break after no more than six hours of work. You are required to take a total of 30 minutes break if your total working time is more than six but not more than nine hours, or a total of 45 minutes if total working time is over nine hours. Breaks must be taken during working time (in other words they may not be taken at the very start or very end of a shift) and may be split into separate periods of at least 15 minutes long.

- There is a Maximum Nightly Working Time of 10 hours. 'Night Time' is defined as the hours between midnight and 04:00 hours for crew of goods vehicles or 01:00 and 05:00 for crew of passenger vehicles. If any of your shift encroaches on these hours, it will be deemed that you are a night worker for that shift. However, under a 'Collective or Workforce Agreement' the Maximum Nightly Working Time can be extended.
- All night workers must have medical check ups made available to them. These medicals are not compulsory though workers may be asked to sign a declaration to say that this has been offered to them.
- Periods Of Availability (POA) are periods of time when the driver is available for work, but not actually working, and is not required to remain at the workstation (for a driver this will usually be your vehicle). This does not mean that you MUST leave your vehicle if you do not wish to do so for whatever reason, but you should be free to do so if you should wish (unless you have to stay in the vehicle for reasons of safety or security). You must not undertake any other work during this time, but should be available to undertake work should you be requested to do so. The tachograph mode should then be re-set if this should occur. POA can include: Time spent waiting to be loaded and unloaded or queuing at depots, time spent with a broken down vehicle (provided you do not have to direct traffic or undertake any other work), time spent as second driver (though not driving), delays at customs or delays due to traffic prohibitions.
- For POA to be valid the period of availability and its forseeable duration must be known in advance. If you typically expect to be delayed for a specific period of time, this will qualify as being known in advance. Where delays extend beyond the expected or notified period, there is nothing to stop another period of availability being recorded after the first if you have sufficient information. For example, you arrive at an RDC and are told there will be a 30-minute delay when you arrive. If at the end of the 30 minutes you are then told there will be further 45-minute delay this second period can also be counted as a POA provided you are not going to do any work and are free to leave your vehicle (unless it is unsafe or unsecure to do so).
- POAs must be recorded on the tachograph using the square sign (or 'packing case' symbol.) If the driver is not in possession of a vehicle, the period must be recorded manually. Failure to record POA properly will mean that the time is likely to be

classed as 'Working Time'. This could result in the driver running out of working or driving hours. Ensure that everyone who requests or requires a copy of your tachograph chart or Record Of Work receives them every week.

- At the time of writing, every employee must have four weeks paid leave per year. This is known as 'Statutory Leave' and may include bank holidays. Any leave in excess of the statutory minimum is 'Contractual Holiday' and will vary from company to company.
- There are special rules that apply when you are absent due to: statutory annual leave; sick leave; maternity; paternity; adoption; or parental leave. When your employer calculates working time over the reference period, they must add in 48 hours for each fixed week of leave taken. When you have not been absent for a full fixed week, eight hours for each individual day is added.
- 'Occasional Workers' do not come under the jurisdiction of the RTD. An 'Occasional Worker' is one that drives or is a member of the vehicle crew of a vehicle in-scope of the EU drivers' hours rules on no more than 10 occasions in any Reference Period that is shorter than 26 weeks or 15 occasions in a reference period of at least 26 weeks. Occasional workers will be subject to the rules of the main directive and/or HAD. If the driver exceeds his restricted number of 'Driving Occasions' allowed within a Reference Period he becomes subject to the full RTD Rules.
- Self Employed Drivers are not covered by the RTD until 2009. However, the definition of Self Employed Driver is very tightly restricted. A Self Employed Driver is one whose main occupation is the transportation of goods or passengers for hire or reward, one who is not tied to any employer by any contract, one who is free to organise his own relevant working activities, one whose income depends directly on profits made and who is free to have commercial relations with several customers.

Main Directive – Non-mobile workers

- Employees cannot be made to work more than an average 48 hours per week over the reference period. However, at the time of writing, opt out agreements signed individually by each employee can be made available to those in operations not subject to EU Rule. The agreement can be cancelled with seven days notice. This opt out agreement system is likely to be reviewed by the European Commission.
- Reference Periods of 16 or 17 weeks are used to calculate the average weekly working time. An employee's total working time over the whole reference period is added up and an average is worked out. Under certain circumstances, the reference period can be extended to 26 or 52 weeks subject to a Collective or Workforce Agreement. This agreement allows for more flexible and varied working times.
- Working time includes meetings, working lunches, job training and work (including overtime), It does not include rest or breaks, travelling to and from work, college or university classes.
- Night time is the period between 23:00 and 06:00. This can be varied with a Collective or Workforce Agreement but it must be less than seven hours and include the period between midnight and 05:00. If one third of the employees working time is spent working at night, he is classed as a night worker. Mobile workers in operations subject to EU Rule should refer to the RTD for information regarding Night Workers.
- Non-Mobile night workers are restricted to an average of eight hours in a 24-hour period. If the work is particularly strenuous workers may be restricted to eight hours only per 24 hours (rather than the average). In certain circumstances, the night limits may be dis-applied if a relevant agreement exists.
- Night workers must have annual medical check ups made available to them. These medicals are not compulsory though workers will be asked to sign a declaration to say that this has been offered to them.
- Non-Mobile workers should have 11 hours of rest in every 24-hour period. Mobile Workers not subject to EU Rule are entitled to 'adequate rest'. (Drivers should also see British Domestic Hour Rule.)
- Non-Mobile workers are entitled to one whole day off per week or two hours per fortnight in addition to paid annual leave. Mobile Workers not subject to EU Rule are entitled to 'adequate rest'. (Drivers should also see British Domestic Hour Rule.)
- Non Mobile Workers are entitled to a 20-minute break during six hours of work. This must not be taken at beginning or end.
- At the time of writing, every employee must have four weeks paid leave per year. This is known as 'Statutory Leave' and can include bank holidays. Employers can stipulate when Statutory Leave is taken.

DRIVING HOURS

EU Rules
Introduction

From 11th April 2007, Modified EU rules (set out below) will apply to all drivers operating within their jurisdiction. The EU rules have been 'simplified' to lessen confusion and to better 'mesh' with The Working Time Regulations. Maximum penalties for violations of these rules are a maximum fine of £2,500 per infringement. If a record is deemed to be deliberately falsified the maximim penalty increases to £5,000 or up to two years in prison

- As with the RTD, the fixed week begins 00:00 Monday and ends 24:00 Sunday.
- You can drive for a maximum of nine hours per day. This can be extended to 10 hours twice a week
- You must drive for no more than 56 hours in a week, and no more than 90 hours in a fortnight.
- After four-and-a-half hours of continuous or accumulated driving you must take a total of 45 minutes' break, unless beginning a daily or weekly rest period.
- Breaks can now be taken in TWO parts only (rather than three.) The first part can be taken at any time up until the time that a total of four-and-a-half hours of driving has been reached, the last part should be taken at the time (or just before the time) that the four-and-a-half hours is reached. The first part must now be a minimum of 15 minutes and the second part a minimum of 30 minutes. Do not set your tachograph to the square (packing case) symbol and record 'POA' in place of 'break'. You must be able show a visible record of your breaks and their times.
- Normally, Daily Rest Periods must consist of at least 11 consecutive hours taken within 24 hours from the end of your last daily or weekly rest. This may be shortened to nine hours no more than three times between any two weekly rests. Reductions in Daily Rest Periods no longer have to be 'paid back' in following weeks.
- Daily Rest Periods can additionally be split into two portions. If this is done, the first portion of Daily Rest must consist of a minimum of three hours, the second a minimum of nine hours. Making a total minimum of 12 hours of Daily Rest.
- There must be no more than six 24-hr periods (144 hrs) between weekly rests.
- Normally, Weekly Rest periods should consist of 45 consecutive hours, which can be reduced to a minimum of 24 hours. (The driver no longer has to be away from base to do this.) In any two consecutive weeks, you must have at least two weekly rests and one of those must be at least 45 hours long. If weekly rest is reduced then the reduced amount must be paid back in one chunk by the end of the third week following the week in which it was taken.
- If at any time the journey involves driving partly off road (such as on a building site) the driver is no longer able to class this driving as 'Other Work'. It must now count towards driving hours.

Work for other employers

Your main employer should monitor any time you have spent in his employ doing 'Other (non driving) Work' or driving a vehicle exempt from EU Rule. However, the driver himself is responsible for declaring, monitoring, recording and providing information relating to all work done for other employers. You must record any other work undertaken during the week in which you work for any other employer on either a tachograph chart, a printout from a digital tachograph or as a manual entry using the data input facility on a digital tachograph. On any day that you drive or work for another employer you must have had your proper weekly rest for the previous week, daily rest for that day and weekly rest for that week and must ensure that you are compliant with whatever regulations apply to all work undertaken for all employers.

Multi-Manning

- Multi-Manning means that during each period of driving there are at least two drivers in the vehicle to do the driving (though for the first hour of the driving period, the presence of another driver is optional).
- Daily Tachograph and Working Time breaks can be taken by the 'second driver' on a moving vehicle, provided that he or she is not required to carry out any other work.
- Each driver must have a daily rest period of no less than nine hours in every 30-hour period. This rest must not be taken on a moving vehicle.
- The vehicle may be driven for up to 20 hours (maximum of 10 hours per driver) but the working day must not exceed 21 hours.

Ferries and Trains

On occasions when the driver is taking an 11-hour rest on a train or ferry, this rest may be interrupted twice due to customs formalities. These interruptions must not exceed a total of 1 hour.

Emergencies
Provided road safety is not jeopardised a driver is permitted to exceed the rules in order to reach a safe stopping place to the extent necessary to ensure the safety of persons, vehicle and or its load. On arrival at the safe stopping place the driver must immediately indicate the reason manually on his tachograph chart or digital printout.

Operations exempt from EU Rule
Changes to Operations Exempt From EU Rule are due to be brought in on April 11th 2007. These changes involve limiting and amending those operations and allowing individual EU member states to adjust them according to their needs. Listed 1 to 11 below applies to operations in the UK, EU and internationally. 12 to 29 applies to operations within the UK only.

1. Vehicles exceeding 3.5 tonnes MGW that are used for the carriage of goods.
2. Vehicles with no more than nine seats (including the driver's seat) that are used for the carriage of passengers.
3. Vehicles used for the carriage of passengers on regular services with a route of not more than 50km.
4. Specialist vehicles used for medical purposes (such as screening units).
5. New or rebuilt vehicles not yet in service.
6. Vehicles undergoing road tests for repair, maintenance or technical development.
7. Vehicles not capable of exceeding 40kph.
8. Vehicles owned or hired without a driver by the armed services, civil defence, fire services and forces responsible for maintaining public order, when the carriage is a consequence of their assigned tasks and is under their control.
9. Emergency and rescue vehicles and those transporting humanitarian aid non-commercially.
10. Specialist breakdown vehicles operating within 100km radius of base.
11. Vehicles or combinations of vehicle not exceeding 7.5 tonnes being used for non-commercial carriage of goods.
12. Vehicles used in connection with flood, sewerage, water, gas, electricity maintenance services, highways maintenance and control, door to door

household refuse collection and disposal, telegraph and telephone services, radio and television broadcasting and detection of radio or television transmitters or receivers.
13. Specialist vehicles transporting circus and funfair equipment.
14. Vehicles being used for milk collection from farms or delivery to farms of milk containers or milk products intended for animal feed.
15. Vehicles used by agriculture, horticulture, forestry, farming or fisheries for the use of carrying goods as part of their own entrepreneurial activity within 100km radius of base.
16. Agricultural and forestry tractors being used within 100km of base.
17. Vehicles carrying animal carcasses or waste not intended for human consumption.
18. Vehicles used to carry livestock to markets or slaughterhouses and vice versa within a radius of up to 50km.
19. Certain historical or vintage vehicles not being used for the commercial carriage of goods or passengers. (The list of vehicles included in this category is very specific. Individuals may have to consult the Department for Transport for further clarification.)
20. Vehicles with between 10 and 17 seats (including the driver's seat) used exclusively for non-commercial carriage of passengers.
21. Vehicles used by a public authority to provide public services not in competition with professional road hauliers. This list is under revision though in the UK it currently includes:
    a. Ambulance service vehicles used to carry patients staff and medical supplies
    b. Vehicles employed to provide certain social services
    c. Coastguard, lighthouse and harbour authorities (within the limits of the harbour)
    d. Airport authorities within the perimeter of the airport
    e. Railways Authorities, Transport for London, passenger transport executives or local authorities for railway maintenance
    f. British Waterways Board for purposes of maintaining waterways.
22. Vehicles specially fitted as a 'mobile project vehicle' the primary purpose of which is use as an educational facility when stationary. This could include vehicles such as play buses and mobile libraries.

23. Vehicles or combination vehicles of not over 7.5 tonnes being used by the driver within 50km radius of base for carrying materials used in the course of his work and where driving does not constitute the driver's main activity.
24. Vehicles operating on an island not exceeding 2,300sq km and not connected to Great Britain by a bridge, ford or tunnel.
25. Gas or electrically propelled vehicles used for the carriage of goods not exceeding 7.5 tonnes operating within a 50km radius of base.
26. Vehicles being used for solely driving instruction and/or examination with a view to obtaining a driving licence or CPC.
27. Vehicles being used by the RNLI to haul lifeboats. (This is currently under revision.)
28. Any vehicle which is propelled by steam.
29. Vehicles used exclusively within hub facilities such as ports, airports and railway terminals.

British Domestic Hours Rules

British Domestic Hours Rules apply to drivers on journeys within the UK who are exempt or excluded from EU Rule. Drivers will be either expected to use a tachograph with which to record their hours or be asked to keep a 'Record Book'. Make sure you know how to use this if one is provided.

- Daily driving limit 10 hours in any 24-hour period
- Daily duty limit 11 hours in any 24-hour period. Any time spent on break, (known as 'meal relief') is not classed as duty time.
- Part time drivers should not exceed four hours of driving in any 24-hour period.
- There are currently no requirements for daily rest periods or meal relief breaks under British Domestic Hours Rule. However, breaks should be taken in accordance with the 'Horizontal Amending Directive' and any current health and any legislation applicable to the company you are working for. (You should ask your company for clarification of this.)
- Under British Domestic Hours Rules a Weekly Rest Period is not required. However, The Horizontal Amending Directive should be followed.
- The British Domestic Hours week begins at 00:00 Monday and ends 24:00 Sunday.

Emergencies

British Domestic Hours Rules Limits can be exceeded in the following circumstances:

Events that cause or may cause:
- A danger to life or health of a person or animal or where events are likely to cause damage to property in a way that immediate action must be taken.
- A serious interruption in water, gas, electricity, drainage, telecommunications, use of roads, railways, ports and airports.

Exemptions to British Domestic Hours Rules and EU Rule

- Drivers of vehicles used by the armed forces, police and fire brigades
- Drivers who always drive off the public road
- Private driving unconnected with any employment.

Light vans and dual-purpose vehicles

Drivers of vans not exceeding 3.5 tonnes MGW when engaged solely in the use of certain professional activities, i.e. such as those used by doctors, dentists, nurses, midwives, vets, sales reps, employees of the AA, RAC and RSAC and persons using their vehicles to assist in carrying out any service of inspection, cleaning, maintenance, repair, installation or fitting are subject to the 10-hour driving regulations stated opposite. Also included is cinematography, radio or television broadcasting staff.

Driving under mixed EU and British Domestic Rules

This occurs when a driver operates a vehicle covered by EU Rules and another covered by British Domestic Rules within the same day or the same week. He must be aware that:
- Driving time under the EU Rule does not count as off duty time under the British Domestic Rules
- Driving time under British Domestic Rules cannot count as Break or Rest Period under the EU Rules.
- Driving under the EU Rules counts towards driving and duty limits under the British Domestic Hour Rules.
- Mixed driving on the same day limits the driver to British Domestic Hour Rule Duty and Driving times. (10 hours Driving and 11 hours of Duty Time, though in Northern Ireland Duty Time limit is 14 hours.)
- When driving under EU Rules, the driver must observe EU Daily and Weekly Rest requirements.
- When driving under EU Rules, all driving done on the same day under British Domestic Hour rule should be marked on the tachograph chart as 'Other Work' by manual entry.

DIGITAL TACHOGRAPHS

Introduction

Digital Tachographs are fitted to all vehicles first used on or after 1 May 2006. Although there is no general requirement to fit older vehicles with the digital equipment, these will have to be fitted to *most* PCVs and LGVs should the analogue tachograph unit have to be replaced in the event of its complete failure. (There are specific rules and exemptions regarding this matter.)

The Digital Tachograph (known as the VU or Vehicle Unit) looks a little like the old analogue tachographs. It has two slots for insertion of the Smart Cards and a slot where the printer paper comes out. It also has an LED display and various mode and menu buttons.

Information is entered into the VU by the driver (such as mode and starting location) and other information is copied from the inserted card into the VU. Different types of information are stored both within the VU and the Drivers' Card(s). (There are four types of card, but we will come to those later.)

Information can later be accessed from the VU and from the cards using external 'plug in equipment' or 'card reading' equipment owned by the fleet holder. The driver may also need to create a printout of his working period each day, this printout (like with the analogue tachograph chart) may be a legal document and should be stored in a cool dry place along with any analogue charts for that day away from heat and sunlight to prevent degradation.

Operating the Vehicle Unit (VU)

The Siemens VU (shown here below, bottom) allows you to slide the card into the appropriate slot and it then takes it in and reads it. With Siemens VU, ignition must be on before you insert the card.

The Stoneridge VU (below, top) works differently. You have to press the button for the slot you wish to use and this opens a card tray like a CD tray on a computer or DVD player. You then insert the card and press the button again to close the tray and start the read process.

Once the card has been read, your name and the time will appear on the display. Then it will

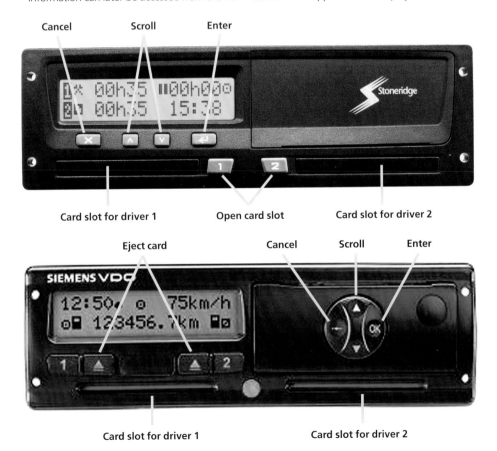

Cancel   Scroll   Enter

Card slot for driver 1   Open card slot   Card slot for driver 2

Eject card   Cancel   Scroll   Enter

Card slot for driver 1   Card slot for driver 2

tell you when the card was last withdrawn from the VU. Then, it will prompt you to make a manual entry. (It will do this if you have spent any period of time away from a VU-equipped vehicle such as when you have been on a daily or weekly rest period.) To make a manual entry just follow the instructions on screen. Manual entries are only stored on the drivers' card and include:

• Start and end location (see list of country codes)
• Specific conditions such as when you are on a ferry or driving vehicle off road
• If you want to enter work done before or after card was inserted or work done away from a VU-equipped vehicle
• Any rest periods since the card was last used.

If you move your vehicle before completing the manual entries, the procedure will be terminated. This also happens if the card is removed or inserted, no keys are pressed for more than a minute or a long press of the cancel button occurs on the Stoneridge VU.

If any of these things occur, the missing data must be entered onto the printout at the end of the day.

UTC (Universal Standard Time) also known as Greenwich Mean Time (GMT) is what is used on *all* Digital Tachographs. Drivers must take this into consideration when entering data during British Summer Time. Be aware that some companies may adjust the VU unit's 'display time' to local time and not UTC. Don't let it catch you out, check your watch and remember to deduct one hour from GMT during British Summer Time in order to work out UTC.

It is very important that the driver selects the correct mode at all times and at the time that each condition applies. Co-Driver cards automatically default to 'POA' when the vehicle is in motion. Driver cards automatically default to 'Other Work' after any period of Driving. Wrong mode selection will need to be manually written on the back of a digital printout.

When double manning, cards must be re-positioned in the VU in order to record rest periods for the No. 2 driver as the rest mode cannot be selected for the No. 2 position when the vehicle is in motion.

It is important to note that the driver card can only be released from the VU when the vehicle is stationary.

You can drive with a malfunctioning VU under certain specified circumstances, but if you have a problem notify your manager as soon as possible to ensure it is rectified as soon as circumstances permit.

Information stored within the VU includes:

1. Distance travelled
2. Speed and any instances of speeding where the vehicle's own speed limiter (usually set at around 56mph) has been exceeded
3. Date and times of driving
4. Periods of other work and POA recorded in real time
5. Driver card issue number with dates and times of insertion and removal
6. Date, time and duration of driving without a card or functioning card
7. Data recorded on the places at which the daily work period began and ended
8. Faults of recording equipment along with dates, times and driver card number
9. Faults in the Driver Card along with dates, times and driver card number
10. Workshop card data with VU and recording equipment inspection information and dates
11. Control card number with dates of insertion, type of action undertaken (i.e. downloading, printing, displaying)
12. Time and adjustment with data, time and card issue number
13. Driving status (single or multi manning, etc).

Information is stored within the VU for approximately 365 days. After this time it is overwritten.

VU Warnings

Your VU may provide you with warning notices that you will have to acknowledge by pressing the OK/Enter button. These are some of the warnings it will give you.

• **Break! 4 hrs 15 mins drive** (This means a break is due within the next 15 minutes)
• **Break! 4 hrs 30 mins drive** (This means you must take a break now!)
• **Stop for break** (repeats every 15 mins showing current drive total – Seimens only)
• **Overspeeding** (When your vehicle's set speed limiter is exceeded for longer than 60 seconds)
• **Driving without card** (If you are driving with no card)
• **No Data** (This occurs when you request a printout from the VU with no card inserted)
• **Wrong card type** (Check you haven't inserted your bank card by mistake!)
• **No paper**
• **Printout not possible** (Check ignition is on)
• **Please enter** (OK/Enter has not been pressed during manual entry procedure)

VU display and Printout Pictograms

There are 38 pictograms that can be found on your printout or LED display, in addition to which there can also be 46 combinations of pictograms. Below are listed the most common. You should familiarise yourself with these.

◘	Available	☻	Clock
O	Drive	☐	Display
ᑋ	Rest	⊥	External storage
⅄	Work	÷	Power supply
‖	Break	▼	Printer/Printout
?	Unknown	Ⅱ	Sensor
24h	Daily	♣	Vehicle/Vehicle Unit
I	Weekly	×	Fault
‖	Two	◆	Location
✦	From or To	⌷	Security
1	Driver slot	☻	Time
2	Co-driver slot	Σ	Total/Summary
▯	Card		

Note: Additional pictograms may be specific to the VU manufacturer.

Printouts will provide the following

1. Driver card number and expiry date
2. Name of cardholder
3. Details of all breaks and rest
4. Details of all driving times
5. Periods of other work and POA
6. Registration numbers of current and previous vehicles for the last 27 days with distance travelled per vehicle per day
7. Time adjustments
8. Faults relating to sensors and power supply
9. Any driving done without card
10. Details of information stored concerning the driver
11. Start and finish locations
12. Faults in recording equipment
13. Faults with the driver card
14. Times and details when control card was used and the card number
15. Overspeeding
16. Summary reports

Cards:

Cards are available from the DVLA at a cost of £38 for a new card or £19 for a replacement or renewal card. You can apply using the dedicated phone line 0870 8501074 or by completing an Application form (D779B) available from the DVLA, DVLA Local Offices and VOSA Testing Stations. The completed form along with any relevant documentation and the fee should be

Country Codes

These are Start and End locations and must be entered manually into the VU when requested.

A	Austria	MC	Monaco
AL	Albania	MD	Republic of Moldova
AND	Andorra		
ARM	Armenia	MK	Macedonia
AZ	Azerbaijan	N	Norway
B	Belgium	NL	The Netherlands
BG	Bulgaria		
BIH	Bosnia and Herzegovina	P	Portugal
		PL	Poland
BY	Belarus	RO	Romania
CH	Switzerland	RSM	San Marino
CY	Cyprus	RUS	Russian Federation
CZ	Czech Republic		
D	Germany	S	Sweden
DK	Denmark	SK	Slovakia
E	Spain	SLO	Slovenia
EST	Estonia	TM	Turkmenistan
F	France	TR	Turkey
FIN	Finland	UA	Ukraine
FL	Liechtenstein	UK	United Kingdom, Alderney, Guernsey, Jersey, Isle of Man, Gibraltar
FR	Faeroe Islands		
GE	Georgia		
GR	Greece		
H	Hungary		
HR	Croatia		
I	Italy	V	Vatican City
IRL	Ireland	YU	Yugoslavia
IS	Iceland	UNK	Unknown
KZ	Kazakhstan	EC	European Community
L	Luxembourg		
LT	Lithuania	EUR	Rest of Europe
LV	Latvia	WLD	Rest of the world
M	Malta		

Note: UK may be found under G for GB even though is displayed as UK

Spanish Regions

AN	Andalucia	EXT	Extremadura
AR	Aragón	G	Galicia
AST	Asturias	IB	Baleares
C	Cantabria	IC	Canarias
CAT	Cataluña	LR	La Rioja
CL	Castilla-León	M	Madrid
CM	Castilla-La-Mancha	MU	Murcia
		NA	Navarra
CV	Valencia	PV	Pais Vasco

sent to DVLA, Swansea, SA99 1ST. For more information and notes on applying for a Driver Card go to www.dvla.gov.uk, then 'Driver information' and scroll down to 'Digital Tacho Card Issuing and Company Cards'.

Driver Card (White in colour)
Owned by the driver

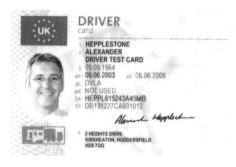

- Identifies the driver by his photograph, full name, date and birthplace, driving licence number, home address and signature. It also shows the issuing Authority, Country, dates of validity and serial number. This data is also stored within the card's chip.
- The driver card is valid for no more than 5 years.

The card currently stores approximately 28 days worth of information at any given time, this includes:
1. Vehicles used by the driver, date and time of last use and vehicle odometer readings at that time
2. Driver activity data and modes selected
3. Start and finish places
4. Card faults and VU faults experienced
5. Data regarding any recent information downloads and printouts made. (This way any printouts cannot be 'discarded' by the driver since evidence that printouts have been made is stored on the card)
6. Dates and times card has been inserted.

The VU reads from the card when inserted information necessary for it to:
1. Identify card type, holder, previously used vehicle date and time of last usage and mode selected at the time
2. Check that the last 'session' was properly closed
3. Add up the driver's continuous driving time, cumulative break and driving times for previous and current week
4. Create a printout if one is requested
5. Download information into 'plug in' or 'external equipment'.

Note that in case of a reading error, the VU will try 3 times before declaring the card faulty and invalid.

Lost stolen or damaged driver cards
The driver must make a printout at the start and end of his journey. He must manually record details of any activity during his daily working period (i.e. between rests) on these printouts. He must also manually record on each printout enough detail to enable him to be identified (such as driver card number, name, driving licence number) then the driver must sign the printout. Loss or theft should be reported to DVLA as soon as possible and within seven working days. They will issue a replacement within five days. If the card was lost or stolen abroad, the driver must also report it to the 'competent authority' within that country.

Drivers may continue to drive without a card for a maximum of 15 calendar days or longer if necessary to return the vehicle to its premises. During this period, drivers must produce two daily printouts as detailed above.

Drivers' Responsibilities
1. Ensure you have a valid Driver Card and carry it with you even when you are using an analogue tachograph. Failure to bring your card to work may mean that you will not be able to drive on that day!
2. You should have only one card at any time. Do not let anyone else use your card and keep it safe. Your company may offer to keep your card for you, but it is best that you take responsibility for it yourself.
3. You must produce your card to the police or VOSA if requested and sign any printouts you are requested to sign
4. You must allow your employer to download from your card

5. You must report lost, stolen, damaged and malfunctioning cards and apply for replacement
6. You should understand how to enter all data and how the unit and printer works
7. You should understand the pictograms (see above) and data produced on the printout
8. You should always carry spare print rolls
9. You should keep 15 calendar days (prior to the current week) tacho printouts and/or analogue tachograph charts on you and be in possession of any tachos or printouts for that current week. This is due to be changed to the current day plus 28 days' tachograph charts and/or printouts on 1 January 2008
10. Agency drivers should ensure that their agency is regularly supplied with photocopies of printouts and tachographs.

Company Card (Yellow in colour)
Owned by fleet operators

Valid for five years. Coupled with 'plug in equipment' and 'card readers', Company Cards enable fleet owners to download, display and print the information stored within the VU and recording equipment.

Workshop Card (Red in colour)
Owned by workshops and fitters

Issued to recording equipment manufacturers, vehicle manufacturers and qualified fitters in a VOSA approved workshop. The workshop card enables the cardholder to test, calibrate and download information from the VU. It is valid for one year. Each fitter should own one and a pin number is required to operate the card.

Control Card (Blue in colour)
Owned by enforcement authorities (such as police, DVLA and VOSA)

Valid for two years, the Control Card identifies the official body and cardholder and allows them access to data stored in the VU or in the recording equipment enabling printouts to be made.

ANALOGUE TACHOGRAPHS

How to correctly complete an analogue tachograph chart

• Surname and first name must be entered in full. Initials and/or abbreviations are not acceptable.

• Recognisable start and finish journey place-names (such as a town or village) must be entered on the front and rear of the tachograph chart. The rear face should be completed in exactly the same way as the front for this particular part of the field.

• Date and place where the use of the chart starts and ends must both be entered, as date, month and year. If you use more than one vehicle, times of vehicle changes should also be entered if space is provided for this on the back of the tachograph chart.

• The full vehicle registration for each vehicle driven must be entered. Any fleet codes are not acceptable.

• Enter full odometer figures for the start and finish of a journey in each vehicle, with the total for each vehicle in the space beneath.

• Start of working period and end of working period should be clearly marked with a straight line. Take care not to mark the tachograph chart trace. To be on the safe side, mark your line at some point between 5 and 15 minutes before and after the start and end of the trace. If you are completing a manual trace, a straight line will not be necessary.

• At no time should the writing spill out from the central field so that it interferes with any written information or cover any part of a tachograph chart trace. This is a tachograph offence.

Remember that different companies or agencies

TACHOGRAPH CHART [MANUAL TRACE]

Note: Both examples shown here were created under British Domestic Hours Rule, not EU Rule.

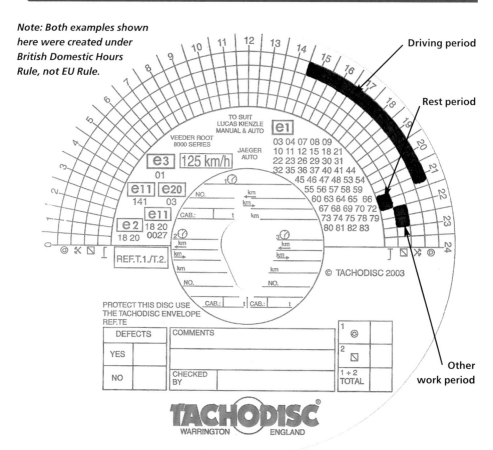

Driving period

Rest period

Other work period

may have different tachograph chart completion requirements. Make sure you know how your company or agency likes to have its tachograph charts presented before you begin driving for them.

You must record every period of activity during your shift that isn't shown and recorded by the tachograph. As demonstrated in the examples below, you should either manually trace on the rear of the tachodisc, or use two small lines on the edge of the front of the tachodisc and write between them words such as 'Rest' or 'OWP' (other work period) to indicate the type of work or rest undertaken. But ask first what's required of you.

Only one tachograph chart should be used for each driving period within a time frame of 24 hours. Exceptions are as follows:
• If the tachograph chart is damaged either in or out of the vehicle and another is required to continue recording the working or driving

period. In instances such as these, the replacement tachograph chart should be clipped to and handed in along with the damaged one.
• If you're driving more vehicles than your tachograph chart will allow you to record details of on the reverse or on vehicles where the chart is not compatible with both tachographs. Again, they should be clipped together and both handed in.

Other rules you should be aware of
• You must not use a chart to record more than 24 hours of information
• You are required to be able to produce at the roadside charts and any legally required printouts and manual records for the current fixed week and the previous 15 calendar days, together with your driver's smart card if you hold one.
• A tachograph chart is a legal document. Look after it and buy a tachograph chart pouch,

TACHOGRAPH CHART [FRONT FACE]

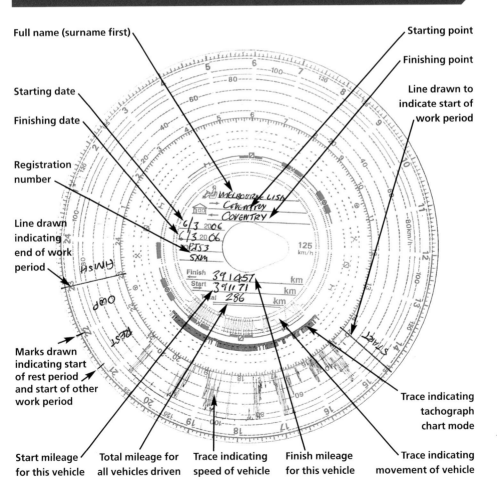

Full name (surname first)
Starting point
Finishing point
Starting date
Line drawn to indicate start of work period
Finishing date
Registration number
Line drawn indicating end of work period
Marks drawn indicating start of rest period and start of other work period
Trace indicating tachograph chart mode
Start mileage for this vehicle
Total mileage for all vehicles driven
Trace indicating speed of vehicle
Finish mileage for this vehicle
Trace indicating movement of vehicle

available from all good truckstops and truckers' shops.

- You should not remove a tachograph chart from the tachograph to check driving times without writing a note in the comments box on the reverse of the disc.
- If you are stopped by the police, ensure that they sign your tachograph chart after checking it.
- If a tachograph develops a fault indicated by a 'v' on the tachograph display or a red light at the bottom of the odometer face (not to be confused with the 'maximum speed reached'

light) this should be noted on the rear of the tachograph chart in the comments or defects box, and the defect reported immediately to your depot manager.

- If your tachograph becomes faulty or has been reported as faulty before leaving the yard and a trace is not visible on the front of the tachograph chart, a manual trace of your working day must be made on the back. Keep a note of your driving, resting, POAs and loading times in order for you to be able to complete this accurately at the end of your day.

HOW TO RECORD YOUR DAY CORRECTLY

DRIVING	This mode is automatically selected when your vehicle moves. If your tachograph does not show this symbol, use the cross hammers symbol. The actual driving times will record on the tachograph chart.
REST OR BREAK	1 Break from driving in accordance with regulations (eg 45 minutes after 4 and a half hours of driving). 2 Daily or weekly rest in accordance with regulations.
PERIOD OF AVAILABILITY	1 Delays due to traffic prohibitions (including queues on site). 2 Waiting for someone else to load or unload a vehicle where the driver does not have to be in attendance and is free to use his time as and where he wishes. Expected delay time must be reported and recorded by your depot. 3 Delays at customs where the driver does not have to be in attendance and is free to use his time as and where he wishes. Again expected delay time must be reported and recorded by your depot. Once you go beyond that estimated time, it is classed as normal other work time. 4 Time spent with a broken-down vehicle at the roadside awaiting repairs or recovery. Expected delay time must be reported and the driver should not undertake any other duties during this time.
OTHER WORK	1 Walk round vehicle checks. 2 Cleaning and maintenance of a vehicle. 3 Securing the load. 4 Livestock attendance. 5 Driving a forklift. 6 Administration duties. 7 Any other work away from driving that you are required to do.

ALSO:
1 Where the driver knows the likely duration of the delay in advance, but it is safer to remain inside the cab, this will not disqualify them from being able to record this time as a period of availability. Only if the driver is required to stay with the vehicle, should he have to record it as normal working time.
2 Time that satisfies the definition of 'period of availability' can instead be used towards taking breaks from driving or working time requirements.

MOBILE PHONES

It is now illegal to make calls or to text using your hand-held mobile phone whilst driving, *unless you are using it to make a 999 call*, in which case you are permitted to do so if you are unable to stop. In order to make and receive any other type of call or to text using the handset, *you must be stationary, parked in a safe place (not the hard shoulder of a motorway) with the engine switched off.* However, there are things you can do or which are permitted, and here is a list of them:

- You may have a phone on 'silent' or switched off, with a voicemail system in place to pick up calls for you.
- You can use a voice-activated headset (non-cordless or cordless such as Bluetooth) to make calls, and a 'button on the headset' activated device to receive calls, *but if you have to actually pick up the phone to do either of these things, you are breaking the law.*
- You are permitted to use phone systems that are built into the vehicle or ones where you sit your phone in a cradle on the dashboard.

If the company you work for offers you a phone for use in your work and it is not compatible, do not use it whilst driving. The penalties for doing so include 3 penalty points and fines which start from £60 and rise to £2,500 (for drivers of lorries or buses) if contested. You can also face prosecution for failing to be in proper control of a vehicle (even whilst using hands-free equipment) and careless, dangerous or reckless driving – with penalties ranging from a fine to a ban and imprisonment – if using a phone affects your control of your vehicle. (See fines and endorsements section.)

Your company can also be prosecuted under health and safety laws and face unlimited fines and charges of individual or corporate manslaughter if you flout the law.

VEHICLE SIZE AND BRIDGES

The law regarding oversized vehicles

If your LGV and its load are over a certain size, special conditions apply. This may mean having to fit markers, carry an attendant, and notify the police. These conditions may apply if:

- Your load is more than 2.9 metres (or 9ft 6in) wide.

- If any part of your load projects more than 305mm (12in) on either side.
- If your load projects by more than 1m (3ft 3in) from the rear of your vehicle.
- If your vehicle and load have a combined rigid length of more than 18.65m (61ft 2in).

You must comply with the requirements of the Special Types Order if your vehicle and load fall within the following description:

- If your vehicle is more than 2.55m wide (8ft 4.5in) or together with its load either:
- Exceeds the gross vehicle weight or gross train weight allowed by the Construction And Use Regulations or Authorised Weight Regulations for ordinary lorries and/or the vehicle and its load are more than 4.3m (14ft 1in) wide.

You must apply to the Department for Transport for permission to move your vehicle if:

- The weight of the vehicle and its load exceed 150 tons (147.6 tonnes).
- Its width is more than 5m (16ft 5in).
- Its rigid length is more than 27.4m (89ft 11in).

The address to write to is: Department for Transport, VSE5 Zone 2/01, Great Minister House, 76 Marsham Street, London, SW1P 4DR.

If your vehicle is over 16ft 6in high you'll need to make Special Routing Arrangements with regard to the clearance of overhead power cables and bridges. These arrangements will have to be made with:

- Each local highways agency
- British Telecom (if over 17ft 6in)
- The National Grid plc
- Scottish Power
- Scottish Hydro Electric Power

The law regarding bridges

If you hit or even scrape a bridge, you are legally required to stop. Failure to do so is an offence and could result in a heavy fine for you and a weakened bridge that becomes a danger to life.

Look for a sign mounted on the outside of the bridge or near it. This should show the exact location and a telephone number to contact. You should also immediately dial 999 and inform the police of the bridge strike. Do not leave the scene. Wait for the correct authorities to arrive and only leave when you have been given permission to do so.

If you approach a bridge that is lower than the height of your vehicle, you are legally required to stop. If you are unable to turn your vehicle, phone the local police authority of that area for advice or assistance. (See under 'Government Bodies' in the index).

Advice regarding bridges

Every year hundreds of rail bridges are hit by truck drivers who are lost or don't know their vehicle height. Here are a few points to note so that you can avoid this happening to you:

- It is a legal requirement that every truck over 3m (9ft 6in) tall should display a sign stating vehicle height in the cab. If you get into a truck and this is not displayed, make it known and ask for the height of the vehicle before you leave the yard. If it is displayed only in either feet or metres, check the Imperial to Metric conversion table below for the missing figures.
- Buy and use a trucker's atlas to plan your route. These are obtainable from any good book store, and these days also from most motorway service stations.
- Remember that any bridge with a clearance height of over 5.03m (16ft 6in) is unsigned and you will be able to drive safely under it, provided you are not driving an over-height vehicle.
- Avoid using unnumbered roads, as any low bridges will not be marked on your trucker's atlas.
- The heights of arched bridges are displayed in a triangle warning sign to advise of the safe clearance height for LGVs. You may also find white lines painted on the road to guide your passage through. Wait until it's safe for you to go – don't try to squeeze through alongside other traffic. Take your time and use all the space in the middle of the road.
- When picking up a trailer, check your trailer height. The height may or may not be written on the trailer. When it is, the height given is that which it would be if coupled to an average height 5th wheel. Afterwards you should adjust your height indicator in the cab if necessary.

METRIC / IMPERIAL CONVERSION TABLE

To Convert	Multiply by	To Convert	Multiply by
Inches to Centimetres	2.5400	Cu Feet to Cu Metres	0.0283
Centimetres to Inches	0.3937	Cu Metres to Cu Feet	35.3100
Feet to Metres	0.3048	Cu Yards to Cu Metres	0.7646
Metres to Feet	3.2810	Cu Metres to Cu Yards	1.3080
Yards to Metres	0.9144	Cu Inches to Litres	0.0163
Metres to Yards	1.0940	Litres to Cu Inches	61.0300
Miles to Kilometres	1.6090	Gallons to Litres	4.4560
Kilometres to Miles	0.6214	Litres to Gallons	0.2200
Sq Inches to Sq Centimetres	6.4520	Grains to Grams	0.0648
Sq Centimetres to Sq Inches	0.1550	Grams to Grains	15.4300
Sq Metres to Sq Feet	10.760	Ounces to Grams	28.3500
Sq Feet to Sq Metres	0.0929	Grams to Ounces	0.0352
Sq Yards to Sq Metres	0.8361	Pounds to Grams	453.600
Sq Metres to Sq Yards	1.1960	Grams to Pounds	0.0022
Sq Miles to Sq Kilometres	2.5900	Pounds to Kilograms	0.4536
Sq Kilometres to Sq Miles	0.3861	Kilograms to Pounds	2.2050
Acres to Hectares	0.4047	Tons to Kilograms	1016.00
Hectares to Acres	2.4710	Kilograms to Tons	0.0009
Cu Inches to Cu Centimetres	16.3900	Fahrenheit to Centigrade	(°F -32) x 0.56
Cu Centimetres to Cu Inches	0.0610	Centigrade to Fahrenheit	(°C x 1.8) +32

VEHICLE HEIGHTS, WEIGHTS AND DIMENSIONS

Height
The normal travelling height of your vehicle should be clearly marked. If you're driving a rigid without drawbar trailer, this height should be a fixed height and displayed prominently in the cab. It's normally somewhere between 9ft 6in and 14ft. If you're driving a solo unit the height will normally be between 13ft and 14ft 6in.

Trailer heights may or may not be marked on the trailer. However, when they are given they're stated on the understanding that the trailer is coupled to a fifth wheel plate height of approximately 4ft 6in. This is the average height of most fifth wheels. Trailer heights when coupled may vary wildly, between 14ft and around 16ft.

You should always check the height of your vehicle and its trailer before you leave the yard.

Maximum weight of Class C1 rigid vehicles
• 7.5 tonnes MGW.

Maximum weight of Class C1+E vehicles (Combination of C1 rigid vehicle and drawbar trailer)
• 12 tonnes MGW.

Weight of Class C rigid vehicles
• Two axles: 18 tonnes MGW
• Three axles: 26 tonnes MGW
• Four or more axles: 32 tonnes MGW.

Weight of Class C+E vehicles
• Three axle artic: 26 tonnes MGW
• Four axle artic: 38 tonnes MGW
• Four axle rigid and drawbar trailer combination: 36 tonnes MGW
• Five axle artic/rigid and drawbar trailer combination: 40 tonnes MGW
• Six axle artic/rigid and drawbar trailer combination: 44 tonnes MGW.

Please note that weights given above are a general guideline and not a hard and fast rule. Specialist vehicle dimensions may vary from these guidelines. For the correct legal maximum load weight for your vehicle or for the un-laden weight of your vehicle, you should check the MoT plate/s and tax disc.

Length
• Class C1: Minimum 5 metres
• Class C1 + E: Combined length of between 8 and 12 metres
• Class C: Between 8 and 12 metres
• Class C+E Rigid and drawbar trailer combinations: 18.75 metres maximum
• Class C+E Artic and unit combination: 16.5 metres maximum
• Trailers with 4 or more axles being drawn by vehicle of over 7.5 tonnes MGW: 12 metres maximum length
• All other drawbar trailers: 7 metres maximum length

Width
• Unit and trailer/rigid and drawbar trailer combination: 2.55 metres maximum
• Refrigerated trailer/rigid and drawbar trailer combination: 2.6 metres maximum
• Trailer drawn by 3.5 tonne rigid: 2.3 metres maximum.

COLLISIONS WITH OTHER ROAD-USERS, PEDESTRIANS, DOMESTIC ANIMALS OR PROPERTY

The law regarding accidents

The law states that if you become involved in an accident where other road-users, pedestrians or domestic animals are injured or property damaged you must do each of the following:

• Stop.
• Give your own name and address and the name and address of the vehicle owner or company that owns the vehicle, plus the registration number of the vehicle to those persons who would require it.
• If you do not do this at the time of the accident – say, for example, you were in a collision with an unknown domestic animal – you must report the accident to the police immediately. You are allowed only 24 hours in which to do this, but must do it as soon as possible. Domestic animals include: horses, donkeys, cows, sheep, goats, deer, pigs, chickens, ostriches and dogs.
• In cases where other persons are injured you must also produce your insurance certificate to the police at the scene. If this is not possible you will be given a producer and asked to present all documents to your local police station within seven days.

Advice regarding accidents

If you're involved in an accident or stop to assist others you should:

• Use your hazard warning lights.
• Turn off your engine and ask others to do the same.
• Use the emergency telephones on the motorway or your mobile phone to contact the emergency services that you require. Use the marker posts placed every 100yd on a motorway to pinpoint your exact location. Don't forget to inform the emergency services of the nature of the accident and the condition of any casualties.
• Move uninjured persons as far away from the carriageway and hard shoulder as possible.
• Do not move any casualties from their vehicles unless they are in danger from fire or explosion.
• Do not remove a motorcyclist's helmet unless in an emergency (say, for example, in order to resuscitate the individual if you're otherwise unable to reach the mouth). If you do have to remove the helmet, this should be done with great care and the neck should be supported at all times.
• Administer First Aid wherever possible.
• Stay at the scene until the emergency services arrive.
• If you have a camera or camera phone, take photographs. These can be of great use to any insurer. Also note the exact time and location of the accident, the position of any vehicles involved, the conditions of the road, and visibility. Take the names of any witnesses and the personal and/or insurance details of any persons involved. This will help you later if you need to complete any paperwork regarding the accident.

Accidents involving dangerous goods vehicles

Vehicles carrying dangerous goods will be displaying plain orange reflective plates. Vehicles carrying tanks full of dangerous goods will be displaying hazard-warning plates which state the nature of their contents. If you or anyone else is involved in an accident with a vehicle carrying dangerous goods you should also:

• Switch off engines and extinguish all cigarettes.
• Do not use a mobile phone in close proximity to the vehicle.
• Do not be tempted to rescue casualties as you yourself could become one.

- Call the emergency services and give as much information as you can about the labels and markings on the vehicle.

- Return and wait – behind the barrier, away from the vehicle – for the breakdown services to arrive.

BREAKDOWNS ON THE MOTORWAY

For more information regarding breakdowns, see the section 'Troubleshooting, and what to do when things go wrong' on p.85. If your vehicle breaks down:

- Attempt to leave at the next exit or service area.
- If this is not possible, pull onto the far left-hand side of the hard shoulder and turn your wheels towards the verge.
- Try to stop close to an emergency phone (placed at one-mile intervals along the hard shoulder).
- Use your lights and hazard warning lights to alert other drivers.
- Leave the vehicle by the passenger door.
- Any horses or livestock must remain in the vehicle, except in an emergency, when they should be properly controlled on the verge.
- Do not attempt to repair your vehicle by the roadside.
- Contact the local motorway police from the emergency phone, stating the nature of the breakdown.
- Contact the transport department of the company you are driving for, or ask the motorway police to do so.

ALCOHOL

As a professional driver, you should not be drinking and driving and here's why. The penalties listed below are pretty much the final nail in the coffin lid for any LGV driver. Any employment agency or haulage company is highly unlikely to employ a driver with these types of endorsement on their licence.

Failing to provide a roadside breath test (Code DR70)

Penalty: Fine up to Level 3 (£1,000), four penalty points on your licence. Disqualification is at the discretion of the Court.

Driving/Attempting to drive with excess alcohol (DR10)

Penalty: Fine up to Level 5 (£5,000) and/or up to six months' imprisonment. Mandatory disqualification for at least 12 months for first offence. Mandatory disqualification for at least three years for second offence within ten years.

Being in charge of a motor vehicle with excess alcohol (DR40)

Penalty: Fine up to Level 4 (£2,500) and/or up to three months' imprisonment. Ten penalty points on your licence. Disqualification is at the discretion of the Court.

After Driving/Attempting to drive refusing to provide samples for analysis (DR30)
Penalty: Fine up to Level 5 (£5,000) and/or six months' imprisonment. Mandatory disqualification for at least 12 months for first offence (18 months tends to be the norm, as you are considered to have been trying to avoid being found guilty). Mandatory disqualification for at least three years for second offence within ten years.

After being in charge of a motor vehicle refusing to provide samples for analysis (DR60)
Penalty: Fine up to Level 4 (£2,500) and/or three months' imprisonment. Ten penalty points on your licence. Disqualification is at the discretion of the Court.
The police can request a breath test or sample from anyone who is believed to have been involved in an accident or who is driving, attempting to drive, *or in charge of any motor vehicle parked in a public place,* including car parks and lorry parks. So having a few pints before you bunk-up for the night can result in disaster.
   It's worth remembering that:
• One pint of normal strength beer will take approximately two hours to work through the body.
• A single whisky or half a pint of beer will take one hour to work through.
• Smaller men and women are more greatly affected by alcohol, as their body's water content is lower.
• Nothing can be used, taken or done to eliminate alcohol from the blood faster than its normal rate. Four pints of beer will take eight hours regardless of how much coffee you drink or how many cold showers you take.

And for the technically minded here are the legal alcohol driving limits in scientific terms:
• 35 micrograms of alcohol per 100 millilitres of breath.
• 80 milligrams of alcohol per 100 millilitres of blood.
• 107 milligrams of alcohol per 100 millilitres of urine.

It is usually considered that approximately 2 pints of normal strength beer equate to the examples given above. But this is not the same for everyone and it would be far safer not to drink at all.
   It is worth remembering that the recommended number of alcohol units per week for women is 14 and men it is 21. A glass of wine, champagne, a single measure of spirits or a normal strength beer all equate to 1 unit each. Cocktails equate to 2 units.

DRUGS
Penalties for drugs are the same as those for

SPEED LIMITS

Type Of Vehicle	Built Up Area	Single Carriageway	Dual Carriageway	Motorway
Cars and Motorcycles	30	60	70	70
Cars towing Caravans or Trailers	30	50	60	60
Buses and Coaches	30	50	60	70*
Goods Vehicles not exceeding seven and a half tonnes	30	50	60	70
Goods Vehicles exceeding seven and a half tonnes	30	40	50	60**

*restricted to 62   **restricted to 56

alcohol (see endorsements list above), though the methods for testing are different. Skin, blood and urine samples are used for this, and although you may think you'll get away with it because drug taking is not easily detected by smelling it on the breath, you can still be asked for a sample at almost any time if you're in charge of a vehicle or if you've been involved in an accident. Remember that some

drugs remain in the blood for up to 28 days. My advice is simple, if you value your licence and your life, DON'T DO IT!

For further detailed information on the law and best practice in road transport see the Freight Transport Association's web site (www.fta.co.uk) or their Driver's Handbook available by calling 08717 11 11 11.

FINES AND ENDORSEMENTS

Offence	Imprisonment	Fine	Disqualification	Penalty points
Causing death by dangerous driving	10 years	Unlimited	Obligatory, minimum of 2 years	3–11 points (if exceptionally not disqualified)
Dangerous driving	2 years	Unlimited	Obligatory	3–11 points (if exceptionally not disqualified)
Causing death by careless driving under the influence of drink or drugs	10 years	Unlimited	Obligatory, minimum of 2 years	3–11 points (if exceptionally not disqualified)
Careless or inconsiderate driving		£2,500	Discretionary	3–9 points
Driving while unfit through drink or drugs or with excess alcohol; or failing to provide a specimen	6 months	£5,000	Obligatory	3–11 points (if exceptionally not disqualified)
Failing to stop after an accident or failing to report an accident	6 months	£5,000	Discretionary	5–10 points
Driving while disqualified	6–12 months	£5,000	Discretionary	6 points
Driving after refusal or revocation of licence upon medical grounds	6 months	£5,000	Discretionary	3–6 points
Driving without insurance		£5,000	Discretionary	6–8 points
Driving otherwise than in accordance with licence		£1,000	Discretionary	3–6 points
Speeding		£1,000–£2,500 for motorway offences, or fixed penalty	Discretionary	3–6 points
Traffic light offences		£1,000	Discretionary	3 points
No MoT Certificate		£1,000		
Seat belt offences		£500		
Dangerous cycling		£2,500		
Careless cycling		£1,000		
Cycling on pavement		£500		
Failing to identify driver of a vehicle		£1,000	Discretionary	3 points

THE TRUCK

Walk-round vehicle check

There are certain things on a truck that need to be checked every day to ensure its roadworthiness and legality. Do not rely on the previous driver – he may not have looked either! Here is a list of the checks:

• **Fuel:** Make sure that you have enough to get you to your destination and back again (if required). It would be wise to remove the cap on the tank and check the level manually. Older vehicles may have unreliable fuel gauges. Remember that if you are driving a refrigerated vehicle or trailer, the fuel level for this will also need to be checked.

• **Oil:** The dipstick is usually found under the front grille or behind the driver's cab, though in many modern vehicles the oil level can only be checked using the 'dashboard diagnostics' before the engine has been started. The diagnostics can be accessed using buttons on the stalk, a push in dial or buttons on the dashboard. The 'hardware' may vary though all you need to find are the methods of 'scrolling', 'entering' and 'exiting' through the menu. Oil level will be in there somewhere.

• **Fluid in Radiator:** The radiator is almost always located under the front grille. Grilles are usually opened from the front using a couple of latches just under the lip, but some simply pull straight up and out, without having latches.

• **Washer water:** Either under the front grille or in the driver or passenger stairwell leading up to the cab.

• **Lights:** Make sure all of them work, including those on the trailer. You'll need help to check the brake lights on unit and trailer. Don't forget to also check the marker lights down the side and at the top corners of your trailer and unit. All lights should be clean and not obstructed.

• **Curtains:** Check that they close, open, and strap down correctly.

• **Doors and retainers:** Make sure they can be correctly secured.

• **Tail-lifts:** Make sure that they're correctly stowed away.

• **Load:** Check that it is secure before you pull away.

• **Tyres and wheels:** Look out for any excessive or uneven wear (your tread depth should be no less than 1mm for vehicles over 3.5 tonnes (1.6 for less than 3.5 tonnes) and should apply to three quarters of the width of the tyre and all around the circumference). Look for scrubbing, bald patches, punctures, peeling or cracking of the tyre wall or any dents in the wheel rims. If any of your vehicle's axles have two tyres on one wheel, look at them from behind and check that the tyres are not 'kissing'.

• **Windscreen:** Check for cracks and chips. Severe cracks may require immediate attention. Make sure that the screen is clean inside and out.

• **Mirrors:** See that they're clean and undamaged.

Many drivers would be unaware of how many pounds per square inch their vehicle's tyres should have and with good reason. Many companies do not not display the PSI requirements for their vehicles' tyres anywhere on the vehicles or trailers themselves. Also, the correct PSI for tyre pressures may vary enormously from vehicle to vehicle. Below is an APPROXIMATE guide of what your tyres should be. This guide should only be used if you have no other information regarding your tyre pressures available to you.

Type of Vehicle	Front Tyres	Middle Tyres	Rear Tyres
Tractor Unit	95	105	100
Trailer for Tractor Unit	95–115	95–115	95–115
26 Tonne Rigid	125	100	100
17 Tonne Rigid	120	N/A	100
7.5 Tonne Rigid	95	N/A	100

- **Wheel nuts:** Most have yellow fluorescent markers that should all be pointing opposite each other. Check for any that are missing or damaged and look for rust marks around the nuts, this could indicate that they may be loose.
- **Brakes:** When you're hooked up to your trailer, listen for any hissing sounds, as this could indicate a serious air leak. If your ABS is working correctly, a light (usually green) should come on – provided it's working – at the bottom driver's side corner of your trailer when you press the brake pedal.
- **Number plates:** Ensure that your unit has two (front and rear) and your trailer has one, and that they're undamaged, clean, and visible.
- **Service leads and fittings on unit and trailer:** Check that they're not damaged, split, or leaking.

- **MoT plates:** Check the one on the trailer (on the trailer body, beneath the floor) and the one in the cab. Make sure they're valid and correct.
- **Tax and O licence:** Displayed in the windscreen of the cab. Check the dates.

- **Fire extinguisher, spill kit, eye kit, First Aid kit:** If it's required that you carry these, check that they contain the items they should and that they appear to be in working order. With fire extinguishers check that they haven't been used and not replaced.
- **Height indicator:** Check that your vehicle has one and that it is correct for the type of trailer you are pulling. Your trailer

height (when coupled to an average 5th wheel height) should be displayed somewhere on the trailer (usually at the front). If your cab is not displaying the correct height, adjust the indicator (so you don't forget what it is). If your cab is not displaying a height indicator at all, report it as a defect.

- **Wiper blades:** Make sure they aren't split, cracked, or bent.
- **Seat belt:** If one is provided, make sure that it's undamaged and working correctly.
- **Horn:** Check that it works.
- **Tachograph:** If you have an analogue tachograh, check that it's set on the right time and isn't showing any obvious faults or fault lights. Don't forget to make sure that if you only have one tachograph chart inserted you should switch the second driver mode to 'Break'. If you have a digital tachograph check for any pictograms showing a fault with the unit.
- **Odometer:** If your vehicle has an electronic odometer, check that it is set on km and not miles since all odometer readings should be written in kilometres on your tachograph chart. If in doubt check the readings on the tachograph itself (if it has an LED display) as these are always shown in km.
- **Interior:** Look for anything broken, damaged, or missing and notify your manager.
- **Dashboard diagnostics:** If, when you turn on the ignition, your vehicle diagnostics tell you that there's a problem with the vehicle or trailer, check it manually. Remember that after you've just coupled up to a new trailer, or if the vehicle has been sitting for a while, the air pressure will be low and will take some time to reach normal levels. If after a few minutes of idling or a few yards of driving your diagnostics system is still showing red lights, or if the red lights return or are intermittent, stop and get the vehicle looked at immediately. Don't drive on red lights! If the diagnostics system shows an orange ABS light for the trailer this may be due to a fault within the unit's or trailer's ABS system, or the ABS service lead may need replacing. Check with your company's workshop, as driving with faulty ABS systems can cause damage to the tyres when cornering or cause the vehicle to skid when braking. If your braking system is working correctly a green light will usually illuminate in the bottom corner of the front of your trailer when you brake, but remember that this light may not be working even if your ABS is.

Your vehicle's equipment

Using a pallet truck

For first-time users, pallet trucks can be pretty awkward things. If you push the handle to the right the forks move left, and vice versa, so manoeuvring them can take a little getting used to. Here are a few tips on how best to use one:

- To check if your pallet truck is working correctly, run your finger around the 'neck' of the handle where it joins the base of the forks. If this is wet and leaking oil profusely, the pallet truck is faulty and shouldn't be used. If it appears to be only slightly greasy, push the pumping lever down and away from you and pump the handle up and down. If it rises quickly and falls swiftly when you pull the pumping lever towards you, then it's in good working order. Check that the wheel and fork rollers are clear of debris in order to ensure free movement.
- If you're struggling to get the forks through the base of the pallet, push down on the handle as you push the forks through. This will lift the front end of the forks up and clear of any obstructions. Ensure that the forks are fully 'let down' before you attempt this.
- A pallet truck is much easier to control if the handle is pointing towards chest level. Any lower or higher and the forks will be harder to direct, forcing your load to wobble around all over the place.
- Some pallet trucks have a brake lever. This is usually situated on the opposite side or next to the pumping lever. It is a rare but useful addition, enabling you to stop the progress of the load without having to pull in the pumping lever and drop it onto the deck.
- A pallet truck cannot be used over kerbs, on cobbles, or on gravel, untarmacked, or uneven surfaces. Nor should it be used on sloping ground without assistance. Steep slopes should be avoided at all costs. The load should be broken down and taken into the premises piece by piece.
- The back of the trailer should be swept clean regularly. Even small chips of wood can abruptly halt the progress of a loaded pallet truck.
- If you're off-loading on a slope, use your tractor unit and trailer suspension to 'level out' the angle of the trailer and/or tail-lift. This should help to avoid instances of back injury through trying to pull a load uphill, and should help prevent accidents caused by being swept off your feet by a loaded, runaway pallet truck.
- To secure your pallet truck in transit, place the forks through the base of a loaded pallet or a pile of empty ones and pump the handle until the forks touch the pallet. Do not lift the pallet itself. This should be enough to hold the pallet truck in place on your journey. To ensure absolute security, run a strap through the handle and secure tightly to either side of the trailer. If you have no strap and no pallets, turn the pallet truck upside-down on the floor of the trailer. This should only be done as a last resort, as it will weaken the hydraulic seals in the pumping mechanism.
- You may come across pallets that can only be approached from two sides, the openings on the other two being too narrow to push the forks through. These types of pallets are often oddly shaped. If they're narrower than the length of the forks, you shouldn't push the forks all the way through and out the other side – you may end up picking up the next pallet in line and damaging it in the process. Also, narrow pallets have their cross-members in different places to what you would expect. If you start pumping

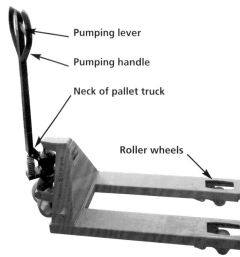

Pumping lever

Pumping handle

Neck of pallet truck

Roller wheels

up the pallet truck when the roller is resting on one of these cross-members, you'll split the pallet. If in doubt, a quick glance underneath should tell you where your rollers are.

Shrink-wrapping and securing pallets

Pallets should be wrapped from the base upwards. Pull out a length of shrink-wrap and twist it. Tie the twisted length in a knot around a chock at the base of the pallet. Beginning with the base, circle the load several times holding both ends of the shrink-wrap. Work upwards gradually towards the top of the load. This will make you dizzy, but persevere. Keep the wrap as taught as possible and use liberally – it's better to over-wrap a pallet than under-wrap it. To break shrink-wrap, use a knife or your nails – don't pull it, as it will only stretch and not break.

Handballing goods

Handballing – the manual handling of goods – is becoming less frequent as more companies become aware of the safety implications and the time wasted in removing goods from a vehicle by hand. The sort of places that you are most likely to encounter goods that need to be handballed are bakeries and those places where deliveries are made to the front of a shop. Even then, such goods will often be in cages or on wheels these days.

If you're delivering goods in stacks of plastic tubs or trays they can be moved fairly efficiently using a 'pulling bar'. This is a metal bar with a hook at one end and a handle at the other. The hook is positioned under the lip of the lid on the tray or tub. Using this method a whole stack can be moved at a time. However, great care should be taken to avoid twisting your body. If you have to do any lifting, manual handling techniques and guidelines must be followed.

Using cages

These are wire containers on wheels, used for transporting loose goods. Many supermarkets use them. They should be moved carefully and stored well. Don't off-load cages on a slope, and be sure to strap them in well during transit. Curtain-sided vehicles should never be used to transport cages unless they have been specially designed to do so. If your cages have foot brakes or braking bars, use them.

Using wheeled platforms

Many bakeries use these to move tall stacks of trays containing bread. Trays or tubs are placed on them and secured inside box trailers by means of retaining bars. However, stacks of goods on wheeled platforms are very unstable and should be manoeuvred carefully, as they have a tendency to topple over or separate. If moving a wheeled stack over a lip or gap, a foot should be placed on the bottom of the stack close to the wheeled platform in order to stabilise it.

Using retaining bars

Spring-loaded bars can be a little awkward to use and are not always very secure, as the sides of the trailer move and flex during transit, so if you have straps use them as well. You'll find most of them have handles to make for easier insertion. First place the spring-loaded end in one of the holes on the side of the trailer, then pull back towards the side forcing the spring-loaded section to compress. This will enable you to insert the other end into one of the holes on the other side. When using bars, try to make them as straight across as possible and do not set them at an angle.

A superior system that can withstand much abuse is the 'cup and bar'. To fit the 'cups' which carry the bar, tilt the end of the cup nearest to you upward, and it should slot into the hole and drop into place. Do the same with the cup on the other side (make sure they're as accurately opposite each other as possible). The ends of the bar simply fall into the cups and a small retaining clip pops over the top to stop them falling out in transit. If the clip is missing, don't use that cup.

'Clipped bars' are very difficult to use and are unreliable when they become old and bent. To use them, first drop the lip of the end of the bar into the slot on the wall of the trailer. Lift the other end of the bar upwards and do the same. The retaining clips should flick forward to hold the bar in place. If they don't, choose another bar or try another slot. Unfortunately this system often jams

when weight is pressed against it. If this occurs, close the back of the trailer, then drive forward a few feet slowly and brake hard. This should throw your load forward enough to release the bar.

Using chocks, blocks and stillages

Very large goods are often placed on the deck of the trailer using blocks. These are long thick planks of wood placed widthways across the trailer, which the goods sit on top of. This keeps them off the deck and allows forks to go underneath to lift them off.

Chocks are triangular-shaped blocks often used in the securing of very large cylindrical loads, such as reels of paper for printing works. The chocks are placed either side of the cylinders to prevent movement.

When not in use, chocks and blocks should be stored at the front of the trailer or in a locker along the side of the trailer body if provided.

Stillages are large metal containers on legs used to transport loose items. They come in all shapes and sizes but can often be stacked two or more high. They should, however, always be securely strapped down.

Using internal and external straps

Additional internal or external straps should be used with all load carriers and retainers to ensure the security of the load. Be sure that you are using the correct type and number of straps to hold the weight of your load. Remember, it is always better to use too many rather than too few.

Ratchet straps

These are used to secure loads likely to move in transit. The strap itself threads through a spindle in the ratchet mechanism. Each part of the strap (one short piece attached to the ratchet and one long piece) has a hook at either end which fits into any number of holes along the sides of the trailer. If the strap is being used as an 'over the top' external strap on a curtain-sided vehicle, the hooks should be clamped beneath the body of the trailer. To move the ratchet mechanism, pull the clip towards you to release it. Keep hold of the threaded strap and move the ratchet back and forth to tighten the strap into place. Remember that ratchet straps are extremely powerful and can bow the sides of a trailer inward if tightened too greatly. If you're using your ratchet straps to secure over the top and down the sides of a load, the easiest way to get them over the top (without climbing over the load) is to separate the two parts of each strap and wind the long end into a snail-like coil. Keeping hold of a free 3ft length of it, throw the remainder of the coil over the top of the load (make sure no-one is standing on the other side when you do this) and then fasten it under the body of the trailer on either side.

External straps

Similar to ratchet straps, these are normally used to secure loads inside a box trailer. You may find some that are attached to the walls of the trailer itself. This helps to prevent theft, but also means

that when a strap is damaged it isn't always replaced. Check that the ones you are intending to use are in full working order. External straps are tightened in a similar way to ratchet straps but don't have a ratchet mechanism. Stronger types are secured with a clip whereas others just fold over. Remember with all box-sided trailer strapping that the straps should be clipped to the walls a foot or so in front of the back end of the load. This will hold the load more securely.

Internal straps
Internal straps are only used on curtain-sided vehicles, where they hang from a bar across the roof of the trailer. They can be used to prevent sideways or backwards movement of the load. To prevent sideways movement, the straps should hang vertically down either side of the part of the load you wish to hold in place, and be secured by clipping the strap beneath the body of the trailer (usually where the curtain straps go). Movement of the strap along the top ring is only prevented by the tightness of the strap and its inability to move along the body of the trailer by being 'hemmed in' by the curtain straps. To prevent rear movement of the load, the straps should again hang vertically down in line with the back end of the load. They should then be diverted across the back of the load diagonally (see picture) towards the front of the trailer – if possible threaded through the base of the pallets – and should be fastened tightly beneath the body of the trailer.

Balancing the load
There may be occasions when you will have no opportunity to supervise the loading of your vehicle or trailer, but whenever you load it yourself try to ensure that the heaviest-weight items are placed over the axles – that is, about 6ft from the front of the trailer and about 6–9ft from the back doors. Also try to ensure that the load is evenly balanced from one side to the other. Do not place all the light items on one side and all the heavy items on the other, or be tempted to place the load on the rear of the trailer for easy removal. Both these actions will make the vehicle very unstable around corners.

Door seals
Electronic seals consist of a panel on the rear of the doors (usually covered by a protective plastic flap) with a thick wire running from it through the door handle and back to the panel. The panel has an LED display and a plastic lever with a red button on it. The plastic lever is used to hold the wire securely in place, and the red button, when pressed, gives you your seal number.

Plastic seals consist of a simple red tag that has to be pulled hard to be broken. A number is printed on the seal, which should be recorded on your paperwork.

Metal seals can be very difficult to remove, although they are very secure. To remove, pull downwards on the seal and wiggle the joining point up and down until it snaps. Don't try to twist off a metal seal, or you'll be there for a very long time!

Note that inbound and outbound seal numbers to and from all your destinations should always be recorded on your paperwork. Some shops and warehouses insist on removing the seal themselves, so this shouldn't be attempted until you've been given permission.

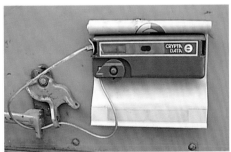

Anatomy of a truck

Getting into the back of your vehicle

This isn't always as easy as it may seem, and if you have no tail-lift it can be a bit of a struggle. Inside your trailer or at the rear of your rigid there should be a handle on the right- or left-hand corner strut, about 2ft up from the deck. It may be either a cord strap or a metal handle. Place your foot on the T-bar beneath the rear lights, grip the handle, and haul yourself up. You should also check beneath the rear of the trailer, as some of them have built-in pull-out ladders. If you use this ensure that it's fully stowed before you drive off.

Trailer interior light

Some newer trailers have interior lights. The switch usually comes in the form of a grey pad situated either outside or inside the trailer, close to the tail-lift control box. Not all trailers have them, and in those that do they often

don't work. With some interior lights, the vehicle headlights may have to be switched on in order for them to work.

Tail-lifts

These vary enormously from brand to brand and vehicle to vehicle. If you're unsure of yours, ask someone to show you how to use it before you leave the yard. Be aware that some tail-lifts have an isolator switch either on the dashboard in the cab or on the tail-lift control box. If a key is required to operate the tail-lift or to open the control box, make sure you have it before you

leave! Some tail-lifts also require you to keep a button pushed in on the control box while you're using the lift from outside the trailer. These complications are all designed to confuse and deter potential thieves (as well as the driver) so make sure you secure your tail-lift if you're parking in a public place overnight.

It's also important to remember that all tail-lifts have a series of buttons inside the trailer

TAIL-LIFT CONTROLS

 Moves up and under tail-lift out from its stored position

 Moves up and under tail-lift back into its stored position

 Moves tail-lift up

 Moves tail-lift down

 Tilts tail-lift when used in conjunction with up or down arrow

 This button needs to be held in when using tail-lift outside of the trailer

 This is representing a red push-in lock often found near tail-lift control panels. If you have to use this, be sure you have the key.

with a 'mode' switch that controls the inside and outside operation. Don't forget to push this switch back across after operating the tail-lift from inside the trailer, otherwise once you've got out and shut the back doors you'll be unable to stow your tail-lift without opening the doors again.

Some tail-lifts have a three-pronged lead that looks a little like a service lead and connects to the trailer in a similar way, which provides an electric feed to the lift. But most tail-lifts rely on an Anderson lead, a two-pronged double-ended lead which is fixed on the service lead frame and clips into a housing on the front of the trailer. Note that Anderson Clips come in more than

one size. Check that your lead fits into both ends correctly. Another similar type is called the Cow Bell. This again is a lead attached to the service lead frame that clips into a housing on the front of the trailer, and is held in place by a pull-down lever. When not being used both these leads should either be removed and stowed in the cab or tied around the service lead cradle.

When your tail-lift is in operation remember to keep your hands and feet well clear of the moving parts and the platform, and don't allow inexperienced persons into the back of your trailer or onto the tail-lift except in an emergency.

The up-and-under tail-lift

With its multitude of buttons this can be pretty complicated to use, but the rules are fairly simple. Move the tail-lift down about 6in before you move it out. When it's at is fullest extension it will make a 'straining' noise. From here, operation varies. Some up-and-unders will automatically flip the rest of the tail-lift out, some require you to use the tilt buttons to make the rest of the tail-lift present itself, and others need to be folded out manually (these can be quite heavy, so take care). However, most up-and-unders fit beneath the trailer in their

entirety and require no more unfolding (apart from the ramp stoppers).

To store your up-and-under, simply repeat the process in reverse, ensuring that the tail-lift is fully tucked under as far as it will go before you drive away. You may also find (though these are rare) that your particular up-and-under tail-lift has an additional feature that allows it to be operated using two rubber buttons on the tail-lift itself. These can be a little awkward if moving large loads on and off the tail-lift as the load itself can get in the way and accidentally activate the buttons.

The cantilever tail-lift

This type is fairly large and sits flat against the

back of the trailer doors. It is fairly simple to use and requires no manual handling. Firstly, you should check whether or not it has any additional safety features, such as a pull-out lever on the side of the lift which holds it in place and stops it from flopping down should the hydraulics fail. Pull this lever out, then press the 'down' and 'tilt' buttons at the same time until the lift is at right-angles to the back of the trailer. Then lower, lift, and tilt it as desired. To store, raise the tail-lift to its fullest height and press the 'up' and 'tilt' buttons at the same time until the lift is flat against the back doors.

same time pull the top edge of the tail-lift down and outwards. When it reaches right angles with the back of the trailer, a small wedge at the base of the lift's nearside hinge should pop into place and hold it at that angle. You then just use the up and down buttons to operate the lift. To store, push down on the floor of the tail-lift and pull up the handle or flip the wedge at the base of the hinge. The floor should try to spring upwards into its stored position. Push it all the way up until it clips securely into place. Press the up button until it stops moving. A retainer at the top will prevent it from falling down in transit.

The column tail-lift

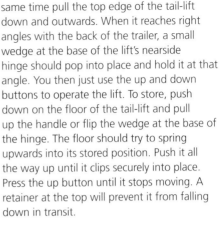

Again, a very simple tail-lift with usually only two buttons to worry about. Press the down button until the bottom of the tail-lift reaches just above knee-height. Check the edge of the lift and you should find a release clip or latch. Undo this and at the

The insider tail-lift
These are found on double-deck trailers and bread delivery trucks. The tail-lift is incorporated inside the trailer itself, acting as part of the floor when in the fully up position. It generally uses only up and down buttons and there may not be any externally accessed control panel.

Using a tail-lift on a slope
You should make efforts to avoid having to do this, but it is occasionally necessary. If your

vehicle is facing an uphill slope, lower the cab suspension and lift the trailer suspension. This should make things a little more even. If you're facing a downhill slope you should lift the cab and lower the trailer. If you're driving a rigid or an artic with no adjustable suspension don't attempt to off-load if the cab is facing an uphill slope, particularly if you're off-loading wheeled goods or palletised goods – a runaway pallet truck accident is not a pretty sight!

Take care to ensure that your goods remain on the floor of the tail-lift and don't slide backwards or forwards off it and under the rear of the truck, or out into the street, as you begin raising it.

Using a tail-lift around pedestrians

If you make deliveries to the front of a shop, be very aware of pedestrian complacency. I've seen people walk beneath, into and over tail-lifts, and even, in a drunken fit of bravado, attempt to climb onto them. If you drive onto pedestrian precincts take great care. You'd be surprised how unconcerned your average man in the street can be about seeing a 38-tonne truck trundling towards him.

Be sure always to use stoppers and safety rails if you have them. If possible, when off-loading make it difficult for pedestrians to walk close to your tail-lift. Block the surrounding area with boxes, tubs, cones, or anything else you have to hand. You'll normally be provided with some assistance if you're delivering to the front of a shop, and you should make good use of this second pair of eyes: ask them to watch out for any miscreants acting foolishly or dangerously around your tail-lift.

Stoppers and safety rails

Stoppers and rails are there to help you and prevent accidents. If provided, they should be used, particularly if you're off-loading wheeled goods. A stopper is a retainer of some description on the widest outside edge of the tail-lift that stops goods from sliding off when the tail-lift is in use. Some tail-lifts provide stoppers on all three edges or additional rails. Here is a description of those most commonly used and a few tips on how to operate them:

Folding ramps

The most common type of stopper. When folded out they provide an upright barrier on the edge or edges of the tail-lift. To use them as

ramps, they should be lifted upwards and outwards until they drop down towards the floor. If your tail-lift has three ramps, take care when stowing as they need to fall in a certain order to sit flush on the floor of the lift.

Flaps

These sit at the outer edge of the tail-lift and are normally flush against the floor. To activate them you most often have to apply weight on one side of each, which will tip them upright. Other flap stoppers are activated by pushing across a lever in the floor (next to the stopper itself) with your foot, which springs them upright. To close, simply stand on the stopper.

Removable safety rails

Some tail-lifts contain holes in the floor at the two short edges. These are for holding removable safety rails which prevent goods (and drivers) from falling off the edge. If your tail-lift has these, look in the back of the trailer or a side locker for the rails. If you're unloading wheeled goods, these can be a real lifesaver.

Trailer door security

Barn doors

'Barn doors' comprise two large doors at the back of the trailer that open outwards, secured by two or four vertical bars that fasten at the top and bottom. They're secured in place by twisting two or four levers, located at head height, towards the outer edges of the trailer. This turns the clips at either end of the bars into locking mechanisms at top and bottom. The levers are

right, which pushes the clip into a hole in the floor. Keep pulling the handle round till it comes up hard against a stopper. A securing latch should then pop in over the top of the handle. If it doesn't do this, it isn't secure.

Fridge doors

These are usually barn doors secured using flat door clips that have a 'push-in' bit in the centre of the handle to release the door. Remember that fridge doors are airtight and often difficult to open and close, so be certain they're secure before you drive off.

then positioned in clips on the door to hold them in place. Such doors can often be very stiff, but it's important to ensure that the clips at both top and bottom are fully secured and that the levers are fully seated within their clips.

Roller shutter doors

These normally use one of two types of lock. The first is the swing-over latch, which is a bar at the back of the trailer that rotates from left to right in order to secure the door and pushes a clip through a hole in the floor. Be sure to check that the door is fully down before you swing the latch across, otherwise it won't clip down. To be certain it's secure, try to pull the door upwards after you've secured it. If it won't budge, it's safe. If it has a Yale lock on the back, also remember to check that you have the keys before you leave the yard.

The other type of lock is a swinging catch. To secure this, simply pull the handle around to the

Types of door retainers

When a door is open it's important to use retaining clips at all times, as a swinging barn door is an accident waiting to happen. You'll find your retainers about 3ft from the back of the trailer, just under the floor. Some are metal bars on springs which pull out and hold back the open door, some are looped wires which clip through a loop on the bottom of the barn door catches. With box trailers you may find that they're attached to the side of the trailer itself

rear passenger side of a trailer. It can be swung upwards to the left or right to raise or lower the suspension. With the modern black-handled version, the lever must be pulled outwards to level the ride height. With older versions, the lever must simply be placed centrally. To adjust the suspension in your unit you'll find an adjustment panel inside the cab, near the floor to the right of the driver. If this is of the small square type, the top centre button activates the panel, the up and down keys raise and lower the suspension, and a button with an arrow pointing forwards (or in some cases a green button with arrows facing towards each other)

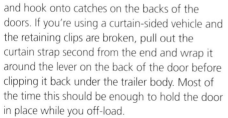

and hook onto catches on the backs of the doors. If you're using a curtain-sided vehicle and the retaining clips are broken, pull out the curtain strap second from the end and wrap it around the lever on the back of the door before clipping it back under the trailer body. Most of the time this should be enough to hold the door in place while you off-load.

Adjusting the height of a trailer or unit

Adjustable suspension
Most modern trailers have this. It is usually in the form of a black or silver handle found at the

returns you to ride height. If it's of the large rectangular type, both switches should be in the central position to return you to ride height.

Dump valves
A dump valve is used to release all the air from the trailer suspension. Dump valve buttons are usually black and are sometimes located in the same place as the trailer brake (don't mistake them for the trailer brake!) or else at the front of the trailer. Occasionally you'll find them at the back, but they're almost always on the passenger side. A prolonged release of air is usually heard when the dump valve is used.

If you have no air suspension on your trailer

This only occurs with very old trailers. If you're attempting to couple up to a trailer that's too low for your unit and you're unable to adjust your cab suspension so that you can fit beneath it, you must raise the trailer manually. This is achieved by pushing in your leg-winding lever. This changes the gearing on the winder and allows you to very slowly raise the trailer. You can also use this technique if your trailer feet seem to be stuck in the floor and you're unable to raise them in the conventional way.

Trailer brakes

Most trailers have brakes that are fairly easy to locate. They're normally one-third of the way from the front of the passenger side of the trailer. Sometimes they're located in a little rectangular box mounted onto the body under the trailer floor. Trailer brake buttons are normally red, though this isn't always the case. A sharp release of air is normally heard when you engage a trailer brake. Don't confuse the trailer brake with the shunt button, which is usually (though not always) blue.

Lift axles on units, rigids and trailers

Some tractor units and trailers have lift axles. This is where one axle of a three-axled unit or trailer can be lifted clear of the ground. Axles should only be lifted when the vehicle is not fully loaded. Lifting axles will save on wear and tear of the tyres but will make the vehicle unstable if it's carrying a full load, and places enormous strain on the other axles. To lift a tractor unit or rigid axle, look for a button in the cab that resembles a couple of off-set zeros (see 'Know your cab instrumentation and equipment'). You should ensure that your vehicle's systems are full of air and that your engine is running or the ignition is on.

Automatic lift axles on a trailer are controlled by a sensor within the trailer's ABS system and will automatically rise when the trailer is empty, and lower when the trailer is fully loaded. If this doesn't occur, there may be a fault with the ABS system. Get it checked.

The functions of service leads

You usually have five, or occasionally six, types of service lead running from the tractor unit to the trailer. Each performs a different function:

- **Red air lead:** This provides all the air to the unit and trailer systems, including brakes, suspension, clutch, driver's seat, and so on.
- **Yellow air lead:** The purpose of this lead is a little hard to define but the best analogy I can give is that if you imagine the red air lead as a tap that lets water into a sink (the 'sink' being the trailer and unit air tanks), then the yellow air lead is the valve that increases and restricts the flow of the water in accordance with requirements.
- **Black electric leads:** There are two of these, providing lights for the trailer.
- **ABS (anti-lock braking system) lead:** This provides anti-lock braking for the trailer, to help prevent skidding. It is black in colour and has a clip on it which is used to secure the coupling. If your trailer does not have an ABS coupling but your unit has an ABS lead, the lead should be either removed and stored in the cab, wound around the service lead cradle, or stored coupled into a dummy holder.
- **Tail-lift lead:** Some units and trailers have permanently attached tail-lift leads that look a little like service leads but only have three pins. Unlike Anderson leads or Cow Bells, these do not need to be removed or securely stored when the vehicle is in transit.

Battery isolator switch

This is a small red switch located at thigh height on the passenger side just behind the cab. Not all units have one. It is used to help prevent load or vehicle theft and also to prevent drainage of the battery on cold nights. Note that when this switch is employed all power to the vehicles systems from the battery is cut.

Know your cab

Adjusting your driving position

You'll find all of your seat adjusters on the right-hand side and front of your seat. Those at the front (usually consisting of pull-up or slide-across bars) adjust the seat backwards and forwards, while those at the side control height, angle, suspension, and lumber. The most comfortable driving position you can attain is one where the seat is tilted slightly backwards. Avoid using too much lumber support as this can tire the muscles in the lower back. To avoid having to stretch as you turn it, bring the steering wheel as close as is comfortable. It is often better to have your knees either side of the steering column rather than behind them, and position your height so that you can see out of the windscreen clearly yet still reach the pedals comfortably. Avoid putting too much 'bounce' on the seat. If you are of small build, this will throw you into the cab roof! The controls perform the following functions:

 Lumbar support: Provides support for the lower back and in some cases also for the sides of the body.

 Seat suspension: Brings the seat up to the ride height you've selected or drops it to the floor.

 Seat-back adjuster: Adjusts the back of the seat from laid-back to bolt upright.

 Heated seat: Unfortunately not all seats have this, but on cold winter days it's a blessing (even if it does make you feel as though you've just wet yourself!).

 Seat tilt: Tilts the front of the seat up or down. Instead of a button at the side of the seat, this can sometimes be found in the form of a paddle at the front edge of the seat.

 Seat height adjuster: Adjusts the height of the seat.

 Seat springiness adjuster: Allows you to adjust the suspension according to your weight and personal preference. If you're light, you should have this set to minimum.

Steering wheel

It's important to get the position of your steering wheel correct and comfortable. If it's too far away, this will cause a strain on your arms, shoulders, and lower back, and if it's too close it may impair your ability to turn the wheel rapidly. Most are fully adjustable, with about four different types of adjusters:

- **The wheels:** There are two wheels, one on either side of the steering column, that you have to undo. Once loosened, one will pull the steering wheel towards you and the other will lift it up and down. These adjusters are often very stiff, as they have to be tightened firmly to stop the steering wheel moving in transit.
- **The lever:** This is found either on the front of the steering column close to the driver's knees, or at the side at knee height. It can be a push-in button, a lift-up button, a lift-up lever, or a twist-back-and-forth lever. The steering wheel can be adjusted in all directions when applied.
- **The floor button:** This is to be found either in the centre of the floor or on the right-hand side close to the base of the seat. The driver has to push it in with his heel in order to adjust the steering wheel. Not to be confused with an exhaust brake.
- **The pedal:** Situated above the accelerator or clutch pedal, this looks like a miniature brake pedal. When pushed in, the steering wheel can be fully adjusted.

Dashboard buttons, lights and dials

The symbols found on your dashboard will vary greatly from vehicle to vehicle. However, I've provided diagrams and explanations of the most popular ones that you're likely to encounter in the course of your working day:

 Overhead lighting: This provides full lighting for the cab. Should not be turned on whilst driving.

 Overhead red nightlight: Provides the driver with dim, red illumination inside the cab. This can be used whilst driving.

Headlight adjuster: Raises and lowers the angle of the headlights. Only to be used to lower the headlights when the vehicle is fully loaded.

  Rear and front fog lights: Apply only when visibility is considerably reduced. On some vehicles you may have to pull out the dipped headlight switch to activate fog lights.

 Inspection light: This allows you to couple and uncouple more easily in the dark. It may sometimes be necessary for your vehicle's head or sidelights to be on in order for the inspection light to work.

 Dashboard light brightness switch: This is usually a dimmer switch type dial. It enables the driver to see his dashboard dials and buttons better in the dark.

 Exhaust brake: May need to be used along with a lower gear when descending a steep hill. The exhaust brake may come in the form of a button on the dashboard, a flat button on the floor, or a feature on one of the steering column stalks, when it is usually displayed as a circle with a dotted crescent around each side. Make sure this is not stuck on when you're accelerating, as you'll not get anywhere fast!

 Cruise control: This is usually featured on one of the steering column stalks. To activate cruise control, you generally have to get to top speed and then pull the stalk towards you. It is deactivated either by braking or by pressing an off switch on the stalk. Configurations for cruise control vary greatly so you may have to play with it a bit.

 Dif lock: Only to be used to move the vehicle if it is momentarily unable to grip the road or surface. It must be turned off immediately the moment it has served its purpose.

 Reverse warning alarm: This silences the reverse warning alarm and should only be used between 23:00–07:00 hours.

 Tank bleeder: If your vehicle runs out of diesel, the system will need to be bled of air. Very few vehicles have a tank-bleeding switch, so try to avoid running out of fuel! The alternative is a costly breakdown bill.

 Tank heater: In this country you're unlikely to ever require this. Under extremely low temperatures it's possible for diesel to freeze, and a tank heater will prevent this from happening.

 ABS light: This is a light on your dashboard that may appear orange if your ABS lead is faulty or if the ABS systems of your truck or trailer are faulty. In the case of an ABS lead, this can often be caused by nothing more than a bent pin within the lead's couplings. Get this checked. Failure to do so may result in wheel-locking and tyre-scuffing when you brake. It will light up red if you have a serious fault with your ABS system. If this happens while you're driving, stop. If it appears when you're in the yard and doesn't turn off after you've driven a few yards, don't leave.

 Brake light: This will appear in red if you have your handbrake on or if you don't have enough air in the system, in which case you won't be able to move. If it comes on when you're driving, stop immediately (though you may not have much choice in this, as the brakes will automatically be applied anyway).

 Raise lift axles: This button raises and lowers your unit or rigid's lift axles. A similar button showing the circles set at the same level, lowers it again.

Air pressure dials: These tell you how much air you have in your vehicle's brake, clutch and suspension tanks. If the needle falls within the red section of the dial on either tank you won't be able to move the vehicle, as the pressure is too low.

MoT plates

MoT plates are positioned both in the cab and on the trailer. These will tell you the make of your vehicle and registration, the maximum gross weight, year of manufacture, and train weight – this is its maximum weight when connected to a trailer. It also tells you when the vehicle or trailer's next inspection is due. In the cab the plate is usually found behind the driver or passenger seat, on the dashboard, or on the rear wall. On a trailer it can be found attached to the chassis, or at the front near the service lead couplings.

Tax and O licence

This is displayed in the windscreen of every vehicle. It shows your company's operators' licence number, the vehicle registration, and the expiry date.

Fuses

Usually found where you'd expect to find the glove box on a car. Fuses often blow following a power surge or a short-out (such as a bulb blowing). Inside the lid of the fuse box there's normally a diagram stating which fuse does what. This also shows you where the spare fuses are kept.

Broms Brake

Only found in Volvos, this is a secondary brake – situated below the normal handbrake – that automatically comes on when the unit is very low on air, and will remain on until released manually. To release the brake, push the knob inwards.

Cab heaters

These are used to warm the cab in cold weather when the engine isn't running. I wouldn't advise  using these while you sleep, as they're powered by diesel from your tank and can dry the air so much that you could find yourself waking up with an awful headache. It's also worth remembering that there's a delay between turning on or adjusting

a heater and it actually doing what you just asked it to do. This makes it difficult to be sure exactly what your heater's doing.

Most cab heaters have a timer switch that you can adjust using arrow keys, enabling you to set it to come on at a certain time. They also have a dial switch to control the 'fan', and many have a temperature switch. The more sophisticated even have an alarm clock built in. However, they're all different, so you may have to play with it to find out what yours does. (At least it gives you something to do before bedtime.)

Uncomfortable seat belts

With older vehicles you'll often find that the seat belts are secured very high up on the side of the cab, and if you're small you may find that the belt will cut right across your neck. However, there is a solution: pull the seat belt out across your chest, longer than is needed, twist the end round and round several times to alter its position across your body, and then clip it in.

Remember that if a seat belt is provided in the cab, you must wear it.

Positioning your mirrors to maximise your vision

Normal mirrors should be positioned so that you can see a small proportion of the trailer, three-quarters ground level, and one-quarter sky. Wide-angled mirrors should be positioned so that slightly more of the trailer is visible. This will help to reduce the size of any blind spots. Kerb mirrors (the ones that hang over the top of the passenger door) should be positioned so that they point straight down without being angled towards the front or rear. Only a small part of the side of the cab should be visible.

The worst blind spots for a truck are the area extending approximately 25ft from the rear of the trailer, the area just behind and beside the passenger door, and a smaller area below and behind the driver's door. There's also another area that extends approximately 5ft in front of the cab. The mirrors themselves also obstruct your view when approaching a roundabout or crossroads, so be aware of this and check the area several times before you pull away.

Different types of tachograph

Type 1

This is the conventional type of tachograph. It is built in as part of the speedometer and is opened by turning a  key above the speedometer dial and pulling it towards you. The tachograph will fold out on a hinge. Tachograph charts should be placed in this type of tachograph with the trace facing upwards. The tachograph mode selectors are found at the bottom of the speedometer, close to the hinge. Always ensure that this type of tachograph is fully closed afterwards. If it isn't, a tiny red warning light should appear at the bottom corner of the speedometer when you're stationary. To adjust to British Summer Time, turn the white cogwheel inside the tachograph until you reach the correct time.

Type 2

Fairly uncommon but usually found in older Volvos. This type of tachograph is hidden behind a panel in the top edge of the dashboard that's opened by twisting a lever found between the mode selectors above the speedometer. The tachograph chart should be placed facing towards you so that its edge falls into the green slot at the bottom. The lever should then be twisted back so that the whole mechanism is hidden again.

Type 3

Becoming more popular in modern vehicles. You could be forgiven for mistaking this type of tachograph for a radio, as it is normally placed

above the driver's head. To open it, turn on your ignition and press the button that looks like an eject button. The front should flop open after about five seconds. If this doesn't happen, push it in, as it may be on a spring catch. Pull the open tray towards you and down and insert your tachograph chart facing upwards. Ensure that it is seated below the guide on the top left-hand side of the tray. To close, push the tray upwards and in until it clicks. You then select your mode using the '1' button (if you're the only driver) and watch the LED display for the various mode symbols. Remember to select the correct mode before you drive off. With this type of tachograph it is impossible to know which mode you are in once the vehicle is moving. If 'break mode' was last selected and you later become stuck in traffic, your tachograph chart will show readings of hundreds of 'mini breaks' taken. This is a tachograph offence and will be noticed.

Type 4

Specific to the Mercedes Actros, this type of tachograph consists of two slots below the speedometer (one for each driver). To use, turn on the ignition and simply insert your prepared disc into slot one in the same way you'd insert a CD into an in-car stereo system, with the trace side facing upwards. The tachograph will do everything else for you; all you have to do is select your mode. Note that this type of tachograph uses a 120 type of tachograph chart as opposed to a 125 used by most other tachographs.

Understanding your gearbox

Manual

Straight 5 or 6 (with or without splitter), rigids only

This is basically much like a car gearbox. It has no high or low ratio gears, though it may have a splitter providing half gears. Those with splitters are usually found on rigids used for towing trailers. With the old type of Iveco gearboxes these can occasionally jump out of gear when going over a bump.

Four over four

The most common type of gearbox. Contains four low ratio forward gears and four high ratio forward gears. This type of gearbox may or may not contain a splitter providing half gears.

Three over three

Same as a four over four, but with only three low and three high ratio gears.

Four beside four

Sometimes known as 'eight with a gate'. Most commonly found in Ivecos and Renault Premiums, this contains four forward gears on the left-hand side of the box. The driver then has to push the gearstick through a gate in the middle to reach the other four higher ratio gears. This can be a very fast gearbox and may or may not contain a splitter providing half gears. It can also be a very stiff and awkward gearbox. The trick is not to attempt to force it into submission. Allow the gearlever to find its way from neutral into the correct gear with the maximum amount of guidance and minimum amount of force. Note that this type of gearbox can be very easily, accidentally put into reverse. If possible, try to choose your start off gear before you have fully stopped at a junction.

Crash

Eaton Twin Splitter

Every new driver's worst nightmare, the Eaton Twin Splitter is rarely seen these days and usually found only in older ERFs, Fodens and DAFs. Some informal training may be required in order to operate one of these.

The configuration is 12 gears in a four over four type of configuration. Each of the four gearstick positions contains three gears that are selected using a three-position splitter lever (towards the driver, in the middle, and away from the driver). When changing gear using the splitter lever only, or changing up through the gearbox using a combination of the splitter and the gearstick, it isn't necessary to use the clutch. It's vital that, whatever you're doing, your revs are within the green band or the gearbox won't select the gear. Down changes made while the vehicle is still travelling should be made gear by gear, though if you've stopped or almost stopped you can block change.

The changing-up technique from standstill goes something like this: pre-select splitter position, put in clutch, rev engine into the green band and move gearstick: the gearbox will select the gear. Pull away. When revs are at the top of the green band, pre-select next higher splitter gear, take your foot off the accelerator, change the gearstick position (if necessary) and while revs are in the green band the gearbox will select the gear. It's the same for changing down, though you'll often find yourself braking then clutching and revving in order to get the box to select a gear. The Eaton Twin Splitter has a lot of power in the lower gears, and unless carrying a heavy load you're unlikely to need to pull away in any gear lower than fifth or sixth. Once fully proficient, a driver can change up and down the box hardly using the clutch at all.

Fuller Road Ranger
This behaves similarly to the Eaton Twin Splitter in that the revs must be within a certain range in order to change gear. The gear configuration is the same as that of a four over four gearbox

with a high and low splitter lever. The main difference between the behaviour of these two gearboxes is that with the Fuller you must use the clutch until you've become fully proficient as it doesn't pop into gear as easily as the Eaton. It also has the added scary function of a 'clutch brake'. This means that if you push the clutch all the way to the floor you won't be able to change gear. This gearbox is now considered to be very archaic, therefore you're unlikely to come across it.

Automatic

Keypad (mostly found in refuse trucks)
This type of gearbox is almost idiot proof. The gear-changing system consists of a keypad situated in the centre console with one drive gear (represented by 'D'), a first and second gear for slow forward motion, a neutral gear (represented by 'N'), a gear for when the vehicle is parked (represented by 'P'), and a reverse gear (represented by 'R'). It's important to note that with this type of gearbox, when the vehicle is placed in any forward or reverse gear the engine is engaged automatically and the vehicle will begin to move. There isn't a clutch, so when not moving neutral or park should be selected.

Actros Automatic

A clutchless gearbox, specific to the Mercedes Actros. In newer models the gearstick is situated on the end of the armrest, while in older models it's attached to the side of the seat. Unlike the Keypad gearbox, the vehicle won't pull forward when a drive or reverse gear is selected. Instead the vehicle will behave as though it's in neutral, so brakes must be applied – it will only move when you press the accelerator. Be aware that because of the nature of this gearbox moving backwards on a slope can be a buttock-clenching experience, since you have no clutch to regulate your vehicle's movement.

The gearbox contains an automatic or manual switch mode. When manual is selected, forward gears are activated by pushing the gear knob forwards and backwards to change up and down the 'box. If automatic is selected, you'll only be required to push the gearlever forward once, to take the vehicle out of neutral. Everything else is decided by the gearbox. If, however, you wish to change into a lower gear than that selected by the 'box, you should push down on the lever attached to the neck of the gear knob. This will put you into the next lowest gear. If you wish to select the next highest gear, pull this lever upwards. To select neutral press the button on the left of the gear knob, and to select reverse push the button on the right of the gear knob and pull back on the stick at the same time.

Iveco Stralis

A clutchless gearbox specific to the Iveco Stralis. So far there have been no modifications to this gearbox. It can be operated in either automatic or semi-automatic mode, which are selected by using the right-hand button on the top of the gear stick. The LED display will tell you which mode and gear you're in. If automatic is selected you'll only need to push the stick forward once, to take the vehicle out of neutral – the gearbox will decide everything else for you. As with the Actros Automatic, the vehicle won't move in either direction until you press the accelerator. If semi-automatic is selected you'll need to push the stick forwards and backwards in order to change up and down. To select neutral, press the button on the left of the gear stick, and to select reverse pull up on the collar at the base of the gearstick while at the same time pulling the 'stick backwards.

Volvo Automatic

A clutchless gearbox similar in appearance to what you would find in a car. This makes it instantly familiar and user-friendly. To change your mode, pull in the button under the gear stick and select either reverse, neutral, automatic, manual or low (indicated by 'R', 'N', 'A', 'M', and 'L'). If you select manual you change gear using the buttons at the sides of the top of the gearstick. If you select automatic you simply press the accelerator to go. The gearstick will also fold out of the way for easier access to the passenger side of the vehicle. Press 'Fold' on the top of the gearstick and push it down.

Renault Opti 2

A clutchless gearbox found in the new Renault Magnum. This is quite unlike most other gearboxes and not easy to understand by sight alone. To select manual or automatic modes, push the gearstick to the left. To select neutral, push the gearstick hard to the right. To remove from neutral hold down the button on the right-hand side of the gear knob at the same time as

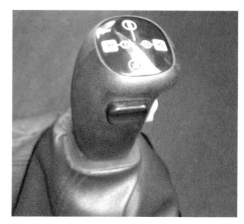

pulling the gearstick back across to the left. If in manual mode push the gearstick forward or backward to change up and down the 'box, and if in automatic mode simply push forward once and the gearbox will select the appropriate gear. As with other automatics, the vehicle will not move until you press the accelerator and behaves as though in neutral. To select reverse hold in the button at the front and pull the gearstick backwards.

Semi-automatic

EPS 1
Specific only to Mercedes, the EPS 1 is the earliest type of EPS gearbox. Its main difference from the EPS 2 is that there's no lever with which to manually select a lower or higher gear because, unlike the EPS 2, the computer won't automatically calculate and block change for you. Instead it will only select the next higher or lower gear to the one you're in. To block change up or down, you must push the lever backwards or forwards more than once before you engage the clutch.

EPS 2
Specific only to the Mercedes Actros, the EPS 2 semi-automatic is an excellent gearbox, easy to use and great for city work. It has a clutch used in the conventional way when the gear is actually changed. The gear 'stick' consists of a box in the centre console. On top of the box is a forward and backward handle, attached to which there is a lever with a button on either side at the top.

To begin the gear changing process you push the handle forward (without having the clutch pushed in at the time). The onboard computer block-changes for you and usually selects second or third gear if you're stationary on level ground. You then push the clutch in to actually engage the gear. To change down gears pull the handle backwards instead of forwards. To select neutral press in the button on the top left-hand side of the handle, and to select reverse push in the button on the top right-hand side of the handle at the same time as pulling the lever backwards. For both neutral and reverse you should be stationary and have the clutch pushed in. If you wish to select a lower gear than the one the computer has chosen, push down on the lever attached to the handle and then push the clutch in again (you won't often need to do this). If, however, an alarm sounds when you attempt this you've selected too low a gear. Don't let the clutch out – instead, alter your selection and try again. Occasionally, the gearbox may throw you into neutral. To resolve this push the clutch in and the lever forward at the same time. The computer should then select the correct gear.

Comfort Shift
Usually found in new MANs, the Comfort Shift looks and behaves like a normal four over four gearbox with one difference: it has two clutches! The conventional one is where you'd expect it to be, while the other takes the form of a thumb-operated button on the top right-hand side of the gear knob. This means that as you begin to change gear, you press in the button at the same time instead of pushing the clutch down. However, you shouldn't leave either the button or the clutch pushed in for any length of time (say, for instance, if you're sitting in traffic), as this will use air and will momentarily disable the clutch.

Fuelling up

FUELLING UP

Automated card bunkering systems

These are used at unmanned fuel bunkers and many truck stops. Some garages also provide a bunkering system out of hours. Here are a few basic tips on how to use one:

- Check that the card you have is accepted at the pump (search the guide in the front half of this book or look on both sides of your card for any logos matching those displayed at the bunker).
- Pull up to the pump and undo fuel cap.
- Look for an electronic machine on a stand next to either of the pumps (it'll look a little bit like an oversized intercom system with a keypad on the front).
- Find the slot where the card goes. This is sometimes hidden under a flap.
- Insert card in the manner indicated on the machine.
- The machine will ask you for your pin number (be sure that you've been given this by your company).
- The machine will then ask you for information

regarding your vehicle, such as odometer reading and registration number. If necessary you should write these down before getting out of the cab, as the machine will only wait a short while before 'timing you out': you'll then have to reinsert your card and start again.

- The machine will next ask you to choose your pump. Numbers are usually clearly marked on the sides of bunker pumps.
- You should now be free to draw fuel. Be careful not to overfill. Only fill to just below the neck, not the top of it.
- When complete, the machine may ask if you'd like a receipt (this is usually an additional option). Press 'enter' or 'yes' and a receipt should emerge.
- You should now be free to remove your card if the machine hasn't already instructed you to.

On-site key systems

Many large distribution centres provide a fuel pump for drivers using their vehicles. Check your key ring for any strange-looking plastic keys or fobs – these are used to draw fuel from this type of system. If you're driving a hire vehicle you

AdBlue and the new Euro 4 and 5 Legislation

European legislation to reduce vehicle emissions and consumption began in 1990 with 'Euro 0' regulations. In October 2006 we reached 'Euro 4.' This legislation is ongoing and Euro 5 comes out in 2008. In order for trucks to be able to meet the Euro 4 legislation, two new systems of reducing emission and consumption have been created. One of these is known as the SCR (Selective Catalytic Reduction) system and uses a liquid called AdBlue. The liquid itself is clear, non-toxic, non-hazardous and non-flammable. AdBlue is the product name so you may see it advertised under other trademarks such as Air1. If you are given a new vehicle, ask if it uses AdBlue. If in doubt, check around the vehicle. You should clearly see an additional tank near the fuel tank. This will be marked AdBlue. Inside the vehicle you will also find gauges telling you how full the AdBlue tank is. You should always keep your AdBlue tank topped up, failure to do so could result in expensive damage to the vehicle's catalytic converter. AdBlue will be available at the pumps in most truck stops, dealerships and LGV-friendly petrol stations. It is also available in 10 litre cans (which will enable you to drive approx 600km) or most haulage firms are supplying it at the pumps in their depots.

Do not put AdBlue in your diesel tank or vice versa. There should be safeguards in place to prevent this happening (such as different sized nozzles and tank necks) but be very careful not to get them mixed up!

The other system of reducing emissions is being used by MAN and *most* Scanias. This is known as the EGR (Exhaust Gas Re-circulation) System and requires no action from the driver.

may have to ask for a key from the transport division.
• Pull up to the pump and undo the fuel cap.
• Look for the electronic machine on a stand next to either of the pumps.
• Find the hole where the key goes. This may be under a flap.
• Insert key into the hole or press against the electronic reader. Keys will often only fit in a certain way and those that actually look like real keys often have to be turned to the right after insertion.
• The machine will then ask you for information regarding your vehicle, such as odometer reading and registration number.
• The machine will next ask you to choose your pump, and either re-show your fob or remove your key.

• You should now be free to draw fuel. Be careful not to overfill. Only fill to just below the neck, not the top of it.

Red diesel/Green diesel

Be very careful when choosing your pump if you're working for a company that transports refrigerated good, as they may have a red diesel pump on site. Don't put red diesel into your tractor unit tank – this is a very serious offence and your company can be prosecuted for it. Red diesel, known as 'Green diesel' in Ireland, (or gas oil) must only be used in the fuel tanks of refrigerated trailers or shunter vehicles. If you've been provided with one of these, be sure to fill it up at the end of the day. White (normal) diesel can also be used to run refrigerated trailers if red isn't available, but red is preferred as it's much less expensive.

Coupling a unit and trailer

1 Check that your tractor unit is roadworthy, legal, and in full working order. Check the fluid levels in your unit before you move it. (See 'Walk-round vehicle check'.)

2 Reverse the back of the unit up to the front of the trailer. Arrange the unit and trailer so that they're both pointing at the same angle and are perfectly lined up.

3 Apply the parking brake and get out of the unit to check the trailer over. If it isn't in a bay, check that the back doors are closed and secure (if not still being loaded). Check that the trailer is roadworthy and has a valid licence (you should find this beneath the body of the trailer on the passenger side, about three-quarters of the way towards the back, or at the front of the trailer).
    If the curtains are open, close and fasten them securely (provided it is not required that the load be re-checked before leaving the yard).

4 Notify anyone loading the trailer that you're about to reverse under it. Many sites will not allow you to reverse under a trailer whilst it is being loaded, so check first that it is OK for you to do this.

5 Check that the trailer brake has been applied; if not, apply it. Remember, pull to park.

6 Check the height of the unit and ensure that the fifth wheel plate will fit beneath the trailer. If the unit is too high or low, adjust the air suspension in the cab. If your cab has no air suspension you'll need to adjust the trailer height manually. (See 'Adjusting the height of a trailer or unit' on p.46.)

7 Reverse part of the way beneath the trailer.

8 Apply the parking brake, get out of the cab and check the height again.
    The fifth wheel plate should be flat and pushed hard up against the bottom of the trailer. If it is not, adjust the suspension. Remember that if your cab suspension is too low or your trailer is too high, the fifth wheel may miss the pin altogether and you will find

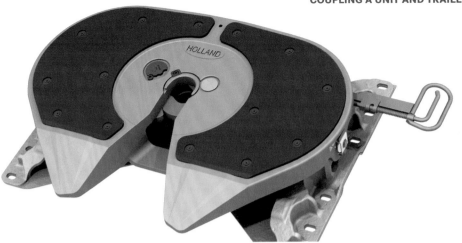

yourself reversing the back of your cab into the front of the trailer. This is a very costly mistake, so it is imperative that you get this right.

9 If you know that the unit and trailer are so close coupled that you'll be unable to squeeze in between in order to put the service (Suzie) leads on, you can do that at this point, though I'd not recommend it unless you have no other choice. If the trailer brake has been applied, it shouldn't move. However, it is wise to exercise great caution when doing this. Do not attempt it on a slope. Be sure that the trailer legs are not off the ground while executing this technique and ensure that you insert the yellow air lead first.

10 Reverse carefully under the trailer until you hear a loud click. This is the sound of the pin on the trailer slotting into place and being secured.

11 Put the vehicle into a low forward gear and try to pull away. You shouldn't be able to go anywhere. Try this several times. If you are able to move the unit out from under the trailer then the pin has not been caught. If you are lining the trailer and unit correctly and you have positioned the unit and trailer at the correct height but this continues to happen, it may be that the spring in the catch has gone. Line up, and reverse back under the trailer until you can reverse no more. Put the unit into park and get out of the cab. Pull the fifth wheel lever across to your left – it may spring inward into place. Get back into the cab and try to pull forward. If you are unable to, then you know you've correctly picked up the trailer. You should, however, remember to report this fault as a defect as soon as possible.

12 Apply the parking break and get out of the cab. Go under the driver's side of the trailer near the fifth wheel plate and attach the safety catch from the fifth wheel lever. This is of vital importance and is your insurance that you've correctly coupled the unit to the trailer. Your unit may also, or instead, have a metal retainer that pops down over part of the fifth wheel lever when the trailer has been securely coupled to the unit. If this metal retainer is not in place then the unit and trailer haven't been properly coupled. Some of these types of retainers don't have a conventional safety clip on a chain, the fifth wheel handle being released by pulling on the wire attached to the retainer at the same time as pulling the lever to the right. If you're unable to pull the lever across to the right or out, your trailer is securely coupled.

13 Fold back any wind deflectors at the side of the unit (some pull out and towards you, some pull out and forward).
  Use the steps at the side of the unit to mount the footplate. Attach the leads furthest from you first. This will prevent the spread of

fifth wheel grease over your clothing. If you struggle with the yellow and red air leads, attach them first. This may involve some interesting acrobatics in order to keep yourself clean; however, you can stand on the service leads to keep them from brushing against you, though you may just end up with the grease all over your boots instead. If you find the leads particularly tough, get right behind them and find something to rest your foot on, then grip the leads, wedge your elbow against your knee and push hard. This should be enough to insert them.

If you're still having difficulty, turn off your engine (if it's running) and pump the foot brake for a short while. This will expel air from the system and make insertion easier. If your leads have been left looking like a mass of spaghetti, stand on the floor and pull them all across the footplate towards one side and stretch them out. This is by far the best way to untangle them.

If your leads have been stowed in 'dummy holders' at the back of the unit, this can be a little confusing for a new driver, who may not be able to tell which is the dummy and which is the genuine clip. Remember that the dummy holder will have no leads running to it at the back. It is important to note that when inserting your electric couplings into the headstock on the trailer, you should always ensure that the spring-loaded flap covering the couplings falls back over the top of them. Failure to do this may result in your electric leads 'popping out' in transit. It is important to note also that if you are driving a fully automatic tractor unit, it may be wise to couple up your air leads with the engine running as many of the vehicle's systems on an automatic are linked to the air supply and a massive loss of air from the unit to the trailer as the vehicle attempts to fill the trailer's tanks and systems may result in an inability to even so much as start the tractor unit after coupling up. Once you have fully coupled-up your leads, dismount from the footplate backwards and walk back to the cab.

14 Turn on ignition, lights, and hazard lights. Check all of these are working on the trailer. Report and correct any defects.

15 Go to the leg-winding handle on the passenger side of the trailer. Occasionally you may find this on the driver's side). Detach the

handle from its housing (you can use your foot to do this if it's stiff) and wind the handle forwards towards the unit (forwards to go, backwards to stay). You may occasionally find that this action is reversed. If the handle won't budge, turn the ignition and raise the cab suspension, then try again. If you don't have air suspension on your cab, you'll have to alter

the gearing on the winding handle (see 'Adjusting the height of a trailer or unit' on p.46), and free the feet of the winding legs bit by bit manually. Wind the legs up as far as they'll go – usually so that you can no longer see the oily or rusty parts of the legs. Stow the handle correctly, don't leave it dangling. If there is no safe way of stowing it, secure it to the body or cross-member using cable ties or string.

16 Check that your vehicle brake is on and release the trailer brake.

17 Check the back of your vehicle if you're in a loading bay and make sure that your load is secure and that it's safe for you to pull out. If you have roller shutter doors, close them securely before you pull out of the bay.

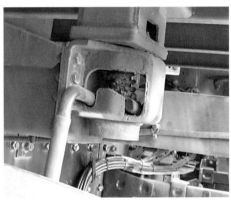

18 If your trailer is carrying a drop-box, check that the twist locks are in the correct position. The red handle should be pointing up and down the length of the vehicle, not out towards the side (see 'Changing boxes on a rigid and drawbar trailer' on p.73).

19 If you have barn doors, pull forward so that you have enough room to securely close them.

20 Affix any seals required.

21 Affix number plate to the back of the trailer. If the number plate is missing, report it and have one made up. Do not leave the yard without a number plate of some sort.

22 If you were in a loading bay and were unable to check the rear lights before, turn on the ignition and do it now.

Uncoupling a unit and trailer

1 If your trailer has barn doors and you're reversing into a loading bay, open them first and use the retainers to hold them back.

2 Remove the number plate and stow it in the cab.

3 Reverse carefully into your allocated bay or parking space.

4 Apply the parking brake and get out of the cab. Walk to the side of the trailer and apply the trailer brake. Some sites prefer you not to leave the trailer brake on after you have uncoupled, but always apply it anyway in order to do this.

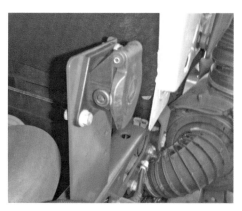

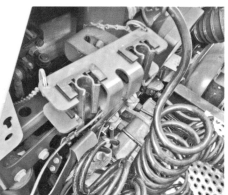

side of the footplate and stretch them out. When done, stow them safely using the 'dummy clips' if provided, or, if not, tie them as securely as possible over the back of the service lead frame.

5 Mount the footplate and, starting with those nearest to you, remove the leads from their clips on the trailer. Take great care with the red and yellow air lines, as these will spit back at you. If the lines have become tangled and you have room to untangle them, pull them to the

6 Wind down the legs using the winding handle. Extend them until they are sitting about 1 inch above the ground and re-stow the handle.

7 Undo the safety clip and pull the fifth wheel plate handle across to the right and out, then across to the right again until it slots into its open position. With some newer units you'll also have to pull on a wire that opens a little retainer at the same time as pulling the handle across and out. With older units (these usually have shorter, less accessible handles) you may have to pull the handle out first then across. If you have difficulty pulling out the handle, get back into the cab and reverse the unit against the trailer; this technique should enable you to then pull out the handle. If this doesn't work, try a forward gear instead and pull away from the trailer. You should then be able to pull out the handle. If neither of these techniques work, seek help.

8 Once uncoupled, drive forward slowly, part of the way out from under the trailer. Stop and apply the parking brake. Lower the unit suspension all the way down before commencing full exit from under the trailer. This prevents damage to the trailer legs and wheel covers on the back of the unit.

9 Raise the unit back to normal ride height before parking up or refuelling.

Coupling a rigid and drawbar trailer

1 Check that your rigid is roadworthy, legal, and in full working order. Check the fluid levels in your rigid before you move it. (See 'Walk-round vehicle check' on p.34).

2 Reverse the back of the rigid up to the front of the trailer. Arrange the rigid and trailer so that they're both pointing at the same angle and are perfectly lined up.

3 Apply the parking brake and get out of the unit to check the trailer over. If it isn't in a bay, check that the back doors are closed and secure (if not still being loaded). Check that the trailer is roadworthy and has a valid licence (you should find this beneath the body of the trailer on the passenger side, about three-quarters of the way towards the back, or at the front of the trailer). If the curtains are open, close and fasten them securely (provided it is not required that the load be re-checked before leaving the yard).

4 Notify anyone loading the trailer that you are about to reverse up to it. Check first that it is OK for you to do this.

5 Check that the trailer brake has been applied; if not, apply it. Remember, pull to park.

6 Check the height of the rigid and ensure that the drawbar eye of the trailer is lined up with the 'guide funnel' (cup) of the rigid. If the rigid is too high or too low, adjust the air suspension in the cab. If your cab has no air

suspension you'll need to adjust the height of the trailer manually. (See 'Adjusting the height of a trailer or unit on p.46).

7 You will notice that your rigid can be fitted with a coupling which is either manually opened or have a partially or fully air-activated system that operates the pin. You will also find that your vehicle will have one of three different types of operating mechanism. These are described in detail below.

For all of these types of coupling, the pin should be in the raised position before coupling can commence.

The manual lever type
If you are facing the 'guide funnel' of the coupling mechanism, you will see on its top, left-hand side a small lever. Lift the lever until the coupling pin is raised into the latched open position, a small red indicator button just in front of the lever will pop out. This shows that the pin is up and the mechanism is ready for coupling.

The plunger and handle type
Take a look along the side of the rigid, near the back and you will find an exposed valve box which has a handle and a black plunger knob on top. To open the coupling pull the plunger knob upwards and at the same time turn the handle through 90° to lift the pin.

The control box type

Again, in roughly the same sort of place as you would normally find the 'plunger and handle type' you should instead see a small box with a hinged lid. Inside this box will be found a red air tap and located beside it is a yellow control valve. Fold the valve handle down and press on the spring part beneath it. At the same time turn the handle anticlockwise through 90° to open the coupling.

Do not touch the red lever within the box. This is for the use of mechanics only.

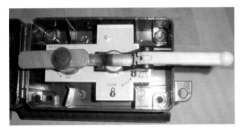

Check the 'guide funnel.' If you see any debris inside, remove it as this could prevent the pin from dropping completely. (Use a stick for this don't under any circumstances use your hands.) Check the eye of the drawbar trailer for excessive wear or damage. Faults such as a worn eye or wear pad, debris or grease in the guide funnel are some of the primary reasons why coupling can be made difficult and why trailers can detatch themselves in transit. (You don't want this happening to you!) If you find grease on the coupling or eye, either clean it off or defect the vehicle. (Couplings should be maintained using oil, not grease as this is too thick.) Check for damage and air leaks in and around the coupling, control box or behind the plunger and handle (you should be able to hear these).

8 If you have a rear camera monitor in the cab, turn it on. Reverse the vehicle so that the drawbar eye is inside the guide funnel. The pin should automatically drop down into place.

9 Get out of the cab and walk to the coupling. If you have the manual lever type, look at the lock indicator button. If it's flush with its housing and not exposed the coupling is locked. If the red button is exposed, carry out the uncoupling procedure and then try to re-couple. If the red indicator button will not sit

flush with its housing even after a few attempts at re-coupling, defect the vehicle. You should not drive the rigid or tow the drawbar trailer. Neither should you use the release handle as an indicator that it is coupled up as it could be fitted in the wrong position on the cross shaft.

If you have a 'plunger and handle type' make sure that the plunger is down and the lever is pointing towards the floor. Check that the handle is functioning correctly and that excessive play is not present. If you suspect a fault, do not drive the vehicle or tow the drawbar trailer.

If you have a 'control box type' put the yellow lever back in its closed position inside the box. If you cannot close the control box lid and the yellow valve is not folded and stowed properly, then you are not properly coupled up. Carry out the uncoupling procedure and try again. If you are still unable to stow the yellow handle and close the control box, there is a fault. Do not drive the vehicle or tow the drawbar trailer.

With all of these mechanisms do not use a pull test to find out whether you are properly coupled up or not. If the pin hasn't dropped properly you will damage the coupling!

10 Attach the air/electric service lines from the rigid to the trailer. If at any time the trailer is not being used, the service leads are double ended and should be unclipped from the rigid and stored in the cab. If you find that when you attach the leads from the rigid to the trailer they drag on the ground, use a piece of string and tie a loose loop around the drawbar encircling the leads to hold them away from the floor.

Do not allow your leads when uncoupled to drop onto the ground. The ends could become damaged and debris or water could get into the system.

11 Turn on ignition, lights, and hazard lights. Check all of these are working on the trailer. Report and correct any defects.

12 Go to the leg-winding handle and detach the handle from its housing (you can use your foot to do this if it's stiff). Wind the handle forwards towards the rigid (forwards to go, backwards to stay). Remember that occasionally you may find this action is reversed. If the handle won't budge, turn the ignition and raise the rigid's rear suspension, then try again. If you don't have air suspension on your rigid, you'll have to alter the gearing on the winding handle (see 'Adjusting the height of a trailer or unit' on p.46), and free the feet of the winding legs bit by bit manually. Wind the legs up as far as they'll go – usually so that you can no longer see the oily or rusty parts of the legs. Stow the handle correctly, don't leave it dangling. If there is no safe way of stowing it, secure it to the body or cross-member using cable ties or string.

13 Check that your vehicle brake is on and release the trailer brake.

14 Check that all twist locks holding the box to the chassis are in the correct position and not pointing outwards away from the centre of the vehicle. (This means they are undone.)

15 Check the back of your vehicle if you're in a loading bay and make sure that your load is secure and that it's safe for you to pull out. If you have roller shutter doors, close them securely before you pull out of the bay.

16 If you have barn doors, pull forward so that you have enough room to securely close them.

17 Affix any seals required.

18 Affix number plate to the back of the trailer. If the number plate is missing, report it and have one made up. Do not leave the yard without a number plate of some sort.

19 If you were in a loading bay and were unable to check the rear lights before, turn on the ignition and do it now. If your trailer usually has a Moffat forklift on the back but is not carrying one now, make sure that the lights are in the driving position, not stored to one side. To bring lights to the driving position, pull up the pin on the hinge, swing the lights towards the rear of the trailer and replace the pin.

Uncoupling a rigid and drawbar trailer

1 If your trailer has barn doors and you are reversing into a loading bay, open them first and use the retainers to hold them back.

2 Remove the number plate and stow it in the cab.

3 Reverse carefully into your allocated bay or parking space. Remember that it is always easier to 'pick up' a trailer on level ground, so always try to avoid dropping a trailer on an uneven surface.

4 Apply the parking brake and get out of the cab. Walk to the side of the trailer and apply the trailer brake. Some sites prefer you not to leave the trailer brake on after you have uncoupled, but always apply it anyway in order to do this.

5 Remove leads from their clips. If you're not coupling up to another trailer, remove the leads from the trailer too and stow them in the cab. Do not allow your leads when uncoupled to drop onto the ground. The ends could become damaged and debris or water could get into the system.

6 Wind down the leg using the winding handle. Extend it all the way to the ground and re-stow the handle.

7 Raise the pin using one of these three methods:

The manual lever type

If you are facing the 'guide funnel' of the coupling mechanism, you will see on its top, left-hand side a small lever. Lift the lever until the coupling pin is

raised into the latched open position, a small red indicator button just in front of the lever will pop out. This shows that the pin is up and the mechanism is ready for uncoupling.

The plunger and handle type

Take a look along the side of the rigid, near the back and you will find an exposed valve box which has a handle and a black plunger knob on top. To open the coupling pull the plunger knob upwards and at the same time turn the handle through 90° to lift the pin.

The control box type

Again, in roughly the same sort of place as you would normally find the 'plunger and handle type' you should instead see a small box with a hinged lid. Inside this box will be found a red air tap and located beside it is a yellow control valve. Fold the valve handle down and press on the spring part beneath it. At the same time turn the handle anticlockwise through 90° to open the coupling.

Do not touch the red lever within the box. This is for the use of mechanics only.

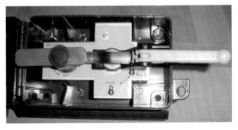

8 Once uncoupled, drive forward slowly.

9 Lower the pin within the coupling, using one of the three methods shown in paragraph 9 of 'coupling a rigid and drawbar trailer.'
It is vitally important always to drive with the pin down. This keeps the area around the pin clear of rust and debris.

Opening and closing curtains

Opening curtains

1 Only undo one curtain at a time. If you open both and it's windy, the wind will blow straight across the trailer and make it very difficult to close the curtains again.

another where you pull down on the strap to release the clip (strap type 2), and a simple fold-down type usually only found on rigid vehicles. The last is not very strong and should be done up extremely tightly.

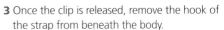

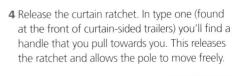

3 Once the clip is released, remove the hook of the strap from beneath the body.

4 Release the curtain ratchet. In type one (found at the front of curtain-sided trailers) you'll find a handle that you pull towards you. This releases the ratchet and allows the pole to move freely.

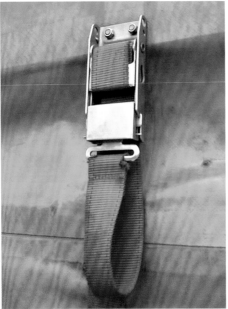

2 Release the straps. There are three different types, one that you push up (strap type 1),

In type two you'll need to pull on the shorter handle to release the ratchet. (These are often held in place with a clip.)

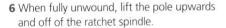

5 Pull the curtain hard and it should unwind from the pole.

6 When fully unwound, lift the pole upwards and off of the ratchet spindle.

7 Go to the other end of the trailer and pull on the curtain straps. Continue pulling back every sixth strap or so (less if on a rigid), working towards the freed pole, until the entire curtain is folded at one end.

8 Fold the pole backward. Pull out some of the folds from behind it and fold them around in front. This will better secure the pole and stop it swinging in the wind while the  forklift driver unloads your vehicle. You may find some lengths of strapping attached to the inside struts of your curtain sides. These are for pulling out and around the curtain to secure it to the outside door latches. This will hold the curtain in place while unattended.

Moving the central bar

There are many different types of central bar and many different ways of releasing it. With some you must pull up a lever and the bar will come away from the trailer floor and slide across on a runner in the roof. The one I've shown here is the most simple. The bar is released by pulling a catch across to the right and swinging the bar outwards. This way, goods can be easily lifted behind the bar with a forklift truck when the curtains are open. To close, simply reverse the procedure, ensuring that the catch is fully pushed home.

Safety of the load

A curtain is not a solid restraint and shouldn't be expected to behave like one. Unless the trailer

has been specially designed to take cages, only immovable or palletised good should be transported in a curtain-sided vehicle, though even many of these may also need to be strapped, certainly in the case of stillages or stacks of pallets.

Closing curtains

the trailer and the curtain is tightened as you pull on the ratchet. Continue working the ratchet until the curtain is as tight as you can get it.

1 Pull on the straps at the free end of the curtain. Keep going until the curtain is taut along the length of the trailer.

5 Secure the strap hooks beneath the body of the trailer. If they won't reach, loosen the straps.

2 Angle the pole downwards and into the groove. Push it up the groove until it slots in at the top.

6 Pull on the loose end of the strap and work the strap clip up and down a couple of times in order to tighten it before you clip it down. Remember that if it's too tight you'll be unable to clip it. It will also be difficult if there are any bits of strap in the way. If your straps are tucked up under the clip and you're finding it difficult to fasten the clip, untuck the straps before fastening.

3 Continue lifting the pole upwards and drop it onto the spindle above the curtain ratchet.

4 With type 1, the curtain is tightened as you push on the ratchet. With type 2, the short lever should be secured against the body of

7 Tuck the loose end behind the rest of the strap to hold it in place and stop the ends fraying.

Pulling a double-deck trailer

Correct loading

A double-deck trailer should be loaded with the heaviest goods on the bottom deck and over the axles. Top-heavy loading will result in the trailer being extremely unstable on corners and in high winds.

Dangers of raising the suspension

When the suspension of any trailer is raised, the airbags inflate. Because a double-deck trailer sits so low, this means that the airbags almost touch the ground. Therefore such trailers should not be moved with the suspension in the raised position.

Reversing a double-deck trailer

Almost all double-deck trailers have a steering rear axle. This makes forward turning easier as the trailer doesn't cut across corners as much, but it makes reversing much harder. Your trailer may have a rear axle steering lock. This should only be applied when the trailer and unit are directly in a straight line with each other.

When used, it makes reversing easier as it prevents the trailer's rear wheels from going all over the place.

How do they handle?

In a word, badly! Double-deck trailers are very unstable on corners and roundabouts, so take it slowly. Be careful on winding country lanes and take particular care in high winds. If fully loaded they can also be extremely heavy. Watch your downhill speed and make good use of your exhaust brakes and half gears, to avoid straining the engine or causing excessive wear on the brakes.

Raising and lowering the deck

Inside the trailer is a control box for raising and lowering the deck, internal tail-lift (if it has one), and suspension. You should not be expected to operate this without some informal training, so if in doubt, ask.

Pulling a refrigerated trailer

Refrigerated trailers do not handle any differently to any other kind of trailer. However, it should be noted that the refrigerated units are temperamental, and I'd advise that on long journeys you should regularly check your electric temperature monitor within the cab

that the fridge has stopped working altogether. If you're driving an artic, don't forget to check the fuel level indicator on the side of the trailer's tank before you leave

Continuous running mode

On and off modes

Enter button to program settings

Whisper mode (for night time running)

De-frost mode

Raise and lower temperature

or the electric or manual control gauge on the front of the trailer (if driving an artic), to ensure that the temperature isn't dropping. If it is, this could indicate either a faulty fridge generator or

the yard. Don't pull away without removing the electric lead from your refrigerated trailer and remember to plug it back in when you arrive back at base.

Pre-system check, to check for faults

For finding out warning codes

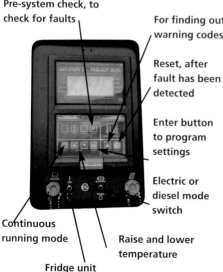

Reset, after fault has been detected

Enter button to program settings

Electric or diesel mode switch

Continuous running mode

Raise and lower temperature

Fridge unit on/off switch

Using frozen, chilled and ambient dividers

If you're carrying goods that need to be stored at different temperatures you may find that your trailer has insulated dividers that hang from the roof. These can be lifted up and stored in the roof, and can be moved up and down the trailer as necessary. The coldest part in a divided trailer is at the front, the warmest at the rear near the doors. Dividers aren't solid, and goods should not be secured to them – retaining bars should be used as a 'front wall' against which to secure goods. To lift dividers, look for a piece of cord or a section at the bottom edge which folds towards you. This will provide a handgrip enabling you to swing the divider upwards like a garage door.

Driving a rigid and drawbar trailer

A rigid and drawbar is a very different animal to a unit and trailer. Besides the ride being a bumpier one you'll also find that the manoeuvring capabilities are vastly different. It follows around corners more tightly, making city driving a joy, but if you're used to a unit and trailer you'll find that reversing a wagon and drag requires the patience of a saint. Its trailer whips round more quickly and you need much more space at the front of your lorry, as the turning circle of a rigid is significantly larger.

Changing boxes on a rigid and drawbar trailer

Dropping a box

1 Ensure that you're on very level ground before you attempt to drop a box.

2 Raise the suspension height of the front and rear of the vehicle. This is done by using the keypad inside the cab to raise the height of

the rear, and the right-hand side pull-in-and-out button (situated behind the cab) to raise the height of the front.

3 Lift the latch holding the front legs in place and pull them towards you. They may be quite stiff if they're not used often. When the legs are fully pulled out they should drop towards the ground.

4 If the legs aren't hanging straight down, they're not fixed. To be sure they're secure, try to kick the legs forwards towards the cab or backwards towards the rear of the vehicle. They shouldn't move. If the legs haven't dropped all the way down, raise the suspension a little more. If you're still unable to secure the legs you may have to stow them away briefly and move the vehicle to more level ground.

6 Move the twist locks holding the box to the chassis so that the red handles are pointing out towards the sides of the vehicle.

5 If your rear legs are similar to those shown in the photographs, you'll need to pull the lever towards the floor. The legs should drop down. You may have to lift them up a little in order to position the lever into one of the notch holes on the leg. Wherever possible try to put it into the last notch hole, and push the lever skyward to secure the legs in place.

7 Lower the front and rear suspension of the vehicle. The body should come away from the chassis and be held up by the legs.

8 Check that the legs are securely supporting the box and that it is free of the chassis, and slowly drive the vehicle out from beneath it. Return the vehicle to normal ride height.

Picking up a box

1 Lower the front and rear suspension of your vehicle.

2 Reverse the chassis slowly beneath the box, making sure that the V-shaped grooves are either side of the ridge of the chassis. You should get out and check this several times as you're reversing. When you're all the way under, the box will hit the front of the chassis and you'll be able to go no further.

3 Raise the chassis at the front and rear so that the box legs lift off the ground.

4 Secure the twist locks so that the red handles are lying flush against the centre of the chassis and pointing forwards and backwards, not out towards the sides.

5 Lift up the handle on the sides of the front legs and lift the legs upwards. Push them in towards the vehicle and flip the clip over to secure them in their stowed position.

6 Do the same for the rear legs and ensure that they're correctly stowed and secure.

7 Return the vehicle to normal ride height.

Acting as a banksman

How to be safe and remain visible

Everyone needs a banksman at times, even the most experienced drivers. It's always courteous to offer if you can see that a driver is struggling.

Wear your high visibility vest and make sure you can see the driver in his mirrors at all times: if he's reversing in the conventional manner, then he'll have difficulty seeing the whole of the nearside of his trailer and unit, and the front and rear offside corner. If he's reversing blindside he'll experience trouble seeing just about everything!

Many different signalling methods are employed by different companies to direct their drivers. However, some are universal. Whatever hand signals are used, they should be clear and easily seen from a distance.

• **Move towards me:** This is an exaggerated beckoning motion with both arms.

• **Stop:** Hold up one hand high and shout stop!

• **Your trailer needs to go to the right:** This is a continuous jabbing motion to the right.

• **Move away from me:** This is a continuous jabbing forward motion with both hands.

• **Your trailer needs to go to the left:** This is a continuous jabbing motion to the left.

Parking: against a kerb

When parking tight against the side of a road, a manoeuvre called a 'swan neck' is used. This involves driving your cab towards, then away from, then towards and level with the side of the road. This should enable you to pull your trailer in level.

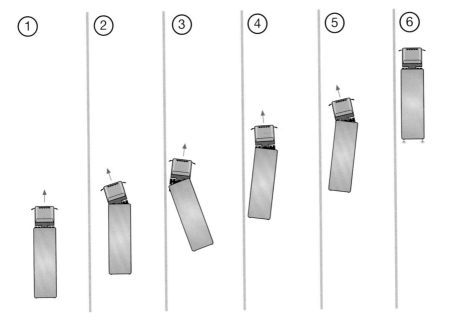

Parking: reverse parallel

This is a difficult manoeuvre that shouldn't be attempted by an inexperienced driver without the aid of a banksman. However, this type of reversing is often necessary if attempting to park in a designated loading area on the side of a road. Take your time and don't let anyone rush you. Mistakes can be costly if there are other vehicles nearby. First you should assess the space, to ensure there's plenty of room. Drive forwards, inwards, and out, then position the front of the cab at an angle pointing slightly towards the kerb before you attempt the manoeuvre.

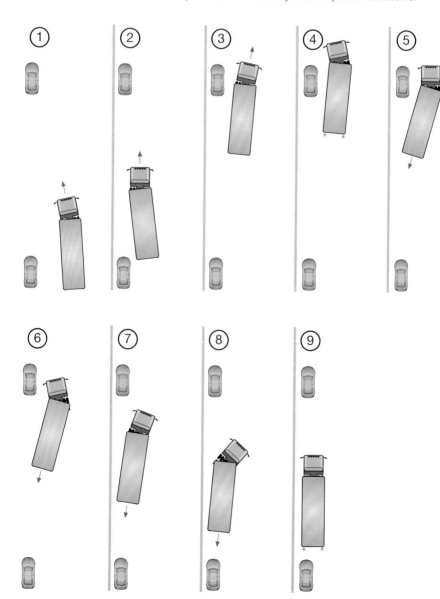

U-turns and tight corners

The dangers of U-turns and tight turns

U-turns and sharp corners are fine manoeuvres to make in a yard, where you have plenty of room, but there are certain things you should be aware of, particularly while executing them on a public highway.

- If you're turning in an extremely tight circle of 180°, your trailer will actually go into reverse. This can place you in something of a predicament if you haven't allowed space for it. Also, the trailer corner opposite to the direction in which you're turning will swing out wildly. Be very aware of this if you're turning a tight corner at a junction or roundabout, and close the lanes down on approach by straddling two of them. This should allow you more room to manoeuvre and prevent any unsuspecting car drivers from being squashed.
- If your leads are particularly tangled, the extreme action of a 180° turn can actually pull them out, particularly if you have anything on the front of your trailer that they can catch on (such as a cow-bell housing). If you can, it's best to stop and check afterwards.
- If you have to do a right-hand U-turn at a road junction, shut down as much of the junction as possible. If it's a dual carriageway cut a slightly diagonal swathe across as many lanes as you can with your cab pointing slightly towards the left. Don't let anyone get on the inside or outside of you. If necessary wait until all other traffic near you has gone. Take the angle wide first, then hard right, making sure that you allow enough space for the back of the trailer to clear the central reservation. This should get you round. Remember that U-turns on public roads are fraught with danger and should be avoided if at all possible. If one has to be attempted, don't try it if there are any 'No U-Turn' signs on the traffic lights or central reservation.

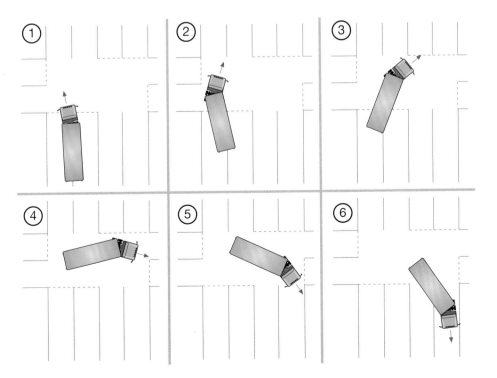

Reversing into loading bay

Check the area

If entering a yard that's unknown to you, it's wise to check the area before you drive in – if you're an inexperienced driver, this could help you to avoid getting yourself into a situation you're unable to get out of. If it looks tight, ask the staff how other drivers normally manoeuvre in. Check the width and length available to you. Make a note of any height restrictions and obstacles and be sure that you can actually fit into the space. Use all the room available, ask for assistance if you're unsure about reversing. Stop if you hear any noises you are unsure about or feel any 'resistance' to your momentum. Don't allow others to rush you and take it slowly – you'll do less damage if you hit something at a low speed! Some loading bays have guiding lines or metal lining-up posts on

the floor to help you aim in the right direction. Most loading bays have large rectangular blocks of hard rubber screwed to the wall to prevent damage to both the back of the trailer and the loading bay. You should also have rubber blocks on the rear of your trailer or unit. When reversing you should aim the rear of your trailer centrally between the rubber blocks on the loading bay

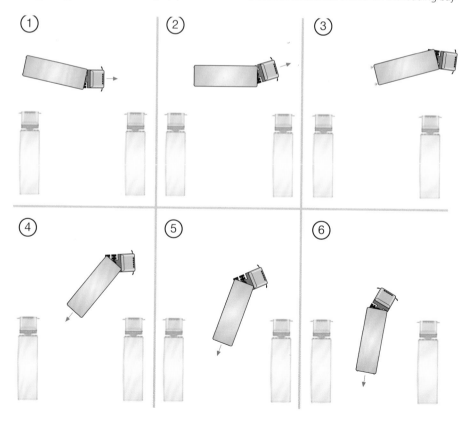

wall. Once hard up against the rubbers, pull forward an inch or two to prevent damage to your vehicle as it rises and falls during off-loading. If your vehicle or trailer has a cantilever tail-lift, check the loading bay. You may find a rectangular hole in the bottom of the loading bay. This is for your cantilever tail-lift. First line up your vehicle before lowering your tail-lift so that it sits about 1ft off the floor before completing your reverse manoeuvre.

It is also vital to note that if at any point you are not in attendance of your vehicle while it is being off-loaded be sure to check that your door is fully closed and your load is secure before you leave the yard.

Reversing blindside

Reversing blindside is an extremely difficult manoeuvre even for an experienced driver, because your view in your nearside mirror is obscured by the trailer once it goes beyond a certain angle with the tractor unit.

Wherever possible you should approach a loading area from its right-hand side so that you can clearly see the offside (driver's side) of your trailer as you manoeuvre backwards, even if this means driving past the loading area and turning your vehicle around.

If you have no other choice but to reverse in blindside, position your nearside (passenger side) wide-angled mirror outwards a little and pull back the curtain covering your cab's rear window (if you have one). This should give you an improved view of the side of your trailer and the area you're reversing into.

Check the area within which you have to manoeuvre, and make a note of the distances between you and any potential obstructions. Get help, even if only from a passer-by: ask them to stand in a safe place and shout if you're about to hit anything behind or to either side of you. Wind down your windows and move very slowly. If you're using a banksman, stop if he disappears from your view.

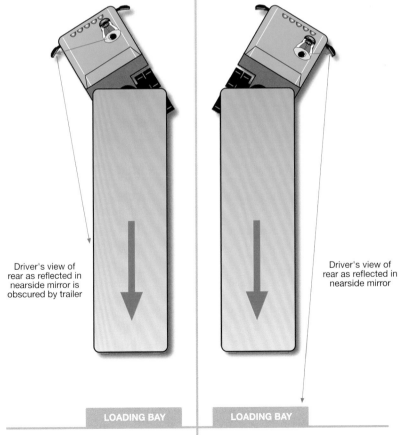

Driver's view of rear as reflected in nearside mirror is obscured by trailer

Driver's view of rear as reflected in nearside mirror

LOADING BAY

LOADING BAY

BLINDSIDE REVERSING MANOEUVRE

NORMAL REVERSING MANOEUVRE

Adverse driving conditions and hazards

Night driving
Some drivers love it and others hate it. Of course, the advantages are obvious – less traffic and fewer hazards than day driving. However, it can take a toll on your eyes. The human body isn't designed to function in low light levels, so it's important to have regular eye-tests and take plenty of Vitamin A. Avoid staring directly at oncoming traffic and try instead to focus on the full extent of the area illuminated by your lights and beyond. Watch out for nocturnal animals and cats when driving through rural areas or along residential streets. Make sure the headlights are clean and bright. If they seem too dim, get them checked. Remember, you should never drive using sidelights – they're only designed for use when parked or stopped on unlit streets.

Narrow roads
For new drivers these can be very unnerving, and only experience will help you overcome this. Just bear in mind that all A-roads are designed to take two trucks side by side in most places. If the road is about to narrow so that this isn't possible, you'll be warned – look out for triangular road narrowing signs or any indication of tight bends up ahead, and slow down. You may have more room than you realise anyway: check your nearside mirror regularly – you may be surprised how much space there is.

Residential streets and parked cars
The hazards are obvious: children and animals running out from between cars, pedestrians crossing, and car drivers opening doors. Take great care when driving through residential areas.

Drive below the speed limit and keep your wits about you. Turn off the stereo and wind down the window. If you have to pass pedestrians or cyclists on the side of the road, give them plenty of room and check your nearside mirror as you pass. Don't be rushed or hurried into any manoeuvre – take your time and drive carefully.

Snow
Hopefully you'll never have to do this, but in regularly snowbound parts of the country your company may supply you with snow chains. Make sure you're trained on how to fit them correctly. Failing that, take great care to ensure that your tyres are in good condition. It can take a truck almost ten times the normal distance to stop safely on a snow-covered road. Avoid braking sharply. Drive very slowly, and if you have traction control or a dif lock, switch it on when required.

Fog
In reduced visibility, use rear fog lights and front fog lights if you have them. Don't forget to turn them off when visibility returns to normal. Slow down and maintain a safe distance. Don't 'hang on the lights' of the vehicle in front of you. If driving in built-up areas, wind down the window and listen for oncoming traffic at junctions, or children playing nearby.

Cold or icy conditions
Before leaving the yard ensure that your screen and mirrors are entirely clear of ice and aren't misted up. If you don't possess a windscreen scraper climb up the front of the cab and use the edge of cassette box or unused credit/loyalty card to scrape off the ice. Don't use the windscreen wipers until the screen has fully cleared, as this will damage them. If you have heated mirrors, use them. Run the engine until the cab heats up and you can clearly see ahead of you before you drive off. Remember to keep a safe distance between you and the vehiclein front.

Heavy rain
Turn on your lights and wipers. Slow down and maintain a good distance from the vehicle in

front. Try to stay out of the spray of other vehicles, avoid overtaking, and don't tailgate.

Steep hills

When descending a steep hill, slow down at the top, change into a lower gear and use your exhaust brake if your vehicle has one. On a more gentle slope, drop down one or two gears and again use the exhaust brake. If approaching a steep incline, change down one gear before starting – you should lose power less quickly: don't wait until the engine is straining before you change down through each gear or you'll struggle before you reach the top. If you have to stop on a steep incline, choose your first lowest gear or crawler gear to move off in. If you lose traction, switch on the dif lock. This should be enough to get you up the hill. Don't forget to turn it off at the top.

High winds

Many a curtain-sided vehicle has been blown over in high winds while driving across exposed parts of the country. Take particular care if you're pulling a double-deck trailer. If the trailer is empty, pull back the curtains and secure them well to the rear of the trailer using any external straps that you have available. Internal straps

should be folded back and secured along with the curtains so that they don't flap or fly about in the wind. Safely stow anything loose in the trailer, such as blocks or chocks. If the trailer is full, try to stick to low ground and roads that aren't so exposed.

Other obstructions or hazards you may encounter

Horses

Take particular care around horses. Keep your revs low and even, keep well back until the opportunity to overtake presents itself, and pass slow and wide. A spooked horse can kill itself, its rider, and possibly even you.

Overhead obstructions

Be aware of overhead cables, low canopies, hanging branches (particularly after a storm), and overhanging wall signs on pedestrianised streets. These can all take the top off your cab's wind deflector or trailer.

Ground-level obstructions

Watch out for bollards, posts, high kerbs, low walls, and holes in the ground. If you're in a pedestrianised area, everything from litter-bins to trees can be a problem, so remember to get out of the cab and take a good look around before reversing.

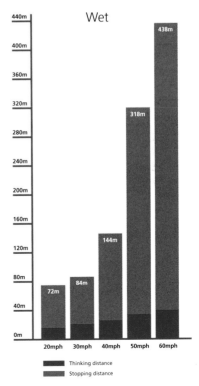

Tramlines

These are indentations in the road (usually the first lane of a motorway) that the wheels of a truck often fall into (sometimes with alarming ferocity). They can even be capable of pulling the steering wheel clean out of the driver's hand.

Contraflows and Roadworks

You may encounter many different types of hazard within roadwork's or contraflows, so it is vital that you stay alert and stick to any temporary speed limits imposed. These hazards may include: Road maintenance staff crossing the carriageway, uneven or loose road surfaces, ramps, uneven cambers, poor lighting, inconsistent road markings, missing barriers and very narrow lanes. If in doubt, slow down and don't be rushed.

Gritter Lorries

On a motorway, these vehicles will normally occupy the middle lane in order to spread grit more evenly. Pass slowly and give the vehicle plenty of room. Remember motorbikes and cyclists will be trying to give any gritter lorries a wide birth. Be prepared for them slowing down or moving further away than you expect.

Abnormal Loads

On a motorway, an abnormal load may be too large to fit into one lane and will straddle the first two. In these instances it is acceptable for an LGV driver to pass in the third lane. If the vehicle is gingerly occupying the first lane only, pass slowly and allow him plenty of room, straddling lanes two and three if you feel it is necessary.

AVOIDING LOAD THEFT, DAMAGE, AND PERSONAL ATTACKS

- Where possible use truck stops, transport cafés and motorway services stations, preferably with CCTV, floodlights, and/or security guards. Keep to well-lit areas and avoid parking overnight in lay-bys.
- If your trailer is empty, or if you're carrying unmovable goods (such as sheet steel), open a back door and fasten it securely. This will deter thieves from slashing open your curtains just to get a look at your load.
- Even on extremely hot nights, it's not wise to leave your window open. A determined thief may break in and assault you in order to steal your load. Other tactics include using ether to knock out the sleeping driver, or gassing him using carbon monoxide from a car exhaust attached to a pipe pushed through the cab window. Instead of leaving a window ajar,

open the sunroof if you have one. You should find anyway that once the sun goes down, the inside temperature of the cab will drop dramatically. If it's a particularly warm day try to park your cab in the shade of a wall or hedge. This should cool the cab more quickly.

- If you have a locking fuel cap on your tank, make sure it's locked before you park up for the night. A truck holds many hundreds of pounds-worth of fuel. In some parts of the country siphoning is common. I've even heard of instances where the entire fuel tank was removed during the night!
- Don't leave valuables in plain sight. Remove from the dashboard anything that can be seen from outside.
- When delivering in public places (at the back or front of a shop, for instance) lock the vehicle and keep mobile phones and CDs hidden. This rule should be observed even when using a filling station or bunker. Remember that thieves fuel up too.
- Women in particular should take great care when parking overnight. Don't park alone. Make yourself known to your male neighbours in the lorry park and remove anything on or in your vehicle that singles you out as being female.

PARKING UP FOR THE NIGHT

- Avoid parking on a slope wherever possible – this can make your night a very uncomfortable one. If it can't be avoided, sleep with your head at the highest end and your back sloped into the wall of the cab. Choose a quiet, traffic-free spot away from entrances or exits and as far from refrigerated lorries as possible (unless you're used to that sort of thing).
- With most truck stops you pay on entry. With most motorway services, a warden is normally in attendance somewhere on the premises (usually in a little yellow hut). If you can't find anywhere to pay, ask in the shop or café; they should be able to point you in the right direction. You'll find that you can purchase two types of ticket, one for parking only and one for parking plus a meal voucher. Don't forget to get a receipt or your company may not be able to reimburse you.
- Before you pay to park, check out the facilities and make sure that everything is working. It isn't much fun to find out in the morning that there's no working shower or hot water.

Troubleshooting, and what to do when things go wrong

'I've released the handbrake but the vehicle won't pull away.'
- Check trailer brake isn't on.
- Check that there's enough air in the braking system (you'll find dials for this on the dashboard: they should display how much air should be present). Normally an alarm will sound when the air is particularly low. Gently increasing the engine revs will enable the system to fill with air more rapidly.
- Make sure that the air leads are correctly coupled and listen for sounds of escaping air. If you have an air leak, you won't be able to pull away.
- If you're driving a Volvo, look for a Broms Brake (a push in/pull out knob) close to the handbrake on the dashboard. This must be pushed in before the vehicle can pull away.

'I can't push the clutch in.'
- Again, check that you have enough air in the system, as the clutch is also air assisted.
- Check for any obstructions beneath the pedal.
- If driving an old Iveco, be aware that their clutches are particularly stiff.

'The gear lever won't move.'
- If your engine is cold, be gentle with it. A truck has a very large gearbox and a cold one takes a little time before it is moving smoothly and fluidly. Run the engine for a short while before putting it into gear and moving off.
- If the gearbox feels jammed, put the lever into neutral position and shift it into high then low ratio a couple of times (with the clutch in of course) this usually frees a stuck box.
- If your gearlever is completely floppy, it may have become disengaged or its linkage broken. Seek help from a mechanic or fitter.

'I can't adjust the seat.'
- Once again, if height is the problem, check that there's enough air in the system, as seats too are air assisted. If, however, you are driving a DAF push the seat backwards a little

as the tube supplying the air to the seat occasionally gets trapped. Once the seat is at its correct height you can pull it forward again.
- If you're unable to move it back and forth, use your weight and use lots of force. Also make sure you have the lever fully pulled up.

'I can't pull out the lever to release the pin from the fifth wheel.'
- Check that your lever isn't a pull out, pull across type. This variety usually has a shorter, less accessible handle.
- Reverse the unit towards the trailer. If this doesn't work put the unit into first and try to pull forward. Either of these motions should free a stuck lever and enable you to pull it out. (Be sure that the trailer brake is on before you attempt this.) If neither of these methods is successful, try pulling out the lever after the cab suspension has been raised or lowered, occasionally this does work. If all of these things fail, seek help.

'I can't push the air leads in.'
- Check you have the collar pulled back and/or the notch lined up.
- Rest your foot on something and push, bracing your elbow against your knee.
- If there isn't enough room for you to squeeze in, refer to the 'How to couple and uncouple a unit and trailer' section on p.58–63.
- If all of these fail, switch off the engine and pump the footbrake to release air from the system.

'My mirrors keep dirtying in the rain and I can't see behind me.'
- Switch on your heated mirrors if you have them. If you're unsure where the switch is, see the 'Know your cab instrumentation and equipment' section on p.48.
- If you have no heated mirrors, or if they're not working, tie a small strip of cloth around the stanchion above the top of the mirror. The movement of the air around the cloth will flick it over the mirror, constantly wiping it.

'The trailer is too low to reverse under and I have no adjustable cab suspension.'
- You'll have to manually adjust your trailer height. See the section on 'Adjusting the height of a trailer or unit' on p.46.

'The lights don't work on my trailer.'
- If there's more than one light not working, check that your trailer electrics are correctly coupled to your trailer and that the leads and couplings don't appear to be damaged.
- If there's one defective light, tap it gently and see if it comes back on. If it does, you may have a loose connection behind the light. If not, then it may be a blown bulb or defective couplings.
- Check fuses to make sure none have blown.

'My tail-lift isn't doing anything when I press the buttons.'
- Check that the electric feed for your tail-lift is undamaged and fully clipped in.
- Look for a tail-lift isolator switch in the cab. This is normally a very obvious 'added on' switch on the dashboard.
- Check there's not an additional switch at the rear of the trailer near to or inside the control box, which you must keep pressed in order for the tail-lift to work.
- Check your key ring or the control box for any weird-looking keys or bits of plastic. These could be tail-lift isolator keys.

'I can't open/close the trailer doors.'
- If you're opening or closing refrigerated trailer doors, these are airtight and require some considerable force. Make sure you're attempting to close or open them in the correct sequence. The one with the overlapping rubber strip closes last.
- With barn doors, unclip and open in the correct sequence, one at a time. When closing check that the clips top and bottom are fully seated correctly. If your trailer is fully loaded, ensure that you are on level ground. An uneven surface will cause the trailer frame to twist. This will make it more difficult to open and close the barn doors.
- With roller shutter doors, check the wires that run up and down the side of the door about one foot in from either edge. If these are slack or appear to be off kilter, the door may be broken. Remember that some roller shutter doors are also very stiff when old and/or if they have a few rollers missing. If your door appears to be broken, get

help to open it and/or defect the vehicle or trailer if necessary (see Glossary). Check that the door rope (the strip of cord you pull on to close the shutter) isn't caught in anything.
- As with all doors, check there are no obstructions preventing you from opening or closing them (such as chips of wood, door ropes, or parts of your load).

'Help! I've hit something.'
- Don't panic. Follow the advice set out in the section on 'Collisions with other road-users, pedestrians, domestic animals or property' on p.28.
- If you've hit a domestic, non-domestic or wild animal such as a pet cat or a badger, stop. If the pet has an address tag, use it to contact the owner. Don't leave any injured animal to suffer. Call the RSPCA immediately. You can find their 24-hour emergency number in the 'Useful contacts' list.
- If an animal is dead it won't be breathing, its gums will turn pale very rapidly, and there'll be no reflex response if you tap the inside corner of its eye. Even an unconscious animal gives this response. If the animal is alive, resuscitation techniques can be followed in the same way as for a human, with the exception that you close the mouth and administer rescue breaths down the nose. For very small animals the infant technique should be followed. Many animals (with the exception of birds) don't survive a collision with a vehicle and die within a few minutes from shock. If this doesn't happen, attempts should be made to keep the animal alive until the RSPCA arrive or until the animal can be driven to a veterinary clinic.
- A dead animal should be moved away from the road, but not out of sight. Badgers are the exception to this rule. If you're able, move a badger well out of sight of the road. Though illegal, badger baiting still occurs in this country, and a baiter can trace a whole family from one dead badger.

'I've broken down on an A-road.'
- Move the vehicle out of the way of passing traffic as much as possible.
- Put on your lights and hazard warning lights. If you have a warning triangle, use that too.
- Get out of the cab on the passenger side and take with you your mobile phone (if you have one), high visibility vest, phone number of your transport department, and any warm clothing you have.
- If you're causing a serious obstruction hazardous to other road-users, call the police immediately.

Put on your high visibility jacket and walk up the road the way you came. Find a safe place from which to warn other drivers of the obstruction.

- Call the 24-hour phone number for your transport division and/or the breakdown number if one is displayed in the cab, and let them know the nature of the breakdown and your exact location. If you're not provided with a breakdown number, your company may give you a number to call, or will get their breakdown assistance provider to call you. If you don't have a mobile you should walk to the nearest house or business with a light on, or attempt to flag down a passer-by.
- Stay out of the cab. Remain in a safe place on the roadside verge (even if it's raining) until assistance arrives.

'I've broken down on a motorway.'
- For motorway breakdown rules see the section on 'Breakdowns on the motorway' on p.29.

'I'm at a filling station and I don't have the fuel cap keys.'
- Call your transport division and let them know what's happened. They may advise you to attempt to return to your transport yard. If the orange fuel light comes on, contact them again for further instructions.
- If they are sending someone out to you with the keys, drive out of the way of the pumps to a place where you can't cause an obstruction and wait for them to arrive.
- If it appears the keys have been lost, your transport division may send a breakdown service out to you.
- Under no circumstances should you attempt to remove the fuel cap yourself unless you've been expressly given permission by someone in authority.
- To remove a fuel cap, you either need to damage the lock or prise off the cap using a screwdriver and hammer (or heavy solid object). There's every chance that parts of the cap may fall into the fuel tank. If this happens, the workshop should be notified.
- Take great care not to damage the neck of the tank whilst doing this. A damaged neck means replacement of the whole tank.
- When you've removed the now damaged fuel cap and filled up you'll need to seal the tank again. Place the damaged fuel cap back onto the neck and place a latex or surgical glove

over the top and secure under the lip of the tank's neck with a cable tie.

'An orange light has appeared on my dashboard.'
- Stop at the next service station or lay-by and ring your transport division. They should be able to advise you what to do. Note that a few makes of truck use an orange light to tell you that it is checking the air tanks. These lights will feature close to the air tank gauge and will alternate continuously between the two tanks to demonstrate which one is being checked. If you are unsure that this is what you are observing, ask.

'A red light has appeared on my dashboard.'
- Stop immediately and ring your transport division. Continuing to drive when a red light is present may cause significant damage to the vehicle. Note, however, that some vehicles have a few interesting quirks when it comes to diagnostics systems. If you have not long switched off your vehicle and everything was fine but now it is giving you every warning light under the sun, switch it off again and leave it for about 30 seconds. This re-sets the diagnostics back to normal.

'There's no clip to hold my number plate in place.'
- Use whatever you can – string, a bulldog clip, several cable ties or rubber bands. Don't leave the yard without a number plate on your trailer.

'My truck wont start.'
- Check your key fob for any unusual looking items that could possible act as an immobiliser key then check your dashboard for a 'lock' to put it into. Immobilisers' 'locks' often come with a little flashing light above them that change colour when deactivated by pushing the key into them for about 3–5 seconds.
- If your vehicle does not have an immobiliser, check that you are not in gear and/or do not have the clutch pushed in when you are trying to start the vehicle. Some vehicles have a safety mechanism built in that prevents you from starting it in gear.
- Check that the battery isolator switch is not engaged. This is usually a red 'twist around' knob located outside of the cab near the battery cover.
- If all these fail, turn the key so the ignition is on and check that you have headlights and a horn. If you have neither of these, it is quite likely that your battery is flat.

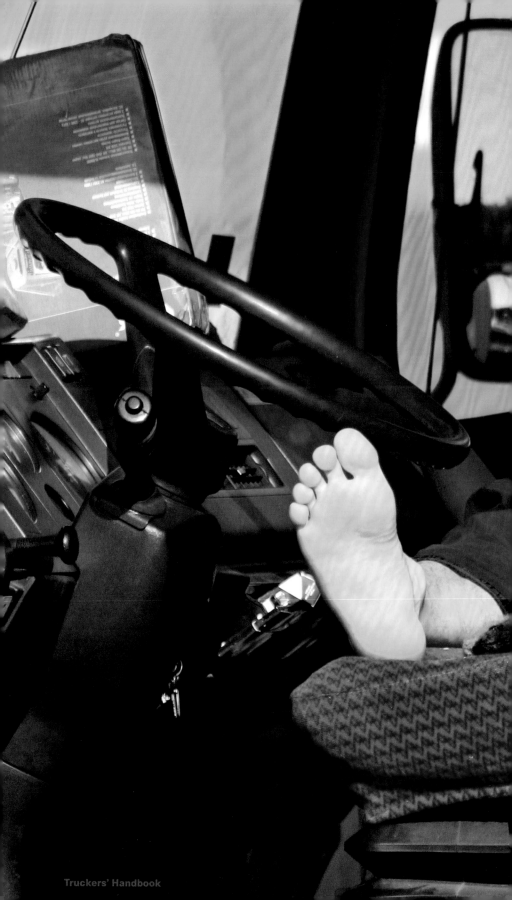

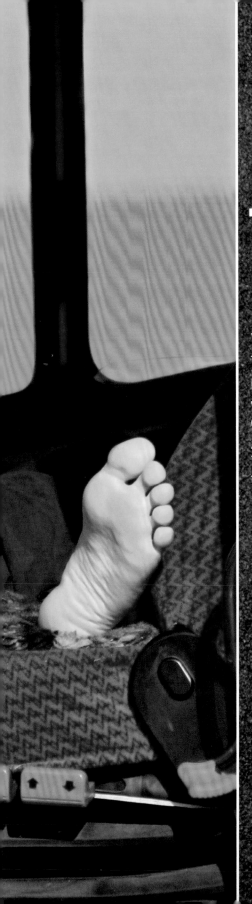

THE DRIVER

Your personal health

WHAT YOU SHOULD AND SHOULD NOT EAT

Well, we all know what these are, even if we don't always follow the advice. But just so you can be certain of what's recommended, here's a list of the *average* Guideline Daily Amounts (GDAs) for adults:

- **Calories:** Up to 2,500 for men, 2,000 for women (though this may be less) and for those on a diet it's around 1,500).
- **Fat (non saturated):** 70g.
- **Saturated fat:** 20g.
- **Salt:** 6g.
- **Total sugars:** (composed of complex and simple carbohydrates) 100g.

Check out the amounts listed on the packaging of your favourite foods and you may be surprised to see how much fat, sugar, and salt we consume in our everyday diets. As a general rule (although I'm sure you've heard it all before), the best advice I can give is:

- Cut down on refined sugar (that's anything containing cane or beet sugar – these cause the pancreas to work overtime and can lead to Type 2 diabetes in later life).
- Keep fats to a minimum and grill rather than fry. If you have to fry or use additional fats stick to high quality oils.
- Buy smaller, leaner cuts of meat.

- Eat fresh fruit and vegetables whenever possible.
- Supplement with fruit rather than sugary snacks.
- Avoid sugary drinks and replace with fresh (no added sugar) fruit juice or water.
- Stay away from processed foods and ready meals whenever possible and plump for freshly prepared food.
- Buy organic whenever you can.
- Reduce cholesterol by opting for soya-based dairy and meat alternatives.
- Cut down on salt where possible and use sea salt rather than rock salt. It tastes nicer and contains more useful minerals.
- Don't eat anything you can't identify.

I'd personally recommend supplementing any diet with vitamins. However, some 'supermarket' and mass-produced vitamins aren't all they appear to be: rather than coming from Mother Nature's fair hand many are made in a lab using artificial ingredients. The best types to buy are natural vitamins and chelated minerals, which can be found in all good health food stores, or try www.gandgvitamins.co.uk, their 'daily packs' are particularly good.

DRINKING FLUIDS

This is something that truck drivers don't do enough of. Let me tell you a little story from my own personal experience to demonstrate how dangerous this can be.

Several years ago I was making a delivery late in the afternoon on a very hot day, to a site on private land which had just closed up for the night. I'd been provided with a key and told where to make the delivery. This involved taking palletised goods off a tail-lift while perched precariously on a steep slope and moving them downhill across an uneven surface to the front of the shop. This took a long while and was exhausting. I had no water with me, as I'd run out some hours before, and as I delivered the last pallet I fainted in the doorway from dehydration. Fortunately I wasn't injured in the fall and came to fairly quickly. I spent the next half-hour lying in front of their mineral water fridge with the door open. Fortunately, as I left I found someone at home in an on-site residence and was able to get a drink. It took *three pints* before I felt normal again!

Water is vital to the health our bodies, and when I say water I mean *water*. Not tea, juice, squash or anything else. Without it our urinary tract becomes infected, our kidneys cease to function, and major organ failure will ensue. You should be drinking at least eight glasses a day, and in hot temperatures or when exercising you can almost double that figure. For those particularly susceptible to urinary infections I can highly recommend cranberry juice capsules, which can be purchased from any health food shop. For those drivers who handball in high outdoor temperatures I'd also recommend tissue salt and potassium capsules. Don't try eating spoonfuls of pure salt – you'll just vomit!

About tea and coffee

Other than the obvious fact that tea and coffee (even decaffeinated brands) contain a certain amount of caffeine, there are other things you should know about these beverages.

Although both have many beneficial properties (tea contains flavanoids, documented as beneficial in the fight against heart disease, while coffee contains ingredients believed to help lower the risk of liver cirrhosis), there's one inescapable fact common to these popular national institutions: they're diuretics – that's to say, that they make you urinate far more than you've consumed by taking fluid out of the body where it's needed and flushing it through the bladder. Aside from the obvious inconvenience to a truck driver, this also increases the likelihood of dehydration in hot weather and may in turn increase the risk of urinary tract infections. Tea has also been known to affect the absorption of iron into the body and it's believed that some types of coffee can increase blood cholesterol.

So, although tea and coffee is greatly enjoyed and consumed by many drivers (including myself) the dangers of over-consumption are obvious and should be taken into consideration. One or two cups a day is more than adequate.

There are, however, many alternatives to your average cuppa. If you're looking for naturally caffeine-free, try Rooibos or Red-bush tea. This is also high in antioxidants and can be found in

many flavours. Some supermarkets and most health food shops now stock it in its basic form, but for more unusual varieties check out www.bluemoontea.com. If you feel very adventurous you could opt for the fruit or herb teas found in most major supermarkets. These are an acquired taste but contain none of the previously mentioned harmful substances.

GETTING ENOUGH SLEEP

Doctors recommend at least eight hours of sleep per night with good reason. The consequences of sleep depravation are a horrific catalogue of unwanted symptoms. These can include:
• Reduced life expectancy
• Heart palpitations
• High blood pressure
• Increased risk of organ failure
• Irritability
• Irrationality
• And for professional drivers, the possibility of falling asleep at the wheel.

Solutions to insomnia

I wouldn't personally recommend any drugs, over the counter or otherwise, and the reason becomes clear if you read the packaging. They're potentially dangerous for you, as a person and as a driver, with side effects that include not only drowsiness but also depression, heart palpitations, increased blood pressure, headaches, nausea and vomiting.

However, there are alternative solutions. These include:

Taking a walk a couple of hours before bedtime

A walk around a local park or an area where there are people and/or interesting things to look at will distract you from whatever's going on in your mind. It's also good exercise and should help you sleep more restfully.

Avoiding caffeine and other stimulants

All drugs, including caffeine, behave in the same way. A little bit will stimulate, a lot will sedate, and too much will kill (though in the case of liquids containing caffeine, the amount would be undrinkably vast!). Even when decaffeinated, tea, coffee and some soft drinks contain a certain amount of caffeine unless they're naturally caffeine free. It's important to avoid even decaffeinated drinks for several hours before you sleep. The same applies to alcohol and drugs. In the case of these, if you consume a generous amount you'll become sedated, but as they work through your system you'll become re-stimulated and artificially 'woken up'. You'll also use vitamin B1 more rapidly if you take any kind of stimulant. This can result in nightmares, restless sleep, and terrible headaches.

Food before bedtime
Avoid eating a large meal any time within three hours of going to bed, as this won't settle easily in the stomach and can cause trapped wind or indigestion. It may also produce an uncomfortable bloated sensation and make sleep more difficult. Very light snacks are OK, but try to have nothing more substantial than a biscuit or a piece of fruit.

Taking control of your environment
To reduce the chances of being disturbed, ensure you're sleeping in an area which is quiet and away from the noise of traffic. Ensure that the curtains in your cab go all the way round, and cover any gaps by draping a towel or used clothing inside the window. Ensure that the temperature is not too hot or cold: 17–20° Celsius is recommended. Keep a thermometer in the cab if necessary.

I wouldn't recommend using a cab heater all through the night. They're good for heating the cab before bedtime and for half-an-hour before you get up (if you can figure out how to work the timer), but many of them are noisy, use diesel to power up, and dry the air in the cab so that it becomes very stuffy very quickly. They also cause dramatic fluctuations in the warmth of the cab. I'd instead recommend a very high quality sleeping bag and/or large duvet.

Smells can act as mild stimulants and produce headaches and/or a sense of unease, so avoid the use of scented washing powders and softeners on your bedding and night things – I'd personally recommend Ecover liquid and softener. Don't ever use air fresheners in your bedroom or cab, for the same reason.

Personal equipment
Earplugs (foam are the best) and eye masks are essential to shut out light and noise. Both take a little getting used to and feel strange at first, but persevere. You'll find the advantages well worth the initial discomfort. To avoid infections, they should be washed on a regular basis, and earplugs should be replaced once every six months.

In extreme weather conditions remember that you lose the majority of your body heat through your extremities. A woolly hat and bedsocks may look strange but they'll keep you warm if the weather is particularly chilly.

Taking vitamins and minerals before bed
It is well documented that the use of 100 mg or less of vitamin B1 before bed time (no more than this or you will become very alert) along with vitamins B5 and C can aid restful sleep (provided that you already supplement with vitamins daily, otherwise a dose of around 50mg of B1 should be taken), as does a drink of calcium and magnesium (commonly known as Cal-Mag). Both of these can be purchased from any health food store. Remember to check that the powdered Cal-Mag formula you purchase has been mixed with an edible acid, as this will aid its absorbtion into the body. And do not take either on a completely empty stomach.

HOW TO AVOID FALLING ASLEEP AT THE WHEEL

When you should stop
Other than when you are legally required to, if you're on a long journey or didn't sleep well the night before you should stop at the next available opportunity if you notice these things occurring:

• An increased difficulty focusing.
• An inability to keep looking straight ahead for more than five minutes.
• Itchy, sweaty or clammy skin.
• A slight feeling of nausea.
• A feeling of fogginess or lack of concentration.

These are all symptoms of sleep depravation and of the body preparing to shut down. Night drivers are particularly susceptible, as they have to fool their bodies into staying awake at times when their senses, metabolism and hormones are telling them to sleep.

If you have the opportunity to stop safely, you should sleep. Even 20 minutes can help, while a good two-hour nap makes quite a difference. In a cab without a bunk this should be attempted by tilting the seat back as far as it'll go. If you're really sleepy you may nod off quite quickly. Afterwards it's important to get out of the cab and walk around for 10 or 15 minutes. This should wake you up again. Remember to set an alarm (use your mobile phone if you have one), or ask your base to ring and wake you after a certain time. Failure to do either may result in you sleeping for longer than intended.

Where you can stop and sleep in an emergency

Of course, it's always best to get yourself to a service station or truck stop, but if that's not possible without running the risk of falling asleep at the wheel there are other places where you're allowed to stop if in dire need:

- Lay-bys: The obvious choice for many, but be aware that the law requires sidelights to remain on if you park in a lay-by. This is particularly important if you park in one that has no kerb or verge separating it from the road.
- At the top of a motorway slip road: Provided you've passed the 'motorway start and end' sign, this is legal though not ideal. If you're not taking a legally required break, you can be moved on. Try and choose a quiet and seldom-used junction, with a wide roundabout at the top. Again, leave your sidelights on – and remember, don't do this on a 'motorway regulations still apply' junction.
- Any road that isn't a red route and doesn't have double yellows or other parking restrictions – but use your common sense. Don't stop on the sides of dual carriageways or along unlit roads (except in lay-bys), where you'll cause an obstruction and possibly an accident. Avoid residential roads if possible and head for industrial estates where signposted. And remember, it's illegal to park on the wrong side of the road at night, since your rear reflectors will be facing the wrong way and won't be seen by approaching traffic.

HOW TO PREVENT BOREDOM ON LONG JOURNEYS

Audio books

Though the very nature of the job involves staring straight ahead when you're driving on a motorway, try to take a look about you as you go along, since the mind is a highly sophisticated mechanism and gets bored pretty quickly. For the professional driver, being behind the wheel of a truck for four-and-a-half hours in a straight line doesn't take up too much attention, so I'd recommend listening to tape or CD 'audio books' to help the journey pass more

quickly. You can borrow these from any library for around three weeks at a time. Some are abridged versions whereas others are presented in their entirety. Choose the same sort of books that you'd normally enjoy reading.

Radio

Some music has the effect of lulling us to a sleep, so I'd advise sticking to radio stations that consist mostly of talking. This tends to keep you alert and involved in what's being discussed. Radio 4 and Steve Wright's afternoon slot on Radio 2 are good examples. Avoid aggressive music as this can have an antagonising effect, and if you're sleepy avoid music that's too relaxing. Agency drivers should take their own personal stereos or MP3 players as they tend to get given vehicles with no stereos on a regular basis.

METABOLISM

Regardless of whether you're a day walker or a night stalker, the body's metabolism is affected by daylight! The hours of daylight, and particularly the first half of the day, are when our bodies burn energy fastest. Even if you work nights and sleep until 2pm your body will demand most of its energy in the few hours before nightfall. This is why a hearty breakfast is so important. A good rule of thumb is: breakfast like a king, lunch like a prince, and supper like a pauper.

EXERCISE IN AND OUT OF THE CAB

The recommended daily requirement for adults is half an hour of cardio-vascular exercise per day. This can be anything from a very brisk walk to a fast run. Basically, anything that gets you slightly out of breath for 20 minutes or more will help towards maintaining a healthy heart. Even taking the dog for a walk, jogging to the shops, or cycling to work can make a difference. The benefits of exercise are more than just strengthening your heart, circulation and cardiovascular system. It also increases energy levels and endurance, lowers blood pressure, improves muscle tone, strengthens bones, reduces anxiety levels, improves sleep and boosts self-esteem.

There are a couple of exercises you can perform while driving, to reduce the possibility of aching shoulders and deep vein thrombosis (blood clots forming in the legs due to long periods of inactivity), though I'd only advise that you attempt these on a motorway:

Shoulder shrugs
Keeping your back straight, lift your shoulders up and forward towards your ears. Release your shoulders down and back in a smooth circular motion five times. Repeat the action in the opposite direction a further five times.

Ankle circles
If you have room in the foot-well, point the toe of your left foot towards the floor then upwards and circle the foot in an anticlockwise motion five times, then repeat the action in the opposite direction five times. If you have cruise control you can do this with the right foot too.

SMOKING

By now everyone knows the dangers of smoking. Not only does it seriously damage the health and life expectancy of the smoker, but it is also a highly anti-social habit which affects the immediate and long-term quality of life of all those in the vicinity of the smoker. The list of diseases, disorders and cancers that can result from tobacco addiction is too long and well-known to need repeating here, but note that most of these conditions can impact particularly severely on the working-life of a truck driver, who gets little exercise.

There are many ways of giving the habit up

and you probably know them all. Patches, gum and cold turkey all have their success stories. Just type 'smoking' into any computer search engine – there's a lot of help out there. Check out www.givingupsmoking.co.uk or see your GP for more advice.

COMMON COMPLAINTS AND AILMENTS OF TRUCKERS

Foot problems

Chilblains
The symptoms of chilblains include itching, redness and skin on the toes that is often swollen and painful to touch. Chilblains are caused by exposure to cold conditions and then rapid re-heating of the affected area. It is exacerbated by poor circulation (something drivers do suffer from greatly).

Preventing Chilblains can be difficult once at least one attack has occurred, however, a change of diet to include healthier, fresher foods can help, so can regular exercise and the use of warmer socks containing natural fibres. When the feet have become chilled try to resist heating them too rapidly. Choose a warm footbath rather than sticking them on the radiator for half an hour. Avoid rubbing and scratching the affected area, as this will create an infection under the skin that may require treatment from your GP.

Athlete's Foot
Extremely common among wearers of trainers or steel toe capped boots, athlete's foot appears as a creamy white and slightly cheesy smelling covering between the toes that can spread to other areas of the foot. Athlete's foot is a fungus that grows in warm damp conditions and therefore easily treatable when mild. When severe it can show up as blistering in other areas and cracking and swelling on the soles of the foot. This can be extremely painful and is usually the sign of a secondary infection within the skin that will require treatment. Avoiding athlete's foot entirely though may prove very difficult, particularly if your toes are set very close together. Regularly washing your feet and changing your socks and shoes can help as can ensuring that whenever your feet become wet, that you dry very thoroughly between each toe. Try wearing sandals in the summer and walking barefoot whenever possible this should help to allow the skin to breathe and 'drying out' to occur.

Toenail Fungi

If you have athlete's foot, chances are that your toenails will also become infected. This looks thoroughly unpleasant and causes the nails to turn white, yellow or black (in severe cases.) They may also appear distorted, thick or crumbly. This infection spreads quickly across the nails so get it treated.

Foot Eczema

A less common condition than athlete's foot, foot eczema is also worsened by warm damp conditions such as those found in trainers, steel toe capped or rubber boots. Visible symptoms can include tiny blisters, though more often than not it begins with dry itchy skin that becomes red, swollen and infected after it has gone hard, cracked and bled. Once this has happened, treatment may be required from your GP.

Prevention is the same for that of athlete's foot with the addition that keeping the feet quite cold really does seem to help. Moisturise the skin where possible using a simple unperfumed cream that contains few chemicals. This should help to prevent cracking and blistering.

Dry skin, eczema and acne

Driving trucks plays havoc with the skin, with constant exposure to the elements and pollution inside and outside the cab. Taking care of the skin on your face and hands is therefore important, so here are some useful tips for combating problems you're likely to encounter.
- Carry a lip balm. Harsh weather will cause lips to dry, crack, bleed and peel.
- Use intensive hand cream daily to avoid cracked, sore and bleeding hands.
- Try to bathe, rather than shower, once a week. Bathing is better for the skin and helps to prevent it flaking and itching.
- Use a natural moisturiser on any affected parts of the face or body.
- Switch to a nylon/cotton glove with textured rubber hand grip. These will allow the skin to breathe more easily.
- Avoid directing the warm air vents of the truck at any infected area, as this will heat up and dry out the skin.

If you suffer from mild or irritant eczema or acne, avoid using chemicals (look at the 'ingredients' on the back of any bottle of shampoo or shower gel to see the long list).
- Buy your toiletries from your local health food

shop. Try Dead Sea Salt products or check out www.organicguys.com.
- Replace household cleaners, washing powders and washing up liquids with an 'eco-friendly' type, which will avoid chemicals.

Urinary tract infections

Whether we like it or not, many of us (particularly women) are prone to these. If you do a job – such as driving a truck – which involves having to remain seated for much of your day or regularly having to 'hold it in' you may find you are more likely to suffer. Symptoms will include:

- Increased desire to urinate
- Increased difficulty passing water
- Only being able to pass small amounts each time
- Eye-watering levels of discomfort when you make the attempts.

Possible methods of prevention include: Drinking more water, more often, wearing looser underwear made with natural fibres, washing after intercourse (though not too vigorously or using a strong soap) and learning to spot the warning signs so that over the counter medicines can be used to solve the problem. If left unchecked they can result in more serious conditions such as kidney infections. If you're suffering from any of these symptoms, seek medical help as soon as possible (preferably within 24 hours). Urinary tract infections can worsen rapidly and cause excruciating abdominal pain.

Headaches

Something of an occupational hazard for truck drivers, headaches are at best an irritation and at worst can lead to nausea and an inability to sleep, concentrate or think rationally. The usual causes of headaches include dehydration, poor diet, allergies, lack of vitamin B1, lack of sleep, confusion, anxiety or simply trying to remember too much. (The solution to the latter is to simply write things down.)

If you're alone, an excellent drug-free therapy is to get out of the cab and take a walk. Look at things (near and far) in great detail and enjoy them. You may find that your headache will lift. If you have friends who're particularly good at cracking jokes, ring them up. Or if you have a portable DVD player in your cab, take some good comedy DVDs with you and watch them when you park up for the night. Laughter is a wonderful cure. As I've mentioned previously, smells can also stimulate a headache, so avoid aftershaves and scented toiletries, air fresheners, and scented washing powder or softener.

Backache

This too is something that many drivers suffer from, due to long periods of inactivity followed by short bouts of strenuous activity. To help prevent the possibility of injury, exercise well and often. Yoga in particular will help to keep the body strong and supple. Other aids I'd recommend are a hot-water bottle or hot wheat pack applied to the affected area. These can both be purchased from any major drug store.

It's best to try and sleep flat on your back at night, with a low but supportive pillow for the neck and head. When driving during the day, position your seat to tilt slightly backwards. This will push you further into the seat and provide more support to your lower back.

Coughs, colds and flu

Anyone regularly stepping out of a warm environment into a cold one is likely to suffer from coughs, colds and flu. Although this action in itself will not cause even so much as a cold, it does make a person more miserable and lowers their sense of well being, in turn making them more likely to pick up a virus. Prevention is the best cure. I personally believe that if you eat and sleep well, supplement with vitamins, and don't smoke, you shouldn't suffer too greatly. Take bed rest when you have flu and avoid contact with children or the elderly. (Remember that flu is often accompanied by extreme tiredness and nausea and isn't just 'a very bad cold'.) If you have a cold or a sore throat, get lots of rest and allow fresh air into the room while you sleep – this should relieve a stuffy nose. For both of these ailments take plenty of vitamin C and drink lots of water.

Constipation

Another occupational hazard for truckers caused by a diet lacking in fibre and long periods of physical inactivity. Since the body requires physical movement to keep the digestive system operating correctly, regular daily exercise can help remedy this. If you particularly suffer from this complaint try switching to high fibre bread and eating fresh fruit and veg whenever

possible. If you can stomach it, prunes or prune juice can be highly effective. Failing that 'Ortisan Fruit Cubes' from your local health food shop are an excellent alternative and can be used every night before bedtime without any of the harmful side affects that laxatives bring. However, do not exceed the stated dose or your constipation may be relieved more rapidly than you would hope for!

About medicines and painkillers

Be aware that all painkillers – even paracetamol and aspirin – reduce a person's level of awareness to some degree. Even mild, over-the-counter drugs can induce a sense of fogginess, making the person more susceptible to accidents and mishaps and lowering their sense of well-being. Stronger prescription painkillers are definitely out of bounds for truck drivers. Many of them carry explicit warnings that they 'May cause drowsiness. If affected, do not drive or operate machinery.' It's worth noting that even seemingly innocuous drugs such as cold and flu remedies and antihistamines may have similar warnings printed on their packets or in the information leaflets that come with them. Always check! Never just assume that yours will be OK.

DRESSING FOR THE JOB

Footwear

Probably one of the most important items of clothing you'll ever own is a pair of steel toecap boots. Anyone who's experienced that terrifying moment of having a forklift truck roll over their feet will understand what I mean. Don't be tempted to go to work in trainers on a hot day – the risks aren't worth it. If you really suffer in warm weather then purchase a pair of steel toecap shoes (rather than boots or trainers), obtainable from most good work-wear shops. Check out www.arco.co.uk for a large selection of styles. For vegetarian steel toecaps see www.heavenlysoles.com. Both of these suppliers provide shoes in men's and women's sizes.

Gloves

Again, essential for the job, not just for protection but also as a barrier against dirt and grease. Many truckers prefer leather or a suede-and-cloth mix glove, which are fine – until they get wet. There's nothing worse than putting on wet gloves! Even drying them off on the dashboard isn't always possible if they're particularly wet and you're making several drops. Personally, I prefer a reinforced rubber type with a cloth cuff, for many reasons:

- They're completely waterproof.
- You can buy textured varieties which offer more grip.
- They're fully washable (though you must turn them partly inside out and hang them upside down in order to dry them).
- They provide adequate protection whilst still allowing some feeling in the fingers.

Their only disadvantage is that when they're new they shed bits inside the glove, and your hands will sweat and smell in them before they've been washed. They can also cause mild skin disorders in those prone to such things.

High-visibility clothing

Every driver should personally own and wear a high-visibility vest at all times. This should incorporate both a fluorescent colour and grey light-reflective strips. Such vests can be purchased from all good work-wear stores and suppliers. If you're provided with additional high visibility garments, wear them! They're for your protection. Remember that transport yards and even warehouses can be dark, dingy places, and no one wants to run over their staff or colleagues in a truck or forklift.

Other protective equipment

Different sites have different requirements. You may be asked to wear (and be provided with) additional protective items including safety hats, ear protectors and eye protectors (which should fit over any prescription glasses). Make sure they fit and use them. You may feel like a prat, but they're provided for a reason. Don't forget to return them when you leave.

KEEPING WARM AND DRY

Hell hath no fury like a cold, wet lorry driver! But you can take simple steps to avoid this. Wear layers of thinner clothing closer to the body, and tuck in T-shirts or polo shirts so they're close to the skin and trap air. If you can find thin polo-neck tops these are even better. Wear at least one close-fitting thick layer on top and always carry a hooded waterproof jacket that falls below the groin. (In the autumn or spring months you can substitute this for a pac-a-mac.) In particularly bad weather you could also benefit from wearing waterproof leggings over your trousers.

Jeans are great, but they don't retain body heat when they get wet. Corduroy, army combat trousers, or men's work-wear trousers are better. Some have the added advantages of extra pockets.

To keep shoes and boots waterproof, coat them in wax. Many types can be bought from any outdoors store, but the best ones are those which are easy to apply.

Socks are also important. Thermal ones may be necessary at times. You can also purchase thermal undergarments and long johns for men and women. I'd highly recommend these for drivers who spend much of their time out of the cab in all weathers. Try your local outdoors store or check out www.millets.co.uk, though their thermal supplies may be limited during the summer months. You can, however, find these all year round by typing 'thermal clothing' into any computer search engine.

And of course, a woolly hat is essential! A great deal of our body heat is lost through the head, particularly if you don't have much hair, and you may be surprised the difference that a hat can make.

The truckers' code of conduct

1 **Keep to site speed limits and observe pedestrian walkways and crossing points.** Follow any and all regulations on the site, including use of protective headgear, high visibility vests, ear protectors and eye protectors. Hand in your keys if required and don't use any equipment you're not authorised to.

2 **Assist other drivers to reverse or manoeuvre if they're having difficulties.** Don't wait to be asked, just do it unless site restrictions expressly forbid it.

3 **Be courteous.** If anyone offers you assistance, thank them and return the favour where possible. Be polite and well-mannered. Don't moan and whinge about being kept waiting – remember, a well-liked driver is a well-respected driver.

4 **Always offer to assist in the loading and off-loading of your vehicle.** Even it you know your help is not likely to be required, your offer will be appreciated. If for any medical reason you're unable to do this, ensure that your employer is made aware.

5 **Always ensure that you park considerately**. Don't block entrances or thoroughfares. Avoid creating an obstruction to road-users or pedestrians by parking either on the kerb or too far away from it.

6 **Fuel up your vehicle at the end of the day.** No one likes to get halfway to their destination and find that they have an empty tank.

7 **Keep your vehicle clean.** Even if it's filthy, isn't yours, and you have it for only one day, remove any rubbish and don't add to the dirt inside. If it's required that you clean it, don't grumble. No one likes to get into a dirty vehicle. Maintain high standards. It won't go unnoticed.

8 **Do not drive an unroadworthy vehicle.** If the vehicle you've been given has what you'd consider to be a serious fault or defect, do not drive it. Remember, it's your licence that will be revoked as well as the operators' licence of the company you're working for. There are instances where vehicles develop faults within their own diagnostics systems, so if in doubt get help to check manually. A vehicle with any obvious major defect like faulty brakes and damaged tyres, or a huge oil leak, should be taken off road.

9 **'Flash in' other drivers.** This includes coach drivers and towing vehicles on motorways and dual carriageways when it's

safe for them to pull across into your lane. This is particularly important in low visibility conditions or at night, as it's more difficult to judge the length of a trailer. Avoid using the flash for other purposes except to warn oncoming drivers of a hazard ahead of them (if it is daylight give the oncoming driver the 'thumbs down' sign at the same time). You can also use a flash of your lights to beckon someone through a small gap. If you are 'flashed in' from behind, use your own judgement to decide whether it's safe to pull across or not and don't forget to acknowledge. This is usually done with one blip to either side with your indicator.

10 Warn traffic behind you of difficulties in front of you.
Use your hazard lights to warn of heavily braking vehicles ahead. Remember, you're in a position to help prevent accidents.

11 If you see an accident happening in front of you, stop and offer assistance.
If no one has been hurt leave your name and contact details so that you can be reached. If there are injured parties, don't be afraid to take control. Use the First Aid advice in this book. Call the emergency services immediately and remain until they arrive. If there's a possibility that persons could have been injured in an accident that seems to have happened a little while ago but the emergency services are not yet in attendance, call them anyway. They'd rather have more than one genuine call than none.

12 If you see an injured animal, stop and help.
Call the RSPCA for assistance if required (see the list of 'Useful contacts' on p.136 and the section headed 'Help! I've hit something').

13 If you come across a large obstruction in the road, remove it if possible.
If this is too dangerous – say, for example, if the obstruction is on a motorway or fast-moving dual carriageway – stop as soon as you can and call either 999 if there's a risk to life, or the local constabulary if there's no immediate danger. (You'll find their numbers in the 'Government bodies' section.) Remember to state the exact location and nature of the obstruction.

14 Maintain a safe environment.
If you see or experience a potential hazard, report it and/or (if possible) remove it. In doing so, you will help to keep your environment safe for yourself and your colleagues.

15 Keep to the LGV speed limits.
Take particular care in built-up areas where there may be children and other hazards. Avoid cutting through towns and villages. No one likes to have a truck rumbling past their window.

16 Maintain good communication with your transport division or agency.
If anything goes wrong with you, your vehicle, load or delivery point, they're your first point of contact. Keep their phone number with you at all times.

17 Always do your vehicle checks.
Even if you're pushed for time, this is of vital importance. Any defects or damage should be noted, since no one wants to be blamed for something they haven't done. Levels are particularly important to the correct running of the vehicle and any problems should be rectified and/or reported before you leave the yard.

18 Be green!
Block change where possible, keep your revs in the green band, use cruise control and your exhaust brake where safe and appropriate to do so, pull away in the correct gear and make sure your vehicle is well maintained. All these pointers will help cut down on fuel consumption and save your company money.

19 Set a good example.
Turn up for work on time and leave only when you've been given permission. Take your breaks, remain legal and alert, but don't waste time. Remember that people are relying on you to make your deliveries. Be patient when you're kept waiting, be productive when you're working. Help others whenever you can and retain a cheerful outlook. Maintain your integrity and don't be taken advantage of. If you commit yourself to a task, follow it through, or don't commit yourself in the first place. Remember that you're a professional in your field – act like one!

First Aid for motorists

A road traffic collision could be one of the most traumatic situations that you'll ever experience, and potentially one of the most dangerous. The following information is a guide to dealing with an accident scene safely and efficiently. In all the actions that you take at the scene of an accident, remember that your own safety is paramount. You should never put yourself at risk.

These tips are no substitute for a thorough knowledge of First Aid. St John Ambulance holds First Aid courses throughout the country. To contact your local St John Ambulance County Headquarters, call 08700 10 49 50 or visit www.sja.org.uk.

This section is the copyright of St John Ambulance 2005. It provides guidance on initial care and treatment but must not be regarded as a substitute for medical advice. Every effort has been made to ensure that the material reflects the relevant guidance from informed authoritative sources, which is current at the time of publication. First Aiders are advised to keep up to date with developments and to obtain First Aid training from a qualified trainer.

ASSESS THE SITUATION

- Survey the scene. Do not approach the scene of an accident unless it's safe to do so.
- Check for hazards – what could prove a potential danger? Look for leaking fuel, smoke or fire, hazardous chemicals, etc.
- Find out what happened. Are there any witnesses? Try to gather as much information as you can. This is important because it highlights what action you should take and will give you the information you need to pass on to the emergency services.
- How many casualties are there, and what type of injuries do they have? Check for 'wandering wounded' or for motorcycle pillions who may have been thrown well clear of the scene. Rear foot pegs down on a motorcycle may indicate the presence of a passenger.

QUESTIONS TO ASK ON THE SCENE

- **Location:** What type of road, motorway or country lane? Different road types require different actions.
- **Position of vehicles:** Are they in a dangerous position? Do they present a risk?
- **Casualties:** How many are there? Where are they and what is the nature of their injuries?
- **Communication:** If you don't have a mobile where is the nearest phone?
- **Bystanders and witnesses:** How can they help?
- **Getting help:** Which emergency services are required and what information can you give them?

MAKING SAFE

- Look after yourself – don't put yourself at risk.
- Warn approaching traffic. If there are others at the scene, send them in both directions to warn oncoming traffic.
- At night or in poor visibility, if possible use lights on undamaged bikes or vehicles to illuminate the accident scene.
- Avoid chemical or fuel spillages.
- Battery acid may also be a hazard at the scene. It will cause burns.
- Apart from being an indicator of a potential fire, smoke at the scene of an accident may contain noxious or poisonous fumes. Minimise your exposure to smoke wherever possible.
- If there's a fire, keep clear. Fuel tanks are an obvious risk, but gas struts, shocks and suspension units can also explode in a fire.
- Take care around damaged vehicles, watch out for sharp edges, broken glass, etc.
- Airbags and seat belt pre-tensioners can go off at any time, causing additional injury. Avoid leaning into a vehicle where the airbag has not obviously been activated.
- Don't climb on or into unstable vehicles.
- Wherever possible leave as much vehicle

debris as you find it. If you need to move it make a mental note of where it was.

- Often police don't get the contact details of the person who performed First Aid. To help the emergency services, make sure you give your details to the police.
- If you're taking charge of the scene, ask bystanders to call the emergency services by dialling 999 or 112. Always ask for the police. Information provided will help the operator to advise other emergency services.
- Calling 999 or 112 from a mobile doesn't necessarily put you through to your local operator. The operator may not have local knowledge so will require precise details of your location.
- **REMEMBER** – Wherever possible do not leave a casualty. If you're on your own at the scene of an accident, and you don't have a mobile phone, it may be necessary to leave the scene to call for assistance. Alerting the emergency services will be your priority in these circumstances.

INFORMATION FOR EMERGENCY SERVICES

- Location of the incident.
- Type and seriousness of the incident.
- Number and type of casualties.
- Any specific hazards which may be present at the scene.
- Any specific care needs (pregnancy, infants, elderly).
- Consider the route – is it blocked?

It is a legal requirement for anyone involved in the accident to remain at the scene. If you're aware of any vehicle leaving the scene try to make a note of any details.

CASUALTIES

- Don't do too much. You can't effectively treat all the casualties at once.
- Assess the needs of the casualties. This will help decide your priorities – such as a casualty needing immediate resuscitation.
- Use disposable gloves if you have them. They'll protect you and your casualty from infection.
- Quickly assess the casualty or casualties.
- Give emergency aid.

If there's more than one casualty, treat in the following order:

1 Unconscious – carry out the resuscitation sequence ('DRABC' – see below).
2 Serious bleeding.
3 Fractures.
4 Other injuries.

Only move casualties if they're in immediate danger as a result of their current position, eg in the middle of the road, near a fire or chemical hazard.

- When moving casualties be aware of possible neck or back injuries. Don't give a casualty anything to eat or drink, or allow them to smoke.
- Get help. Use bystanders to call for help – get them to dial 999 and give the following information:

1 Full address or location of the accident, as clearly and precisely as possible.
2 Describe what has happened.
3 Describe the injuries found.

THE RESUSCITATION SEQUENCE

Remember the mnemonic **DRABC**:
Danger – check for danger.
Response – check response.
Airway – check airway.
Breathing – check for breathing.
Circulation – check for signs of circulation.

If the casualty is

Conscious and breathing
- Check circulation (including a check for severe bleeding).
- Treat any injuries.
- Get help if necessary.

Unconscious and breathing
- Place the casualty in the recovery position.
- Check circulation (including a check for severe bleeding).
- Treat any life-threatening conditions.
- Call for an ambulance.

Unconscious and not breathing
Circulation is present, and the condition is due to injury, drowning or choking:
- Give ten rescue breaths.
- Call an ambulance, return to casualty and follow resuscitation sequence again, acting on your findings.

If the infant or child is

Conscious and breathing
- Check circulation (including a check for severe bleeding).
- Treat any injuries.
- Get help if necessary.

Unconscious but breathing
- Place infant/child in the recovery position.
- Check circulation (including a check for severe bleeding).
- Treat any life-threatening conditions.
- Call an ambulance.

Unconscious, not breathing but has circulation
- Give 20 rescue breaths.
- If the infant or child is small enough, carry them to the telephone and call for an ambulance.
- If you've left the infant or child to call an ambulance, follow the resuscitation sequence again on your return.
- If the infant or child is still unconscious and not breathing, continue to give rescue breaths until help arrives.
- Check for circulation after every 20 breaths.

Circulation is present, and the condition is not due to injury, drowning or choking:
- Call for an ambulance, then continue to give rescue breaths until help arrives.
- Check for circulation after every ten breaths.

Circulation is absent, and the condition is due to injury, drowning or choking:
- Perform CPR for one minute.
- Call an ambulance, then return to casualty and follow resuscitation sequence again, acting on your findings.

Circulation is absent, and the condition is not due to injury, drowning or choking:
- Call for an ambulance, then continue to perform CPR until help arrives.

DIFFERENCES FOR INFANTS AND CHILDREN

(For the purposes of these instructions an infant is considered to be less than one year old and a child one to seven years inclusive.)

Unconscious, not breathing and has no circulation
- Perform CPR for one minute.
- If the infant or child is small enough, carry them to the telephone and call for an ambulance.
- If you've left the infant or child to call an ambulance, follow the resuscitation sequence again on your return.
- If the infant or child is still unconscious, not breathing and has no circulation, continue to perform CPR until help arrives.

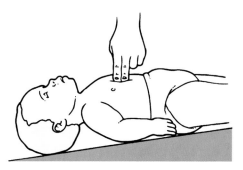

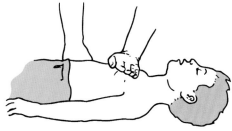

UNCONSCIOUS CASUALTIES

Recovery position – adult

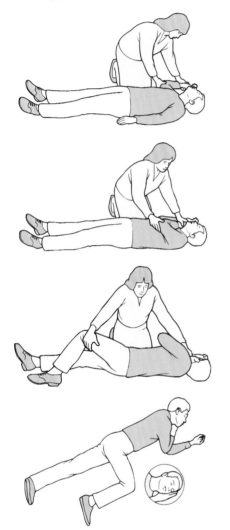

Jaw thrust technique

1 Kneel behind the casualty and support their head in a neutral position.
2 Place your hands either side of the casualty's head, fingertips at the jaw.
3 Gently lift and support the jaw taking care not to move the head.
4 Monitor breathing and circulation constantly. If breathing stops follow the resuscitation sequence DRABC (see above).
5 Keep a close eye on a casualty who's sustained a head injury for the next 24 hours, and if you're at all worried seek medical advice.

Recovery position – infant

1 Cradle the infant in your arms, with his head tilted downwards.
2 Monitor breathing, level of response and pulse until medical help arrives.
3 For children over one year old, the adult recovery position should be used.

An unconscious casualty who is breathing and has no other life-threatening conditions should be placed in the recovery position.
1 Turn casualty onto their side.
2 Lift chin forward in open airway position and adjust hand under the cheek as necessary.
3 Check casualty cannot roll forwards or backwards.
4 Monitor breathing and pulse continuously.
5 If injuries allow, turn the casualty onto other side after 30 minutes.
Note: *if you suspect spinal injury, use the jaw thrust technique described below to maintain an open airway.*

HEAD INJURIES

If the casualty has fallen and knocked their head and is not unconscious, treat any external injury first by applying firm, even pressure to the wound with a clean pad if you have one; otherwise use your fingers. If there are any loose flaps of skin gently replace them. Once the bleeding has stopped, secure the pad with a bandage.

With a head injury there may be things you can see, or there may be no clue as to how bad the injury is – so check the casualty's level of response by asking simple questions. If the responses seem impaired for more than three minutes, dial 999 for an ambulance. Check breathing and circulation every ten minutes.

Whether you think the injury is serious or not, get the casualty to lie down for a short while with the head supported in a neutral position. If they lose consciousness, follow the resuscitation sequence DRABC (see above) using the jaw thrust technique.

If the casualty is breathing, use the jaw thrust technique to maintain the open airway.

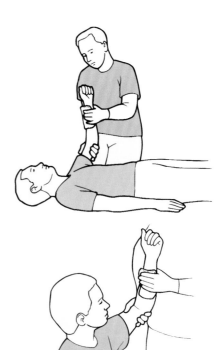

BLEEDING

Minor cuts, scratches and grazes
Treatment
• Wash and dry your own hands.
• Cover any cuts on your own hands and put on disposable gloves.
• If dirty, clean the cut under running water. Pat dry with a sterile dressing or clean lint-free material. If possible, raise affected area above the heart.
• Cover the cut temporarily while you clean the surrounding skin with soap and water and pat the surrounding skin dry. Cover the cut completely with a sterile dressing or plaster.

Severe bleeding
Treatment
• Put on disposable gloves.
• Apply direct pressure to the wound with a pad (eg a clean cloth) or fingers until a sterile dressing is available.
• Raise and support the injured limb. Take particular care if you suspect a bone has been broken.

• Lay the casualty down to treat for shock.
• Bandage the pad or dressing firmly to control bleeding, but not so tightly that it stops the circulation to fingers or toes. If bleeding seeps through first bandage, cover with a second bandage. If bleeding continues to seep through bandage, remove it and reapply.
• Treat for shock.
• Dial 999 for an ambulance.
Remember
• Protect yourself from infection by wearing disposable gloves and covering any wounds on your hands.
• If blood comes through the dressing do not remove it – place another bandage over the original.
• If blood seeps through both dressings, remove them both and replace with a fresh dressing, applying pressure over the site of bleeding.

Objects in wounds
Where possible, swab or wash small objects out of the wound with clean water. If there's a large object embedded:
Treatment
• Leave it in place.
• Apply firm pressure on either side of the object.

- Raise and support the wounded limb or part.
- Lay the casualty down to treat for shock.
- Gently cover the wound and object with a sterile dressing.
- Build up padding around the object until the padding is higher than the object, then bandage over the object without pressing on it.
- Depending on the severity of the bleeding, dial 999 for an ambulance or take the casualty to hospital.

Fractures
Treatment
- Give lots of comfort and reassurance and persuade them to stay still.
- Do not move the casualty unless you have to.
- Steady and support the injured limb with your hands to stop any movement.
- If there's bleeding, press a clean pad over the wound to control the flow of blood. Then bandage on and around the wound.
- If you suspect a broken leg, put padding between the knees and ankles. Form a splint (to immobilise the leg further) by gently, but firmly, bandaging the good leg to the bad one at the knees and ankles, then above and below the injury. If it's an arm that's broken, improvise a sling to support the arm close to the body.
- Dial 999 for an ambulance.
- If it doesn't distress the casualty too much, raise and support the injured limb.
- Don't give the casualty anything to eat or drink in case an operation is necessary.
- Watch out for signs of shock.
- If the casualty becomes unconscious, follow the resuscitation sequence DRABC (see above).

BURNS AND SCALDS

Severe burns
Treatment
- Start cooling the burn immediately under running water for at least ten minutes.
- Dial 999 for an ambulance.
- Make the casualty as comfortable as possible. Lie them down.
- Continue to pour copious amounts of cold water over the burn for at least ten minutes or until the pain is relieved.
- Whilst wearing disposable gloves, remove jewellery, watch or clothing from the affected area – unless it is sticking to the skin.

- Cover the burn with clean, non-fluffy material to protect from infection. Cloth, a clean plastic bag or kitchen film all make good dressings.
- Treat for shock.

Minor burns
Treatment
- For minor burns, hold the affected area under cold water for at least ten minutes or until the pain subsides. Remove jewellery etc and cover the burn as detailed above.
- If a minor burn is larger than a postage stamp it requires medical attention. All deep burns of any size require urgent hospital treatment.

Clothing on fire
Treatment
- Stop the casualty panicking or running – any movement or breeze will fan the flames.
- Drop the casualty to the ground.
- If possible, wrap the casualty tightly in a coat, curtain or blanket (not the nylon or cellular type), rug, or other heavy-duty fabric. The best fabric is wool.
- Roll the casualty along the ground until the flames have been smothered.

On ALL burns DO NOT
Use lotions, ointments and creams.
Use adhesive dressings.
Break blisters.

SHOCK

In the case of a serious accident, once you've treated any obvious injuries and called an ambulance watch for signs of shock:
- Pale face.
- Cold, clammy skin.
- Fast, shallow breathing.
- Rapid, weak pulse.
- Yawning.
- Sighing.
- In extreme cases, unconsciousness.

Treatment
- Lay the casualty down and support their legs.
- Use a coat or blanket to keep them warm – but not smothered.
- Don't give them anything to eat or drink.
- Check breathing and pulse frequently. If breathing stops, follow the resuscitation sequence DRABC (see above).
- Give lots of comfort and reassurance.

What every driver should wear or carry

WEAR
- Steel toecap boots.
- High visibility vest or jacket.
- Any other protective clothing if required.
- A strong pair of trousers that will offer some protection.
- Clothing suitable to the weather conditions.

CARRY
- A good strong bag, preferably a rucksack.
- Gloves.
- Any equipment required for the job, such as a pulling hook.
- Cash, cashpoint card or credit card.
- Phone.
- Hands-free kit and phone charger (if necessary).
- MP3 player or personal stereo and CDs or tapes of your choice.
- Reading material (if long waiting times are likely).
- Licence (both parts).
- Timesheets.
- Maps, your own and any that are provided by the company you're working for.
- The phone number of your agency and a 24-hr number for the company you're working for.
- Fuel card if required.
- All keys required for the vehicle.
- Any paperwork or export documents.
- A disposable camera or camera phone (provides evidence in the event of an accident or incident).
- Food and water.
- Several very thin strips of rag to tie to the tops of your mirrors (as they move in the wind they'll wipe rain from the surface).
- Disposable surgical gloves (even untangling Suzie leads can be pretty messy).
- Cable ties.
- Mini roll of Duct Tape.
- A screwdriver or two.
- Bulldog clip (to secure a number plate if the clip is missing).
- A small pair of pliers.
- A packet of tissues.
- Tachograph charts and pouch.
- Driver Card for digital tachographs.
- Print rolls for digital tachographs.

- Pens and notepaper.
- Stanley knife (to rip shrink wrap).
- Waterproof mac or, in colder weather, a waterproof coat with a hood.
- Waterproof leggings for extremely wet weather (if you spend much of your day outside off-loading).
- Plasters.
- A digital watch or timer to count the amount of accumulated time you've been driving.
- At least one item of clothing that can be rolled up and used as a pillow or spread over you and used as a cover.
- A tie-back if you have long hair.
- Ice scraper (in cold weather).
- Sunglasses (in sunny weather).
- A miniature screwdriver and spare screws if you wear glasses, in case the screw that holds in the lens pops out (this has happened to me on many occasions).
- Felt-tip pen (for drawing manual traces if required).
- A mini torch.
- A calculator (to calculate total kilometres on tachograph chart).
- Tyre depth gauge and tyre pressure gauge.

IF YOU DO OVERNIGHT WORK OR TRAMPING
- Sleeping bag, duvet and pillow.
- Hand cream.
- Food and drink.
- Personal washing equipment, towel.
- Sleepwear, earplugs and eye mask.
- Alarm clock (or use mobile phone).
- Cab shoes (for in the cab or the washrooms).
- Thermometer (if required).
- Nailbrush, nail clippers, scissors.
- Cab cleaning equipment.
- Large water container (if you're likely to be stuck overnight without washing facilities).
- Small washing-up bowl (useful for many purposes).
- A bottle of tea-tree oil lotion (to cleanse cuts or to disinfect when diluted in water).
- At least two bin liners.
- A shovel, if driving in snowy conditions.

Additional qualifications and training

CPC (FREIGHT) CERTIFICATE OF PROFESSIONAL COMPETENCE

Everyone involved in road transport who operates vehicles for hire and reward must demonstrate evidence of professional competence, in compliance with the Goods Vehicle (Licensing of Operators) Act 1995.

The certificate itself requires that you sit and pass exams regarding issues such as:
• Employment law.
• Transport law.
• Vehicle law
• Financial management.
• Marketing.
• Safe transportation of goods.
• Documentation.
• Advertising.
• Man management.

HAZARDOUS FREIGHT QUALIFICATIONS (ADR)

All drivers required to move hazardous substances by road in tanks, tank containers and packages must hold a valid ADR licence. The licence is valid for a maximum period of five years, and you can take a course covering any one of nine different groups of Hazardous Freight. This may include radioactive material, explosives, flammable goods, etc. Courses must be taken to obtain this licence. You must pass exams to ensure that:
• You have sufficient knowledge and information to enable you to operate safely, respond to and deal effectively with emergency situations.
• To ensure you know and understand the current legislation and how the legislation impacts upon you.
Refresher courses must be taken before the end of each 5 year licence expiry period.

HI-AB (LORRY LOADER OR MOBILE CRANE)

Drivers required to lift goods using a mobile crane or lorry loader on the back of their vehicle must complete a Hi-Ab or lorry loader course. General contents of the course are as follows:
• Health and safety.
• Types of lifting gear.
• Inspection of lifting gear and loader.
• Hand signals.
• Practical training on loader including inspection of area.
• Setting vehicle up for loading/unloading.
• Written and practical test.
Refresher courses must be taken before the end of each 5 year licence expiry period.

FORKLIFT LICENCE

Anyone required to operate a forklift must hold a valid licence for the type of forklift they're operating. This can be one of the following types:
• Counterbalance.
• Reach truck.
• Ride on pallet truck.
• Side-loading forklift truck.
• Moffat (Quap licence).
Training includes both practical and theory exams and covers all aspects of health and safety regarding the use of forklift trucks. You also require specialist training to operate an EPT (electric pallet truck).
    Refresher courses must be taken before the end of each 5 year licence expiry period.

IPAS (POWERED ACCESS LICENCE)

Trains the individual to operate scissor lifts and cherry pickers. This licence has to be renewed every four years. The two-day course includes:
• Written and practical exams.
• Health and safety training.
Refresher courses must be taken before the end of each licence expiry period.

Types of work

AGENCY WORK

Requirements
Must be reliable, polite, well presented and responsible. Must be willing to work flexible hours.

Nature of work
Agency workers may be asked to work for almost anyone and drive and deliver almost anything within their realm of experience. Agencies may keep individual drivers on certain long-term placements or place the driver with a different company every day. Some agencies even have a temp-to-permanent arrangement with a few of their clients. Agency work is ideal for new drivers, as they'll acquire a great deal of experience quickly. Most agencies are willing to take on new drivers or those with some points on their licence. This type of work would also suit experienced drivers looking for part-time work or flexible hours. Some smaller agencies are willing to offer work to self-employed drivers.

FLATBED WORK

Requirements
Experience and informal training on roping and sheeting and beaver-tailed trailers (if required). Driver must be fit and physically strong. If using a low-loader trailer the driver may also need additional qualifications that allow him to transport abnormal loads or plant vehicles.

Nature of work
You may be asked to transport almost anything from caravans to aircraft parts. This type of work should only be undertaken by an experienced driver, as they must know the correct methods of securing and covering a whole variety of cargoes. This type of work is hard, physical, and often very dirty.

TANKER (MILK) WORK

Requirements
Informal training on the 'fixtures and fittings' of a milk tanker, competency as a driver, and (if collecting from farms in a class C vehicle) a strong stomach. Drivers should also be aware of the Domestic Hours Regulations regarding the collection of milk from farms.

Nature of work
If collecting from farms you'll be required to reverse in and out of small awkward spaces. You should be provided with protective clothing, as farms are not the cleanest of places. Milk collection is messy, smelly work, often involving long hours and many collections. If delivering milk in an artic from dairy to dairy be aware that your safe stopping distance is less than a conventional lorry, as your liquid load will hit you hard from behind when braking.

TANKER (HAZARDOUS SUBSTANCES) WORK

Requirements
A valid ADR licence. Ideally, drivers should also be very experienced and used to transporting liquid loads. Drivers should not possess a dislike of strong smells if transporting fuel.

Nature of work
If delivering fuel to garages, this type of work often involves reversing in and out of awkward spaces and can be rather dirty. However, it is extremely well paid and the hours are not usually particularly long. The vehicles used are normally new (though sometimes a little fragrant).

TRADEPLATING

Requirements
A good deal of experience driving many different types of vehicle. Drivers must be polite, intelligent, clean, well presented and good communicators. They must also possess an uncanny sense of both direction and adventure.

Nature of work

This is a driving job like no other. The driver must be willing to hitch-hike all over the country (and be good at it), collecting vehicles (as opposed to cargo) and delivering them as and where required. He must be prepared to sleep out and carry his whole life in a rucksack on his back. The hours are long and the wages not outstanding by comparison, but you won't find any other job like it anywhere.

GENERAL HAULAGE

Requirements

A fairly good level of experience of securing loads and using curtain-sided vehicles, a good general knowledge of the UK, and a willingness to work nights if required.

Nature of work

You'll be asked to collect and deliver almost anything to and from anywhere. Most general haulage involves the use of curtain-sided vehicles, though in some instances flatbed trailers are used. This is almost always artic work. The hours are long, the pay is good to average, and the work can be hard and a little dirty. You may also often be asked to wait for long periods of time in order to off-load.

HI-AB (LORRY LOADER) WORK:

Requirements

A valid Hi-Ab licence. Drivers must be fit and strong, willing to work outside in all weathers, and have good general knowledge of safely securing loads on a flatbed trailer.

Nature of work

Much Hi-Ab work involves delivering and collecting to building sites or builders' suppliers and merchants. The work is not usually long distance but it's physical and dirty.

SUPERMARKET DELIVERIES

Requirements

Most supermarkets (though not all) require that you've held your C+E licence for at least two years. You should have good knowledge of transporting both ambient and refrigerated goods and be a well-presented, polite, patient and competent driver. An induction course and assessment is usually given.

Nature of work

Delivering to stores and dealing with paperwork. You may have to reverse in and out of some very awkward loading bays (depending on whether you're working for a large or small supermarket chain). The goods are usually palletised or caged. Minimal effort is required and sometimes you won't even be expected to off-load yourself. Supermarket work is some of the cleanest and easiest of all lorry-driving work, though you may often be asked to wait for long periods of time. The vehicles provided are normally clean and new, the work is well paid, and the hours are average.

SHOP DELIVERIES

Requirements

Good knowledge of tail-lifts and wheeled, caged and palletised goods. The driver should be polite, diplomatic, well-presented, patient, capable of directing others, safety conscious and able to take control of a vehicle and its load in a public thoroughfare.

Nature of work

More like that of a company representative than a lorry driver. Shop deliveries can be very physical, the pay is average to good, and the hours are long (particularly if delivering in a class C vehicle). Deliveries are sometimes made at the

front of the shop during opening hours, and drivers have to be prepared to handle every type of possible scenario which may arise from this.

REFRIGERATED VEHICLE OR TRAILER WORK

Requirements
Some informal training is required. Drivers should be competent, safety conscious, intelligent and hard-working. They shouldn't suffer from poor circulation of the hands or feet and should have good working knowledge of tail-lifts and delivering palletised goods.

Nature of work
This type of work involves spending time in the back of a vehicle with a temperature of anything from –5° to –30°. (In the winter this is no joke!) The work usually involves delivering to supermarkets, food manufacturers and shops and can involve reversing into and out of any number of tight spaces. It is fairly clean work and not particularly physical, the pay is good to average, but the hours in a class C can be long.

BAKERY DELIVERIES

Requirements
Drivers should be extremely fit and strong and have good working knowledge of tail-lifts, retaining bars, and wheeled goods.

Nature of work
You'll often be required to manoeuvre stacks of bread weighing anything up to 20 stone (that's about 130kg), so this type of work shouldn't be undertaken by anyone with a previous back injury. You'll often be required to drive older types of vehicles, though the work itself is not too dirty. The hours, however, can be long, and the pay is good to average. There may be a degree of waiting time involved at depots. On the plus side, bakery workers are usually a cheery bunch and very helpful to a new driver.

TRUNKING

Requirements
Good knowledge of the UK and of coupling and uncoupling many different kinds of trailers. The driver must also be fairly experienced and willing to work nights if required.

Nature of work
Almost always class C+E, trunking is by far the easiest of all lorry-driving work. It mostly consists of one or two long-distance drops, rarely involves any off-loading (normally you just swap trailers), and is usually undertaken at night. The work is not normally too dirty, the vehicles are fairly new and clean, the pay is good to average, but the hours are long.

SKIP WORK

Requirements
Some informal training is required. The driver should be diplomatic, capable of handling cash, and very safety conscious, particularly since it's been known for people to be found asleep inside skips.

Nature of work
Skip work is extremely dirty and often involves driving a class C vehicle into all sorts of places. The driver will be required to deliver to anywhere, from a building site to a school. You'll often be required to collect cash from private addresses and to understand how to secure your skip and its contents correctly. The work is physical, dirty, and not particularly well paid.

TIPPER WORK

Requirements
Some training is required. The driver should be competent and fairly experienced. He must also be extremely good at finding his way around.

Nature of work
Tippers come in all shapes, sizes and types. The work is fairly dirty, particularly if delivering building or resurfacing materials. Delivering feed or grain, however, is usually cleaner, unless delivering to farms. Hours are average to long and pay is average to good. You'll sometimes be expected to deliver to places that aren't even on a map, so a good knowledge of the area would be an advantage.

TRANS-CONTINENTAL WORK

Requirements
Only to be attempted by highly experienced drivers. Multilingual capabilities would be a great advantage, as would excellent map-reading skills. You may also be expected to drive a left-hand-drive vehicle.

Nature of work

You'll be expected to drive a vehicle on the wrong side of the road in countries with alien road systems and inconsiderate drivers. Although facilities for truck drivers in Western European countries are better than those in Britain, the further east you go the more alien the customs and 'ways of the road' become. In colder countries you'll be expected to cope with extreme weather and difficult border crossings. You'll find yourself very much on your own. The hours are long and lonely, and although the wages can be very rewarding forget having any kind of home life.

BIN LORRY WORK

Requirements

You should be a skilled and confident class C driver. You must be very safety conscious and extremely social. You should be happy with early starts and not be bothered by strong smells.

Nature of work

You'll be expected to drive and reverse your vehicle into impossibly tight spaces with ease. You need to enjoy the company of your loaders and work happily as part of a team. Bin work is extremely dirty, and even though you'll be sitting at the wheel the whole time your companions will make for very fragrant, grubby company. The hours are fairly short, though the pay is not good and the smell can be terrible!

CAR TRANSPORTERS

Requirements

Drivers should be experienced, but will receive thorough informal training. They should be safety conscious and prepared to work nights.

Nature of work

You'll often be required to deliver on the roadside, and to drive vehicles safely up and down ramps and secure them correctly. Mistakes are extremely costly and you and your load are always at risk from theft and attack. The work can be fairly well paid though physical, and the hours are long.

SHUNTER WORK

Requirements

You should be a competent driver and great at reversing. You should have an LGV C+E or Shunter licence. You should not mind being out in all weathers and getting covered in fifth wheel grease. Training on specialised shunter vehicles would be an advantage.

Nature of work

Shunter work can be very tedious, as you don't actually get to go anywhere. As long as you don't leave the private property of your yard you can acquire a shunter licence without having an LGV licence, though the shunter licence is specific only to the yard you're working from. Shunter work is very much a love it or hate it kind of job. The pay is average, hours can be long, and the work is very dirty indeed.

The Scania Experience

Jeremy Clarkson once said there are two types of truck drivers: Those who drive a Scania, and those who want to! Naturally, we wouldn't disagree with Britain's leading motoring journalist, but we would just like to point out that there is much more to Scania than just its vehicles.

We call it *The Scania Experience*, an extensive and unrivalled set of factors – some tangible, some less so – which together combine to form one of the most satisfying ownership experiences imaginable. Exceptional products, exceptional performance and exceptional operating economy, all play key roles here.

But there's more, much more too. Round-the-clock support from Scania Assistance, for example, plus a service network that literally blankets the UK and Europe with aftermarket-cover providing operators with the peace of mind that's essential in today's demanding operating environment.

Other elements include our highly trained dealer staff, the most skilled in the industry, the application of leading-edge transport technology wherever it benefits our operators and our unshakable commitment to road safety. And that's not to mention our range of Scania Support Programmes, financial packages, Scania Truck Rental and the many other products and services available from Scania today.

To find out more about each of these exciting initiatives, and everything else that adds up to The Scania Experience, why not pay a visit to our website, www.scania.co.uk? The site contains full details on everything about our products and us. It's also regularly updated with our latest news – so if you want to stay abreast of all the latest happenings in the world of Scania, make sure you bookmark the page on your favourites list today!

WHAT'S IN A NAME?

Scania is one of the world's oldest automotive manufacturers with a long history that stretches back well over 100 years to 1891. Then, a company called Vabis was making railway rolling stock in the town of Södertälje, (pronounced 'Soda-tell-yer'), which is located approximately 20 miles south of Stockholm and is still Scania's home today.

A few years later, a second Swedish company began assembling bicycles designed by the British manufacturer Humber in its workshops in Malmö in southern Sweden. That firm was called Scania after the Latin name for the province of Skåne in which Malmö is situated.

By the turn of the 20th Century, Vabis and Scania were successfully establishing themselves as motor manufacturers. While each began with cars, by 1902 both had built their first trucks.

In 1911 the two companies merged to form Scania-Vabis, a name that would become synonymous with leading-edge commercial vehicle design for the following half century and more.

Back in Great Britain, the European Free Trade Association agreement of the mid-1960s saw the door open to foreign imports for the first time. An early arrival was the Scania-Vabis LB76 truck, a vehicle which wooed drivers with its heated cab, power-steering and ten-speed twin-lever synchromesh gearbox.

In 1969, Scania merged once again, this time with Saab, at which time the Vabis name was dropped. The Saab-Scania organisation went on to develop a number of award winning trucks, including the LB110s and 140s, the LB111s and 141s, the GPRT range, the 3-series and the 4-series.

Soon after the launch of the 4-series, Saab was sold to General Motors and Scania became an independent company, which is how it stands today.

Scania's long history is reflected in its logo, which is widely recognised as one of the automotive world's best-known and most-respected symbols. Its centrepiece is the Griffin, a mythical creature which has

been associated with Scania for more than 100 years because of its qualities of strength, durability and courage.

But the logo also reveals something of the company's past: Take a look at the shape surrounding the Griffin – it represents a bicycle pedal crank, an image that harks back to the pioneering days when Scania was busy establishing its reputation as a vehice producer of considerable renown.

NEW SCANIA V8 ENGINES: Top of the range, highest status

UNRIVALLED PRESTIGE

Your Business: long distances, heavy loads, mountains to climb, schedules to meet.

It's a competitive world. Your customers are demanding. Door-to-door, just-in-time means that nobody can be kept waiting. What are your options?

Scania offers plenty of choice. For example, this is the new Scania R 620. Our top-of-the-range truck.

That V8 620 engine is supreme. Our most powerful truck engine ever, with up to 3000 Nm of torque. Perfect for fast, effortless journeys, rewarding driving, and consistently good economy.

The Scania Topline cab offers the most when it comes to space, comfort, equipment and prestige.

It's the complete truck. In fact, this R620 is one of four new possibilities. There is a choice of three sleepers and the spacious day cab. Choosing which is right for you may be a tough call. After that, everything else is easy.

Power with economy. Tradition with Innovation.

For more than thirty years, Scania has been committed to the use of V8 engines for its biggest and most powerful trucks. The arrival of these Euro 4 and Euro 5 V8s marks yet another major landmark in development.

What has been achieved?

Firstly, these new Euro 4 and Euro 5 V8 engines will deliver the same outstanding operating economy as comparable Scania Euro 3 engines.

Secondly, driveability is further enhanced – something you will appreciate the instant your fully laden truck takes to the road and demonstrates its brisk performance.

To accomplish such beneficial gains over highly successful Euro 3 engines is a formidable achievement.

The heart of the matter.

Like all Scania engines, the new V8s capitalise on the thrifty efficiency derived from the Scania modular combustion concept. All these engines exhibit enhanced output characteristics. Both power and torque build more rapidly. The economical green band provides a wider window of flexibility.

The optimised torque curve is broader and higher, yielding the very best combination of driveability and on-the-road performance ever delivered by Scania engines.

Proven V8 technology for Euro 4 and Euro 5.

Scania has developed SCR (Selective Catalytic Reduction) for V8 engines. Why? Because it offers an attractive solution for vehicles engaged in moving heavy loads over long distances, and where cruising speeds can be maintained for long periods. Precisely the applications associated with powerful engines.

The technology has been tried and tested by customers in comprehensive field trials. The objectives were to test reliability and integrity of the SCR system to measure operating economy, and to assess driveability and performance.

Customer feedback has been very enthusiastic. All measurement criteria confirm that high standards of performance and economy traditionally associated with Scania engines have been further enhanced.

More of what you need.

Scania V8s are special. But pure emotion is not enough. You need sound economic and practical reasons for wanting an engine as powerful as 500 hp, as mighty as 560 hp or as awesome as 620 hp.

It must be a business decision. So leave the emotion aside and look at it this way. The heavier the load, the quicker the journey, the higher the uptime, the lower the overall cost, then the greater your productivity and profitability. Scania V8s deliver on every count. They always have done, but now even more so.

How much power? How much torque?

Common characteristics of all engines are the steeply rising power curves and fast build up of torque that holds its peak across a broad rev range.

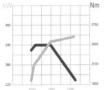 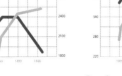 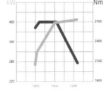 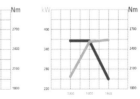

Euro 4
500 V8 (16-litre)
Maximum power: 500 hp
(368 kW) at 1900 r/min
Maximum torque: 2400 Nm
between 1100 and 1400 r/min

Euro 4
560 V8 (16-litre)
Maximum power: 560 hp
(412 kW) at 1900 r/min
Maximum torque: 2700 Nm
between 1100 and 1400 r/min

Euro 4
620 V8 (16-litre)
Maximum power: 620 hp
(456 kW) at 1900 r/min
Maximum torque: 3000 Nm
between 1100 and 1400 r/min

Euro 5
500 V8 (16-litre)
Maximum power: 500 hp
(368 kW) at 1800 r/min
Maximum torque: 2500 Nm
between 1000 and 1350 r/min

SCANIA UK DEALER NETWORK

Aberdeen – Scania Aberdeen
01224 896312

Banbury – Scania Banbury
01295 272857

Bedford – The Pip Bayley
Truck Centre
01767 641111

Bellshill – Scania Bellshill
01698 841994

Boston – Scania Boston
01205 460841

Bridgwater – Scania
Bridgwater
01278 685060

Bristol – Scania Bristol
0117 937 9800

Burton-On-Trent – Keltruck
Limited
01283 510011

Cardiff – Silurian Scania
02920 224671

Carlisle – Graham
Commercials Limited
01228 529149

Cheltenham – Keltruck Limited
01242 252140

Chepstow – Silurian Scania
01291 431715

Corby – TruckEast Limited
01536 443883

Coventry – Keltruck Limited
02476 644 664

Crick – TruckEast Limited
01788 823930

Cross Hands – Silurian Scania
01269 844855

Darlington – Scania Darlington
01325 480713

Deeside, North Wales –
Deeside Truck Services
01244 547202

Didcot – Scania Didcot
01235 834933

Dover – Scania Dover
01304 831730

Droitwich – Keltruck Limited
01905 777060

Dumfries – Scania Dumfries
01387 250502

Dundee – Scania Dundee
01382 455556

Edinburgh – Scania Edinburgh
0131 333 2362

Ellesmere Port – Ellesmere
Port Scania
0151 355 0199

Ely – TruckEast Limited
01353 666503

Exeter – Scania Exeter
01392 824474

Fareham – Scania Fareham
01489 886800

Felixstowe – TruckEast
Limited
01394 676625

Glasgow – Scania Glasgow
0141 886 5633

Grimsby – Scania Grimsby
01472 346913

Groby – Keltruck Limited
01530 243133

Haydock – Haydock
Commercial Vehicles Limited
01942 714103

Heathrow – Scania Heathrow
01784 240777

Hull – Scania Hull
01482 626880

Inverness – Scania Inverness
01463 729400

Kings Lynn – TruckEast
Limited
01553 771877

Knighton – West Pennine
Trucks Limited
01547 528600

Lancaster – S.J. Bargh Sales
and Service Limited
01524 770439

Larne – Road Trucks Limited
028 2827 9611

Leeds – Scania Leeds
0113 231 1411

Lewes – Scania Lewes
01273 479123

Lincoln – Scania Lincoln
01522 681222

Lingfield – Scania Lingfield
01342 837373

Lutterworth – Keltruck Ltd
01455 550740

Macclesfield – West Pennine
Trucks Limited
01625 0869208

Manchester – West Pennine
Trucks Limited
0161 653 9700 (24hrs)

Manchester – West Pennine
Trucks Limited
0161 877 7708

Milton Keynes – TruckEast
Limited
01908 242448

Newark – Keltruck Limited
01636 700203

Newbury – Scania Newbury
01635 871157

Newcastle-Upon-Tyne –
Scania Newcastle
0191 256 1900

Newry – Granco
028 3026 6335

Normanton – Scania Normanton
01924 228800

Northampton – TruckEast
Limited
01604 874747

Norwich – M & K
Commercials Limited
01603 748995

Nottingham – Keltruck Limited
0115 986 5121

Omagh – Road Trucks Limited (West)
028 82259 198

Oswestry – West Pennine Trucks Limited
01691 671500

Peterborough – TruckEast Limited
01733 555233

Poole – Scania Poole
01202 533978

Preston – Preston Scania
01772 698811

Purfleet – Scania Purfleet
01708 257400

Redruth – Scania Redruth
01209 820820

Ross-on-Wye – Silurian Scania
01600 891257

Rugby – Keltruck Limited
01788 571 959

Scunthorpe – Scania Scunthorpe
01724 289088

Sheffield – Scania Sheffield
0114 262 6700

Shepton Mallet – Scania Shepton Mallet
01749 880088

Sittingbourne – Scania Sittingbourne
01795 430304

Skipton – Scania Skipton
01756 797197

South Mimms – Scania South Mimms
01707 649955

Southampton – Scania Southampton
02380 734455

Spalding – Scania Spalding
01775 713707

Stansted – Scania Stansted
01279 758088

Stoke-On-Trent – West Pennine Trucks Limited
01782 577955

Stowmarket – TruckEast Limited
01449 613553

Sutton-In-Ashfield – Keltruck Ltd
01623 559559

Swindon – Scania Swindon
01793 715100

Tamworth – Keltruck Limited
01827 330100

Telford – West Pennine Trucks Limited
01952 587222

Thetford – TruckEast Limited
01842 763400

Thirsk – Scania Thirsk
01845 573500

Washington – Scania Washington
0191 4188500

Wellingborough – TruckEast Limited
01933 303303

West Bromwich – Keltruck Limited
0121 524 1800

Widnes – Halebank Scania
0151 423 8601

Willenhall – Keltruck Limited
01902 637777

Witham – TruckEast Limited
01376 503003

Worksop – Scania Bus & Coach
01909 500822

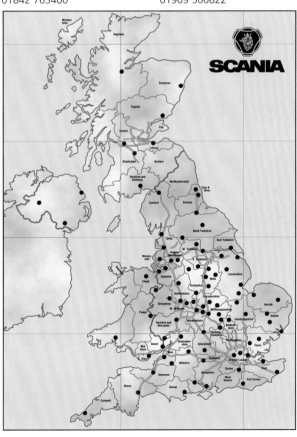

POWER

NAME: Sadurski Rafal   AGE: 27   NATIONALITY: Polish   FAVOURITE PLACE TO ST

SCANIA
www.scania.co.uk/truckgear

Home   FAVOURITE ROUTE: M1 Minsk-Moscow   WEARS: Wind Proof Flannel Shirt

SCANIA TRUCK GEAR

Truck dealerships, service centres and fitters

DAF UK, Eastern Bypass, Thame, Oxfordshire, OX9 3FB
Tel: 00 (44) 1844 261111, Fax: 00 (44) 1844 217111, www.daftrucks.co.uk
DAFaid UK: 0800 919395

A Herring Ltd, Toc H Yard, Old Road, Chesterfield, Derbyshire, S20 2RG	Tel: 01246 234213
A M Bell Ltd, Hawkshead Quarry, Leek Old Road, Sutton, Macclesfield, Cheshire, SK11 0JB	Tel: 01260 253232
Aberystwyth Automotive Services, Unit 3, Glan Yr Afon Industrial Estate, Aberystwyth Automotive Services, Dyfed, SY23 3JQ	Tel: 01970 615830
Adams Morey Ltd. Bournemouth, Yeomans Way, Yeomans Industrial Park, Bournemouth, Dorset, BH8 0BJ	
Adams Morey Ltd. Isle of Wight, 1-2 Riverway Industrial Estate, Newport, Isle Of Wight, PO30 5UY	Tel: 01983 522552
Adams Morey Ltd. Portsmouth, Burrfields Road, Portsmouth, Hampshire, PO3 5NN	Tel: 02392 691122
Adams Morey Ltd. Salisbury, Stephenson Road, Churchfield Industrial Estate, Salisbury, Wiltshire, SP2 7NP	Tel: 01722 412171
Adams Morey Ltd. Southampton, The Causeway, Redbridge, Southampton, Hampshire, SO15 0DR	Tel: 02380 663000
Aire Valley Commercials Ltd, Railway Goods Yard, Cross Hills Road, Keighley, West Yorkshire, BD20 7DA	Tel: 01535 634067
Barnes Daf. Cowley, 18 Pony Road, Horspath Trading Estate, Cowley, Oxford, Oxfordshire, OX4 2SA	Tel: 01865 749899
Barnes Daf. Guildford, Slyfield Industrial Estate, Woking Road , Guildford, Surrey, GU1 1RT	Tel:01483 594900
Barnes Daf. Reading, Station Road, Theale, Reading, Berkshire, RG7 4AG	Tel: 01189 300900
Barnes Daf. Shoreham, 44 Dolphin Road, Shoreham, West Sussex, BN43 6PB	Tel: 01273 454887
Barr Truck Services, Braehead, Barhill, Girvan, Ayrshire, KA26 0QR	Tel: 01465 821300
Basingstoke Commercials Ltd, Whitney Road, Daneshill Industrial Estate, Basingstoke, Hampshire, RG24 8NS	Tel: 01256 811414
Brewers Daf, Hammonds Drive, Eastbourne, East Sussex, BN23 6PW	Tel: 01323 745700
Brian Currie. Bedford, 3 Brunel Road, Barkers Lane Industrial Estate, Bedford, Bedfordshire, MK41 9TL	Tel: 01234 211241
Brian Currie. Bleak Hall, Chesney Wold, Bleak Hall, Milton Keynes, Bedfordshire, MK6 1LH	Tel: 01908 663991
Brian Currie. Northampton, Gayton Road, Northampton, Northamptonshire, NN7 3AB	Tel: 01604 858810
Cardiff Daf Truck Centre, Leckwith Industrial Estate, Whittle Road, Cardiff, South Glamorgan, CF1 8AT	Tel: 02920 308595
Cawsey Commercials Ltd, Unit 11, Newport Industrial Estate, Launceston, Cornwall, PL15 8EX	Tel: 01566 772805
Cayton Commercials, 1 Main Street, Scarborough, North Yorkshire, YO11 3RU	Tel: 01723 582697
Channel Commercials Ltd. Ashford, Brunswick Road, Cobbs Wood Estate, Ashford, Kent, TN23 1EH	Tel: 01233 629272
Channel Commercials Ltd. Canterbury, Unit 18, Cooting Road, Aylesham, Canterbury, Kent, CT3 3EP	Tel: 01304 841111
Channel Commercials PLC. Sevenoaks, North Downs Business Park, Pilgrims Way, Dunton Gr, Sevenoaks, Kent, TN13 2TL	Tel: 01732 469469
Channel Commercials PLC. Strood, Whitehall Road, Medway City Industrial Estate, Strood, Kent, ME2 4DZ	Tel: 01634 296686
Chassis Cab Truck Centre. Ipswich, Addison Way, Great Blakenham, Ipswich, Suffolk, IP6 0RL	Tel: 01473 833003
Chassis Cab-Truck Centre. Bury St Edmunds, Northern Way, Bury St Edmunds, Suffolk, IP32 6NL	Tel: 01284 768570
Chatfields. Leeds, Grangefield Industrial Estate, Pudsey, Leeds, West Yorkshire, LS28 6SD	Tel: 01132 571701
Chatfields. Manchester 1, 40 Ashton Old Road, Manchester, M12 6NA	Tel: 0161 2737351
Chatfields. Manchester 2, Mellors Road, Manchester, M17 1PB	Tel: 0161 8772519
Chatfields. Sheffield, 7 Orgreave Drive, Handsworth, Sheffield, Derbyshire, S13 9NR	Tel: 01142 548854
Chatfields. Tyne Tees 1, Drum Road, Barley Mow, Birtley, County Durham, DH3 2AF	Tel: 0191 4921155
Chatfields. Tyne Tees 2, Teesway, North Tees Industrial Estate, Stockton on Tees, North Yorkshire, TS18 2RS	Tel: 01642 637660
Commercial Fleet Services Daf, Richmond House, Wainwright Street, The Heartlands, Birmingham, West Midlands, B6 5TJ	Tel: 0121 3266985
Comprehensive Commercials Services Ltd, Masters Yard, Railway Terrace, Kings Langley, Hertfordshire, WD4 8JA	Tel: 01923 262199
Cousins & Sharp Ltd, Algores Way, Wisbech, Cambridgeshire, PE13 2TQ	Tel: 01945 461316
Double Drive Engineering, 1-5 Johnsons Way, 841 Coronation Road, Park Royal, London, NW10 7QB	Tel: 0208 9657400
Doves Truck Centre, Leeds Road, Huddersfield, West Yorkshire, HD2 1UR	Tel: 01484 300500
Drummond Motor Company Ltd, Ferrard Road, Kirkcaldy, Fife, KY2 5RZ	Tel: 01592 201555
Euroway Daf. High Wycombe, Central Workshops, Unit B, Lincoln Road, Cressex, High Wycombe, Buckinghamshire, HP12 3RH	Tel: 01494 465464
Euroway. Warrington, Geodis House, Holmsfield Road, Farrel Street Industrial, Warrington, Cheshire, WA1 2DR	Tel: 01925 629116
F & G Commercials Ltd, Unit 2, Barkston Road, Carlton Industrial Estate, Carlton, Barnsley, Yorkshire, S71 3HU	Tel: 01226 731870
F W Abbott Ltd, Unit 10, Orion Way, Kettering Business Park, Pytch, Kettering, Northamptonshire, NN15 6	Tel: 01536 517704
Fairwood Truck Centre, Afon Ebbw Road, Rogerstone Park, Risca, Newport, Gwent, NP10 9HZ	Tel: 01633 891991
Ford & Slater Daf. Coventry, Rowley Road, Coventry, Warwickshire, CV3 4FL	Tel: 02476 302856
Ford & Slater Daf. Kings Lynn, Maple Road, Kings Lynn, Norfolk, PE34 3AH	Tel: 01553 764466
Ford & Slater Daf. Leicester, Hazel Drive, Narborough Road South, Leicester, Leicestershire, LE3 2JG	Tel: 0162 632900
Ford & Slater Daf. Lincoln, Sleaford Road, Bracebridge Heath, Lincoln, Lincolnshire, LN4 2NQ	Tel: 01522 518170
Ford & Slater Daf. Newark, Unit 12A, Newark Storage Co, Bowbridge Road, Newark, Nottinghamshire, NG24 4EX	Tel: 01636 674441
Ford & Slater Daf. Norwich, Longwater Business Park, Norwich, Norfolk, NR5 0JS	Tel: 01603 731600
Ford & Slater Daf. Peterborough, Newark Road, Eastern Industrial Estate, Peterborough, Cambridgeshire, PE1 5YD	Tel: 01733 295000

Ford & Slater Daf. Spalding, 58 Station Road, Donington, Spalding, Lincolnshire, PE11 4UJ	Tel: 01775 820777
G B Fleetcare Ltd, C/O Fine Lady Bakeries, Southam Road, Banbury, Oxfordshire, OX16 2RR	Tel: 01295 270072
G Mutch Mechanical Services, Shore Road, Perth, Pershire, PH2 8BH	Tel: 01738 626688
Grant Welsh Commercials, Unit B12, Olympic Business Park, Drybridge Road, Dundonald, Ayrshire, KA2 9BL	Tel: 01563 851015
Greenhous Daf. Shrewsbury, March Way, Battlefield Enterprise Park, Harlescott, Shrewsbury, Shropshire, SY13 3JE	Tel: 01743 467904
Greenhous Daf. Willenhall, Neachells Lane, Willenhall, West Midlands, WV13 3SF	Tel: 01902 305090
Halesfield Truck & Van Hire, Haybrook, Halesfield 9, Telford, Shropshire, TF7 4QW	Tel: 01952 586454
Harris Daf. Grays, 601 London Road, West Thurrock, Grays, Essex, RM20 4AU	Tel: 01708 864426
Harris Daf. Waltham Cross, 1 Station Approach, Waltham Cross, Hertfordshire, EN8 7YD	Tel: 01992 651155
Harris Truck & Van Ltd, 5 Wheaton Road, Witham, Essex, CM8 3UJ	Tel: 01376 533680
Heathrow Daf, Spedition Park, Lakeside Industrial Estate, Bath Road, Colnbrook, Slough, Berkshire, SL3 0ED	Tel: 01753 681818
Holyhead Truck Services, The Garage, Llanfaethlu, Holyhead, Anglesey, LL65 4NW	Tel:01407 730759
Ian Gordon Commercials, Schawkirk Garage, on the B730, Ayr, Ayrshire, KA5 5JA	Tel: 01292 591764
J D S Trucks, Broadgate, Broadway Business Park, Chaderton, Oldham, Cheshire, OL9 9NL	Tel: 0161 9471400
J E Douglas & Sons, Station Road Industrial Estate, Duns, Berwickshire, TD11 3HS	Tel: 01361 883411
Kettlewell Commercials, Station Depot, Melmerby, Ripon, North Yorkshire, HG4 5EX	Tel: 01765 640913
Lakeland Trucks Ltd, Carnforth Industrial Estate, Lodge Quarry, Carnforth, Lancashire, LA5 9DW	Tel: 01524 734544
Lancashire Daf, Unit 223-224, Walton Summit Centre, Bamber Bridge, Preston, Lancashire, PR5 8AL	Tel: 01772 338111
Lex Commercials Ltd. Barford, Wellesbourne Road, Barford, Warwickshire, CV35 8DS	Tel: 01268 290680
Lex Commercials Ltd. Bristol, Days Road, St Philips, Bristol, North Somerset, BS2 0QP	Tel: 01179 557755
Lex Commercials Ltd. Cumbernauld, 8 Southward Park Court, Wardpark South, Cumbernauld, North Lanarkshire, G67 3HE	Tel: 01236 727771
Lex Commercials Ltd. Derby, Ashbourne Road, Mackworth, Derby, Derbyshire, DE22 4NB	Tel: 01332 825300
Lex Commercials Ltd. Doncaster, Brooklands Road, Carcroft, Doncaster, North Yorkshire, DN6 7BA	Tel: 01302 727040
Lex Commercials Ltd. Frome, Unit 12 Moreacres, Marston Trading Estate, Frome, Somerset, BA11 4RL	Tel: 01373 468521
Lex Commercials Ltd. Glasgow, 131 Bogmoor Road, Govan, Glasgow, G51 4TH	Tel: 0141 4251530
Lex Commercials Ltd. Halesowen, Park Road, Halesowen, West Midlands, B63 2RL	Tel: 01384 424500
Lex Commercials Ltd. Hull, Hedon Road, Hull, North Humberside, HU9 5PJ	Tel: 01482 795111
Lex Commercials Ltd. Nottingham, Beacon Road, Boulevard Industrial Park, Beeston, Nottingham, Nottinghamshire, NG9 2JR	Tel: 01559 677077
Lex Commercials Ltd. Rhostyllen, Wrexham Road, Rhostyllen, Wrexham Road, Flintshire, LL14 4DP	Tel: 01978 346100
Lex Commercials Ltd. Scunthorpe, Midland Industrial Estate, Kettering Road, Scunthorpe, South Humberside, DN16 1UW	Tel: 01724 282444
Lex Commercials Ltd. Stoke on Trent, Leek New Road, Cobridge, Stoke on Trent, Staffordshire, ST6 2DE	Tel: 01782 276600
Lex Commercials Ltd. Sutton in Ashfield, Fulwood Road South, Fulwood Road Ind. Est., Sutton in Ashfield, Nottinghamshire, NG17 2JZ	Tel: 01623 516735
Lex Commercials Ltd. Swindon, Radway Road, Stratton, Britannia Trading Park, Swindon, Wiltshire, SN3 4ND	Tel: 01793 835200
Lex Commercials Ltd. York, North York Trading Estate, Auster Road, Clifton Moorgate, York, Yorkshire, YO3 8XD	Tel: 01904 692909
Lothian Daf, Pentland Industrial Estate, Loanhead, Mid Lothian, EH20 9QH	Tel: 0131 4404100
Luton Daf, 166 Camford Way, Sundon Park, Luton, Bedfordshire, LU3 3AN	Tel: 01582 505464
Lynch Truck Services Ltd, Barnfield Way, Altham Business Park, Altham, Accrington, Lancashire, BB5 5YT	Tel: 01282 773377
M C A Commercials Ltd, Dockyard Road, Ellesmere Port, Cheshire, CH65 4EG	Tel: 0151 3551076
Marshall Motor Group Ltd, Airport Garage, Newmarket Road, Cambridge, Cambridgeshire, CB5 8SQ	Tel: 01223 377900
Morgan Elliott Daf. Belvedere, Crabtree Manor Way North, Belvedere, Kent, DA17 6BT	Tel: 0208 3197800
Morgan Elliott Daf. Croydon, 93 Beddington Lane, Croydon, Surrey, CR0 4TD	Tel: 0208 6836200
Mutch Tayside, Block 9, Nobel Road, Wester Gourdie Industrial Estate, Dundee, Angus, DD2 4UH	Tel: 01382 611166
Norden Truck Centre, 3 Avon Industrial Estate, Butlers Leap, Rugby, Warwickshire, CV21 3UY	Tel: 01788 579535
Norscot Truck & Van Ltd. Aberdeen, Norsot House, The Parkway, Bridge of Don, Aberdeen, Aberdeenshire, AB23 8JZ	Tel: 01224 824444
Norscot Truck & Van Ltd. Inverness, The Truck Centre, 52 Seafield Road, Inverness, Inverness-shire, IV1 1SG	Tel: 01463 712000
North West Trucks. Huyton, Huyton Industrial Estate, Wilson Road, Huyton, Liverpool, Merseyside, L36 6AJ	Tel: 0151 4800098
North West Trucks. Northwich, Griffiths Road, Lostock Gralam, Northwich, Cheshire, CW9 7NU	Tel: 01606 818088
Ontime Rescue & Recovery Ltd, Cranes Close, Cranes Farm Road, Basildon, Essex, SS14 3JB	Tel: 01268 290680
Parrys Commercials Ltd, Craig Road, Glan Conwy, Conwy, LL28 5RA	Tel: 01492 580303
Pelican Engineering Company Ltd, Rhine Park Industrial Estate, Altofts Lane, Castleford, Wakefield, North Yorkshire, WF10 5UB	Tel: 01924 227722
Perfect Engineering, Harfreys Road, Harfreys Industrial Estate, Great Yarmouth, Norfolk, NR31 0	Tel: 01493 657131
Saltash Daf, HMG House, Channon Road, Moorlands Estate, Saltash, Cornwall, PL12 6LX	Tel: 01752 848359
Sheriffmill Motor Company, Sheriffmill Road, Elgin, Inverness, Inverness-shire, IV30 3UH	Tel: 01343 547121
Simmons Commercials, Clarke Street, Poulton le Fylde, Lancashire, FY6 8JR	Tel: 01253 884521
Solway Daf Carlisle, Kingstown Broadway, Kingstown Industrial Estate, Carlisle, Cumbria, CA3 0HD	Tel: 01228 539394
Solway Daf. Dumfries, Irongray Road, Lochside Industrial Estate, Newbridge, Dumfries, Dumfriesshire, DG2 0JE	Tel: 01387 720820
Solway Daf. Penrith, Gillwilly Lane, Gillwilly Industrial Estate, Penrith, Cumbria, CA11 9BN	Tel: 01768 892938
Solway Daf. Workington, 6G Reedlands Road, Solway Road, Clay Flatts, Workington, Cumbria, CA14 3YF	Tel: 01900 66927
Stevens Daf. Crawley, Flemming Way, Manor Royal Industrial Estate, Crawley, West Sussex, RH10 2NS	Tel: 01293 540054
Swansea Truck Centre, Unit 43, Cwmdu Business Centre, Fforestfach, Swansea, Carmarthenshire, SA5 8LG	Tel: 01792 582255
T B F Thompson Daf Trucks. Belfast, 19 Michelin Road, Hydepark Ind. Est., Mallusk, Newtownabbey, Belfast, BT36 8PT, Northern Ireland	Tel: 02890 342001
T B F Thompson Daf Trucks. Coleraine, 6-10 Killyvalley Road, Garvagh, Coleraine, BT51 5JZ, Northern Ireland	Tel: 0282 9558353
T B F Thompson Portadown, Diviny Drive, Carn Industrial Estate, Portadown, BT63 5WE, Northern Ireland	Tel: 028 38393300
Taunton Daf, 148 Priorswood Road, Taunton, Somerset, TA2 8DW	Tel: 01823 331275
Truck Services Of Grimsby, Estate Road No 2, South Humberside Industrial Estate, Grimsby, North East Lincolnshire, DN31 2TG	Tel: 01472 362929
Universal Garage Daf, 67 Hall Barn Road, Isleham, Ely, Cambridgeshire, CB7 5QZ	Tel: 01638 780642

Wade's Truck Services, Balthane Industrial Estate, Ballasalla, Isle of Man, IM9 2AD	Tel: 01624 825559
Watts Truck & Van Centre, Unit F, Moreton Park, Moreton on Lugg, Herefordshire, HR4 8DS	Tel: 01432 763900
Watts Truck Centre Ltd. Broomhall, Bath Road, Broomhall, Worcestershire, WR5 3HR	Tel: 01905 829800
Watts Truck Centre Ltd. Gloucester, Mercia Road, Gloucester, Gloucestershire, GL1 2SQ	Tel: 01452 508700
Wessex Daf, 1 Roundhead Road, Heathfield Industrial Estate, Newton Abbot, Devon, TQ12 6EU	Tel: 01626 833737
Windrush Daf, Burford Road, Minster Lovell, Witney, Oxfordshire, OX29 0RB	Tel: 01993 702131
Wynne Phillips Truck Centre, Station Road, Whitland, Carmarthenshire, SA34 0QE	Tel: 01994 240820

FODEN, Foden Trucks, Moss lane, Sandbach, Cheshire, CW11 3YW
Tel: 01270 758400, Fax: 01270 762758 , www.foden.com,
FODEN ASSIST (FROM A LANDLINE): 0800 591101 FODEN ASSIST (FROM A MOBILE): 01922 646136

Acorn Truck Sales Ltd., Acorn Ind. Park, Crayford Road, Crayford, Kent, DA1 4AL	Tel: 01322 556415
Adams Morey Foden, Burrfields Road, Portsmouth, Hampshire, PO3 5NN	Tel: 02392 691122
Albany Motors, Saltmeadows Road, Gateshead, Tyne & Wear, NE8 3AH	Tel: 0191 4770501
Aquila Truck Centres Manchester, 52 Kansas Avenue, Salford, Manchester, M5 2GL	Tel: 0161 873 8048
Birmingham Truck Centre Ltd., Vinculum Way, off Armstrong Way, Willenhall, West Midlands, WV13 2RG	Tel: 01902 637777
Brian Currie. Bedford, 3 Brunel Road, Bedford, Bedfordshire, MK41 9TL	Tel: 01234 211241
Brian Currie. Northampton, Milton Trading Estate, Gayton Road, Milton Malsor, Northampton, Northamtonshire, NN7 3AB	Tel: 01604 858810
Carrow Commercials. Ipswich, c/o Van Ommeren Tank Terminal, Landseer Road, Ipswich, Suffolk, IP3 0BG	Tel: 01473 218524
Carrow Commercials. Wymondham, South Side, Ayton Road, Wymondham, Norfolk, NR18 0RA	Tel: 01953 600999
Cawsey Commercials Ltd., Unit 11, Newport Industrial Estate, Launceston, Cornwall, PL15 8EX	Tel: 01566 772805
Charnwood Truck Services, Hillside, Gotham Road, Kingston-on-Soar, Nottingham, Nottinghamshire, NG11 0DF	Tel: 0115 983 0093
Cumbria Truck Centre Ltd., Leabank Road, Kingstown, Carlisle, Cumbria, CA3 0HB	Tel: 01228 536405
Danby Engineers, Dalton Street, Cleveland Street, Kingston upon Hull, East Yorkshire, HU8 8BB	Tel: 01482 226795
Fairwood Truck Centre, Afon Ebbw Road, Rogerstone Park, Risca, Newport, Gwent, NP10 9HZ	Tel: 01633 891991
Foden. Heathrow, Spedition Park, Lakeside Industrial Estate, Bath Road, Colnbrook, Berkshire, SL3 0ED	Tel: 01753 682282
Foden. Ireland, Baldonnel Business Park, Baldonnel, Dublin 22, Ireland	Tel: 00353 (0) 1403 4100
Foden. Luton, 166 Camford Way, Sundon Park, Luton, Bedfordshire, LU3 3AN	Tel: 01582 590903
Foden. Norscot, Norscot House, The Parkway, Bridge of Don, Aberdeen, Aberdeenshire, AB23 8JZ	Tel: 01224 824444
Foden. Wessex, 1 Roundhead Road, Heathfield Industrial Estate, Newton Abbot, Devon, TQ12 6UE	Tel: 01626 834444
Ford & Slater. Donington, 58 Station Street, Donington, Spalding, Lincolnshire, PE11 4UJ	Tel: 01775 820777
Ford & Slater. King's Lynn, Marple Road, King's Lynn, Norfolk, PE34 3AH	Tel: 01553 764466
Ford & Slater. Leicester, Hazel Drive, Narborough Road South, Leicester, Leicestershire, LE3 2JG	Tel: 0116 263 2900
Ford and Slater. Peterborough, Newark Road, Peterborough, Cambridgeshire, PE1 5YD	Tel: 01733 295000
Foulgers Garage, Melda Farm, Elliot Drive, Melbourn, Royston, Hertfordshire, SG8 6DF	Tel: 01763 262826
Gallows Wood Service Station Ltd., Melton Road, Barnetby, North Lincolnshire, DN38 6DW	Tel: 01652 688259
H & H Commercial Truck Services Ltd., Nevada Close, Sneyd Industrial Estate, Burslem, Stoke on Trent, Staffordshire, ST6 2NT	Tel: 01782 575522
H W Martin Plant Ltd., Fordbridge Lane, Blackwell, Alfreton, Derbyshire, DE55 5JY	Tel: 01773 813313
Harris Truck & Van Ltd., 5 Wheaton Road, Witham, Essex, CM8 3UJ	Tel: 01376 533685
John Maitland & Sons, Trabboch, Mauchline, Ayrshire, KA5 5HT	Tel: 01292 592000
Joseph Rice Truck Services Ltd., 26A Hempsted Lane, Gloucester, Gloucestershire, GL2 5FH	Tel: 01452 522563
Lex Commercials Ltd. Cumbernauld, 8 South Wardpark Court, Wardpark South, Cumbernauld, Glasgow, G67 3HE	Tel: 0123 672 7771
Lex Foden. Bristol, Days Road, St. Philips, Bristol, North Somerset, BS2 0QP	Tel: 0117 941 4765
Lex Foden. Frome, Unit 12, Marston Trading Estate, Frome, Somerset, BA11 4RL	Tel: 01373 464524
Lex Foden. Glasgow, 131 Bogmoor Road, Govan, Glasgow, Renfrewshire, G51 4TH	Tel: 0141 425 1530
Lex Foden. Stoke on Trent, Leek New Road, Cobridge, Stoke on Trent, Staffordshire, ST6 2DE	Tel: 01782 276600
Lex Foden. Wrexham, Wrexham Road, Rhostyllen, Wrexham, Denbighshire, LL14 4DP	Tel: 01978 346100
Midland Commercial Services Ltd, Hazel Way, Barwell, Leicester, Leicestershsire, LE9 8GP	Tel: 01455 840994
M T C Northwest Ltd, Gores Road, Knowsley Industrial Park, Kirkby, Liverpool, L33 7XS	Tel: 0151 545 4750
Osborn Transport Services, 35A Stanbridge Road, Leighton Buzzard, Bedfordshire, LU7 8PZ	Tel: 01525 383548
Parrys Commercials Ltd, Graig Truck and Van Centre, Glan Conwy, Colwyn Bay, Clwyd, LL28 5RA	Tel: 01492 580303
Parsons Truck Centre, Brenda Road, Hartlepool, Cleveland, TS25 2BJ	Tel: 01429 864876
Pelican Engineering Co Ltd. Sheffield, Unit 11, Monksbridge Trading Estate, Outgang Lane, Dinnington, Sheffield, S25 3QY	Tel: 01909 564215
Pelican Engineering Co. Ltd. Wakefield, Rhine Park Ind. Est., Altofts Lane, Wakefield Europort, Castleford, Wakefield, WF10 5UB	Tel: 01924 227722
R Eastman & Son, The Garage, Newark Road, Torksey, Lincoln, Lincolnshire, LN1 2EJ	Tel: 01427 718638
R P Cherry & Son Ltd., Thrupp Lane, Abingdon, Oxfordshire, OX14 3NG	Tel: 01235 531004
Swansea Truck Centre Ltd., Unit 43, Cwmdu Business Centre, Fforestfach, Swansea, Carmarthenshire, SA5 8LG	Tel: 01792 582255
T B F Thompson Ltd. Garvagh, 6-10 Killyvalley Road, Garvagh, Coleraine, Northern Ireland, BT51 5JZ	Tel: 028 2955 8353
T B F Thompson Ltd. Mallusk, 19 Michelin Road, Hydepark Ind. Est., Mallusk, Newtownabbey, Northern Ireland, BT36 4PT	Tel: 028 9034 2001
T B F Thompson Ltd. Portadown, Diviny Drive, Carn Industrial Estate, Portadown, BT63 5RH, Northern Ireland	Tel: 028 3839 3300
T J Parry & Sons, Wattlesborough Heath Garage, Wattlesborough, Shrewsbury, Shropshire, SY5 9EG	Tel: 01743 885018

Valley Trucks Ltd., Bingley Road, Hoddesdon, Hertfordshire, EN11 0NX	Tel: 01992 441551
Watts Truck & Van Centre. Gloucester, Mercia Road, Gloucester, Gloucestershire, GL1 2SQ	Tel: 01452 508700
Watts Truck & Van Centre. Hereford, Moreton Business Park, Moreton-on-Lug, Hereford, Herefordshire, HR4 8DS	Tel: 01432 763900
Watts Truck & Van Centre. Worcester, Bath Road, Broomhall, Worcestershire, WR5 3HR	Tel: 01905 829800
W M Armstrong Trucks, Nasmyth Square, Houstoun Industrial Estate, Livingston, West Lothian, Scotland, EH54 5GG	Tel: 01506 430000

IVECO/SEDDON ATKINSON, Iveco Ltd, Iveco House, Station Road, Watford, Hertfordshire, WD17 1SR
Tel: 01923 246400, www.iveco.co.uk
ASSISTANCE NON STOP: 0800 590509

A M Phillip. Aberdeen, 218 Auchmill Road, Bucksburn, Aberdeen, Aberdeenshire, AB21 9NB	Tel: 01224 716888
A M Phillip. Broxburn, Simpson Road, East Mains Industrial Estate, Broxburn, West Lothian, EH52 5NP	Tel: 01506 865000
A M Phillip. Dundee, Camperdown Industrial Park, Dryburgh Industrial Estate, Dundee, Angus, DD2 3SN	Tel: 01382 817266
A M Phillip. Forfar, Muiryfaulds Garage, Inverarity, Forfar, Angus, DD8 1XP	Tel: 01307 474000
A M Phillip. Glenrothes, Blackwood Way, Bankhead Industrial Estate, Glenrothes, Fife, KY7 6JF	Tel: 01592 775511
Arm Truck Repairs, Garage Lane Industrial Estate, Setchley, King's Lynn, Norfolk, PE33 0BE	Tel: 01533 810292
Bougourd Ford, Les Grange, St Peter Port, Guernsey, Channel Islands, GY1 3LB	Tel: 01481 724772
Bramall Quicks Trucks, Chester Road, Bretton, Chester, Cheshire, CH4 0DS	Tel: 01244 660681
Brand Of Beccles, Common Lane North, Beccles, Beccles, Suffolk, NR34 9BN	Tel: 01502 718800
Bristol Street Commercials. Bristol, Unit 1, St Andrews Trading Estate, Third Way, Avonmouth, Bristol, South Gloucs., BS11 9YE	Tel: 0117 9382880
Bristol Street Commercials. Gloucester, Bristol Road, Gloucester, Gloucestershire, GL2 5YB	Tel: 01452 314905
Bristol Street Commercials. Swindon, Marshgate Trading Estate, Stratton Road, Swindon, Wiltshire, SN1 2PA	Tel: 01793 422366
Brooklyn Motors, Battens Drive, Redditch, Worcestershire, B98 0LJ	Tel: 01527 405066
C D Bramall Truck. Ardwick, Ashton Old Road, Ardwick, Manchester, M12 6JD	Tel: 0161 2726000
C D Bramall Truck. Bedford, Hudson Road, Elms & Viking Estate, Bedford, Bedfordshire, MK41 0HR	Tel: 01234 340041
C D Bramall Truck. Leicester, 302 Melton Road, Leicester, Leicestershire, LE4 7SL	Tel: 0116 2667721
C D Bramall Truck. Loughborough, Unit C, Belton Road, Chrisie Bradford Industrial Estate, Loughborough, Leicestershire, LE11 0XH	Tel: 01509 264362
C D Bramall Truck. Urmston, Taylor Road, Trafford Park, Urmston, Manchester, M41 7JQ	Tel: 0161 7461903
C D Bramall Truck. Warrington, Unit 12, Clayton Road, Risley, Warrington, Cheshire, WA3 6PH	Tel: 01925 284411
C E M Day Ltd, Beaufort Road, Morriston Swansea, West Glamorgan, SA6 8HR	Tel: 01792 310410
Central Motors Ltd, 105 Carlisle Road, Airdrie, North Lanarkshire, ML6 8AG	Tel: 01236 762881
Chambers Engineering Ltd, Warmstone Works, Warmstone Road, Waddesdon, Aylesbury, Buckinghamshire, HP18 0NF	Tel: 01296 651380
Dagenham Motors Ltd Barking, 51 River Road, Barking, Essex, IG11 0SW	Tel: 0208 5949666
Dagenham Motors Ltd. Chelmsford, Cuton Hall Lane, Springfield, Chelmsford, Essex, CM2 6PB	Tel: 01245 466633
Dagenham Motors Ltd. Hayes, Dawley Road, Hayes, Middlesex, UB3 1EH	Tel: 01208 6061538
Dovercourt Motor Company Ltd, 4 Newcomen Way, Severalls Business Park, Colchester, Essex, CO4 9YR	Tel: 01206 222222
Dragon Truck & Van, Coaster Place, Rover Way, Cardiff Dock, Cardiff, South Glamorgan, CF10 4XZ	Tel: 029 20449660
E W Smith, Unit 1, Chepping Park, Lincoln Road, Cressex Industrial Estate, High Wycombe, Buckinghamshire, HP12 3RB	Tel: 01494 537547
Eakin Brothers Ltd, 48 Main Street, Claudy, County Antrim, Londonderry, Northern Ireland, BT47 4HR	
Edwards Commercials, Stephenson Road, Churchfield Industrial Estate, Salisbury, Wiltshire, SP2 7NP	Tel: 01722 331188
Fishlake Commercials Ltd, Jubilee Bridge Works, Selby Road, Doncaster, East Yorkshire, DN8 4JD	Tel: 01405 740086
Furrows Commercial Vehicles Ltd, Kemberton Road, Halesfield, Telford, Shropshire, TF7 4QS	Tel: 01952 684433
Glenside Commercials, Trecenydd Industrial Estate, Caerphilly, Mid Glamorgan, CF83 2RZ	Tel: 02920 867721
Grays Truck & Van. Croydon, 37-39 Imperial Way, Purley Way, Croydon, Surrey, CR0 4RR	Tel: 0208 6800600
Grays Truck & Van. Guildford, Slyfield Industrial Estate, Woking Road, Guildford, Surrey, GU1 1RY	Tel: 01483 571012
Grays Truck & Van. Reading, 8 Arrowhead, Reading, Berkshire, RG7 4AZ	Tel: 0118 9304044
Guests Trucks Birmingham, 31 Shefford Road, Aston, Birmingham, West Midlands, B6 4PQ	Tel: 0121 359 5888
Guests Trucks. Coventry, Kingswood Close, Holbrook, Coventry, West Midlands, CV6 4BJ	Tel: 01276 584488
Guest Trucks. West Bromwich, Kenrick Way, West Bromwich, West Midlands, B70 6BY	Tel: 0121 5532737
Guest Trucks. Wolverhampton, 55 Willenhall Road, Wolverhampton, West Midlands, WV1 2HL	Tel: 01902 352888
Haynes Brothers Ltd. Ashford, 73-74 Ellingham Way, Ashford, Kent, TN23 6JU	Tel: 01233 667500
Haynes Brothers Ltd. Maidstone, 23 Ashford Road, Maidstone, Kent, ME14 5DQ	Tel: 01622 756781
Haynes Trucks Ltd, Vauxhall Industrial Road, Canterbury, Kent, CT1 1HD	Tel: 01227 783480
Hendy Truck & Van. Eastleigh, School Lane, Chandlers Ford, Eastleigh, Hampshire, SO53 4DG	Tel: 02380 579806
Hendy Van & Truck. Exeter, Grace Road, Marsh Barton Industrial Estate, Exeter, Devon, EX2 8QB	Tel: 01392 276561
Hendy Van & Truck. Poole, Witney Road, Nuffield Industrial Estate, Poole, Dorset, BH17 0GH	Tel: 01202 494700
Hendy Van & Truck. Portsmouth, Quatermaine Road, Portsmouth, Hampshire, PO3 5QH	Tel: 02392 696926
Hendy Van & Truck. Yeovil, 9 Oxford Road, Penn Mill Trading Estate, Yeovil, Somerset, BA21 5HR	
Hilltop Garage, 22 Cranagh Road, Coleraine, County Antrim, Londonderry, Northern Ireland, BT51 3NN	Tel: 02870 343809
Holyhead Motors, The Garage, on the A5025, Llanfaethlu, Anglesey, LL65 4NW	Tel: 01407 730 759
Jacksons Basingstoke Ltd, Rotentgen Road, Daneshill East Industrial Estate, Basingstoke, Hampshire, RG24 8NT	Tel: 01256 461656
Jeffreys Vehicle Service, Swadlincote Road, Woodville, Swadlincote, Derbyshire, DE11 8DD	Tel: 01283 817321

Kenwood Commercials, Kenwood Road, Reddish, Stockport, Cheshire, SK5 6PH
Kerr & Smith. Cumnock, Riverside Garage, Ayr Road, Cumnock, Ayrshire, KA18 1BJ — Tel: 01290 422440
Kerr & Smith. Glasgow, 10 Springhill Parkway, Glasgow Business Park, Glasgow, G69 6GA — Tel: 0141 7733999
La Motte Ford, 14 Rue Des Pres Trading Estate, St Saviour, Jersey, Channel Islands, JE4 8UR — Tel: 01534 636600
Lifestyle Ford, 53-55 Bishopric, Horsham, West Sussex, RH12 1QJ
McKinnin & Forbes Ltd, 48-58 Clark Street, Paisley, Renfrewshire, PA3 1RB — Tel: 0141 8872411
N I Trucks Ltd. Newtownabbey, 1-3 Mallusk Road, Newtownabbey, County Antrim, Northern Ireland, BT36 4XS — Tel: 02890 833040
N I Trucks Ltd. Portadown, 6 Carn Court Industrial Estate, Portadown, County Antrim, Northern Ireland, BT63 5YX — Tel: 02838 362413
Norfolk Trucks. Enfield, Mollison Avenue, Brimsdown, Enfield, Middlesex, EN3 7NE — Tel: 0208 8041266
Norfolk Trucks. Ipswich, Lodge Lane, Great Blakenham, Ipswich, Suffolk, IP6 0LB — Tel: 01473 834200
Norfolk Trucks. Norwich, School Lane, Sprowston, Norwich, Norfolk, NR7 8TL — Tel: 01603 253340
North East Truck & Van Ltd. Bellingham, Cowpen Bewley Road, Haverton Hill, Bellingham, Teeside, YS23 4EX — Tel: 01642 370555
North East Truck & Van Ltd. Carlisle, 49 Parkhill Road, Kingstown Industrial Estate, Carlisle, Cumbria, CA3 0EX — Tel: 01228 404400
North East Truck & Van Ltd. Hull, Staithes Road, Hull, East Yorkshire, HU12 8DX — Tel: 01482 899099
North East Truck & Van Ltd. Immingham, 124 Manby Road, Immingham, North East Lincolnshire, DN40 2LJ — Tel: 01469 565544
North East Truck & Van Ltd. Blaydon on Tyne, Chainbridge Road, Blaydon on Tyne, Tyne & Wear, NE21 5TR — Tel: 0191 4143333
North East Truck & Van Ltd. York, Auster Road, York, Yorkshire, YO30 4XA — Tel: 01904 479123
Northern Commercial Ltd. Brighouse, Armytage Road, Brighouse, West Yorkshire, HD6 1PG — Tel: 01484 380111
Northern Commercials Ltd. Morley, Albert Road, Morley, Leeds, West Yorkshire, LS27 8TT — Tel: 0113 2383110
Parrys Commercial, on the A470, Colwyn Bay, Clwyd, LL28 5RA — Tel: 01492 580303
Paynes Garages, Watling Street, Hinckley, Leicester, Leicestershire, LE10 3ED — Tel: 01455 237777
Pitter Commercials Ltd, Botley Road, West End, Southampton, Hampshire, SO30 3HA — Tel: 02380 477125
Pye Motors Ltd, Ovangle Road, Morcambe, Lancashire, LA3 3PF — Tel: 01524 598598
Sherwood Commercial Vehicles Ltd. Blackwell, Berristow Lane, Blackwell, Derbyshire, DE55 5HP — Tel: 01773 863311
Sherwood Commercial Vehicles Ltd. Nottingham
522 Derby Road, Lenton, Nottingham, Nottinghamshire, NG7 2GX — Tel: 0115 9787274
Sherwood Commercial Vehicles Ltd. Sheffield, Highfield Lane, Sheffield, South Yorkshire, S13 9DB — Tel: 0114 2693230
Sherwood Commercial Vehicles Ltd. Stoke on Trent, Etruria Old Road, Etruria, Stoke on Trent, Staffordshire, ST1 5PE
Southern Vectis Commercials, Nelson Road, Newport, Isle of Wight, PO30 1RD — Tel: 01983 821135
Stormont Truck & Van Ltd. Brighton, Ellen Street, Portslade, Brighton, East Sussex, BN41 1DW — Tel: 01273 430828
Stormont Truck & Van Ltd. Crayford, Thames Road, Crayford, Kent, DA1 5QQ — Tel: 01322 295935
Stormont Truck & Van Ltd. Dunstable, 23 Eastern Avenue, Bedfordshire, LU5 4JY — Tel: 01582 884527
Stormont Truck & Van Ltd. Tonbridge, London Road, Hildenborough, Tonbridge, Kent, TN11 8NN — Tel: 01732 838072
Stormont Truck & Van. Kettering, Bartley Drive, Telford Way Industrial Estate, Kettering, Northamptonshire, NN16 8JN — Tel: 01536 517079
Stormont Truck & Van. Northampton, Jackdaw Close, Crow Lane Industrial Estate, Billing, Northampton, NN3 9ER
T C Harrison. Boston, Riverside Industrial Estate, Marsh Lane, Boston, Lincolnshire, PE21 7RP — Tel: 01205 377117
T C Harrison. Cambridge, Unit 1, Ely Road, Waterbeach, Cambridge, Cambridgeshire, CB5 9PG — Tel: 01223 861371
T C Harrison. Peterborough, Oxney Road, Eastern Industrial Estate, Peterborough, Cambridgeshire, PE1 5YN — Tel: 01733 425555
Truck Care, Unit 3, Perseverance Road, Hereford, Herefordshire, HR4 9SD — Tel: 01432 342679
Umax Crane & Haulage Ltd, 35 Henderson Drive, Inverness, Inverness-shire, IV1 1TR — Tel: 01463 233282
Vospers Commercial Services. Plymouth, Vally Road, Plympton, Plymouth, Devon, PL7 1RS — Tel: 01752 206828
Vospers Commercial Services. St Austell, Victoria Business Park, Roche, St Austell, Cornwall, PL26 8LQ — Tel: 01726 892101
Wades Truck Services, Unit 2, Balthane Industrial Estate, Ballasalla, Isle of Man, IM9 2AQ — Tel: 01624 825559
Walton Summit Truck Centre, 211 Walton Summit Road, Bamber Bridge, Preston, Lancashire, PR5 8AQ — Tel: 01772 334006
Wasdies Motors, A40 Northern Bypass, Eynesham, Oxfordshire, OX29 4EF — Tel: 01865 881367

MAN/ERF, Frankland Road, Blagrove, Swindon, Wiltshire, SN5 8YU
Tel: 01793 448000, Fax: 01793 448265 www.man.co.uk
EUROSERVICE 24 (MAN): Freefone 0800 0287728 or 01793 448044
EUROSERVICE 24 (ERF): Freefone 0800 424333 or 01793 448044
A. N. Richards, The Garage, Froncysyllte, Llangollen, Denbighshire, LL20 7RA — Tel: 01691 777 835
Allied Commercials, 4 Atcost Road, Barking, Essex, IG11 0EQ — Tel: 0208 5947634
Aquila Truck Centre Limited, Westgate, Walsall, Birmingham, West Midlands, WS9 8EZ — Tel: 01922 743783
Beech's Garage Ltd. Stoke on Trent, Shelton New Road, Stoke on Trent, Staffordshire, ST4 7DL — Tel: 01782 848485
Beech's Garage Ltd. Middlewich, Brooks Lane Industrial Estate, Middlewich, Cheshire, CW10 0JH — Tel: 01606 832 930
Borderman Trucks Ltd. Carlisle, 76-83 Black Dyke Road, Carlisle, Cumbria, CA3 0PJ — Tel: 01228 595849
Borderman Trucks Ltd. Penrith, Quarry Garage, Penrith, Cumbria, CA11 0EB — Tel: 01768 865181
B M Trucks, Cromwell Road, Inverness, Highland, IV1 1 — Tel: 01463 231727
Cebron Motors, Cochrane House, Pedmore Road, Dudley, West Midlands, DY2 0RL — Tel: 01384 482002
Clydesdale Commercials, Unit 134, Clydesdale Place, Leyland, Lancashire, PR26 7QS — Tel: 0177 2458274
Frank Tucker Commercials Ltd, Peamore Garage, off the A379, Shillingford St George, Exeter, Devon, EX2 9SL — Tel: 0139 2832662
Hawarden Commercials, Factory Road, Deeside, Flintshire, CH5 2QJ — Tel: 0124 4520853

HRVS, Heage Road Industrial Estate, Ripley, Derbyshire, DE5 3GH	Tel: 0177 3745 311
Husk UK Ltd, The Freight Terminal, Dover, Kent, CT15 7JW	Tel: 01304 831222
Jeffreys Vehicle Services, Swadlincote Road, Swadlincote, Derbyshire, DE11 8DD	Tel: 0128 3817 318
John Arnold Commercials Ltd, Kenneth Way, Bedford, Bedfordshire, MK45 3PD	Tel: 0123 4742 266
Lamb Commercials, 126 Tamnamore Road, Dungannon, Northern Ireland, BT71 6HW	Tel: 028 8772 2111
L C W Truck & Van Centre Ltd, Halifax Road, Halifax, West Yorkshire, HX3 8ER	Tel: 0142 2205618
Leach Commercials, Chichester Street, Rochdale, Lancashire, OL16 2AU	Tel: 0170 6868668
Lex Commercials Ltd. Derby, Ashbourne Road, Derby, Derbyshire, DE22 4NB	Tel: 01332 824999
Lex Commercials Ltd. Luton, Unit 10, Finway, Luton, Bedfordshire, LU1 1TR	Tel: 01582 411244
Lex Commercials Ltd. Norwich, Barnard Road, Norwich, Norfolk, NR5 9JB	Tel: 01603 741741
Lex Commercials Ltd. Peterborough 1, Fengate, Peterborough, Cambridgeshire, PE1 5XG	Tel: 01733 560591
Lex Commercials Ltd. Peterborough 2, Willow Road, Yaxley, Peterborough, Cambridgeshire, PE7 3HT	Tel: 01733 240627
Lex Commercials Ltd. Northampton, 2 Deer Park Road, Northampton, Northamptonshire, NN3 6RX	Tel: 01604 495497
M V Trucks. Maidstone, New Hythe Lane, New Hythe, Maidstone, Kent, ME20 7PW	Tel: 01622 681111
M V Trucks. Gatwick, Salfords Industrial Estate, Redhill, Surrey, RH1 1ES	Tel: 01293 783166
MAN Central, 4 Sunningdale Road, Leicester, Leicestershire, LE3 1UX	Tel: 01162 878317
MAN ERF. Aberdeen, Minto Road, Aberdeen, Aberdeenshire, AB12 3LU	Tel: 01224 875757
MAN ERF. Birmingham, Premier Street, Birmingham, West Midlands, B7 5TP	Tel: 0121 3266555
MAN ERF. Blackburn, Hollin Bridge Street, Blackburn, Lancashire, BB2 4AX	Tel: 01254 682022
MAN ERF. Broxburn, Westerton Road, Broxburn, West Lothian, EH52 5AU	Tel: 01506 858344
MAN ERF Colchester, Westside Centre, London Road, Stanway, Colchester, Essex, CO3 5PB	Tel: 01206 213321
MAN ERF. Enfield, Crown Road, Enfield, Middlesex, EN1 1TH	Tel: 0208 4434949
MAN ERF Fife, Cross Gate Road, Cross Gates, Dunfermline, Fife, KY11 7EG	Tel: 01383 626277
MAN ERF. Gateshead, Earlsway, Gateshead, Tyne & Wear, NE11 0RQ	Tel: 01914 211111
MAN ERF. Glasgow, 30 Clydesmill Drive, Cambuslang, Glasgow, Strathclyde, G32 8	Tel: 0141 641 6172
MAN ERF. Grangemouth, Dalgrain Industrial Estate, Grangemouth, Falkirk, FK3 8EB	Tel: 01324 273700
MAN ERF. Manchester, Irlam Wharf Road, Salford, Manchester, M44 5PN	Tel: 01324 473 700
MAN ERF. Newcastle, Harveycombe, Killingworth, Newcastle upon Tyne, NE12 6QQ	Tel: 0191 2165350
MAN ERF. Northampton, 14 Gambrel Road, Northampton, Northamptonshire, NN5 5BB	Tel: 01604 588555
MAN ERF. Nuneaton, Harrington Way, Nuneaton, Warwickshire, CV10 7SA	Tel: 02476 357800
MAN ERF Scunthorpe, Ermine Street, Brigg, Near Broughton, Scunthorpe, South Humberside, DN20 0QA	Tel: 01652 650404
MAN ERF Sheffield, Shepcote Lane, Sheffield, S9 1FX	Tel: 0114 2012424
MAN ERF Stockton, Bowsfield Lane, Stockton on Tees, TS18 3HJ	Tel: 01642 611812
MAN ERF Tipton, Chimney Road, Tipton, West Midlands, DY4 7BY	Tel: 0121 5201234
MAN ERF Truck Services Swindon, Frankland Road, Swindon, Wiltshire, SN5 8YU	Tel: 01793 448190
Martin Commercials, Quatermaine Road, Portsmouth, Hampshire, PO3 5QG	Tel: 02392 599033
McDougall Commercials, Beeswing, Dumfries, Dumfries and Galloway, DG2 8JF	Tel: 01387 760 612
Mendip Truck & Bus Services Ltd, Crowne Trading Estate, Shepton Mallet, Somerset, BA4 5QQ	Tel: 01749 343 963
Mick Gould Commercials Ltd, The Royal Oak Garage, on the A21, Flimwell, East Sussex, TN5 7PJ	Tel: 01580 879 333
Mike Aven Commercials, 8 Victory Road, Westbury, Wiltshire, BA13 4JL	Tel: 01373 864148
Millbrook Beven, 18-20 Morfa Road, Swansea, SA1 2EN	Tel: 01792 650646
North Yorkshire Commercials, Dalton Industrial Estate, Dalton, Thirsk, North Yorkshire, YO7 3HE	Tel: 01845 578 123
Patrick Uren Commercials, 17 Jon Davey Drive, Redruth, Cornwall, TR16 4AX	Tel: 01209 313377
Pullman Fleet Services. Dundee, Smeaton Road, Dundee, Tayside, DD2 4UT	Tel: 01382 623263
Pullman Fleet Services. Ellesmere Port, Rosswood Road, Ellesmere Port, Cheshire, CH65 3BU	Tel: 0151 355 8355
Pullman Fleet Services. Haydock, Yew Tree Trading Estate, St Helens, Haydock, Cheshire, WA11 9UX	Tel: 01942 402260
Pullmans Truck Centre. Widnes, Waterloo Road, Catalyst Trade Park, Widnes, Cheshire, WA8 0WG	Tel: 0151 4204700
R & A Scott Auto Services, 5 Sandars Road, Gainsborough, Lincolnshire, DN21 1RZ	Tel: 01427 611005
R K Trucks Centre Ltd, Unit 12, Edgar Road, Carryduff, Belfast, Northern Ireland, BT8 8NB	Tel: 02890 813600
R Lawson & Co, Sea lane, Butterwick, Boston, Lincolnshire, PE22 0HG	Tel: 01205 760269
Reliance Commercial Vehicles, Wakefield Road, Brighouse, West Yorkshire, HD6 1QQ	Tel: 01132 389999
Richard Read Commercials Ltd, Monmouth Road, Gloucester, Gloucestershire, GL17 0QG	Tel: 01452 830456
S A Trucks Ltd. Bristol, Third Way, Avonmouth, Bristol, South Gloucestershire, BS11 9RH	Tel: 01179 821241
S A Trucks Ltd. Exeter, 7 Christow Road, Marsh Barton Industrial Estate, Exeter, Devon, EX2 8QP	Tel: 01392 437440
S A Trucks Ltd. St Columb, Moorland Road, St Columb, Cornwall, TR9 6HN	Tel: 01726 860779
Staverton Commercials Services Ltd, Site 14, Bamfurlong Industrial Park, Steverton, Cheltenham, GL51 6SP	Tel: 01452 714610
Steadplan Ltd, Salthill Industrial Estate, Clitheroe, Lancashire, BB7 0QL	Tel: 01200 444000
Testwood Truck & Van Centre, Nutsey Lane, Southampton, Hampshire, SO40 3NB	Tel: 02380 663333
The Mansfield Group, Harpur Hill Business Park, Buxton, Derbyshire, SK17 9JL	Tel: 0129 872399
Thoroughbred Trucks Ltd, Estate Road 2, Grimsby, Humberside, DN31 2TE	Tel: 01472 252455
Torridon Commercial Vehicles Ltd, Littlefair Road, Hull, North Humberside, HU9 5LP	Tel: 01482 790760
Ullswater Road Garage, off Shap Road, Unit 5, Westmorland Business Park, Kendal, Cumbria, LA9 6NS	Tel: 01539 730730
W G Davies (Landore) Ltd, Unit 11, St David's Road, Swansea, West Glamorgan, SA6 8QL	Tel: 01792 795705
W G Davies Ltd, Hazelbrook Garage, off the B4318, Sageston, Tenby, Pembrokeshire, SA70 8SY	Tel: 01646 651417
Welch's Commercials, Granta Terrace, Cambridge, Cambridgeshire, CB2 5DL	Tel: 01223 841703
Wooton Trucks Ltd. Abingdon, Unit 28, Nuffield Way, Abingdon, Oxfordshire, OX14 1RY	Tel: 01235 555520

Wooton Trucks Ltd. Reading, Grange Lane, Reading, Berkshire, RG7 5PT	Tel: 0118 9710071
Worcester Truck Services, Blackpole Trading Estate, Worcester, Worcestershire, WR3 8SG	Tel: 01905 756089
Yorkshire Coast Commercials Ltd, 17 Bridlington Road, Filey, North Yorkshire, YO14 1LR	Tel: 01723 891111

Mercedes-Benz, Burystead Court, Caldecotte Lake Drive, Caldecotte, Milton Keynes, MK7 8ND
Tel: 0870 840500, www.mercedes-benz.com
Mercedes 24 Hour Breakdown: 00800 17777777

A C Price (Engineering) Ltd, Ingleton Industrial Estate, Ingleton, North Yorkshire, LA6 3NU	Tel: 01524 242333
Arthur Ibbett Ltd, River Lane, Great Paxton, St Neots, Cambridgeshire, PE19 6RD	Tel: 01480 473452
Bell Truck Sales. Billingham, Macklin Avenue, Cowpen Lane Industrial Estate, Billingham, Durham, TS23 4BY	Tel: 01642 561333
Bell Truck Sales. Birtley, Portobello Road, Portobello Industrial Estate, Birtley, Tyne and Wear, DH3 2SH	Tel: 0191 410 6514
Bell Truck Sales. Longbenton, Whitley Road, Bellway Ind. Est., Longbenton, Newcastle upon Tyne, Tyne and Wear, NE12 9SW	Tel: 0191 2700787
Bell Truck Sales. Spennymoor, Coulson Street, Spennymoor, Durham, County Durham, DL16 7RS	Tel: 01388 819672
Caledonian Trucks, Whitfield Drive, Heathfield Industrial Estate, Ayr, Strathclyde, KA8 9RX	Tel: 01292 610888
Ciceley Commercials. Blackburn, Commercial Road, Junction 4 Intersection M65, Darwen, Lancashire, BB3 0DB	Tel: 01254 870990
Ciceley Commercials. Carlisle, Peterfield Road, Kingstown Industrial Estate, Carlisle, Cumbria, CA3 0EY	Tel: 01228 544611
Ciceley Commercials. Dumfries, Brownrigg Loaming, Dumfries, Dumfriesshire, DG1 3JT	Tel: 01387 250822
Ciceley Commercials. Preston, Mercedes-Benz House, Queen Street, Preston, Lancashire, PR1 4HH	Tel: 01772 201455
Ciceley Truck & Van Centre, Weston Street, Bolton, Lancashire, BL3 2BZ	Tel: 01204 383835
Commercial Motors South West. Avonmouth, Kings Weston Lane, St Andrews Road, Avonmouth, South Gloucestershire, BS11 9BY	Tel: 0117 938 7770
Commercial Motors South West. Bristol, Days Road, Barton Hill, Bristol, North Somerset, BS5 0AJ	Tel: 0117 955 1571
Commercial Motors South West. Exeter, Heron Road, Sowton Industrial Estate, Exeter, Devon, EX2 7LL	Tel: 01392 360555
Commercial Motors South West. St. Austell, Bucklers Lane, Holmbush, St. Austell, Cornwall, PL25 3JL	Tel: 01726 874200
Commercial Motors South West. Yeovil, Oxford Road, Pen Mill Trading Estate, Yeovil, Somerset, BA21 5HR	Tel: 01935 431883
Enza Motors. Stoke, Chemical Lane, Longport, Stoke-on-Trent, Staffordshire, ST6 4PB	Tel: 01782 820200
Enza Motors. Trafford Park, 717 Trafford Park Road, Trafford Park, Manchester, M171HG	Tel: 0161 8737066
Enza Motors. Warrington, Leacroft Road, Risley, Cheshire, WA3 6NN	Tel: 01925 847100
Euro Commercials. Bridgend, Brynmenyn Industrial Estate, Bridgend, South Glamorgan, CF32 9TD	Tel: 01656 304304
Euro Commercials Cardiff, Ipswich Road, Cardiff, South Glamorgan, CF23 9AQ	Tel: 02920 310310
Euro Commercials Newport, 164 Malpas Road, Newport, Monmouthshire, NP20 5PP	Tel: 01633 764764
Euro Commercials Swansea, Viking Way, Winch Wen Industrial Estate, Swansea, SA1 7DA	Tel: 01792 526526
Fengate Commercials Mercedes-Benz Authorised Repairer, Bretton Way, North Bretton, Peterborough, Cambridgeshire, PE3 8YQ	Tel: 01733 333232
Gerard Mann. Birmingham, 2 Lichfield Road, Aston, Birmingham, West Midlands, B6 5SU	Tel: 0121 326 4200
Gerard Mann. Coventry, Wheler Road, off Humber Road, Coventry, West Midlands, CV3 4LA	Tel: 02476 518300
Gerard Mann. Wolverhampton, Neachells Lane, Willenhall, Wolverhampton, West Midlands, WV13 3RP	Tel: 01902 630317
H & L Garages. Boston, Lealand Way, Riverside Industrial Estate, Boston, Lincolnshire, PE21 7SW	Tel: 01205 311288
H & L Garages. Hull, Henry Boot Way, Priory Park, Hull, East Yorkshire, HU4 7DY	Tel: 01482 577797
H & L Garages. Immingham, Humber Road, South Killingholme, Immingham, Lincolnshire, DN40 3DL	Tel: 01469 571666
H & L Garages. Lincoln, Wrights Way, Off Outer Circle Road, Lincoln, Lincolnshire, LN2 4JY	Tel: 01522 521777
H & L Garages. Scunthorpe, Grange Lane North, Scunthorpe, Lincolnshire, DN16 1BT	Tel: 01724 856655
H & L Garages. York, Outgang Lane, Osbaldwick, York, Yorkshire, YO19 5UP	Tel: 01904 427624
Hughes of Aylesbury, Bicester Road, Aylesbury, Buckinghamshire, HP19 8BL	Tel: 01296 319600
Intercounty Truck and Van. Milton Keynes, 8 Fingle Drive, Stonebridge, Milton Keynes, Buckinghamshire, MK13 0AY	Tel: 01908 228200
Intercounty Truck and Van. Peterborough, Broadway Business Park, Yaxley, Peterborough, Cambridgeshire, PE7 3EN	Tel: 01733 246419
Intercounty Truck and Van Limited, Finedon Road Industrial Estate, Stewarts Road, Wellingborough, Northamptonshire, NN8 4TR	Tel: 01933 232600
John R Weir. Dundee, Kingsway West, Dundee, Tayside, DD2 4TD	Tel: 01382 576600
John R Weir. Inverness, Longman Road, Inverness, Highland, IV1 1RY	Tel: 01463 238008
John R Weir Truck & Van Centre, Hareness Road, Altens Industrial Estate, Aberdeen, Grampian, AB12 3LE	Tel: 01224 871234
Kent and Sussex Truck Centre, Longfield Road, Tunbridge Wells, Kent, TN2 3EY	Tel: 01892 515333
Mercedes-Benz. Colindale, 403 Edgware Road, Colindale, Edgware, London, NW9 0HX	Tel: 020 8205 1212
Mercedes-Benz of North Wales, Conwy Road, Llandudno Junction, Conwy, North Wales, LL31 9BG	Tel: 0845 123 9591 [lo-call]
Mercedes-Benz Truck and Van, Northern Ireland, Mollusc Road, Mallusk, Newtownabbey, County Antrim, Northern Ireland, BT36 4PJ	Tel: 028 9034 2411
Mertrux Limited. Derby, 10 Chequers Road, West Meadows Industrial Estate, Derby, Derbyshire, DE21 6EN	Tel: 01332 290290
Mertrux Limited. Leicester, Knights Road, Leicester, Leicestershire, LE4 1JY	Tel: 01162 361400
Mertrux Limited. Nottingham, Willow Road, Lenton Lane, Nottingham, Nottinghamshire, NG7 2TA	Tel: 01159 248 100
Mertrux Ltd. Mansfield, Plot 2, Fulwood Park, South Normanton, Mansfield, Nottinghamshire, NG17 6AF	Tel: 01623 447599
Mudie-Bond. Brackley, Unit 2, Boundary Road, Buckingham Road Industrial Estate, Brackley, Northamptonshire, NN13 7ES	Tel: 01280 700293
Mudie-Bond. Kidderminster, No. 3 Road, Hoobrook Trading Estate, Worcester Road, Kidderminster, Worcestershire, DY10 1HY	Tel: 01562 864444
Mudie-Bond. Oxford, Eynsham Road, Cassington, Oxford, Oxfordshire, OX29 4DD	Tel: 01865 881581
Mudie-Bond. Tewkesbury, Northway Lane, Newtown Trading Estate, Tewkesbury, Gloucestershire, GL20 8JG	Tel: 01684 295090
North Manchester Commercials Mercedes-Benz, Briscoe Lane, Newton Heath, Manchester, Lancashire, M40 2NL	Tel: 0161 230 6808
Northside Truck and Van Ltd. Bradford, Legrams Lane, Bradford, West Yorkshire, BD7 2HR	Tel: 01274 577311
Northside Truck and Van Ltd. Doncaster, Unit 4 Railway Court, Ten Pound Walk, Doncaster, South Yorkshire, DN4 5FB	Tel: 01302 369351

Northside Truck and Van Ltd. Leeds, Elland Way, Elland Road, Leeds, West Yorkshire, LS11 0EY	Tel: 0113 277 5636
Northside Truck and Van Ltd. Sheffield, Amberley Street, Attercliffe, Sheffield, South Yorkshire, S9 2LU	Tel: 01142 448252
Orwell Trucks. Colchester, Heckworth Close, Brunel Way, Severalls Industrial Park, Colchester, Essex, CO4 9TB	Tel: 01206 751550
Orwell Trucks. Ipswich, 28 Betts Avenue, Martlesham Heath Industrial Estate, Ipswich, Suffolk, IP5 3RH	Tel: 01473 618000
Orwell Trucks. Newmarket, Fordham Road, Pines Industrial Estate, Newmarket, Suffolk, CB8 7LQ	Tel: 01638 720 204
Orwell Trucks. Norwich, 39 Hurricane Way, Airport Industrial Estate, Norwich, Norfolk, NR6 6HE	Tel: 01603 428 000
Pentagon. Southampton (MBCV After Sales), Unit A, Andes Road, Nursling Industrial Estate, Southampton, SO16 0YZ	Tel: 02380 743800
Pentagon. Andover, Scott Close, Walworth Industrial Estate, Andover, Hampshire, SP10 5NU	Tel: 01264 366 224
Pentagon. Fareham, Standard Way, Fareham Industrial Park, Fareham, Hampshire, PO16 8XL	Tel: 01329 286224
Pentagon. Poole, Cabot Lane, Heckworth Close, Brunel Way, Poole, Dorset, BH17 7BX	Tel: 01202 690724
Road Range Commercials, Rathbone Road, Wavertree, Liverpool, Merseyside, L13 1BA	Tel: 0151 330 7000
Road Range Commercials. Deeside, Link 56, Weighbridge Road, Deeside Industrial Park, Deeside, CH5 2LL	Tel: 01244 838280
Rossetts Commercials. Aldershot, Unit 1, Eastern Road, Aldershot, Surrey, GU12 4TD	Tel: 01252 341212
Rossetts Commercials. Crawley, Unit 1 Manor Gate, Manor Royal, Crawley, Sussex, RH10 9SX	Tel: 01293 652560
Rossetts Commercials. Eastbourne, 7 Birch Road, Eastbourne, Sussex, BN23 6PD	Tel: 01323 410192
Rossetts Commercials. Guildford, Unit 1a, Cathedral Hill Industrial Estate, Guildford, Surrey, GU2 5YB	Tel: 01252 341212
Rossetts Commercials. Worthing, Meadow Road Industrial Estate, Worthing, West Sussex, BN11 2RU	Tel: 01903 223400
Rygor Commercials, The Broadway, West Wilts Trading Estate, Westbury, Wiltshire, BA13 4JX	Tel: 01373 855555
Rygor Commercials. Heathrow, Stanwell Road, Bedfont, Feltham, Middlesex, TW14 8NW	Tel: 0208 890 8907
Rygor Commercials. Newbury, Unit 1A, Argent Mere, Newbury, Berkshire, RG14 5XB	Tel: 01635 413165
Rygor Commercials. Swindon, Hunts Rise, South Marston Park, Swindon, Wiltshire, SN3 4TG	Tel: 01793 821820
Rygor Commercials. Wokingham, Unit 2, Molly Millars Lane, Wokingham, Berkshire, RG41 2RX	Tel: 0118 989 1111
S & B Commercials. West Thurrock, Central Avenue, West Thurrock, Essex, RM20 3WD	Tel: 01708 892500
S & B Commercials. Hatfield, Travellers Lane, Welham Green, Hatfield, Hertfordshire, AL9 7HW	Tel: 01707 261111
S & B Commercials. Stansted, Start Hill, Bishop's Stortford, Hertfordshire, CM22 7DW	Tel: 01279 712 200
S G Smith (Motors) Ltd Forest Hill, 812 Old Kent Road, London, SE15 1NH	Tel: 0207 639 2052
S G Smith (Motors) Ltd Croydon, Unit 2 Beddington Cross, 136/138 Beddington Road, Croydon, Surrey, CR0 4XH	Tel: 020 8665 7800
S G Smith (Motors) Ltd. Sydenham, 140-149 Mayow Road, London, SE26 4HZ	Tel: 020 8659 3636
South Cave Tractors Ltd, Ratten Row, Eastgate, North Newbald, York, YO43 4SD	Tel: 01430 827377
Sparshatts of Kent. Ashford, Leacon Road, Brookfield Industrial Estate, Ashford, Kent, TN23 4TU	Tel: 01233 610 400
Sparshatts of Kent. Dartford, Unit H, Acorn Industrial Estate, Crayford Road, Dartford, Kent, DA1 4FL	Tel: 0870 8353637
Sparshatts of Kent Ltd, Unit 10, Eurolink Industrial Estate, Sittingbourne, Kent, ME10 3RN	Tel: 01795 479571
Trevor Haydock, 104 Bush Road, Dungannon, Tyrone, BT71 6QG	Tel: 028 8772 2089
Western Commercial. Belshill, Site C1, Melford Road, Righead Industrial Estate, Belshill, Glasgow, ML4 3LR	Tel: 01698 498999
Western Commercial. Edinburgh, 9 Simpson Road, East Mains Industrial Estate, Broxburn, West Lothian, EH52 5NP	Tel: 01506 208090
Western Commercial. Glasgow, Moor Park Industrial Estate, Broomloan Road, Govan, Glasgow, G51 2JQ	Tel: 0141 272 5000
Western Commercial. Kirkcaldy, Caxton Place, Mitchelson Industrial Estate, Kirkcaldy, Fife, KY1 3LT	Tel: 01592 588388
Western Truck Rental, Roundswell Industrial Estate, Barnstaple, Devon, EX31 3NL	Tel: 01271 345738

RENAULT, Boscombe Road, Dunstable, Bedfordshire, LU5 4LX
Tel: 01582 471122, www.renault-trucks.com
RENAULT TRUCKS 24/24: 0800 626541

A E George & Sons Ltd, Brewham Road Deopt, Bruton, Somerset, BA10 0JH	Tel: 01749 813838
Alex Aiken & Son, Damhead Way, Peterhead, Aberdeenshire, AB42 3GY	Tel: 01779 481030
Alex Aiken & Son, Greenbank Crescent, East Tullos Industrial Estate, Aberdeen, Aberdeenshire, AB12 3BG	Tel: 01224 891655
Allports Truck Centre, Westhill Road, Fradley Park, Lichfield, Staffordshire, WS13 8NG	Tel: 01543 420120
Ballie Brothers Truck Services, Linkwood Industrial Estate, Elgin, Morayshire, IV30 1XB	Tel: 01343 555312
Bicester Commercial Garages Ltd, Unit 40, Murdock Road, Bicester, Oxfordshire, OX26 4PP	Tel: 01869 252222
Boarhunt Garage, Unit A, A1 Fort Walling Industrial Estate, Military Road, Fareham, Hampshire, PO16 8TT	Tel: 01329 289999
Commercial Vehicle Repair, 2 Fir Tree lane, Rotherwas, Herefordshire, HR2 6LA	Tel: 01432 355795
Complete Ltd, Unit 42, Okus Trading Estate, Swindon, Wiltshire, SN1 4JH	Tel: 01793 484999
Co-op Garage Services, 52 Windsor Street South, Birmingham, West Midlands, B7 4JB	Tel: 0121 359 2601
Co-op Garage Services, Marlow Road, Leicester, Leicestershire, LE3 2BQ	Tel: 01162 629692
Coulter Truck & Van, 11 Vicarage Road, Portadown, County Armagh, BT62 4HF, Northern Ireland	Tel: 028 38390160
Coulter Truck & Van, Commercial Way, Mallusk, Newtownabbey, County Antrim, Northern Ireland, BT36 8UB	Tel: 028 90837171
David Phillip Commercials Ltd, Camps Industrial Estate, Kirknewton, Mid Lothian, EH27 8DF	Tel: 01506 882212
Ebor Trucks, Brockett Industrial Estate, Acaster Airfield, Acaster Malbis, York, North Yorkshire, YO23 2PT	Tel: 01904 708 372
Englands Truck Care, Hadfield Road, Cardiff, South Glamorgan, CF11 8AQ	Tel: 029 2023 1355
E T Commercials Ltd, Baythorpe, Boston Road, Swineshead, Boston, Lincolnshire, PE20 3HB	Tel: 01205 821567
E T Commercials Ltd, Estate Road No 5, South Humberside Industrial Estate, Grimsby, North East Lincolnshire, DN31 2TY	Tel:01472 347246
E T Commercials Ltd, Hydra Business Park, Nether Lane, Ecclesfield, Sheffield, S35 9ZX	Tel: 0114 240 0080
Fengate Commercial Services, Bretton Way, North Bretton, Peterborough, Cambridgeshire, PE3 8YQ	Tel: 01733 333232

Fleet Commercial Services, Units 5 & 6, Greenend Industrial Estate, Gamlingay, Sandy, Bedfordshire, SG19 3LB	Tel: 01767 651336
Gerald White Group, Banbury Road, Kislingbury, Northampton, Northamptonshire, NN7 4AW	Tel: 01604 830770
G Mutch Mechanical Services, Block 9, Nobel Road, Wester Gourdie Industrial Estate, Dundee, Angus, DD2 4UH	Tel: 01382 611166
Hawarden Commercials, Factory Road, Engineers Park, Sandycroft, Deeside, Flintshire, CH5 2QJ	Tel: 01244 520853
J C Snell Ltd, Hoyle Mill Road, off Doncaster Road, Barnsley, North Yorkshire, S70 3EZ	Tel: 01226 731234
J D Engineering, Irongrey Road, Dumfries, Dumfriesshire, DG2 0HA	Tel: 01387 720235
J D S Trucks Blackburn, Navigation Garage, Forrest Street, Blackburn, Lancashire, BB1 3BB	Tel: 01254 297299
J D S Trucks Leeds, Howley Park Road, Morley, Leeds, Yorkshire, LS27 0BN	Tel: 0113 393 6788
J D S Trucks Manchester, Broadway, Salford Quays, Salford, Manchester, M50 2UW	Tel: 0161 786 8199
J D S Trucks Oldham, Broadgate, Broadway Business Park, Chadderton, Oldham, OL9 9NL	Tel: 0161 947 1499
John Allan Motors Ltd, Lockavullin Industrial Estate, Oban, Argyll & Bute, PA34 4SE	Tel: 01631 563817
Jordan Commercials Ltd, Farmbeg, Strokestown, County Rosscommon, Ireland	Tel: 00353 (0) 7196 33682
Kenny Commercials, Unit 4, Rollesby Road, Hardwick Industrial Estate, King's Lynn, Norfolk, PE30 4LS	Tel: 01553 692919
K T S Trucks Ltd, East Kent International Freight Terminal, Hernhill, Faversham, Kent, ME13 9EN	Tel: 01227 771111
Perrys of Gobowen, St Martins Road, Gobowen, Oswestry, Shropshire, SY10 7AN	Tel: 01691 679907
Peter Haines Engineers, Thorpe Lane, Banbury, Oxfordshire, OX3 8UT	Tel: 01295 256467
Plymstock Commercials, Unit 14, Central Avenue, Lee Mills Industrial Estate, Ivybridge, Devon, PL21 9ER	Tel: 01752 201400
Rabeys Commercial Vehicles Ltd, Northside, Vale, Guernsey, GY1 6DP, Channel Islands	Tel: 01481 244551
Rabeys Universal Ltd, La Grande Route De St Martin, Five Oaks, St Saviour, Jersey, JE2 7GR, Channel Islands	Tel: 01534 730437
Renault Trucks Carlisle, 20B Millbrook Road, Kingstown Industrial Estate, Carlisle, Cumbria, CA3 0EU	Tel: 01228 547548
Renault Trucks Chiltern, Luton Road, Dunstable, Bedfordshire, LU5 4QF	Tel: 01582 500000
Renault Trucks Essex, Weston Avenue, Waterglade Industrial Park, West Thurrock, Grays, Essex, RM20 3FZ	Tel: 01708 866643
Renault Trucks Felixstowe, Sub Station Road, Felixstowe, Suffolk, IP11 3JB	Tel: 01394 614110
Renault Trucks London, 37-43 Gorst Road, Park Royal, London, NW10 6LA	Tel: 0208 965 9181
Renault Trucks Midlands, Hortonwood 7, Hortonwood, Telford, Shropshire, TF1 7GP	Tel: 01952 677069
Renault Trucks Midland, Power Way, Black Country New Road, Tipton, West Midlands, DY4 0PW	Tel: 0121 505 0300
Renault Trucks South, 1 Normandy Way, Marchwood Industrial Estate, Marchwood, Southampton, Hampshire, SO40 4PB	Tel: 023 8066 0456
Renault Trucks South, Bennett Road, Reading, Berkshire, RG2 0QX	Tel: 0118 975 2355
Renault Trucks South West, Dunns Business Centre, Trusham Road, Marsh Barton, Exeter, Devon, EX2 8LR	Tel: 01392 422114
Renault Trucks South West, Fith Way, Avonmouth, Bristol, South Gloucestershire, BS11 8DT	Tel: 0117 982 0481
Renault Trucks Wellingborough, Ise Valley Industrial Estate, Finedon Road, Wellingborough, Northamptonshire, NN8 4BJ	Tel: 01933 276617
R H Commercial Vehicles, James Irland & Son, Harlaxton Road, Grantham, Lincolnshire, NE31 9QS	Tel: 01476 565259
R H Commercial Vehicles, Lenton Lane, Nottingham, Nottinghamshire, NG7 2NR	Tel: 0115 943 8000
Roy Humphrey Car & Commercial, A140 Ipswich Road, Eye, Suffolk, IP23 8AW	Tel: 01379 870666
Scott Truck Ltd, Penilee Road, Hillington Industrial Estate, Glasgow, Renfrewshire, G52 4UW	Tel: 0141 882 3304
Staffordshire C V, Bute Street, Fenton, Stoke on Trent, Staffordshire, ST4 3PS	Tel:01782 598282
Surehaul Commercials, Ballylynch, Carrick on Suir, County Tipperary, Ireland	Tel: 00353 (0) 5164 0194
Thompson Commercials, Clay Pit Lane, Roecliffe, Boroughbridge, Yorkshire, YO51 9LS	Tel: 01423 322621
Thompson Commercials Teeside, Nuffield Road, Cowpen Lane Industrial Estate, Billingham, Cleveland, TS23 4DA	Tel: 01642 370370
Thompson Commercials, Salvesen Way, Hull, North Humberside, HU3 4UQ	Tel: 01482 322331
Thompson Commercials, Unit B6, Third Avenue, Tyne Tunnel Trading Estate, Willington, North Tyneside, NE29 7SP	Tel: 0191 296 2848
Transport Services Ltd, Ballyvolane, Cork, County Cork, Ireland	Tel: 00353 (0) 2145 97377
Vally Trucks Ltd, Bingley Road, Hoddesdon, Hertfordshire, EN11 0NX	Tel: 01992 441551
W Belben Commercials Ltd, 73 Ringwood Road, Parkstone, Poole, Dorset, BH14 0RG	Tel: 01202 741088
Woodwards Truck & Van Centre, Lock Street, Off Merton Bank Road, St Helens, Cheshire, WA9 1HU	Tel: 01744 20421
Woodwards Truck & Van Centre, Stephens Way, Warrington Road Industrial Estate, Goose Green, Wigan, Lancashire, WN3 6PQ	Tel: 01942 230026

SCANIA, Scania GB Ltd, Delaware Drive, Tongwell, Milton Keynes, MK15 8HB
Tel: 01908 210210, Fax: 01908 215040, www.scania.co.uk
SCANIA ASSISTANCE: 0800 800 660 (IF IN UK), 0044 127 430 1260 (IF ABROAD)

Deeside Truck Services, a division of Haydock Commercial Vehicles Ltd, Pinfold Lane, Alltami, Mold, Clwyd, CH7 6NY	Tel: 01244 547202
Derek Jones Commercials Ltd., Chesney Wold, Bleak Hall, Milton Keynes, Buckinghamshire, MK6 1LP	Tel: 01908 242448
Derek Jones Commercials Ltd, Eldon Way, Crick, Northamptonshire, NN6 7SL	Tel: 01788 823930
Derek Jones Commercials Ltd, Forty Acre Road, Boongate, Peterborough, Cambridgeshire, PE1 5PS	Tel: 01733 555233
Derek Jones Commercials Ltd, Geddington Road, Corby, Northamptonshire, NN18 8AA	Tel: 01536 266638
Derek Jones Commercials Ltd, Kilvey Road, Brackmills, Northampton, Northamptonshire, NN4 7BQ	Tel: 01604 874747
Derek Jones Commercials Ltd, Stewarts Road, Finedon Road Industrial Estate, Wellingborough, Northamptonshire, NN8 4RJ	Tel: 01933 303303
Derek Jones Commercials Ltd, Swan Valley Way, Swan Valley, Northamptonshire, NN4 9BD	Tel: 01604 755969
East Midland Commercials Ltd, 3rd Avenue, Centrum 100, Burton on Trent, Staffordshire, DE14 2WD	Tel: 01283 510011
East Midland Commercials Ltd, Bilton Way, Lutterworth, Leicestershire, LE17 4JA	Tel: 01455 550740
East Midland Commercials Ltd, Brunel Drive, Newark Industrial Estate, Newark, Nottinghamshire, NG24 2EG	Tel: 01636 700203
East Midland Commercials Ltd, Rennie Hogg Road, Riverside Industrial Estate, Nottingham, Nottinghamshire, NG2 1RX	Tel: 0115 986 5121

East Midland Commercials Ltd, Unit 2, Fullwood Road South, Huthwaite, Sutton in Ashfield, Nottinghamshire, NG17 2JZ	Tel: 01623 559559
Ellesmere Port Scania, Haydock Commercials Ltd, North Road, Ellesmere Port, Cheshire, CH65 1BW	Tel: 0151 355 0199
Graham Commercials Ltd, Kingstown Broadway, Kingstown Industrial Estate, Carlisle, Cumbria, CA3 0HA	Tel: 01228 529149
Granco, 26 Downshire Road, Newry, County Down, BT34 1EE, Northern Ireland	Tel: 028 3026 6335
Halebank Scania, Haydock Commercials Ltd, Pickerings Road, Halebank Industrial Estate, Halebank, Widnes, Cheshire, WA8 8XW	Tel: 0151 423 8602
Haydock Commercial Vehicles Ltd, Haydock Cross, Kilbuck Lane, Haydock St Helens, Merseyside, WA11 9XW	Tel: 01942 714103
Keltruck Ltd, Golden Valley, Gloucester Road, Cheltenham, Gloucestershire, GL51 0TT	Tel: 01242 252140
Keltruck Ltd, Kenrick Way, West Bromwich, West Midlands, B71 4JW	Tel: 0121 524 1800
Keltruck Ltd, Unit 8B, Paragon Way, Bayton Road, Exhall, Coventry, Warwickshire, CV7 9QS	Tel: 02476 644 644
Keltruck Ltd, Unit 17-18, Maple Leaf Industrial Estate, Bloxwich Lane, Walsall, West Midlands, WS2 8TF	Tel: 01922 641888
Keltruck Ltd, Unit 28C, North Bank, Berry Hill Industrial Estate, Droitwich, WR9 9AN	Tel: 01905 777060
Keltruck Ltd, Watling Street, Dorden, Tamworth, Staffordshire, B78 1TS	Tel: 01827 330100
M & K Commercials Ltd, 11-13 Morgan Way, Bowthorpe Industrial Estate, Norwich, Norfolk, NR5 9JJ	Tel: 01603 748995
Preston Scania, Haydock Commercials Ltd, Four Oaks Road, Walton Summit Centre, Bamber Bridge, Preston, Lancashire, PR5 8BW	Tel: 01772 698811
Road Trucks Ltd, Circular Road, Larne, County Antrim, BT40 3AB, Northern Ireland	Tel: 028 2827 9611
Road Trucks Ltd, Gortrush Industrial Estate, Great Northern Road, Omagh, BT78 5LU, Northern Ireland	Tel: 028 82259 198
Ro Truck Ltd, 6 Hodgkinsons Road, Felixstowe, Suffolk, IP11 3QT	Tel: 01394 676625
Ro Truck Ltd, Hamlin Way, Hardwick Narrows, King's Lynn, Norfolk, PE30 4NG	Tel: 01553 771877
Ro Truck Ltd, 42 Lancaster Way, Ely, Cambridgeshire, CB6 3NW	Tel:01353 666503
Ro Truck Ltd, Unit 5, Moss Road, Witham, Essex, CM8 3UQ	Tel: 01376 503003
Ro Truck Ltd, Unit 8, Mundford Road, Thetford, Norfolk, IP24 1NB	Tel: 01842 763400
Ro Truck Ltd, Violet Hill Road, Stowmarket, Suffolk, IP14 1NN	Tel: 01449 613553
East Midland Commercials Ltd, Midland Distribution Centre, Markfield Road, Groby, Leicestershire, LE6 0FS	Tel: 01530 243133
Scania Aberdeen, Blackness Road, Altens Industrial Estate, Aberdeen, Aberdeenshire, AB12 3LH	Tel: 01224 896312
Scania Banbury, Unit 2-4, 18A Wildmere Road, Banbury, Oxfordshire, OX16 3JU	Tel: 01295 272857
Scania Bellshill, Melford Road, Righead Industrial Estate, Bellshill, North Lanarkshire, ML4 3LF	Tel: 01698 841994
Scania Boston, Main Road, Wigtoft, Boston, Lincolnshire, PE20 2NX	Tel: 01205 460841
Scania Bridgwater, Unit 10, Dunball Industrial Estate, Dunball, Bridgwater, Somerset, TA6 4TP	Tel: 01278 685060
Scania Bristol, Avonmouth Way, Avonmouth, Bristol, South Gloucestershire, BS11 8DB	Tel: 0117 937 9800
Scania Bus & Coach Ltd, Claylands Avenue, Worksop, Nottinghamshire, S81 7DJ	Tel: 01909 500822
Scania Darlington, Whessoe Road, Drinkfield, Darlington, County Durham, DL3 0XE	Tel: 01325 480713
Scania Didcot, 178A Milton Park, Didcot, Abingdon, Oxfordshire, OX14 4SE	Tel: 01235 834933
Scania Dover, Pike Industrial Estate, Pike Road, Tilmanston, Dover, Kent, CT15 4ND	Tel: 01304 831730
Scania Dumfries, Heathall Industrial Estate, Dumfries, Dumfries & Galloway, DG1 3PH	Tel: 01387 250502
Scania Dundee, Riverside Drive, Dundee, Perth & Kinross, DD2 1UD	Tel: 01382 630033
Scania Edinburgh, Newbridge Industrial Estate, Newbridge, Mid Lothian, EH28 8PJ	Tel: 0131 333 2362
Scania Exeter, Unit E, Denbury Court, Off Silverton Road, Matford Business Park, Marsh Barton, Exeter, Devon, EX2 8NB	Tel: 01392 824474
Scania Fareham, 9 Whittle Avenue, Segensworth West, Fareham, Hampshire, PO15 5SH	Tel: 01489 886800
Scania Glasgow, Clyde Street, Renfrew, Renfrewshire, PA4 8SL	Tel: 0141 886 5633
Scania Grimsby, Estate Road One, South Humberside Industrial Estate, Pyewipe, Grimsby, North East Lincolnshire, DN31 2TA	Tel: 01472 346913
Scania Hatfield, Hatfield Business Park, Frobisher Way, Hatfield, Hertfordshire, AL10 9TR	Tel: 01707 274413
Scania Heathrow, Bedfont Road, Stanwell, Middlesex, TW19 7LZ	Tel: 01784 240777
Scania Hull, Priory Park East, Hull, East Riding Of Yorkshire, HU4 7DY	Tel: 01482 626880
Scania Inverness, Unit 1A, Henderson Road, Longman Industrial Estate, Inverness, Inverness-shire, IV1 1SN	Tel: 01463 729400
Scania Leeds, Royds Farm Road, Beeston Royds Industrial Estate, Beeston, Leeds, North Yorkshire, LS12 6DX	Tel: 0113 231 1411
Scania Lewes, 28 Cliffe Industrial Estate, Lewes, East Sussex, BN6 6JL	Tel: 01273 479123
Scania Lincoln, Plot 5, Whisby Way, Whisby Road Industrial Estate, Lincoln, Lincolnshire, LN6 3LQ	Tel: 01522 681222
Scania Lingfield, Unit 53A, Hobbs Industrial Estate, New Chapel, Lingfield, Surrey, RH7 6HN	Tel: 01342 837373
Scania Newbury, Daytona Drive, Colthrop, Thatcham, Newbury, Berkshire, RG19 4ZD	Tel: 01635 871157
Scania Newcastle, Mylord Crescent, Camperdown Ind. Est., Killingworth, Newcastle upon Tyne, Northumberland, NE12 5UD	Tel: 0191 256 1900
Scania Normanton, Ripley Drive, Normanton Industrial Estate, Normanton, West Yorkshire, WF6 1QT	Tel: 01924 228800
Scania Purfleet, Ensign Estate, Arterial Road, Purfleet, Essex, RM16 1TB	Tel: 01708 257400
Scania Poole, 543 Wallisdown Road, Poole, Bournemouth, Dorset, BH12 5AD	Tel: 01202 533978
Scania Redruth, Wheal Rose, Scorrier, Redruth, Cornwall, TR16 5BX	Tel: 01209 820820
Scania Scunthorpe, Grange Lane North, Scunthorpe, North Lincolnshire, DN16 1BT	Tel: 01724 289088
Scania Sheffield, Don Road, Sheffield, Yorkshire, S9 2TL	Tel: 0114 262 6700
Scania Shepton Mallet, Waterlip, Shepton Mallet, Somerset, BA4 4RN	Tel: 01749 880088
Scania Sittingbourne, 15A Eurolink Industrial Estate, Sittingbourne, Kent, ME10 3RN	Tel:01795 430304
Scania Skipton, Skipton Rock Quarry, Harrogate Road, Skipton, North Yorkshire, BD23 6AB	Tel: 01756 797197
Scania Southampton, Unit C Andes Road, Nursling Industrial Estate, Southampton, Hampshire, SO16 0YZ	Tel: 02380 734455
Scania South Mimms, Bignells Corner, St Albans Road, South Mimms, Hertfordshire, EN6 3NG	Tel: 01707 649955
Scania Spalding, Wardentree Lane, Pinchbeck, Spalding, Lincolnshire, PE11 3UG	Tel: 01775 713707
Scania Stansted, Unit B, Stansted Distribution Centre, Start Hill, Great Hallingbury, Bishops Stortford, Hertfordshire, CM22 7DG	Tel: 01279 758088
Scania Swindon, Faraday Road, Dorcan Industrial Estate, Swindon, Wiltshire, SN3 5PA	Tel: 01793 715100
Scania Thirsk, Thirsk Industrial Park, York Road, Thirsk, North Yorkshire, YO7 3AA	Tel: 01845 573500
Scania Washington, Mandarin Way, Pattinson Industrial Estate, District 15, Washington, Tyne And Wear, NG38 8QG	Tel: 0191 4188500

Silurian Scania, Cross Hands Business Park, Cross Hands, Llanelli, Dyfed, SA14 6RB	Tel: 01269 844855
Silurian Scania, Goodrich, Whitchurch, Ross on Wye, Herefordshire, HR9 6EG	Tel: 01600 891257
Silurian Scania, Penarth Road, Cardiff, South Glamorgan, CF11 8UT	Tel: 02920 224671
Silurian Scania, Unit 55, Severn Bridge Industrial Estate, Caldicot, Chepstow, Monmouthshire, NP26 5PT	Tel: 01291 431715
S J Bargh Sales and Service Ltd, TNT Garage, Hornby Road, Caton, Near Lancaster, Lancashire, LA2 9JA	Tel: 01524 770439
The Pip Bayley Truck Centre, Unit 5, The Ridgeway, Blunham, Bedfordshire, MK44 3DE	Tel: 01767 641111
West Pennine Trucks Ltd, Cross Street, Off Chemical Lane, Longport, Stoke on Trent, Staffordshire, ST6 4PU	Tel: 01782 577955
West Pennine Trucks Ltd, Halesfield 17, Telford, Shropshire, TF7 4PW	Tel: 01952 587222
West Pennine Trucks Ltd, Stakehill Industrial Park, Middleton, Manchester, M24 2RW	Tel: 0161 653 9700
West Pennine Trucks Ltd, Station Road, Knighton, Powys, LD7 1DR	Tel: 01547 528600
West Pennine Trucks Ltd, Unit 1, Circle South, John Gilbert Way, Trafford Park, Manchester, M17 1NF	Tel: 0161 877 7708
West Pennine Trucks Ltd, Unit 19, Mile Oak Industrial Estate, Maesbury Road, Oswestry, Shropshire, SY10 8HA	Tel: 01691 671500

VOLVO, Volvo Trucks Corporation, SE-40508 Goteborg, Sweden
Tel: 0046 3166 6000, Fax: 0046 3151 0465, www.volvotrucks.volvo.co.uk
VOLVO ACTION SERVICE: 0800 929292

A Culpin & Son. Pinchbeck, Northgate Garage, Pinchbeck, Lincolnshire, PE11 3SE	Tel: 01775 725038/9
Crossroads Truck & Bus Ltd. Birstall, Pheasant Drive, Birstall, West Yorkshire, WF17 9LR	Tel: 01924 425000
Crossroads Truck & Bus Ltd. Hull, Valletta Street, Kingston upon Hull, East Yorkshire, HU9 5NP	Tel: 01482 781831
Crossroads Truck & Bus Ltd. Immingham, Redwood Industrial Park, Immingham, North East Lincolnshire, DN41 8DL	Tel: 01469 556930
Crossroads Truck & Bus Ltd. Lincoln, Freeman Road Industrial Estate, Lincoln, Lincolnshire, LN6 9AP	Tel: 01522 684496
Crossroads Truck & Bus Ltd. Rotherham, Canklow Meadows Ind Est, Rotherham, South Yorkshire, S60 2XL	Tel: 01709 365566
Crossroads Truck & Bus Ltd. Scunthorpe, Kendale Road, Scunthorpe, North Lincolnshire, DN16 1BY	Tel: 01724 280724
Truck & Bus Ltd. Tadcaster, C/O Coors Brewery, Tadcaster, North Yorkshire, LS24 9SD	Tel: 01937 830840
Crossroads Truck & Bus Ltd. Thirsk, Stockton Road, Thirsk, North Yorkshire, YO7 1AX	Tel: 01845 522057
Crossroads Truck & Bus Ltd. Wakefield, Wakefield Europort, Normanton, Leeds, WF10 5UB	Tel: 01924 894001
Dennison Commercials Ltd. Coleraine, Longuestown Industrial Estate, Coleraine, County Londonderry, BT52 2NS, Northern Ireland	Tel: 028 70321155
Dennison Commercials Ltd. Dungannon, Derrycreevy Lane, Dungannon, County Tyrone, BT71 6SA, Northern Ireland	Tel: 028 87722220
Dennison Commercials Ltd. Newry, Martins Lane, Newry, County Down, BT35 8PJ, Northern Ireland	Tel: 028 30265425
Hartshorne (East Midlands) Ltd. Burton Upon Trent, Derby Street, Burton upon Trent, Staffordshire, DE14 2LG	Tel: 01283 515777
Hartshorne (East Midlands) Ltd. Nottingham, Beechdale Road, Bilborough, Nottingham, Nottinghamshire, NG8 3EU	Tel: 01159 292211
Hartshorne (East Midlands) Ltd. Somercotes, Ashfield Avenue, Somercotes, Derbyshire, DE55 4QR	Tel: 01773 529400
Hartshorne (Potteries) Ltd. Newcastle under Lyme, Hammond Road, Chesterton, Newcastle under Lyme, Staffordshire, ST5 7RX	Tel: 01782 568600
Hartshorne (Potteries) Ltd. Stafford, Pasturefields, Stafford, Staffordshire, ST18 0RB	Tel: 01889 270600
Hartshorne Ltd. Shrewsbury, Ainsdale Drive, Shrewsbury, Shropshire, SY1 3TL	Tel: 01743 444555
Hartshorne Motor Services Ltd. Birmingham, Hanover Drive, Birmingham, West Midlands, B24 8HZ	Tel: 0121 3801950
Hartshorne Motor Services Ltd. Kingswinford, Dandy Bank Road, Kingswinford, Dudley, West Midlands, DY6 7TD	Tel: 01384 402333
Hartshorne Motor Services Ltd. Walsall, Bentley Mill Close, Walsall, West Midlands, WS2 0BN	Tel: 01922 704600
M C Truck & Bus Ltd. Aylesford, Beddow Way, Aylesford, Kent, ME20 7BT	Tel: 01622 710811
M C Truck & Bus Ltd. Blandford Forum, Higher Shaftesbury Road, Blandford Forum, Dorset, DT11 7TB	Tel: 01258 480404
M C Truck & Bus Ltd. Burgess Hill, Unit 1, Consort Way, Braybon Business Park, Burgess Hill, West Sussex, RH15 9ND	Tel: 01444 230700
M C Truck & Bus Ltd. Lympne, The Link Park, Lympne, Kent, CT21 4LR	Tel: 01303 266864
M C Truck & Bus Ltd. Portsmouth, Dundas Spur, Portsmouth, Hampshire, PO3 5NY	Tel: 023 92662187
M C Truck & Bus Ltd. Southampton, Test Lane, Southampton, Hampshire, SO16 9JX	Tel: 023 80663500
M C Truck & Bus Ltd. West Thurrock, Barclay Way, West Thurrock, Essex, RM20 3FB	Tel: 01708 868956
M C Truck & Bus Ltd. Witham, Eastways, Witham, Essex, CM8 3DH	Tel: 01376 520727
Stuarts Commercials. Exeter, Hill Barton Business Park, off the A3052, Clyst St Mary, Exeter, Devon, EX5 1DR	Tel: 01395 232800
Stuarts Commercials. Plymouth, Crown Hill, Plymouth, Devon, PL6 5JT	Tel: 01752 752233
Stuarts Commercials. Redruth, Carew Industrial Estate, Redruth, Cornwall, TR15 1SP	Tel: 01209 314496
Thomas Hardie Commercials Ltd. Kirkby, Newstet Road, Kirkby, Lancashire, L33 7TJ	Tel: 0151 5493000
Thomas Hardie Commercials Ltd. Manchester, Fifth Avenue, Manchester, M17 1TR	Tel: 0161 9354100
Thomas Hardie Commercials Ltd. Middlewich, Beta Road, Middlewich, Cheshire, CW10 0QA	Tel: 01606 6830100
Thomas Hardie Commercials Ltd. Preston, Unit C23, Red Scar Industrial Estate, Preston, Lancashire, PR2 5NN	Tel: 01772 799000
Thomas Hardie Commercials Ltd. Queensferry, 23 Fourth Avenue, Queensferry, Flintshire, CH5 2NR	Tel: 01244 281004
Thomas Hardie Commercials Ltd. Stockport, Bredbury Parkway, Stockport, Derbyshire, SK6 2SN	Tel: 0161 9356100
Thomas Hardie Commercials Ltd. Wigan, Lockett Road, Wigan, Lancashire, WN4 8DE	Tel: 01942 505100
Volvo Truck & Bus (North) Ltd. Bebside, Ennerdale Road, Bebside, Northumberland, NE24 4RD	Tel: 01670 359999
Volvo Truck & Bus (North) Ltd. Darlington, Lingfield Way, Darlington, County Durham, DL1 4PY	Tel: 01325 355161
Volvo Truck & Bus (North) Ltd. Kingstown, Kingstown Broadway, Kingstown, Carlisle, Cumbria, CA3 0HA	Tel: 01228 529262
Volvo Truck & Bus (North) Ltd. Morecambe, Newgate, Morecambe, Lancashire, LA3 3PT	Tel: 01524 62866
Volvo Truck & Bus (North) Ltd. Washington, Crowther Road, Washington, Tyne and Wear, NE38 0AQ	Tel: 0191 4151111
Volvo Truck & Bus (Scotland) Ltd. Aberdeen, Barclayhill Place, Aberdeen, Aberdeenshire, AB12 4PF	Tel: 01224 781782

Volvo Truck & Bus (Scotland) Ltd. Edinburgh, Drover's Road, Edinburgh, West Lothian, EH52 5ND — Tel: 01506 856892
Volvo Truck & Bus (Scotland) Ltd. Dunfirmline, Kingdom of Fife Parts Centre, Dunfermline, Fife, KY11 4JT — Tel: 01383 625594
Volvo Truck & Bus (Scotland) Ltd. Glasgow, Fifty Pitches Place, Glasgow, Renfrewshire, G51 4GA — Tel: 0141 8102777
Volvo Truck & Bus (Scotland) Ltd. Glasgow 2, 2 Whistleberry Industrial Park, Glasgow, South Lanarkshire, ML3 0ED — Tel: 01698 823300
Volvo Truck & Bus (Scotland) Ltd. Inverness, Longman Drive, Inverness, Inverness-shire, IV1 1SU — Tel: 01463 221177
Volvo Truck & Bus (Scotland) Ltd. Perth, Ruthvenfield Way, Perth, Perthshire, PH1 3UF — Tel: 01738 637256/7
Volvo Truck & Bus (Scotland) Ltd. Prestwick, Highfield Business Park, Prestwick, Aryshire, KA6 5HQ — Tel: 01292 613383
Volvo Truck & Bus (South) Ltd. Basingstoke, Knight Park Road, Basingstoke, Hampshire, RG21 6XE — Tel: 01256 340509
Volvo Truck & Bus (South) Ltd. Bedford, Wolseley Road, Bedford, Bedfordshire, MK42 7SE — Tel: 01234 853877
Volvo Truck & Bus (South) Ltd. Bicester, Souldern Gate Garage, Banbury Road, Bicester, Oxfordshire, OX6 9HT — Tel: 01869 345151
Volvo Truck & Bus (South) Ltd. Bristol, Burcott Road, Avonmouth, Bristol, South Gloucestershire, BS11 8AP — Tel: 01179 823741
Volvo Truck & Bus (South) Ltd. Calne, Clark Avenue, Calne, Wiltshire, SN11 9PZ — Tel: 01249 817345
Volvo Truck & Bus (South) Ltd. Cambridge, Ely Road, Cambridge, Cambridgeshire, CB5 9PG — Tel: 01223 204760
Volvo Truck & Bus (South) Ltd. Chedburgh, Bury Road, Chedburgh, Bury St Edmunds, Suffolk, IP29 4UQ — Tel: 01284 850418
Volvo Truck & Bus (South) Ltd. Coventry, Siskin Parkway West, Coventry, West Midlands, CV3 4PW — Tel: 02476 576100
Volvo Truck & Bus (South) Ltd. Croydon, Beddington Farm Road, Croydon, Surrey, CR0 4XB — Tel: 0208 6655775
Volvo Truck & Bus (South) Ltd. Didcot, Hawksworth, Didcot, Oxfordshire, OX11 7EN — Tel: 01235 519179
Volvo Truck & Bus (South) Ltd. Enfield, Mollison Avenue, Enfield, Middlesex, EN3 7NJ — Tel: 0208 3443700
Volvo Truck & Bus (South) Ltd. Felixstowe, Bryon Avenue, (Off Walton Avenue), Felixstowe, Suffolk, IP11 8HZ — Tel: 01394 674711
Volvo Truck & Bus (South) Ltd. Gloucester, Lower Tuffley Lane, Tuffley, Gloucester, Gloucestershire, GL2 5DP — Tel: 01452 560010
Volvo Truck & Bus (South) Ltd. Great Yarmouth, Gapton Hall Road, Southtown, Great Yarmouth, Norfolk, NR31 0NL — Tel: 01493 443001
Volvo Truck & Bus (South) Ltd. Gurney Slade, on the A37, Binegar, Gurney Slade, North Somerset, BA3 4TQ — Tel: 01749 840777
Volvo Truck & Bus (South) Ltd. Hinckley, Station Road, Earl Shilton, Hinckley, Leicestershire, LE9 6LJ — Tel: 01455 273260
Volvo Truck & Bus (South) Ltd. Ipswich, The Exchange, Foxtail Road, Ipswich, Suffolk, IP3 9RT — Tel: 01473 718223
Volvo Truck & Bus (South) Ltd. Kettering, Pytchley Road Industrial Estate, Kettering, Northamptonshire, NN15 6JJ — Tel: 01536 516311
Volvo Truck & Bus (South) Ltd. King's Lynn, Saddlerbow Road, King's Lynn, Norfolk, PE30 5BN — Tel: 01553 816460
Volvo Truck & Bus (South) Ltd. Milton Keynes, Delaware Drive, Willen, Milton Keynes, Buckinghamshire, MK15 8JH — Tel: 01908 210525
Volvo Truck & Bus (South) Ltd. Newport, Spytty Road, Newport, Gwent, NP9 0QU — Tel: 01633 290929
Volvo Truck & Bus (South) Ltd. Norwich, 24-28 Frensham Road, Norwich, Norfolk, NR3 2BT — Tel: 01603 785100
Volvo Truck & Bus (South) Ltd. Peterborough, Global Centre, Newark Road, Peterborough, Cambridgeshire, PE1 5YD — Tel: 01733 894940
Volvo Truck & Bus (South) Ltd. Pontypridd, Upperboat, Pontypridd, Rhonnda Cynon Taff, CF37 5 — Tel: 01443 841168
Volvo Truck & Bus (South) Ltd. St Albans, 4 Old Parkbury Lane, Colney Street, St Albans, Hertfordshire, AL2 2OZ — Tel: 01923 852950
Volvo Truck & Bus (South) Ltd. Swansea, 21 Viking Way, Swansea, Carmarthenshire, SA1 7DA — Tel: 01792 795462
Volvo Truck & Bus (South) Ltd. Thetford, 34 Howlett Way, Thetford, Norfolk, IP24 1HZ — Tel: 01842 855900

Fuel & bunker card contacts

BP Routex Fuel Cards
BP Oil UK Ltd
Witan Gate House
500-600 Witan Gate
Central Milton Keynes
MK9 1ES
Tel: 0845 6030723
Fax: 01908 852856
www.bpplus.com

Brobot Petroleum Fuel Cards
Brobot Petroleum
Thorpe Road
Melton Mowbray
Leicestershire
LE13 1SH
Tel: 01664 480000
www.brobot.co.uk

C H Jones/Diesel Direct/Key Fuels Cards
Premier Business Park
Queen Street, Walsall
West Midlands, WS2 9PB
Tel: 01922 704455
Fax: 01922 704456
Actionline: 0800 1950588
www.chjones.co.uk

CSC Fuel Cards
CSC Group
14 Trevor Hill, Newry
County Down
Northern Ireland
BT34 1DN
02830 266202
www.cscgroup.org.uk

DCI Fuel Cards Northern Ireland
Unit 7, The Vale Centre
Clooney Road
Eglington
County Londonderry
Tel: 02871 812121
www.dcicard.ie

DCI Fuel Cards Southern Ireland
Purcell House
Claregalway Road
Oranmore
County Galway
Tel: 00353 (0) 1890242324
www.dcicard.ie

EMO Fuel Cards
Clonminam Industrial Estate
Portlaoise
County Laois
Ireland
00353 (0) 578674700
00353 (0) 578674750
www.emo.ie

Esso Fuel Cards
Exxon Mobil House
Ermyn Way
Leatherhead
Surrey KT22 8UX
Tel: 0800 626672
Fax: 01483 774226
www.essocard.com

Fastfuel/Uk Fuels Cards
Texaco Ltd
1 Westferry Circus
Canary Wharf
London E14 4HA
Tel: 01270 655600

Fuelserve/Securicor/PCS Fuel Cards
Richmond House
Sproughton Road, Ipswich
Suffolk IP1 5AW
Tel: 01473 466666
Fax: 01473 749706
www.fuelserve.com

IDS/Q8 Fuel Cards
Burgan House, The Causeway
Staines
Middlesex TW18 3PA
Tel: 01784 467660
Telephone out of hours or outside home country if calling from a landline: 00800 56565656
Telephone out of hours or outside home country if calling from a mobile: 0033 (0) 142990830
www.ids.q8.com

Jet/ConocoPhillips Fuel Cards
Jet Card Centre
PO Box 65
Crewe CW1 6GQ
Tel: 08457 444044
www.jetcard.co.uk

Murco Fuel Cards
Tel: 01727 892400
www.murco.co.uk

Overdrive/Allstar/Dial/ArvalPhh Fuel Cards
Arval UK Ltd
Arval Centre
Windmill Hill
Swindon SN5 6PE
Tel: 0870 4197000
www.arvalphh.co.uk

Petroplus/Routemate UK Fuel Cards
Fuel Card Department
Petroplus Marketing Ltd
Petroplus House
St Marks Court
Teesdale
Stockton on Tees
TS17 6QW
Tel: 01642 736300
Fax: 01642 736004
www.petroplus.co.uk

Shell Fuel Cards
Shell UK Oil Products
Rowlandsway House
Rowlandsway
Manchester
M22 5SB
Tel: 0800 7313131
Fax: 0800 7313130
www.euroshell.com

Statoil Fuel Cards
Fuel Card Services
Statoil Card Centre
Statoil Service Station
Oranmore
County Galway
Ireland
Tel: 00353 (0) 191788116
Fax: 00353 (0) 191795777
www.statoilcard.ie

Total Fuel Cards
Total Card Services
Total UK Ltd
40 Clarendon Road
Watford
Hertfordshire WT17 1TQ
Tel: 0800 147148
www.total.co.uk

Government bodies

DTI Enquiry Unit
1 Victoria Street
London
SW1H OET
Tel: 020 7215500
www.dti.gov.uk
The DTI works to create successful British business and industry, helps companies to become more productive and protects the rights of working people and consumers.

Department for Transport
www.dft.gov.uk
Great Minster House
76 Marsham Street
London SW1P 4DR
Tel: 020 79449643
DFT oversee the delivery of a reliable, safe and secure transport system whilst safeguarding our environment.

DVLA
Longview Road
Morriston
Swansea
SA6 7JL
Tel: 01792 782318
www.dvla.gov.uk
DVLA maintain registers of drivers and vehicles and collect road tax.

Driving Standards Agency
Stanley House
56 Talbot Street
Nottingham
NG1 5GU
Tel : 0115 901 2500
Fax: 0115 901 2510
www.dsa.gov.uk
The DSA is responsible for driving standards, testing car drivers, truckers, motorcyclists and driving instructors. You can even book your test on-line at their website!

European Parliament
Rue Wiertz–Wierzstraat
B-1047 Brussels
Belgium
Tel: 0032 (2) 2842929
www.europarl.eu.int
For written publications covering parliament's plenary sessions call the above contact number or search the web-site for latest truck and driver legislation.

HM Customs and Excise
Tel: 0845 0109000
www.hmce.gov.uk
HM Customs and Excise is a government department with responsibility for collecting billions of pounds in revenue each year in VAT, other taxes and customs duties. They also have a vital front-line role in protecting us from illegal imports of drugs, alcohol and tobacco smuggling, and tax fraud.

Health and Safety Executive
Tel: 0845 3450055
www.hse.gov.uk
Britain's Health and Safety Commission (HSC) and the Health and Safety Executive (HSE) are responsible for the regulation of almost all the risks to health and safety arising from work activity in Britain.

Highways Agency
Tel: 08457 504030
www.highways.gov.uk
The Highways Agency is an executive agency of the Department for Transport (DFT), and is responsible for operating, maintaining and improving the strategic road network in England on behalf of the Secretary of State for Transport. We have a major role in delivering the government's Ten Year Plan for Transport.

Inland Revenue
Tel: 0845 302148
www.inlandrevenue.gov.uk
For specific enquiries, go on-line to find the phone number for the department you require.

Jobcentre Plus
Jobseeker Direct Helpline: 0845 6060234
www.jobcentreplus.gov.uk
In some areas Jobcentre Plus offices are already offering a fully integrated work and benefit service. It will take several years to integrate the entire local office network of Jobcentres and social security offices fully. During this time, services will continue to be provided in local social security offices and Jobcentres, which will be part of the Jobcentre Plus network. Jobcentre Plus will be introduced everywhere by 2006.

Learning and Skills Council
Tel: 0870 900 6800
www.lsc.gov.uk
The LSC exists to make England better skilled and more competitive. They are responsible for planning and funding high-quality vocational education and training for everyone.

Police

www.police.uk
Anti-terrorist hotline Tel: 0800 789 321
British Transport Police (Public Rail Systems)
Tel: 0800 405040
Crimestoppers Tel: 0800 555111

Dial 999 from a landline or 112 from a mobile if:

A. There is a danger to life or risk of injury being caused such as a serious road accident or assault.

B. A crime is in progress, such as a robbery, burglary or theft, and the offender is still on the scene or has just left the area.

C. The Immediate attendance of the police is necessary – such as someone acting suspiciously and obviously about to commit a crime.

Local constabulary contact numbers:
  Avon and Somerset: 01275 818181
  Bedfordshire Police: 01234 841212
  Cambridgeshire Constabulary: 01480 456111
  Central Scotland Police: 01786 456000
  Cheshire Constabulary: 01244 350000
  City of London: 020 7601222
  Cleveland Constabulary: 01642 326326
  Cumbria Constabulary: 01768 891999
  Derbyshire Constabulary: 0845 1233333
  Devon & Cornwall
      Constabulary: 08452 777444
  Dorset Police: 01202 222222
  Dumfries and Galloway
      Constabulary: 01387 252112
  Durham Constabulary: 0845 6060365
  Dyfed Powys Police: 01267 232000
  Essex Police: 01245 491491
  Fife Constabulary: 01592 418888
  Gloucestershire Constabulary: 0845 901234
  Grampian Police: 0845 60057000
  Greater Manchester Police: 0161 8725050
  Gwent Police/Heddlu Gwent: 01633 838111
  Hampshire Constabulary: 0845 0454545
  Hertfordshire Constabulary: 0845 3300222
  Humberside Police: 0845 6060222
  Kent Police: 01622 690690
  Lancashire Constabulary: 0845 1253545
  Leicestershire Constabulary: 0116 2222222
  Lincolnshire Police: 01522 532222
  Lothian and Borders Police: 0131 3113131
  Merseyside Police: 0151 7096010
  Metropolitan Police Service: 020 72301212
  Norfolk Constabulary: 01953 424242
  North Wales Police: 0845 6071002
  North Yorkshire Police: 0845 6060247
  Northamptonshire Police: 01604 700700
  Northern Constabulary: 01463 715555
  Northumbria Police: 01661 872555
  Nottinghamshire Police: 0115 9482999
  Police Service of Northern
      Ireland: 028 90650222
  South Wales Police: 01656 655555
  South Yorkshire Police: 0114 2202020
  Staffordshire Police: 08453 302010
  Strathclyde Police: 0141 5322000

Suffolk Constabulary: 01473 613500
Surrey Police: 0845 1252222
Sussex Police: 0845 6070999
Tayside Police: 01382 200449
Thames Valley Police: 0845 8505505
Warwickshire Police: 01926 415000
West Mercia Constabulary: 08457 444888
West Midlands Police: 0845 1135000
West Yorkshire Police: 0845 6060606
Wiltshire Constabulary: 01380 735735

R.O.S.P.A.

Edgbaston Park
353 Bristol Road
Edgbaston
Birmingham
B5 7ST
Tel: 0121 2482000
Fax: 0121 2482001
www.rospa.co.uk
Provides up to the minute advice and information on safety issues and law.

Traffic Scotland (formerly part of Scottish Executive

National Driver Information and Control System)
Transport Scotland
Meridian Court
5 Cadogan Street
Glasgow
GL2 6AT
Tel: 0131 2447510
www.trafficscotland.org
Provides up to the minute information about Scotland's road conditions, traffic and weather.

UK Passport Service

Tel: 0870 521 0410
www.passport.gov.uk
You can use this number for any passport enquires or to report a lost or stolen passport. Go on-line to find out more about different types of passports or the other services offered by the UK Passport Service.

Vehicle and Operator Services Agency

(V.O.S.A.)
Tel: 0870 6060440
www.vosa.gov.uk
Vosa aims to improve road safety and the environment and enforce compliance with commercial operator licensing requirements. They also have the authority to stop and spot-check HGV's.

Vehicle Certification Agency

VCA Bristol
1 The Eastgate Office Centre
Eastgate Road
Bristol, BS5 6XX
United Kingdom
Tel: 0117 9515151
www.vca.gov.uk
The VCA is responsible for national approval and policy formulation with regard to the enforcement of vehicle safety and environmental standards.

Useful contacts

AA
The AA
Contact Centre
Lambert House
Stockport Road
Cheadle
SK8 2DY
AA roadwatch: 09003 401100
www.theaa.com
AA Roadwatch will send texts or e-mail the latest traffic info to your phone and provide personalised routes and interactive maps for an annual fee. Find out more on line.

ALLMI Training
Second Floor Suite
9 Avon Reach
Monkton Hill
Chippenham
Wiltshire
SN15 1EE
Tel: 01249 659150
Fax: 01249 464675
www.allmitraining.co.uk
ALLMI Training Ltd is the independent training accreditation service and standards body for The Association of Lorry Loader Manufacturers and Importers of Great Britain (ALLMI). ALLMI is the UK's only trade association devoted exclusively to advancing safety and standards in the lorry loader industry.

Drivers Helpline
7 Sinclair Court
Scarborough
Yorkshire
YO12 7DS
Tel: 01723 351425
Mobile: 07791 601307
email: dneale7@aol.com
www.drivershelpline.co.uk
A service offering advice and support for drivers, or the families of drivers who have been arrested abroad. The helpline is a free service and is available 24 Hours a day, 7 days a week.

European Shippers Council
ESC Brussels
Park Leopold
Rue Wiertz 50
B-1050 Brussels
Belgium
Tel: (322) 230 21 13
www.europeanshippers.com
The ESC looks after the interests of companies represented by 15 national transport user organisations and a number of European commodity trade associations.

Lady Truckers Club
7 Sinclair Court
Scarborough
Yorkshire
YO12 7DS
Tel: 01723 351425
Mobile: 07791 601307
www.ladytruckersclub.co.uk
email: dneale7@aol.com
A club aimed exclusively at female truck and coach drivers addressing the particular issues faced by girls on the road.

FERRIES

Brittany Ferries
Tel: 08703 665333
www.brittanyferries.co.uk

DFDS Seaways
Tel: 08705 333000
www.dfdsseaways.com

Fjord Line
Tel: 0870 1436979
www.fjordline.co.uk

Norfolk Line
Tel: 0870 8701020
www.norfolkline.com

P&O Ferries
Tel: 08705 980333
www.poferries.com

SeaFrance Ferries
Tel: 08705 711711
www.seafrance.com

Stena Line
Tel: 0845 0704000
www.stenaline.co.uk

Irish Ferries
Tel: 08705 171717
www.irishferries.com

Norse Merchant Ferries
Tel:0870 6004321
www.norsemerchant.com

P&O Irish Sea
Tel: 0870 2424777
www.poirishsea.com

Swansea Cork Ferries
Tel: 01792 456116
www.swansea-cork.ie

Caledonian MacBrayne
01475 650100
www.calmac.co.uk

NorthLink Orkney & Shetland Ferries
Tel:0845 6060449
www.northlinkferries.co.uk

Orkney Ferries
Tel: 01856 872044
www.orkneyferries.co.uk

Freight Transport Association
Tel: 08171 112222 (Member Service Centre Number)
www.fta.co.uk
Freight Transport Association represents the transport interests of companies moving goods by road, rail, sea and air. Its members range from small and medium size enterprises to multinational public companies and are involved in all modes of transport. FTA members operate over 200,000 goods vehicles – almost half the UK fleet.

Garage Watch
43 Broadway
Shifnal
Near Telford TF11 8BD
Tel: 0870 794 3455
www.garagewatch.co.uk
*Representative body for the
UK's 45,000 independent
garages.*

London Congestion Charge
Customer service enquiries
Congestion Charging
PO Box 2985
Coventry CV7 8ZR
Penalty charge enquiries
Congestion Charging
PO Box 2984
Coventry
CV7 8YR
Tel: 0845 900 1234.
www.cclondon.com

**M6 Toll
(Midland Expressway Ltd)**
Midland Expressway Limited
Freepost
NAT 9069
Weeford
Lichfield WS14 0PQ
Tel: 0870 850 6262
Fax: 01543 267 001
www.m6toll.co.uk
*Call or go on-line to
find out about tags and
charges.*

Network Rail
Network Rail
40 Melton Street
London NW1 2EE
Tel: 020 7557 800
Fax: 020 7557 9000
National Rail Enquiries:
08457 484950
Network Rail Helpline:
08457 114141
www.networkrail.co.uk
*Network Rail is an engineering
company formed to revitalise
Britain's railways. They maintain,
improve and upgrade every
aspect of the rail infrastructure
including tracks, signalling
systems, bridges, viaducts,
tunnels, level crossings and
stations.*

RAC
1 Forest Road
Feltham TW13 7RR
Tel: 020 89172742
Head office: 020 89172500
www.rac.co.uk
*Gives information about mobile
phone law, traffic, weather and*

*route planning for an
annual fee. Alternatively gain
instant access to the latest
traffic by dialling 1740 from any
mobile.*

**Recruitment and
Employment Confederation**
36-38 Mortimer Street
London
W1W 7RG
Tel: 020 24623260
www.rec.uk.com
*The Recruitment and
Employment Confederation is
the body representing the
private recruitment industry in
the UK. They offer services to
employers, jobseekers and
industry observers.*

Road Haulage Association
www.rha.net

*Scotland and Northern
Ireland*
Roadway House
The Rural Centre
Ingliston
Newbridge
EH28 8NZ
Tel: 0131 4724180
Fax: 0131 4724179
scotland-northernireland@rha.net

Northern Region
Roadway House
Little Wood Drive
West 26 Industrial Estate
Cleckheaton
BD19 4TA
Tel: 01274 863100
Fax: 01274 865855
northern@rha.net

*Midlands and Western
Region*
Roadway house
Cribbs Causeway
Bristol
BS10 7TU
Tel: 01179 503600
Fax: 01179 505647
Midlands-western@rha.net

*Southern and Eastern
Region*
Roadway House
Bretton Way
Bretton
Peterborough
PE3 8DD
Tel: 01733 261131
Fax: 01733 332349
Southern-eastern@rha.net

RHA Weybridge (Head Office)
Roadway house
35 Monument Hill
Weybridge
Surrey
KT13 8RN
Tel: 01932 841515
Fax: 01932 852516
weybridge@rha.net
*The Road Haulage Association
provides dedicated
campaigning, advice,
information and business
services specially tailored for the
haulage industry.*

RSPCA
National Hotline:
0870 5555999
www.rspca.org.uk
*Call this number anywhere in
the UK to report a distressed or
injured animal (wild or
domestic). An operator will
advise you on what to do, direct
you to your nearest RSPCA
centre or send an officer to your
location.*

Skills for Logistics
14 Warren Yard
Warren Farm Office Village
Stratford Road
Milton Keynes
MK12 5NW
Tel: 01908 313360
www.skillsforlogistics.org
*Skills for logistics is an
independent UK-wide
organisation run for
employers to help them
tackle the skills and
productivity needs of the
logistics sector.*

T&G
Transport & General
Workers Union
Central Office
Transport House
128 Theobald's Road
Holborn
London
WC1X 8TN
Tel: 0207 6112500
www.tgwu.org.uk
*With over 900,000 members
in every type of workplace
the T&G is the UK's biggest
general union, and has a long
and proud tradition of
representing members in the
workplace.*

Glossary

Abnormal load: Any load that's heavier than 42 tonnes, or wider, longer or taller than the normal size of an articulated vehicle trailer. See 'Vehicle size and bridges' on p.25.

AdBlue: A liquid placed within a separate tank (close to the fuel tank) that reduces emissions in new vehicles. Also see AdBlue p.57.

A-frame: A combination of a 17-tonne rigid and trailer of approximately equal size with a steering front axle and rigid rear axle on the trailer.

ADR (Hazardous Goods): A type of licence required by drivers who have to transport hazardous goods by road. See section on 'Additional qualifications and training'.

Agency: A company which provides drivers with temporary employment and employers with a temporary workforce.

Air brakes: Used to efficiently stop a large vehicle by providing a circuit of air through pipes and valves on the rigid, tractor unit and/or trailer. If the air ceases to flow due to leakage or closure of a valve (such as that operated by braking) the brakes will immediately be applied.

Air suspension (adjustable): Used for adjusting the height or angle of the trailer, unit, or rigid vehicle.

Ambient goods: Transported goods that require no refrigeration or freezing (such as household cleaners and tinned food).

Anderson lead and clip: A black electric lead used to carry current from the tractor unit to the trailer with a male and female clip at opposite ends. Only to be applied when tail-lift is in use.

Articulated vehicle (artic): Any vehicle comprised of two coupled independent and separable parts. 'Artic' is usually a term used to describe a tractor unit and trailer of at least 26 tonnes maximum gross weight.

Banksman: Any person (in an official capacity or otherwise) who assists a driver to safely reverse their vehicle.

Barn doors: Two large doors on the back of a trailer that open outwards.

Beaver tail: Two huge fold-up-and-down ramps on the rear of a flatbed trailer that enable vehicles to be driven on and off.

Block change: Changing gears without going through every single gear or half gear in the 'box. See section on 'How to understand your gearbox' on p.52.

Blocks: Long thick blocks of wood placed beneath large goods to provide a gap through which forks can be inserted to lift the goods from the deck of the trailer.

Bonded goods: Cigarettes and alcohol are the two main ones. These goods come strictly and separately sealed, and deliveries are often timed. Rigid codes of conduct surround bonded warehouses – be aware of this if you have to collect or deliver from or to one.

Bouncing: An action used to describe driving a solo unit without a trailer. See 'Running Bobtail' and 'Running Solo'.

Box trailer: A trailer with hard sides and top.

Break: A standard tachograph break is 45 minutes, following four-and-a-half accumulated hours of driving. See section on 'Laws regarding driving hours' on p.14.

British Domestic Hours Rule: A type of driving hours configuration that applies only to drivers working for certain types of operations. See 'British Domestic Hours Rule' on p.16 and 'Operations Exempt From EU Rule' on p.15.

Broms Brake: A secondary parking brake on Volvo tractor units, situated close to the normal parking brake on the dashboard. It's described as a round pull-out knob. This should be pushed in before driving can commence.

Bunker (fuel): A no-frills fuelling site designed for LGVs. Fuel/Bunkering Cards and their pin numbers are required in order to draw fuel, as many of these sites are unmanned.

Burns kit: Usually provided by companies whose drivers transport hazardous chemicals. The kits are usually kept in the cab. Training is given on their use and application.

Cab heater: Used for heating the cab when the engine is switched off.

Cages: Upright wire containers on wheels used for transporting loose goods. They're awkward to move and often come without brakes. Some can be collapsed for ease of storage.

Canopy: The cover over a filling station or loading

bay designed to protect those below it from the elements. Be sure to make certain your vehicle is low enough to get under it.

Cantilever tail-lift: A large type of tail-lift that folds flat against the rear doors of the trailer. See 'Tail-lifts' section on p.40.

Catwalk: Term sometimes used to describe the footplate at the rear of a tractor unit that you stand on when coupling to your trailer.

Central bar (tautliner trailer): The two central supporting posts that run from deck to roof in a curtain-sided vehicle. These can be unclipped and swivelled or swung out so that goods can be more effectively placed behind them.

Cherry picker: A vehicle with a platform located at the rear that's raised and lowered on an hydraulic arm. This type of vehicle is used for (amongst other things) repairing streetlights.

Chest compressions: A procedure used in resuscitation of unconscious persons. See section on 'First Aid for motorists'.

Chocks: Triangular pieces of wood inserted under each side of a large object to prevent its movement in transit. Also used to prevent movement of vehicles and/or trailers.

Close coupled: Term used to describe a tractor unit and trailer that are joined close together, providing little room for the driver to couple or uncouple the service leads.

Collective or Workforce/Workplace Agreement: Any agreement regarding working hours and times that is drawn up between an employer and his or her employees. All employees have to sign to say they agree with it.

Column tail-lift: Type of tail-lift that folds up against the back doors of the trailer. See 'Tail-lifts' section on p.40.

Construction And Use Regulations: See section on 'Vehicle size and bridges' on p.25.

Contraflow: A traffic directing system created using cones and temporary cat's eyes that directs traffic away from roadworks.

COSHH (Control of Substances Hazardous to Health): Regulations and advice regarding the storage and handling of hazardous substances.

Cow bells: An electric lead used to carry current from a tractor unit to a trailer. This lead has a large, square, bell-like attachment at one end which secures into a housing on the trailer. This should only be connected when the tail-lift is in use.

CPC: A qualification which confirms an individual has the training and authority to run a transport department.

CPCS: A qualification that allows an individual to move and operate plant machinery and to work on a construction site.

Crash box: Any gearbox without a synchromesh, where the driver can only change gear at a certain point on the rev counter. This includes Fuller Road Ranger and Eaton Twin Splitter gearboxes. See section on 'How to understand your gearbox' on p.52.

Cross-members (pallet): The three wooden struts across the base of a pallet.

Cross-members (trailer legs): The diagonal supports that hold the trailer legs in place.

Cruise control: A feature that allows a driver to maintain his speed without using the accelerator.

Cup: The rectangular hole and flange on the rear of a rigid prime mover that the drawbar of a trailer is coupled into to create a rigid and drawbar trailer combination.

Curtain-sider or tautliner: A trailer with strong plastic sides that can be folded back like a curtain to allow goods to be loaded.

Daily driving limit/time: The accumulated hours that anyone is allowed to drive within a 24-hour period. See 'Driving Hours' on p.14 and Working Time Regulations on p.10.

Daily rest period: The number of hours during which a mobile worker has to rest between in two 24-hour periods. See 'Driving Hours' on p.14 and Working Time Regulations on p.10.

Daily working time/working period/duty time: The number of hours in a day that any mobile worker is allowed to be on duty. This includes driving, other work periods, periods of availability and breaks (with EU regulations). See 'Driving Hours' on p.14 and Working Time Regulations on p.10.

Deck: The inside floor of the trailer.

Defect: Term used to describe any fault on a vehicle unit or trailer. Also used to describe the action of writing a report about a particular defect in order to have the vehicle repaired – eg 'I defected that vehicle last week,' meaning 'I wrote a defect report on that vehicle.'

Demountable body: See 'Drop-box trailer'.

DFT (Department for Transport): See section on 'Government bodies'.

Diagnostics system: The tractor unit's onboard computer that tells you if there's something wrong with the braking system, lights or fluid levels. Some systems can be very complex and comprehensive. With some newer vehicles you may only be able to check the truck's condition using the diagnostics system. The menus are usually accessed using the right-hand stalk that branches off from the steering column, or a button/dial on the dashboard.

Dif lock: Allows axles to turn at different speeds, giving grip to one axle if the other is unable to grip in snow or extreme conditions.

Dog clip: See 'Safety Catch'.

Dollies: See 'Wheeled Platforms'.

Domestic hours: See section on 'British Domestic Hours Rule' on p.16.

Door retainers: Clips and bars that hold open trailer doors securely and prevent movement.

Double-deck trailer: A type of trailer with two internal floors and an tail-lift that services both levels. These types of trailer have small wheels and sit very low to the ground. They are also extremely tall.

Doubling the clutch: A procedure used to change gear in a vehicle with a crash gearbox. See section on 'How to understand your gearbox' on p.52.

Drawbar Eye: The coupling attachment on a drawbar trailer. Also see: 'Coupling a rigid and drawbar trailer'

Drop-box: A changeable box or boxes on a rigid or trailer that can be removed, put on legs, stored, or placed on another chassis.

Drop-box trailer: A rigid or articulated vehicle trailer with a system designed so that the body or box of the trailer can be removed from the chassis and stored separately. See 'Driving a rigid and drawbar' on p.73.

DSA (Driving Standards Agency): See section on 'Government bodies'.

DTI (Department of Industry): See section on 'Government bodies'.

Dummy holders/clips: Clips attached to the service lead bar used to safely store and hold service leads and couplings while not being used.

Dump valve: A pull/push lever or handle-type combination (on adjustable suspensions) that releases the air from the trailer suspension in order to lower it.

DVLA (Driver and Vehicle Licensing Agency): See section on 'Government bodies'.

ESC (European Shippers Council): See 'Useful contacts' list.

Exhaust brake: Used instead of or in addition to conventional brakes to slow a vehicle on steep or long hills. Some vehicles feature an automatic exhaust brake which is applied when you decelerate.

External straps: Straps (usually removable) used to secure the load. Can be used around the back of a load in order to push it hard up against the front of a trailer, or over and around the top and sides of a load in curtain-sided vehicles to prevent movement in any direction.

Eye kit: Provided in vehicles that carry hazardous chemicals. Used to wash out the eyes should they come into contact with harmful substances.

Fifth wheel: The large upside-down U-shaped plate on the back of a tractor unit that the trailer rests and swivels on.

Fifth wheel grease: Lubrication grease applied to the fifth wheel plate. This is horrible stuff, very difficult to remove from skin and clothing, but not harmful.

Fifth wheel lever/handle: The handle or lever that has to be pulled in order to release the trailer pin from the fifth wheel.

Flatbed trailer: An open-backed trailer used for transporting large, heavy or abnormal loads.

Fleet codes: Unique code numbers applied by some large companies to their vehicles in order to identify each vehicle within their fleet.

Footplate (see also 'catwalk'): The flat area of the chassis at the rear of the cab next to the fuel tank. Designed for standing on while inserting service leads.

Fork rollers: The roller wheels at the front of the forks of a pallet truck.

Forklift truck: A machine used to mechanically load a vehicle. Stand-on and ride-on forklift trucks all require special licences. See section on 'Additional qualifications and training'.

Fortnightly driving limit: The number of hours that a driver is allowed to drive in a 14-day period. See 'Driving Hours' on p.14 and Working Time Regulations on p.10.

FTA (Freight Transport Association): See 'Useful contacts' list.

Gantry: The structure above a motorway on which signs are displayed.

Gas oil: See 'Red diesel' in Glossary and section on 'Fuelling up' on p.56.

General haulage: A type of work where you may be asked to transport almost any type of goods. General haulage usually involves several drops in a day, covering long distances, and working long hours. Deliveries and collections are often assigned ad hoc.

Guide Funnel: The coupling attachment on a

rigid that the 'Drawbar Eye' slots into. Also see: 'Coupling a rigid and drawbar trailer'

Guide posts: Low-level metal posts concreted into the floor of a loading bay to help guide you into the correct position.

Handballing: See 'Manual handling' in Glossary and section on 'Manual handling' on p.10.

Headstock: The area of the front external wall of a trailer to which the service leads are coupled.

Height indicator: A legal requirement for any vehicle over 9ft 6in or 2.9m. It tells you the height of your vehicle or any normal height trailer it might be coupled to. It is normally situated on the dashboard or behind the sun visor.

HGV (heavy goods vehicle): The old title used to describe any vehicle over 7.5 tonnes.

HGV Class 1: The old title used to describe any articulated tractor unit and trailer combination.

HGV Class 2: The old title used to describe any rigid vehicle above 17 tonnes.

HGV Class 3: The old title use to describe any rigid vehicle between 7.5 tonnes and 17 tonnes.

Hi-Ab: A type of licence required by anyone loading and unloading a vehicle using a crane attached to its rear. See section on 'Additional qualifications and training'.

High visibility clothing: Normally consists of at least a jacket or vest that fits over the top of your outer garments. It usually displays a fluorescent colour and at least one light-reflective strip. This is a site requirement within most yards, distribution centres, and warehouses.

HMSO (Her Majesty's Stationary Office): Publishes and distributes government books and pamphlets such as the Highway Code, Theory Test Books, and others pertaining to transport and employment law.

Horizontal Amending Directive (HAD): See p.13.

HSE (Health and Safety Executive): See section on 'Government bodies'.

HSW (Health and Safety at Work): Legislation and advice on the health and safety of employees in the workplace.

Imperial: Old style of measurement still widely used by lorry drivers. Common imperial measurements include feet and inches, yards and miles, gallons and fluid ounces, pounds, stones, hundredweights and tons. See 'Metric to Imperial conversion table' on p.26.

Insider: Type of enclosed tail-lift most commonly found on bread delivery vehicles. When not in use the tail-lift acts as part of the floor. See 'Tail-lifts' section on p.40.

Internal straps: Fixed load-restraining straps used in curtain-sided trailers. See section on 'Using internal and external straps' on p.38.

Inspection Light: A light at the rear of the cab that enables the driver to couple and uncouple in the dark.

IPAS (Powered Access Licence): A licence that allows an individual to operate cherry pickers and scissor lifts.

Isolator switch (battery): A red switch usually found on the passenger side of the tractor unit at thigh height, just behind the cab. This switch cuts power to the battery and prevents overnight draining in cold conditions.

Isolator switch (tail-lift): A switch normally found inside the cab or within the tail-lift control box at the rear of the vehicle. The tail-lift cannot be used if this switch is not employed.

Kerb mirror: The mirror that hangs over the passenger side door and gives the driver a view of the nearside kerb area.

Kissing (Tyres): Where a wheel has more than one tyre on it, and those tyres are touching because the gap between them is too narrow.

Leg winding handle: Used to raise and lower the legs of a trailer. See section on 'How to couple and uncouple a unit and trailer' on p.58–63.

Legs (trailer and box): The supporting legs used to hold a trailer or a drop-box away from the ground when it's not being pulled by a unit or rigid.

LGV C: A rigid vehicle with a maximum gross weight of between 7.5 and 32 tonnes.

LGV C1: A rigid vehicle with a maximum gross weight of between 3.5 tonnes and 7.5 tonnes.

LGV C+E: Any articulated vehicle with a combined maximum gross weight usually between 12 and 44 tonnes.

Lift axles: Axles on a trailer, unit, or rigid which allow you to raise and lower the wheels when you're not carrying a load. This is employed to save on tyre wear.

Loading ramp or Dock Leveller: The ramp used to close the gap between the rear of the trailer and the loading bay floor. Can be manual or mechanical.

Low-loader: A flatbed trailer which sits close to the ground and normally has more than the usual quota of axles. These types of trailer are often used to transport plant machinery.

LSC (Learning and Skills Council): See section on 'Government bodies'.

Manual handling: Lifting, pulling or pushing any item or animal without mechanical assistance. See section on 'Manual handling' on p.10.

Matrix Signs: Electronic signs on a motorway that display information.

Maximum Average Working Week: The maximum average number of hours that an employee can work over a reference period. Also see 'Working Time Regulations' on p.10.

Maximum gross weight: The sum total weight of a vehicle and its load – for example, a 7.5 tonne vehicle would comprise the vehicle itself, weighing about 4.5 tonnes, plus its load of three tonnes.

Maximum Weekly Working Time: The maximum number of hours that any employee can work in one week. Also see 'Working time Regulations' on p.10.

Mobile worker: Drivers, driver's mates or apprentices and some types of warehouse staff are classed as 'Mobile Workers.' Also see 'Working Time Regulations' on p.10.

Moffat: A brand of forklift truck, designed to ride 'piggyback' on the rear of a trailer or rigid vehicle when not in use.

MoT: An annual test of roadworthiness for all engine-propelled and towed vehicles (excluding car trailers below a certain weight).

MoT plate: A plate displayed within the cab and underneath a trailer that shows the driver (amongst other things) the carrying capacity of his vehicle. See 'Know your cab instrumentation and equipment' section on p.48.

Nearside: The passenger side of a vehicle, the side which is nearest the kerb.

O Licence (Operators' Licence): The licence owned by any transport company that transports goods for payment. See 'Know your cab instrumentation and equipment' section on p.48.

Occasional Drivers: One who drives on no more than 10 or 15 occasions in a reference period. Also see HAD on p.13 for full clarification.

Odometer: Records the speed of a vehicle in miles and kilometres, and in an LGV the distance travelled in kilometres rather than miles.

Offside: The driver's side of a vehicle, the side which is furthest from the kerb.

Operations Exempt From EU Rule: See p.15.

Pallet truck: A hydraulic, manual (and sometimes battery-operated) device used to manoeuvre palletised goods on flat ground.

Pallets: A raised wooden platform to which goods are secured for ease of transportation and storage. Though they come in any number of shapes, sizes and strengths, the most common type is the square blue pallet.

Part Time Drivers: Drivers working under British Domestic Hour Rule who do not exceed four hours of driving in any 24-hour period.

Payload: The weight of the cargo being carried by a vehicle.

Period of availability (POA): See 'Driving Hours' on p.14 and Working Time Regulations on p.10.

Permission to move your vehicle: See 'Vehicle size and bridges' on p.25.

Pictograms: Symbols used by digital tachographs that are shown both on the LED display and on any printout made. These symbols can represent and show anything from breaks taken, speeding events and power failures. Also see 'Digital Tachographs' on p.17.

Pin: Tapered cylindrical metal object beneath the floor of the trailer that is secured between the jaws of the fifth wheel plate when connected to the tractor unit.

Pin (Rigid and Drawbar): The drop down pin which secures a drawbar trailer into the coupling guide funnel. Also see: 'Coupling a rigid and drawbar trailer' on p.64.

Prime mover: A rigid vehicle designed for towing a trailer. Such vehicles often have splitter gearboxes.

Producer: A ticket given to a driver by the police which demands that he take it and any documents requested to a police station of his choice within seven days.

PTPS (Personal Track Safety): A training qualification that allows the individual to collect and deliver railway trackside machinery and equipment.

Pull Test: A method of placing a coupled tractor unit in a low gear and trying to pull forward while the trailer brake is on. This is used to check if a unit is correctly coupled to the trailer. Not to be used on a rigid and drawbar trailer combination.

Pumping handle: See pictures in section on 'Using a pallet truck' on p.36.

Pumping lever: In order to pump up the forks of a pallet truck, this lever should first be pushed away from the user until it clicks before pumping can commence. When pulled towards the user, the pallet truck forks will be released and dropped to the ground. See pictures in section on 'Using a pallet truck' on p.36.

Ratchet: The mechanism used to tighten and loosen the curtains on a curtain-sided trailer. Consists of a spindle which the curtain pole sits upon, and levers which loosen and tighten the curtains.

Ratchet straps: Strong, thick cord straps with metal attachments used to secure movable goods in place during transit. Can be fastened very tightly indeed without too much effort. See section on 'Using internal and external straps' on p.38.

Record Book: A daily log completed by the driver and used by operations exempt from EU rule to keep track of working and driving hours.

Record Of Work: A log kept by drivers working under EU regulations. This is completed by the driver and shows all driving time, working time, rest, breaks and POA.

Recovery position: A position used in resuscitation techniques to prevent a breathing but unconscious casualty from blocking their own airway or choking before they regain consciousness. See section on 'First Aid for motorists'.

Red diesel: Diesel that is of the same quality as white (normal) diesel but for which there is no tax duty to be paid. Red diesel can only be used in vehicles not driven on the public highway. It can also be used to power the generators of refrigerated trailers. A red dye is added to the fuel to stain the tank and internal workings of an engine in order to easily detect misuse. Note that 'Red diesel' is know as 'Green diesel' in Ireland.

Reference period: A period of 17–18 weeks during which a company or agency measures the average working time of its mobile staff. A company can ask for the period to be extended for up to 26 or 52 weeks. See 'Driving Hours' on p.14 and 'Working Time Regulations' on p.10.

Rescue breaths: A method of resuscitating an unconscious person who has stopped breathing. See section on 'First Aid for motorists'.

Retaining bars: Metal bars placed widthways across a trailer to prevent forward or rearward movement of a load. See section on 'Using retaining bars' on p.37.

Reverse parallel parking: The process of reversing a vehicle into a space at the side of a kerb (usually in between two parked vehicles or obstructions). See section on 'How to park against a kerb' on p.77.

Reversing blindside: The process of reversing a vehicle into a space or loading bay from its left-hand side. This is an extremely difficult manoeuvre as the trailer obstructs the driver's view in the nearside mirror. See section on 'Reversing blindside' on p.81.

RHA (Road Haulage Association): See 'Useful contacts' list.

Rigid: A term usually used to describe a non-articulated vehicle of more than 7.5 tonnes, though it can apply to any non-articulated vehicle.

Rollerbed trailer: A specialised type of trailer used for transporting goods that can't be loaded using conventional means. These are normally used for transporting airfreight containers and require some training in their proper use.

Roll-on roll-off: A type of vehicle that can tilt and roll containers onto its chassis from ground level using a hydraulic arm and/or winch.

Roller shutter doors: The rear doors of a trailer that consist of slats held together with hinges and wires and open upwards and inwards on rollers which run along a gutter inside the trailer. See section on 'Trailer door security' on p.44.

Rope and sheet: A process used to cover and protect a large load on the back of a flatbed trailer or low-loader. Training is required for this process.

ROSPA (Royal Society for the Prevention of Accidents): See section on 'Government bodies'.

RSPCA (Royal Society for the Prevention of Cruelty to Animals): See section on 'Government bodies'.

Rubbers (loading bay): Most loading bays have large rectangular blocks of hard rubber screwed to the wall to prevent damage to both the back of the trailer and the loading bay. See section on 'Reversing safely into a loading bay' on p.80.

Rubbers (trailer): Some trailers have strips of rubber on the rear, just below the doors, to help prevent damage to the trailer when it's reversed into a loading bay.

Running bent: Driving or operating a vehicle when you're out of driving or working hours.

Running bobtail: Driving a tractor unit without a trailer attached. Also known as 'running solo'.

Running solo: See 'Running bobtail' above.

Sack truck: A small upright trolley on two wheels, upon which you can stack a small number of items to be taken over rough ground from the vehicle to their delivery point. Can be used up or down a small number of steps, up kerbs, and over gravel and cobbles.

Safety catch: The catch inserted into a hole on the fifth wheel plate handle which ensures that the trailer pin is properly secured within the jaws of the fifth wheel plate. If you're unable to insert the catch, the trailer is not secured correctly.

Safety clip retainer: A metal retainer that pops down over part of the fifth wheel handle when the trailer has been securely coupled to the unit.

Safety rails: Slotted into holes at the edges of a tail-lift in order to prevent goods from rolling off the edge when it's in use.

Scissor lift: Similar to a cherry picker, a scissor lift has a platform which raises and lowers, allowing a person to gain access to streetlights and cables.

Scissor lift 2: Installed where a raised loading bay is not possible, it is a type of platform that the vehicle's load is placed upon. The platform is then mechanically lifted to the same level as the rear of the trailer and the goods loaded on and off.

Self Employed Drivers: See 'Working Time Regulations' on p.10.

Service lead fittings/couplings: Service leads that run from the tractor unit to the trailer using metal couplings and housings at either end, providing an electric feed to the lights and air to the brakes and suspension.

Shrink-wrap: A thin plastic film like a stronger version of cling film. Used to secure goods to a pallet.

Shunt button: A pull out/push in button situated next to the parking brake. Usually blue in colour, though not always. This is used only by mechanics, and should not be used by the driver.

Shunters: Vehicles used to move trailers around a yard. These can be old tractor units or specially designed vehicles. The same term is also applied to the drivers of such vehicles.

Skids: The two ramps mounted on the rear of a tractor unit, which lift a trailer into place and guide it towards the fifth wheel when coupling up.

Special conditions: See 'Vehicle size and bridges' on p.25.

Special routing arrangements: See 'Vehicle size and bridges' on p.25.

Special types order: See 'Vehicle size and bridges' on p.25.

Spill kit: Usually carried by vehicles transporting chemicals, petrol, or oil. Used to mop up and render any spillages harmless.

Split coupling: A term used to describe the technique of coupling the service leads to a trailer before the pin is secured to the fifth wheel plate. This is a risky technique fraught with potential hazards and should only be used when a trailer is close-coupled to its unit owing to a deep pin (one that's set far back from the front of the trailer).

Split daily rest period: The period of rest that a driver must complete between two 24-hour periods, split into two or more parts. See 'Driving Hours' on p.14 and 'Working Time Regulations' on p.10.

Splitter box: Any gearbox with low and high range gears within the same configuration, or half gears within the same configuration. See section on 'How to understand your gearbox' on p.52.

Steering rear axles: Usually found on very long or very short trailers. They allow the driver to take tighter corners without cutting across.

Statutory leave: Compulsory leave that all employees must be granted each year. In the UK this is 20 days and can include bank holidays.

Stillages: Large metal wire containers used to hold loose goods. Only used on curtain-sided vehicles or flatbed trailers and removed using a forklift truck. Can be stacked several high.

Stoppers: Barriers designed to prevent a load from falling off the edge of a tail-lift. See section on 'Stoppers and safety rails' on p.44.

Suspension: Most modern units, trailers, and rigids have adjustable air suspension designed to raise and lower the height of the vehicle and trailer. See section on 'Adjusting the height of a trailer or unit' on p.46.

Suzies: See 'Service lead fittings/couplings' in Glossary.

Swan neck (manoeuvre): A manoeuvre used to bring a trailer and unit tight up against and level with the kerb. See section on 'How to park against a kerb' on p.77.

Swan neck (trailer): The part of a low-loader, flatbed, or double-deck trailer above where the fifth wheel plate is coupled to the unit. It is stepped up above the main level of the deck.

T-bar: The bar at the rear of a trailer or rigid below the lights, designed to prevent cars from sliding beneath the vehicle in an accident.

T&G (Transport and General Workers Union): See 'Useful contacts' list.

Tachograph chart – analogue: A disc of wax-coated paper used to record movement and speed of a vehicle and the working modes of the driver. See 'Know your cab instrumentation and equipment' section on p.48 and 'Tachographs' on p.22.

Tachograph printout – digital: A piece of paper about the size of a till receipt that displays all the details of a driver's working day.

Tachograph – analogue: The recording unit into which the tachograph chart fits. See 'Know your cab instrumentation and equipment' section on p.48.

Tachograph – Digital: A recording unit (also known as a VU or Vehicle unit) into which the driver's card fits enabling him to record his working day. See digital tachographs on p.17.

Tail-lift mode switch: A switch on a panel within the back of a trailer that enables the controls to be accessed from either inside or outside.

Thinking distance: The distance travelled before a driver reacts to an emergency.

Timed out: A phrase used to describe being locked out of an automated bunkering machine for taking too long to enter your details.

Tradeplate drivers: Drivers (often with LGV licences) who hitch-hike around the country collecting and delivering vehicles going on or off hire. They also deliver new, unregistered vehicles out of the factory or showroom, take vehicles to port to be exported, and move vehicles to and from repair shops. The tradeplates themselves are white with red lettering and border. They license the driver to move a roadworthy vehicle without tax, MoT, or a conventional type of insurance.

Trailer brake: Used to hold the trailer in one place. This is usually (though not always) a red pull-out knob situated beneath the floor of or at the front of the trailer. Not to be confused with the shunt button, which is usually (though not always) blue.

Train weight: The total weight of a rigid and trailer plus its load.

Tram lines: Worn ruts in a road (usually the first lane of a motorway) that an LGV's wheels are often pulled into.

Tramping: Work that involves living and sleeping in your lorry for most of the week.

Trans-continental: Work that involves driving an LGV abroad.

Trolleys: See 'Wheeled platforms'.

Trunking: Long-distance driving that usually involves delivering only one load or swapping trailers.

Twist locks: Locks controlled by a handle beneath the body of a drop-box or container, that hold the box to the chassis.

UTC or Universal Standard Time: This is the same as Greenwich Mean Time and is used by all digital tachographs. Also see 'Digital Tachographs' on p.17.

Up-and-under: A type of tail-lift that tucks up and under the rear of the trailer. See 'Tail-lifts' section on p.40.

Urbie: Nickname given to an urban trailer, which is a 32–35ft trailer designed for city and town deliveries. Usually has only one rear axle. Some have a steering rear axle for getting around tight corners.

VCA (Vehicle Certification Agency): See section on 'Government bodies'.

Vehicle Licence (Road Tax): An annual duty paid by any company or individual who owns a vehicle. See 'Know your cab instrumentation and equipment' section on p.48.

VOSA (Vehicle and Operator Services Agency): See section on 'Government bodies'.

Vehicle Unit (VU): Also known as a Digital Tachograph. Also see 'Digital Tachographs' on p.17.

Wagon and drag: A combination of a rigid vehicle and drawbar trailer.

Walking floor: A specialist type of trailer that allows bulk loads that can't easily be palletised (such as paper or textiles) to be moved more easily. This system works by literally 'walking' the load out of the back of the trailer using a mechanism which moves the metal floorboards against one another in an alternating motion using hydraulic pistons below the floor.

Weekly rest period: The legally required period of time that a driver has to rest after no more than six consecutive working days. See section on 'Laws regarding driving hours' on p.14.

Weighbridge: A flat platform laid into the ground that weighs a vehicle and its load. In simple terms the equivalent of a giant set of scales.

Wheeled platforms: Small platforms with a wheel at each corner used to transport stacks of tubs or trays.

Wind deflectors: Plastic body modifications made to a vehicle to improve its aerodynamic properties. Wind deflectors can be found on the roof of the unit and at the sides and rear of the cab.

Working Time Regulations: See p.10.

Workshop: An on-site facility within most transport yards to provide repair support to the fleet.

Foreign dictionaries

ENGLISH	GERMAN	FRENCH	ITALIAN	DUTCH	SPANISH	POLISH	Polish/English pronunciation
a	ein/eine	un	un/uno/una	een	un/una	ten,ta,to	ej, a
abnormal load	Schwertransport/Sondertransport	convoi exceptionnel	carico anormale	abnormale lading	carga anómala	nieprawidłowy ładunek	abnormal lołd
accident	Unfall	accident	incidente	ongeval	accidente	wypadek	akcident
accommodation/bed and breakfast	Unterkunft/Bed&Breakfast	chambre d'hôte	alloggio	onderdak/pension	habitación	zakwaterowanie	akommodejszyn/bed and brejkfest
address	Adresse	adresse	indirizzo	adres	dirección	adres	adres
air pressure	Luftdruck	pression d'air	pneumatici	luchtdruk	presión atmosférica	ciśnienie atmosferyczne	er preszer
airport	Flughafen	aéroport	aeroporto	luchthaven	aeropuerto	lotnisko	erport
alternator	Generator	alternateur	alternatore	dynamo	alternador	prądnica, alternator	alternejte
ambulance	Krankenwagen	ambulance	ambulanza	ambulance	ambulancia	karetka	ambiulans
ample room for manoeuvring	ausreichend Platz zum Manövrieren	assez de place pour faire la manoeuvre	piazzola di manovra	ruim voldoende ruimte om te maneuvreren	sala amplia de maniobras	wygodny pokój	ampyl rum for manuvrin
and	und	et	e	en	y	i	and
animal	Tier	animal	animale	dier	animal	zwierzę	animal
arcade machine	Spielautomat	jeux électroniques	macchina da gioco	fruitmachine	videojuego	automaty do gier	arkejd maszin
area	Bereich/Gebiet/Fläche/Gegend/Stelle	aire	zona	gebied	zona	teren, obszar	arija
articulated vehicle/artic	Gelenkfahrzeug	tracteur trailer/semi-remorque	veicolo articolato	voertuig met aangekoppelde oplegger	camión articulado	samochód ciężarowy przegubowy	artikulejtet vejkal/artik
attack	Angriff	attaque	attacco	aanval	ataque	zaatakowany	atak
bank	Bank	banque	banca	bank	banco	bank	bank
banksman	Einweiser	banksman (une personne qui vous aide reverse votre camion)	manovratore	iemand die aanwijzigingen geeft bij het achteruitrijden	banksman (una persona que ayuda para invertir un camión)	pracownik banku	banksman
bar	Stange	barre	sbarra	stang	barra	bar	bar
barrier	Absperrung/hindernis	barrière	barriera	barrière	barrera	ogrodzenie, barierka	barier
battery	Batterie	batterie	batteria	accu	batería	bateria	bateri

bend	Kurve	virage	curva	bocht	curva	zakręt	bend
bollard	Poller	cônes de signalisation	colonnina	verkeerszuiltje	baliza	pacholek	bolard
bottom	Unterseite	fond	fondo	bodem	fondo	dno, spód	botum
box	Barton/Kasten/Schachtel	boîte	scatola	kist	caja	pudełko	boks
brake	Bremse	frein	freni	rem	freno	hamulec	brejk
break	Pause	break	pausa	pauze	pausa	przerwa	brejk
breakdown	Ausfall/Betriebsstörung	en panne	guasto	storing	avería	awaria, niepowodzenie	brejkdałn
breakfast	Frühstück	petit déjeuner	prima colazione	ontbijt	desayuno	śniadanie	brejkfest
British	britisch	Britannique	britannico/britannica	Brits	británico	brytyjski	Britisz
bureau de change/Euro's accepted	Geldwechsel/Euroannahme	bureau de change/accepte les euros	la ufficio di cambio/accetta eurodollaro	wisselkantoor/ook euro's	la oficina de cambio/aceptar eurodivisa	przyjmujemy Euro	biuro de sząsz/juroł's akseptet
bus	Bus	bus	autobus	bus	autobús	autobus	bas
business park	Gewerbegebiet	business center	parco commerciale	industrieterrein	parque industrial	teren przemysłowy, handlowy	busines pak
button	Knopf/taste	bouton	bottone	knop	botón	przycisk	baton
cab	Fahrerkabine	cabine / tracteur	cabina	cabine	cabina	szoferka	kab
café	Café	café	caffè	café	café	kawiarnia	kafe
cage	Käfig	cage	gabbia	kooi	jaula	klatka	kejdż
canopy	Baldachin	vache	cappa	overhuiving	toldo	zadaszenie, baldachim, sklepienie	kanapi
car	Auto	voiture	macchina	auto	coche	samochód	kar
caravan	Wohnwagen	caravane	roulotte	caravan	caravana	przyczepa mieszkalna	karavan
cashpoint machine	Geldautomat	distributeur d'argent	cassa automatica	pinautomaat	cajero automático	bankomat	kaszpoint maszin
caution	Vorsicht	attention	prudenza	let op	precaución	uwaga	koszion
central reservation	Mittelstreifen	terre-plein	banchina spartitraffico	middenberm	mediana	linia pomiędzy pasami ruchu	sentral reserwejszon
charge	Fracht, Gebühr, Anklage, Aufladung, Honorar, Kosten	tarif	tarriffa	tarief	tarifa	ładować, polecić, obciążać	czardż
city centre	Stadtmitte	centre ville	centro città	stadscentrum	centro de la ciudad	centrum miasta	sity senter
clean	reinigen	propre	pulire	reinigen	lavado	posprzątać	klin
clip	Klammer	pince	fermaglio	klem	grapa	spinacz, uchwyt, zacisk	klip
closed	geschlossen	fermé	chiuso/a	dicht	cerrado	zamknięty	klost
clothing	Kleidung	vêtements	vestiti	kleding	ropa	ubrania	klotin
coach	Reisebus	autocar	pullman	autobus	autobús	autobus	kolcz
coffee	Kaffee	café	caffè	koffie	café	kawa	kofi
congestion	Verkehrsstauung	circulation difficile	congestione	verkeersopstopping	congestión	przeciążenie	kondzesczion
congestion charge	City-maut	péage pour rentrer dans le centre-ville de Londres	tariffa per congestione a Londra	verkeerstarief in centrum van Londen	tarifa por congestión en Londres	opłata od każdego samochodu do zapłacenia w centralnym Londynie	kondzesczion czardż

ENGLISH	GERMAN	FRENCH	ITALIAN	DUTCH	SPANISH	POLISH	Polish/English pronounciation
couple up	ankoppeln	accrocher	agganciare/attaccare	aankoppelen	acoplar	połączyć, podłączyć	kopyl ap
crossing	Fußgängerstreifen	passage piétons	passaggio pedonale	oversteekplaats	paso de peatones	pasy	krosin
crossroads	Kreuzung	carrefour	incrocio	kruising	cruce	krzyżowanie	krosrolds
curtain sided trailer	Anhänger mit plane	remorque a rideaux	rimorchio con lati a tenda	met zeildoek afgesloten aanhanger	camión con cortina	firanka, zasłona	kurtejn sajdet czrejler
customs	Zoll	douane	dogana	douane	aduana	celnik	kustoms
cycle	Fahrrad	vélo/bicyclette	bicicletta	fiets	bicicleta	jechać na rowerze	cajkl
danger	Gefahr	danger	pericolo	gevaar	peligro	niebezpieczeństwo	dendzer
dashboard	Armaturenbrett	tableau de bord	cruscotto	dashboard	salpicadero	błotnik	daszbord
dealership	Händler	concessionnaire	concessionario	dealerbedrijf	representación	sprzedawca samochodów i części	dilerszip
delay	Verzögerung	délai	ritardo	vertraging	demora	opóźniać, wstrzymywać	dilej
diagnostic system	Diagnosesystem	système diagnostic	sistemi diagnostico	diagnostisch systeem	sistema diagnóstico	przegląd, system diagnostyczny w ciężarowce	dajagnostik system
diesel	Diesel	diesel	gasolio	diesel	gasoil	diesel	disel
dispatch department	Versandabteilung	département pour les envois	reparto de spedizione	verzendafdeling	departamento de expedición	oddział wysyłek	dispacz dipartment
diversion	Umleitung	déviation	deviazione	omleiding	desviación	odwrócenie, zmiana kierunku	dajverszion
document	Dokument	document	documenti	document	documento	dokument	dokjument
door	Tür	porte	porta	deur	puerta	drzwi	dor
double yellow lines	durchgezogene gelbe fahrbahnmarkierung	double ligne jaune (route non stop)	doppia giallo linea (sosta vietata)	dubbele gele streep, niet parkeren	doble línea amarilla (prohibido aparcar/estacionarse)	podwójna żółta linia na której nie można parkować	dabyl jelol lajns
down	abwärts/nach unten	en bas	giu'	omlaag	abajo	dół	dałn
driver	Fahrer	conducteur	camionista	chauffeur	camionero/a	kierowca	drajver
drivers washroom	Sanitärräume für fahrer	WC pour camionneurs	bagno per camionista	wasruimte voor chauffeurs	baño para conductor/a	łazienka dla kierowców	drajvers łoszrum
driving licence	Fahrervorschriften	permis de conduire	patente	rijbewijs	permiso de conducir	prawo jazdy	drajvin lisens
driving regulations	Führerschein	règlements de conduite	regolamento per camionista	verkeersregels	normas de conducción	kodeks pracy dla kierowców	drajvin regiulejszyn
dual carriageway	zweispurige Straße	deux voies	doppia corsia	tweebaansweg	carretera de doble sentido	droga dwukierunkowa	dulal kariadżtej
Dutch		néerlandais		Nederlands			
east	Ost/Osten	est	est	het oosten	este	wschód	ist
engine	Motor	moteur	motore	motor	motor	silnik	endzin
entertainment	Unterhaltung	spectacle	intrattenimento	amusement	diversión	rozrywka, przedstawienie	entetejnment
entrance	Auffahrt/Eingang	entrée	entrata	ingang	entrada	wejście	entrens
exit	Ausfahrt/Ausgang	sortie	uscita	uitgang	salida	wyjście	eksit

English	German	French	Italian	Dutch	Spanish	Polish	Pronunciation
factory	Fabrik	usine	fabbrica	fabbriek	fabrica	fabryka	faktori
fax/photocopy facility	Fax-/Kopiermöglichkeit	fax / photocopie	servizio copisteria	Fax/fotokopieermachine	instalación telefax/fotocopiadora	fax, kserokopia	faks/fotokopi fesiliti
female	Frau	femelle	femmina	vrouw	femenino	kobieta	fimejl
ferry	Fähre	ferry	traghetto	veerdienst	trasbordador	przeprawiać	feri
fifth wheel	Sattelkupplung	sellette d'attelage	piattaforma d'inesto	koppelschotel	rueda de repuesto	siodło	fift til
fire service	Feuerwehr	pompier	vigili del fuoco	brandweer	bomberos	straż pożarna	fajer servis
flood	Flut/Überflutung	inonder	inondazione	overstroming	inundación	powódź	flod
floor	Stockwerk	sol	pavimento	vloer	suelo	podłoga	flor
fog	Nebel	brouillard	nebbia	mist	niebla	mgła	fog
food	Essen	nourriture	cibo	voedsel	comida	żywność	fud
foot (ft)	Fuß (ft)	pied (mesure Britannique)	piede (Britanico misure)	Britse voet (0,3048 m)	pie (Británico medida)	stopa	fut (ft)
for	für	pour	per	voor	para/por	za, dla	for
fork lift truck	Gabelstapler	chariot élévateur	carrello elevatore	vorkheftruck	carretilla elevadora	wózek widłowy	fork lift czrak
France		France					
free	kostenlos	libre	gratis	gratis	gratuito/gratis	bezpłatny	fri
French		Français					
fuel bunker	Treibstofftank	station service	pompa di gasolio automatica	branstofreservoir	fuel búnker	miejsce tankowania paliwa	fuel bankier
fuse	Sicherung	fusible	fusibile	zekering	fusible	zapalnik, bezpiecznik	fiuse
fusebox	Sicherungskasten	boîte à fusibles	scatola dei fusibili	zekeringdoos	caja de fusibles	skrzynka bezpiecznikowa	fiuseboks
garage	Autowerkstatt/Garage	garage	officina	garage	garage	garaż	garedz
gearbox	Getriebe	boîte de vitesses	scatola del cambio	versnellingsbak	caja de cambios	skrzynia biegów	girboks
gentlemen	Herren	homme	signori/uomini	heren	caballeros	pan	dzentlemen
german	deutsch	allemand					
Germany	Deutschland	Allemagne					
give way (yield)	Vorfahrt gewähren	céder le passage	dare la precedenza	voorrang verlenen	ceder el paso	ustąp pierszeństwa	giv lej/jild
go	gehen/fahren	aller	avanti	gaan	ir	iść, potrząść się, jechać	gol
goodbye	Auf Wiedersehen	au revoir	arrivederci	tot ziens	adiós	do wiedzenia, żegnajcie	gudbaj
goods inward	Wareneingang	réception de marchandises	articoli in entrata	goederen in	entrada de mercancías	przyjęcie towaru	guds inlord
Great Britain	Großbritannien	grande Bretagne	Gran Bretagna	Groot-Brittannië	Gran Bretaña	Wielka Brytania	Grejt Brityn
gymnasium/gym	Fitnessstudio	gym	la palestra	gymnastieklokaal	gimnasio	szkoła średnia, gimnazjum	dzimnasium/dzim
hard shoulder	Standstreifen	accotement/bande d'arrêt d'urgence	corsia di emergenza	vluchtstrook	andén	pobocze	hard szolder
hazardous goods	Gefahrengüter	matières dangereuses	oggetti pericolosi	gevaarlijke goederen	mercancías peligrosas	substancje niebezpieczne	hazardos guds
he	er	lui	lui	hij	él	on	hi
healthy food menu	gesundes Essen	nourriture saine	menu di cibi sani	gezond menu	menú orgánico	zdrowa żywność	helti fud meniu
heater	Heizer	chauffage	riscaldamento	verwarming	calentador	grzejnik, podgrzewacz, grzałka	hiter
height	Höhe	hauteur	altezza	lengte	altura	wysokość	hajt

ENGLISH	GERMAN	FRENCH	ITALIAN	DUTCH	SPANISH	POLISH	Polish/English pronunciation
hello	hallo	bonjour	ciao	hallo	hola	cześć	hello
help!	Hilfe!	au secours	aiuto!	help!	¡ayuda!	pomocy	help!
HGV/LGV (heavy/large goods vehicle)	LKW	poids lourd	veicolo per transporti pesanti	vrachtwagen	Vehiculo pesado	ciężarówka, naczepa	hevi/lardz guds vejkal
high winds	starker Wind	vent fort	grande vento	harde wind	vientos fuertes	silne wiatry	haj łinds
hill	Hügel	coline	collina	heuvel	colina	wzgórze, górka	hil
Holland		pays bas		Nederland			
hospital	Krankenhaus	hôpital	hospital	ziekenhuis	hospital	szpital	hospital
hotel	Hotel	hôtel	albergo	hotel	hotel	hotel	hotel
how	wie	comment	come	hoe	cómo	jak?	hał
hungry	hungrig	faim	fame	honger	hambriento	głodny	hangri
I	ich	je	io	ik	yo	ja?	aj
ice	Eis	verglas	ghiaccio	ijs	hielo	ja	ajs
identification	Identifikation	identification	documento d'identità	identificatie	identificación	identyfikacja, rozpoznanie, stwierdzenie tożsamości	ajdentifikejszyn
inch (")	Zoll (")	pouce (mesure Britannique)	pollice (Britànico misure)	Engelse duim (2,54 cm)	pulgada (Británico medida)	cal (=2,54 cm)	incz
indicator	Kontrollleuchte	clignotant	indicatore di direzione	richtingaanwijzer	indicador	żółte światło sygnalizacyjne w samochodzie	indikejtor
industrial estate	Industriegebiet	zone industrielle	zona industriale	industrieterrein	zona industrial	teren przemysłowy, magazyny	industrial estejt
information	Information	information	informazioni	informatie	información	informacja	informejszyn
inn	Gasthof	auberge	locanda	herberg	hostal	zajazd, gospoda	in
international newspapers	internationale Zeitungen	journal international	giornale internazionale	buitenlandse kranten	diarios internacionales	gazety międzynarodowe	internaszional niuspejpers
internet	Internet	accès internet	internet	internet	Internet	internet	internet
Italian		italien	italiano/italiana				
Italy		Italie	Italia				
jacuzzi	Whirlpool	jacuzzi	jacuzzi	jacuzzi	jacuzzi	jacuzzi	dżakuzi
junction/exit	Anschlussstelle/Ausfahrt	carrefour / sortie	incrocio/uscire	knooppunt/afslag	cruce/salida	zjazd z drogi	dżankszyn/eksit
keys	Schlüssel	clefs	chiavi	sleutels	llaves	klucze	kijs
kilometre	Kilometer	kilomètre	chilometro	kilometer	kilómetro	kilometr	kilometr
ladies	Damen	femmes	signore/donne	dames	señoras	panie	lejdis
laundry/launderette	Waschsalon	blanchisserie	lavanderia	wasserij/wasserette	lavandería	pralnia	londri/londrete
left	links	gauche	sinistra	links	izquierda	lewo	left
legs	Anhängerständer	jambes	gambe	benen	piernas	nogi, na których stoi naczepa	legs

level crossing	Bahnübergang	passage a niveau	passaggio a livello	gelijkvloerse overweg	paso a nivel	skrzyżowanie kolei z drogą	level krosin
lever	Hebel	levier	leva	hendel	palanca	dźwignia, lewar	liver
lights	Lichter/Leuchten	lumières	luci	lichten	luces	światła	lajts
loading bay	Ladebucht	quai	piazzola di carico	laadruimte	área de carga y descarga	miejsce załadunku	loldin bej
long stay parking	Dauerparkplatz	parking longue durée	parcheggio a lungo termine	lang parkeren	aparcamiento prolongado	parking długiego postoju	long stej parkin
lorry	Lastwagen	camion	camion	vrachtwagen	camión	ciężarówka	lori
lorry park	LKW-Raststätte	parking pour camion	parcheggio per camion	voorzieningen voor chauffeurs	aparcamiento para camiones	parking dla ciężarówek z udogodnieniami dla kierowców	lori park
low bridge	niedrige Brücke	hauteur limitée	ponte basso	lage brug	puente bajo	niski most	lol bridż
lower	Senken/Herablassen/Herabsetzen	plus bas	più basso	laten zakken	bajar	opuszczać, zniżać, zmniejszać	loler
Madam	Frau	Madame	Signora	Mevrouw	Señora	pani	Madam
male	Mann	male	maschio	man	hombre	mężczyzna	mejl
maximum	Maximum	maximum	massimo	maximum	máximo	największy, maksymalny	maksimum
meal voucher	Essensgutschein	ticket restaurant	buono pasto	maaltijdbon	vale de comida	kupon rabatowy na posiłek	mil volczer
mechanic	Mechaniker	mécanique	meccanico	monteur	mecánico	mechanik	mechanik
meter	Parkuhr	compteur	parchimetro	meter	parquímetro	miernik	miter
MGW (maximum gross weight)	MBG (maximales Bruttogewicht)	poids maximum	peso massimo lordo	maximum brutogewicht	Peso total máximo	waga maksymalna	maksimum gros wejt
mile (m)	Meile	mile (mesure Britannique)	miglio (Britanico misure)	mijl (1,60934 km)	milla (Británico medida)	mila (=1609,31 m)	majel
miles per hour (MPH)	Meilen pro Stunde (MPH)	mile a l'heure (mesure Britannique)	miglia all'ora (Britanico misure)	mijl per uur (1,60934 km/u)	millas por hora (Británico medida)	wskaźnik mil na godzinę	majels per aler
minimum	Minimum	minimum	minimo	minimum	mínimo	najmniejszy	minimum
mirror	Spiegel	miroir	specchio	spiegel	espejo	lustro	miror
Miss	Frau	Mademoiselle	Signorina	Mejufrouw	Señorita	panienka	Mys
Mister	Herr	Monsieur	Signor	Mijnheer	Señor	pan	Myster
mobile phone	Mobiltelefon	téléphone portable	telefono cellulare	mobiele telefoon	teléfono móvil	telefon komórkowy	mobajl fohn
money	Geld	argent	soldi	geld	dinero	pieniądze	mani
MoT plate/certificate	TÜV-Plakette	contrôle technique	certificato di revisione	Bewijs van verplichte jaarlijkse keuring	inspección placa/certificado	potwierdzenie sprawności pojazdu (tablica na naczepie i przedniej szybie)	em ot ti plejt,sertifikat
motorcycle	Motorrad	moto	motocicletta	motorfiets	motocicleta	motocykl	motocajkyl
motorway	Autobahn	autoroute	autostrada	snelweg	autopista	autostrada	motortej
nearby	in der Nähe	près	vicino	dichtbij	cercano	pobliski	nirbaj
no	nein	non	no/non	nee	no	nie	noł
no entry	keine Einfahrt	sens interdit / défense d'entrer	senso vietato	verboden toegang	prohibido el paso	brak wjazdu	noł enczri
north	Nord/Norden	nord	nord	het noorden	norte	północ	nort
number plate	Kennzeichen	plaque d'immatriculation	targa	nummerbord	placa de matrícula	tablica rejestracyjna	nambe plejt

ENGLISH	GERMAN	FRENCH	ITALIAN	DUTCH	SPANISH	POLISH	Polish/English pronunciation
oil	Öl	huile	olio	olie	aceite	olej (oil change - zmiana oleju)	ojl
okay	okay	ok	ok	in orde	OK	w porządku	okkej
on site	vor Ort	sur le site	su luogo	op het terrein	en su sitio	na miejscu, na terenie (site-teren,położenie,okolica)	on sajt
one	eins/eine/einen	un	uno/una	een	un/uno/una	jeden	lan
one way street	Einbahnstraße	sens unique	senso unico	straat met eenrichtingsverkeer	calle de sentido unico	ulica jednokierunkowa	lan wej strit
open	öffnen	ouvert	aperto/a	open	abierto	otwarte	olpen
opening times	Öffnungszeiten	heures d'ouverture	orario di apertura	openingstijden	hora de abertura	godziny otwarcia	olpenin tajms
over	über	au-dessus	sopra	over	encima	nad, po, w	olver
overhead	Oberleitungen	au-dessus	sospeso in aria	bovenhoofds	arriba	na górze	olverhed
overnight	über nacht	pour la nuit	durante la notte	nachtelijk	durante la noche	całonocny	olvernajt
pain	Schmerzen	douleur	dolore	pijn	dolor	ból	pejn
pallet	Palette	palette	paletta	pallet	palet	paleta	palet
pallet truck	Gabelstapler	chariot elevateur (Equiptment a utilisé pour déplacer de palettes)	carrello elevatore - muletto	pallettruck	carretilla (equiptment para mover paleta)	paleciak	palet czrak
pardon?	Wie bitte?	pardon?	scusa	pardon?	¿cómo?	słucham?	pardon?
parking space	Parkplatz	place de parking	posto per la macchina	Parkeerplaats	sitio para aparcar	miejce parkingowe	parkin spejs
passport	Pass	passeport	passaporto	paspoort	pasaporte	paszport	pasport
pavement	Bürgersteig	trottoir	marciapiede	trottoir	acera	nawiezchnia drogi	pejwment
pedestrian	Fußgänger	piéton	pedoni	voetganger	peatón	pieszy	pedesczian
petrol station	Tankstelle	station d'essence	stazione di servizio	benzinestation	estación de servicio	stacja benzynowa	peczrol stejszyn
please	bitte	s'il vous plait	per favore	a.u.b.	por favor	proszę	plise
Poland		Pologne				Polska	Poland
police	Polizei	police	polizia	politie	policía	policja	polis
Polish		polonais				polski	polis
port/harbour	Hafen	port	porto	haven	puerto	port	port/harbor
post office	Postamt	bureau de poste	ufficio postale	postkantoor	correos	poczta	post ofis
priority to the right	rechts vor links	priorité à droite	dare la precedenza adestra	rechts gaat voor	dar la prioridad a la derecha	pierszeństwo w prawo	priojoriti tu de rajt
problem	Problem	problème	problema	probleem	problema	problem	problem
pub	Pub	pub	birreria	café	pub	pub	pab
pull	ziehen	tirer	tirare	trekken	tirar	pociągnąć	pul
pump	Pumpe	pompe	pompa	pomp	bomba	pompka	pamp

English	German	French	Italian	Dutch	Spanish	Polish	Pronunciation
puncture	Reifenpanne	crever, crevaison	gomma forata	lekke band	pinchazo	złapać gumę	pankczer
push	drücken/schieben	pousser	spingere	duwen	empujar	pchać	pusz
quarry	Steinbruch	carrière	cava	steengroeve	cantera	kopalnia, kamieniołom	klari
queue	Schlange	file	fila	rij	cola	kolejka	kju
quiet	ruhig	calme/tranquille	silenzioso	stil	silencioso	cisza, spokój	klajet
radio	Radio	radio	radio	radio	radio	radio	rejdiol
rain	Regen	pluie	pioggia	regen	lluvia	deszcz	rejn
raise	heben	soulever	sollevare	heffen	levantar	podnosić, ustawiać	rajz
red diesel	Roter Diesel/Heizöl	gas oil rouge (Diesel pour les véhicules agricoles)	gasolio rosso (gasolio per veicoli agrari)	rode diesel	gasoil teñido (gasóleo por agricultura vehiculo)	paliwo do ciężarówek nieopodatkowane	red disel
red route	absolutes Halteverbot	Route rouge (route non stop)	itinerario rosso (divieto di sosta)	route met stopverbod	rojo ruta (prohibido aparcar/estacionarse)	miejsce, na którym wzbronione jest zatrzymywanie pod grozbą wysokiej kary pieniężnej)	red rut
refrigerated goods/trailer	Kühlwaren/Anhänger	camion frigorifique	camion frigo	gekoelde goederen/aanhanger	mercancías refrigeradas/remolque	towary mrożone, przyczepa_ chłodnia	refridzerated guds/czrejler
repair	reparieren	réparation	riparazioni	repareren	reparación	naprawiać	riper
restaurant	Restaurant	restaurant	ristorante	restaurant	restaurante	restauracja	restarant
restriction	Einschränkung	restriction	limitazione	beperkende bepaling	limitado	ograniczenie	restrikszion
reverse	Umdrehen/Wenden/Rückwärtsgang einlegen	marche arrière	inverso	achteruitrijden	inverso	odwracać	riverse
right	rechts	droite	destra	rechts	derecha	prawo	rajt
rigid and trailer/wagon and drag	Zugmaschine und Anhänger	train routier	camion e rimorchio	vrachtwagen met aanhanger	camión y remolque	ciężarówka	ridżit and czrejler/laon and dzrag
ring road	Umgehungsstraße	périphérique	cironvalazione	ringweg	circunvalación	obwodnica	ring rold
road	Straße	route	strada	weg	carretera	droga	rold
roadworks	Bauarbeiten	travaux	lavori in corso	wegwerkzaamheden	obras	robory drogowe	roldforks
room	Zimmer	chambre	camera	kamer	alojamiento	pokój	rum
roundabout/island	Kreisverkehr/Verkehrsinsel	rond point	rotatoria	rotonde	glorieta	rondo	randabaut/ajlend
route	Route	itinéraire	itinerario	route	ruta	trasa	rut
sandwich	Sandwich	sandwich	sandwich	sandwich	bocadillo	kanapka	santicz
sauna	Sauna	sauna	sauna	sauna	sauna	sauna	sona
seal	Verriegelung	sceau	sigillo	zegel	sellar	pląba, pieczęć	sil
seat	Sitz	chaise	posto	stoel	asiento	siedzenie, miejsce	sit
seat belt	Sicherheitsgurt	ceinture de sécurité	cinture di sicurezza	veiligheidsgordel	cinturón de seguridad	pas bezpieczeństwa	sit belt
secure	sicher	ferme	sicuro	vast	firme	zabezpieczony, zamknięty	sekiur
security guard	Sicherheitswachmann	gardien	guardia giurata	bewaker	guardia de seguridad	strażnik	sekiuriti gard
service leads/suzies	Anschlussleitungen	accouplement électrique	attacci dell'aria e corrente	verbindingskabels	parejas eléctricas	kable pomiędzy kabiną ciężarówki a naczepą	servis lids/suzis

Polish/English pronounciation

ENGLISH	GERMAN	FRENCH	ITALIAN	DUTCH	SPANISH	POLISH	Polish/English pronounciation
services	Tank- und Raststätten	station service	area di servizio	stopplaats met winkels aan de snelweg	servicios	serwis na autostradzie (jedzenie,toalety,parking)	servysys
she	sie	elle	lei	zij	ella	ona	szi
shop	Laden	boutique	negozio	winkel	tienda	sklep	szop
shopping centre/mall	Einkaufszentrum	galerie marchande	centro commerciale	Winkelcentrum	centro comercial	centrum handlowe	szopin center/mall
short term parking	Kurzparkplatz	parking courte durée	parcheggio a orario limitato	kort parkeren	aparcamiento carga y descarga	parking krótkiego postoju	szort term parkin
shower	Dusche	douche	doccia	douche	ducha	prysznic	szałer
shrink wrap	Schrumpffolienverpackung	filmer	incelofanare	krimpverpakking	empaquetar en envase termoretráctil	folia	szrink rap
shunter vehicle	Rangierfahrzeuge	véhicule pour détourner de remorque	motrice rimorchio	rangeerwagen	vehículo para maniobras	samochód używany do przestawiania naczep	syanter wejkal
single carriageway	einspurige Straße	voie simple	solo carreggiata	eenbaansweg	carretera de un solo sentido	pas ruchu	singyl karydżtej
sink	Handwaschbecken	lavabo	lavandino	gootsteen	fregadero	umywalka	synk
site	Standort	site	luogo	terrein	ubicación	miejsce	sajt
slow	langsam	lentement	lento/rallentare	langzaam	decelerar	powoli	slof
snack bar	Imbiss	snack bar	snack bar	snackbar	cafetería	bar	snack bar
snow	Schnee	neige	neve	sneeuw	nieve	śnieg	snoł
south	Süd/Süden	sud	sud	het zuiden	sur	południe	sałt
Spain		Espagne			España		
Spanish		espagnol			Español		
speed camera	Blitzgerät	radar	autovelox	snelheidscamera	radar	aparat robiący zdjęcia samochodom jadącym z niedozwoloną prędkością	spid kamra
speed limit	Geschwindigkeitsbegrenzung	limitation de vitesse	limite di velocità	maximumsnelheid	límite de velocidad	ograniczenie prędkości	spid lymit
spray	Spritzwasser	éclaboussure	spray	stuivend water	spray	woda chlapiąca spod kół samochodu	sprej
standpipe	Standrohr	fontaine	rubinetto pubblico	standpijp	tubo vertical	postój z wodą	standpajp
stay in lane	kein Fahrbahnwechsel	rester dans sa voie	tenere la corsia	baan aanhouden	quedarse en el camino	nie zmieniaj pasu ruchu	staj in lejn
steering wheel	Lenkrad	volant	volante	stuur	volante	kierownica	stiring fil
stop	anhalten	stop	alt	stop	alto	stop	stop
straight ahead	geradeaus	tout droit	sempre dritto	rechtdoor	siga recto	prosto	strajt ehed
strap	Riemen	sangle	tracolla	riem	correa	pasek	strap
supermarket	Supermarkt	supermarché	supermercato	supermarkt	supermercado	supermarket	siupermarket
suspension	Aufhängung	suspension	sospensione	vering	suspensión	wstrzymanie, zawieszenie	sespenszion

English	German	French	Italian	Dutch	Spanish	Polish	Phonetic
tacho disk	Tacho disk	tachydisque	tachidisk	tacho disk	disco diagrama de tacógrafo	tarcza	takodisk/takograf czart
tachograph	Fahrtenschreiber	tachygraphe	tachigrafo	tachograaf	tacógrafo	tachograf	takograf
tail lift	Hebebühne	monte charge	pedana solevatore	autolaadklep	plataforma elevadora	winda na końcu naczepy	tejl lift
take-away	Imbiss zum Mitnehmen	à emporter	piatti pronti	afhaalmaaltijd	comida para llevar	na wynos	tejk-e tej
tank	Tank	réservoir	serbatoio	tank	depósito	zbiornik	tank
tank cleaning facilities	Tankreinigungsanlage	lavage pour camion-citerne	lavaggio per camion cisterna	reiniger voor in tanks	lavado para camión cisterna	myjnia dla cystern i zbiorników (od wewnątrz)	tank klinin fesilites
tea	Tee	thé	tè	thee	té	herbata	ti
telephone	Telefon	téléphone	telefono	telefoon	teléfono	telefon	telefoln
thank you	Danke	merci	grazie	dank u	gracias	dziękuję	tank ju
the	der/die/das	le, la	la/lo/il/le	de/het	los/las/lo	ten, ta, to	de
theft	Diebstahl	vol	furto	diefstal	robo	kradzież	teft
they	sie	ils, elles	loro	zij	ellos/ellas	oni	tej
thirsty	durstig	soif	assetato/aver sete	dorst	sediento	spragniony, chcący się napić	tersti
ticket	Ticket	ticket	biglietto	kaartje	billete	bilet	tiket
tired	müde	fatigué	stanco	moe	cansado	zmęczony	tajerd
t-junction	T-Kreuzung	intersection	incrocio a T	T-kruising	cruce en T	skrzyżowanie w kształcie litery T	ti-dżankszon
today	heute	aujourd'hui	oggi	vandaag	hoy	dzisiaj	tudej
toilet	Toilette	toilette	toilette	toilet	sanitario/aseos/servicios	toaleta	toilet
toll	Maut/Gebühr/Zoll	péage	pedaggio	tol	peaje	opłata, cło	toll
tomorrow	morgen	demain	domani	morgen	mañana	jutro	tumarol
tonnes/tons (British measurement)	Tonnen	tonnes/tons (mesure Britannique)	tonnellata/tonnellata (Britanico misure)	Engelse ton (1016 kg)	tonelada/toneladas (medida británica)	tona	tons
top	Oberseite/Spitze	dessus	cima	bovenkant	cima	uzupełnić, załadować	top
town	Stadt	ville	città	stad	ciudad	miasto	tałn
tractor unit	Sattelschlepper	tracteur	motrice	tractor	tractor	ciągnik siodłowy, ciągnik do naczepy	czraktor junit
traffic lights	Ampel	feux	semaforo	stoplichten	semáforo	światła sygnalizacyjne	czrafik lajts
trailer	Anhänger	remorque	rimorchio	aanhanger	remolque	naczepa	czrejler
train	Zug	train	treno	trein	tren	pociąg	czrejn
tram	Straßenbahn	tram	tram	tram	tranvía	tramwaj	tram
transport department	Transportministerium	département de transport	reparto di trasporto	transportafdeling	sección de transporte	wydział transportu	czransport dipartment
truck	Lastwagen	camion	camion	vrachtwagen	camión	samochód ciężarowy	czrak
truckers accessories	Lastwagenzubehör	accessoires pour les camionneurs	accessorio per camionista	accessoires voor vrachtwagens en chauffeurs	accesorios para camioneros	akcesoria samochodowe	czrakers aksesoris
truckstop	LKW-Raststätte	parking pour camions	area di servizio per camion	chauffeurscafé	parada para camioneros	miejsce postoju z udogodnieniami dla kierowców	czrakstop
truckwash	LKW-Waschanlage	station lavage pour camions	lavaggio per camion	wasplaats voor vrachtwagens	lavado de camiones	myjnia dla ciężarówek	czraktosz

Polish/English pronunciation

ENGLISH	GERMAN	FRENCH	ITALIAN	DUTCH	SPANISH	POLISH	Polish/English pronunciation
tunnel	Tunnel	tunnel	tunnel	tunnel	túnel	tunel	tanel
turn	Kurve	tourne	girare	draai	girar	obracać	tern
tyre	Reifen	pneu	gomma	band	neumáticos	opona	tajer
under	unter	dessous	sotto	onder	debajo	pod	ander
up	auf	vers le haut	su	op	arriba	nad	ap
van	Transporter	camionnette	furgone	bestelwagen	furgoneta	van, furgonetka	van
vehicle and operator services agency (VOSA)	VOSA (britischer TÜV)	VOSA (Le véhicule de gouvernement vérifie l'agence)	polizia stradale	controlebureau voor voertuigen	VOSA (Agencia de vehículo de gobierno)	służby kontroli pojazdów	vekjal and operejtor servisys ajdżensi
wait	warten	attendre	aspettare	wachten	espera	czekać	łejt
warehouse	Lager	entrepôt	magazzino	magazijn	almacén	magazyn	łerhałs
water	Wasser	eau	acqua	water	agua	woda	łoter
waybill	Wiegekarte	lettre de voiture	scontrino bilancia	vrachtbrief	conocimiento de embarque	kwit potwierdzający wagę pojazdu	wejbil
we	wir	nous	noi	wij	nosotros/as	my	łi
weak bridge	schwache Brücke	pont faible	ponte debole	zwakke brug	puente débil	słaby most, ograniczenie wjazdu ciężkim naczepom	łik bridż
weighbridge	Brückenwaage	pont-bascule	bascula	weegbrug	puente basculante	waga samochodowa	wejbridż
west	West/Westen	ouest	ovest	het westen	oeste	zachód	łest
wheel	Rad	roue	la ruota	wiel	rueda	koło	łil
when	wann	quand	quando	wanneer	cuándo	kiedy?	łen
where	wohin	où	dove	waar	dónde	gdzie?	łer
why	warum	pourquoi	perché	waarom	por qué	dlaczego?	łaj
wide load	Schwertransport	convoi exceptionnel	carico largo	brede lading	carga ancha	duży załadunek	łajd lołd
windscreen	Windschutzscheibe	pare-brise	parabrezza	voorruit	parabrisas	przednia szyba	łindskrin
windscreen wipers	Scheibenwischer	essuie-glace	tergicristallo	ruitenwissers	limpiaparabrisas	wycieraczki	łindskrinłajpez
with	mit	avec	con	met	con	z	łit
working	funktioniert	travail	funziona	werkt	operacional	działać, pracować	łorkin
workshop	Werkstatt	atelier	laboratorio	werkplaats	taller	warsztat	łorkszop
yard	Hof	dépôt/chantier	depósito	depot	depósito	miejsce postoju	jard
yard (yd)	Yard	yard (mesure Britannique)	iarda (Britanico misure)	0,914 meter	yarda (Británico medida)	jard (=0,914 m)	jard
yard marshal	Hofaufsicht	chef de chantier	ufficiale per deposito	rangeermeester	Oficial del depósito	osoba kierująca ruchem ciężarówek (nie jest to policjant)	jard marszal
yes	ja	oui	sì	ja	sí	tak	jes
you	du/Sie	vous	tu	u	tú	nie	ju

ENGLISH PHRASE	GERMAN PHRASE	FRENCH PHRASE	ITALIAN PHRASE	DUTCH PHRASE	SPANISH PHRASE	POLISH PHRASE	POLISH/ENGLISH PRONOUCIATION
Where is ?	Wo ist ?	où est ?	dov'è ?	Waar is ?	¿Dónde está ?	Gdzie jest?	ter is ?
I would like	Ich möchte	je voudrais	Vorrei	Ik wil graag	Quiero	Chciałbym… Poprosze…	Aj łud lajk
Do you have ?	Haben Sie ?	avez-vous ?	Ha ?	Heeft u ?	¿Tiene ?	Czy macie…?	Du ju hev ?
I understand	Ich verstehe	je comprends	Capisco	Ik begrijp het	Entiendo	Zrozumiałem	Aj anderstand
I do not understand	Ich verstehe nicht	je ne comprends pas	Non capisco	Ik begrijp het niet	No entiendo	Nie zrozumiałem	Aj du not anderstand
Do you speak ?	Sprechen Sie ?	parlez vous ?	Parli ?	Spreekt u ?	¿Habla usted ?	Czy mówisz po…?	Du ju spik ?
I do not know	Ich weiß nicht	je ne sais pas	Non lo so	Ik weet het niet	No sé	Nie wiem	Aj du not not
Excuse me	Entschuldigen Sie	excuse-moi	Mi scusi	Pardon	Oiga, por favor	Przepraszam	Ekskjus mi
Excuse me	Entschuldigung	Pardon	Mi dispiace	Pardon	Perdone	" "	" "
I do not speak English	Ich spreche kein Englisch	je ne parle pas anglais	Non parli inglese	Ik spreek geen Engels	No hablo inglés	Nie mówię po angielsku	Aj du not spik inglisz
There has been an accident	Es gab einen Unfall	il y a un accident	Ce stato un incidente	Er is een ongeluk gebeurd	Ha habido un accidente	Zdążył się wypadek	Ter has bin an aksident
I have	Ich habe	j'ai	Ho questo	Ik heb	Tengo	Mam….	Aj hev
Can you help me?	Können Sie mir helfen?	pouvez-vous m'aider?	Può aiutarmi?	Kunt u mij helpen?	¿Me puede ayudar?	Czy mógłbyś/mogłabyś mi pomóc?	Ken ju help mi?
I have a problem with	Ich habe ein Problem mit	j'ai un problème avec	Ho un problema con	Ik heb een probleem met	Tengo el problema con	Mam problem z….	Aj hev a problem wit
What is it?	Was ist es?	qu'est-ce que c'est?	Che cosa è questo?	Wat is het?	¿Qué es?	Co to jest?	łot is it?
How much is it?	Wie viel kostet es?	combien cela coûte?	Quanto costa ?	Hoeveel is het?	¿Cuánto es?	Ile to kosztuje? Ile place?	hał macz is it?
I am	Ich bin	je suis	Sono	Ik ben	Estoy/soy	Jestem/nazywam się…	Aj em
Can you give me a receipt?	Können Sie mir eine Quittung geben?	pouvez vous me donner un reçu?	Può darmi una ricevuta ?	Kunt u mij een bonnetje geven?	¿Puede darme un recibo, por favor?	Paragon poproszę	Ken ju giv mi a resit?
The bill please	Die Rechnung bitte	l'addition s'il vous plait	Il conto, per favore	De rekening a.u.b.	La cuenta, por favor	Rachunek poproszę	Te bil plise

SITE
REVIEWS

A5 Service Station, Wallsall

Lime Lane, Pelsall, Walsall
West Midlands WS3 5AR
T 01543 373444

ON THE B4154 If Heading from Bloxwich on the A4124, turn left onto the B4154 and A5 Service Station is 1 mile along on the left. If heading from Brownhills, turn left onto the B4154 and it's 1 mile along on your right.

CREDIT/DEBIT CARDS

FUEL CARDS (see key on page 6)
① ② ㊷

TRUCK FACILITIES
Truck washing facilities

DRIVER FACILITIES
Truckers' accessories

All on-site facilities 06:00-21:30 Mon-Fri, 07:00-17:00 Sat, 09:00-17:00 Sun.　　**F001**

Adastra Service Station, Market Drayton

Chester Road, Ternhill, Market Drayton
Shropshire TF9 3QD
T 01630 638729

ON THE A41 Adastra is close to Market Drayton on the A41 Wolverhampton to Whitchurch road and is on the right-hand side just past the junction with the A53 if heading south.

CREDIT/DEBIT CARDS

FUEL CARDS (see key on page 6)
① ② ③ ④ ⑪ ⑭

DRIVER FACILITIES
Truckers' accessories
Truck dealership nearby

SITE COMMENTS/INFORMATION
Friendly staff

All on-site Facilities 07:00-22:00 Mon-Sun.　　**F002**

Ardleigh South Services, Colchester

Harwich Road, Ardleigh, Colchester
Essex CO7 7SL
T 01206 231174

ON THE A120 Ardleigh is on the A120 Harwich to Colchester road, 3 miles before the interchange with the A12 and on the left-hand side of the carriageway if heading north-west.

CREDIT/DEBIT CARDS

FUEL CARDS (see key on page 6)
① ② ③ ④ ⑨ ⑫ ⑬

TRUCK FACILITIES

DRIVER FACILITIES
Truckers' accessories

All on-site facilities 24 hours　　**F003**

Asda Coryton Services, Cardiff

Asda Supermarkets Ltd
Longwood Drive, Cardiff
South Glamorgan CF14 7EW
T 0292 0616044

M4 JUNCTION 32 If heading Eastbound, exit the M4 at junction 32 and take the 3rd exit from the roundabout. Asda is to your left and the filling station is on the same site.

CREDIT/DEBIT CARDS

FUEL CARDS (see key on page 6)

TRUCK FACILITIES
Ample room for manoeuvring

DRIVER FACILITIES
Accommodation nearby, 600 yards, village hotel and quality friendly hotel

Toilets 06:00-22:30. Other on-site facilities 24 hours

F004

Atlantic Oils Ltd, Tralee, County Kerry

Tralee Road, Ardfert, Tralee
County Kerry, Ireland
T 00353 (0) 667134 192/184/315

ON THE R551 Take the R511 north-westbound out of Tralee. Atlantic Oils is on that road in the middle of the town of Ardfert, on the right-hand side.

CREDIT/DEBIT CARDS

FUEL CARDS (see key on page 6)

TRUCK FACILITIES
Truck washing facilities

DRIVER FACILITIES
Truckers' accessories

Bunker fuel and toilets 24 hours. Other on-site facilities 08:00-21:30

F005

Baglan Service Station, Port Talbot

Swan Road, Baglan, Port Talbot
Carmarthenshire SA12 8LA
T 01639 822898

ON THE A48 If heading north-west, exit M4 at junction 41. Take A48 towards Briton Ferry and Baglan is on the right. If heading south-east, exit at junction 42 and take the A48 towards Port Talbot. Baglan is on the left.

CREDIT/DEBIT CARDS

FUEL CARDS (see key on page 6)

DRIVER FACILITIES
Takeaway food nearby

SITE COMMENTS/INFORMATION
Friendly staff

All on-site facilities 06:30-21:45 Mon-Fri, 08:00-21:45 Sat & Sun.

F006

Barham Services, Canterbury

Folkstone Road, Barham, Canterbury
Kent CT4 6EX
T 01227 831356 www.arterbros.co.uk

ON THE A260 Barham is on the A260 between Folkestone and the A2. If heading towards Dover on the A2, exit at the B2046 Aylesham and A260 Folkestone exits. Head for Folkestone, and Barham Services is half a mile along on the right.

CREDIT/DEBIT CARDS

FUEL CARDS (see key on page 6)
①④㊷

TRUCK FACILITIES
NOT ACCESSIBLE FOR ARTICS

All on-site facilities 06:30-20:00 Mon-Sat, 08:00-20:00 Sun   **F007**

Besthorpe Filling Station, Attleborough

Besthorpe, Attleborough
Norfolk NR17 2LA
T 01953 452441

ON THE A11 SOUTHBOUND Besthorpe is on the A11 southbound carriageway between Wymondham and Attleborough, and 100 yards on from the Little Chef.

CREDIT/DEBIT CARDS

FUEL CARDS (see key on page 6)
⑤⑥

DRIVER FACILITIES
Accommodation nearby, half a mile, Sherbourne Country House Hotel
Takeaway food nearby

All on-site facilities 06:00-21:00.   **F008**

Bishops Meadow Filling Station, Brecon

Hay Road, Brecon
Powys LD3 9WS
T 01874 614 927

ON THE B4602 Bishops Meadow can be found on the B4602, one mile north of Brecon and on the left-hand side if heading towards the A470.

CREDIT/DEBIT CARDS

FUEL CARDS (see key on page 6)
①③④⑨⑫⑭

All on-site facilities 07:00-20:00 Mon-Fri, 08:00-20:00 Sat, 08:30-19:00 Sun   **F009**

Blackpark Filling Station, Inverness

Clachnaharry Road, Inverness
Highland IV3 8QH
T 01463 233632

ON THE A862 (The old A9) If heading north-westbound out of Inverness on the A862 towards Beauly, Blackpark Filling Station is on your left opposite the West side of the Carse Industrial Estate, past B&Q and the canal bridge.

CREDIT/DEBIT CARDS

FUEL CARDS (see key on page 6)

DRIVER FACILITIES
Clothing for sale
Takeaway food nearby

All on-site facilities 06:30-22:00 Mon-Sun.

F010

Blackquarry Service Station, Kilkenny

Benettsbridge Road, Kilkenny
County Kilkenny, Ireland
T 00353 (0) 567761864

ON THE R700 Take the R700 out of Kilkenny towards Bennetsbridge. Blackquarry Service Station is on the right-hand side just before you reach the N10 Kilkenny ring road.

CREDIT/DEBIT CARDS

FUEL CARDS (see key on page 6)

TRUCK FACILITIES
Truck washing facilities
Tyre repair/sales

DRIVER FACILITIES
Drivers' washroom
Takeaway food

All on-site facilities 08:00-22:00

F011

Bournmoor Filling Station, Houghton le Spring

Chester Road, Bournmoor,
Houghton le Spring
Tyne and Wear DH4 6EY
T 01913 852514

ON THE A183 From junction 63 of the A1M, take the A183 towards Sunderland. Bournmoor Filling Station is on the right-hand side just past the turning for the A1052.

CREDIT/DEBIT CARDS

FUEL CARDS (see key on page 6)

DRIVER FACILITIES
Truckers' accessories

SITE COMMENTS/INFORMATION
Very popular with lorry drivers.
Also has a 'Dog Wash' on site!

All on-site facilities 24 hours

F012

Bowhouse Service Station, Falkirk

**Echobank, Maddison, Falkirk
Stirlingshire FK2 0BX
T 01324 711789**

ON THE A801 From the M9, exit at junction 4 and take the A801 south. Bowhouse is on the A801 on the left, just after the junction with the B825. From Junction 4 of the M8, take the A801 north and Bowhouse is on the right just before Maddison.

CREDIT/DEBIT CARDS

FUEL CARDS (see key on page 6)
① ② ③ ⑧ ⑩ ⑮ ㊷ ㊹

All on-site facilities 24 hours

F013

Bridge End Garage, Leek

**Macclesfield Road, Leek
Staffordshire ST13 8LD
T 01538 384250**

ON THE A523 Bridge End Garage is on the outskirts of Leek and on your left-hand side if heading north on the A523.

CREDIT/DEBIT CARDS

FUEL CARDS (see key on page 6)
④ ⑤ ⑧ ⑫

SITE COMMENTS/INFORMATION
Clean site with efficient, friendly and helpful staff

All on-site facilities 07:00-22:00 Mon-Fri, 08:00-22:00 Sat & Sun

F014

Brobot East Bridgeford

**Brobot Petroleum Ltd, Foss Way,
East Bridgeford, Nottinghamshire NG13 8LA
T 01949 21132**

ON THE A46 Brobot East Bridgeford is located on the A46 between Leicester and Newark. It is approximately 10 miles from Newark and is on the right-hand side of the A46 if heading towards Leicester.

CREDIT/DEBIT CARDS

FUEL CARDS (see key on page 6)
① ④ ⑫ ⑬ ⑮ ㊹

SITE COMMENTS/INFORMATION
Friendly, helpful staff

Little Chef open 07:00-22:00. All other on-site facilities 24 hours

F015

Broxden Services, Perth

2 Broxden Avenue, Perth
Perth and Kinross PH2 0PX
T 01738 626332

OFF THE A93 From the roundabout at the end of the M90, take the A93 towards Perth, turn right at the next roundabout and Broxden Services is on the same site as McDonalds and the Park and Ride.

CREDIT/DEBIT CARDS

FUEL CARDS (see key on page 6)

TRUCK FACILITIES
Short-term coach parking (4 spaces)

DRIVER FACILITIES
Takeaway food nearby

SITE COMMENTS/INFORMATION
New site. Clean facilities

All on-site facilities 24 hours.   **F016**

By Pass Filling Station, St Austell

Southbourne Road, St Austell
Cornwall PL25 4RS
T 01726 73274

ON THE A390 From the A30, follow the A391 towards St Austell. Turn right at the T-junction with the A390 signposted towards Truro. The By Pass Filling Station is on the left after the roundabout with Woodland Road.

CREDIT/DEBIT CARDS

FUEL CARDS (see key on page 6)

TRUCK FACILITIES
Truck dealership nearby

DRIVER FACILITIES
Takeaway food

SITE COMMENTS/INFORMATION
Helpful, friendly staff

All on-site facilities 07:00-23:00 Mon-Sun.   **F017**

Calcutt Service Station, Swindon

Calcutt, Cricklade, Swindon
Wiltshire SN6 6JR
T 01793 752272

ON THE A419 This site is located on the left-hand side of the A419 Swindon to Cirencester road. If heading towards Cirencester it's just before the exit for Cricklade.

CREDIT/DEBIT CARDS

FUEL CARDS (see key on page 6)

SITE COMMENTS/INFORMATION
Friendly helpful staff
Always fresh food available

All on-site facilities 24 hours   **F018**

Cooper Brothers, Winshaw

Overtown Road, Newmains, Winshaw
Lanarkshire ML2 8HF
T 01698 385477

ON THE A71 From M74 northbound exit at junction 8 and take the A71 towards Livingstone. Cooper Brothers is at the junction with the A73. From the A8, exit junction 6 onto A73 to Carluke and Cooper Brothers is at the junction with the A71.

CREDIT/DEBIT CARDS

FUEL CARDS (see key on page 6)
① ⑮ ㊹

DRIVER FACILITIES
Truckers' accessories
Phone top ups/accessories
Takeaway food

SITE COMMENTS/INFORMATION
Easy access for LGVs

On-site facilities 07:30-22:00 Mon-Fri, 07:30-21:00 Sat, 09:00-21:00 Sun **F019**

Corrigans Service Station, Moyne

Legga, Moyne, County Longford, Ireland
T 00353 (0) 494335333

ON THE R198 From Longford take the R198 to Arvagh. Corrigans is on that road in the village of Legga on the left-hand side.

CREDIT/DEBIT CARDS

FUEL CARDS (see key on page 6)
⑨ ㉑

TRUCK FACILITIES
Short-term coach parking (1 space)
Truck washing facilities

All on-site facilities 08:30-22:00. Short time parking times unknown **F020**

Creetown Service Station, Creetown

Castle Douglas Road, Creetown
Near Newtown Stewart
Dumfries and Galloway DG8 7DA
T 01671 820233

ON THE A75 Creetown Service Station is on the A75 at the south end of the village of Creetown, 7 miles south-east of Newton Stewart.

CREDIT/DEBIT CARDS

FUEL CARDS (see key on page 6)
① ② ③ ⑨ ⑬

All on-site facilities 08:00-19:00 Mon-Fri, 08:00-18:00 Sat, 09:00-17:00 Sun **F021**

Darcroft Garage & MoT Centre, Bodmin

Fourwinds, Bodmin, Cornwall PL30 4HH
T 01208 821238

ON THE A30 Darcroft Garage is on the A30 about 3 miles from Bodmin, just after the turning for Blisland if heading north-westbound towards Launceston. It is situated just after the dual carriageway becomes a single carriageway and is accessible from both directions.

CREDIT/DEBIT CARDS

FUEL CARDS (see key on page 6)
① ② ④

All on-site facilities 08:30-19:00 Mon-Fri

F022

De Rodes Service Station, Boston

East Heckington, Boston
Lincolnshire PE20 3QF
T 01205 820307

ON THE A17 EASTBOUND De Rodes is on the A17 at East Heckington, west of Boston on the left-hand side if heading east towards Boston and before the junction with the A1121.

CREDIT/DEBIT CARDS

FUEL CARDS (see key on page 6)
① ② ③ ④ ⑤ ⑥ ⑫ ⑬ ㉟ ㊱ ㊲ ㊴

DRIVER FACILITIES
Truckers' accessories

All on-site facilities 07:00-22:00 Mon-Sat. 08:00-22:00 Sun

F023

Southlea Service Station, South Molton

Devon 4x4 Centre Ltd
Bish Mill, South Molton
Devon EX36 3QU
T 01769 550900

ON THE A361 Devon 4X4 is on the main A361 Tiverton to Barnstaple road. If heading towards Tiverton it is on the left-hand side just after the turnings for South Molton.

CREDIT/DEBIT CARDS

FUEL CARDS (see key on page 6)
① ② ④

All on-site facilities 07:00-21:00

F024

Drakes MG Rover, York

York Road, Shiptonthorpe, York
North Yorkshire YO43 3PH
T 01430 871556

ON THE A1079 Drakes Garage can be found at Skiptonthorpe on the A1079 between Market Weighton and Barmby on the Moor, on the right-hand side if heading north-west and about 2 miles from Market Weighton.

CREDIT/DEBIT CARDS

FUEL CARDS (see key on page 6)
① ④ ㉓

DRIVER FACILITIES
Takeaway food

All on-site facilities 07:00-19:00 Mon-Fri, 07:00-18:00 Sat, 09:00-18:00 Sun   **F025**

Dunmoran Service Station, Emyvale

Mullinderg, Emyvale
County Monaghan
T 00353 (0) 4786088/4786108

ON THE N2 Take the N2 northbound from Monaghan towards Aughnacloy. Dunmoran Service Station is in the village of Emyvale, just past the river and on the right-hand side.

CREDIT/DEBIT CARDS

FUEL CARDS (see key on page 6)
② ⑩ ⑰ ⑱ ㉑ ㉔

SITE COMMENTS/INFORMATION
Good quality low priced food
Breakfasts include free tea and toast
Takeaway breakfasts

Bunker fuel 24 hours. Other on-site facilities 07:30-23:00 Mon-Sat, 08:30-23:00 Sun   **F026**

Dynevor Service Station, Nelson

Petrol Express Ltd, Dynevor Terrace
Nelson, Mid Glamorgan CF46 6PD
T 01443 450510

ON THE B4255 If heading from Abercynon to Ystrad Mynach on the A472, Dynevor Service Station is at Nelson on the B4255 a few yards from the roundabout with the A472.

CREDIT/DEBIT CARDS

FUEL CARDS (see key on page 6)
① ⑨

DRIVER FACILITIES
Internet access

All on-site facilities 06:00-22:00   **F027**

Eccleston Green Filling Station, Chorley

**218 The Green, Eccleston, Chorley
Lancashire PR7 5SU
T 01257 452593**

ON THE B5250 From the A581, take the B5250 towards Eccleston. Eccleston Green Filling Station is in the middle of the village on the left-hand side.

CREDIT/DEBIT CARDS

FUEL CARDS (see key on page 6)
❶

DRIVER FACILITIES
Truckers' accessories

All on-site facilities 06:00-22:30.

F028

Emerald Service Station, County Clare

**Ennis Road, Newmarket on Fergus
County Clare, Ireland
T 00353 (0) 61368449/862447150**

ON THE R458 From the N18 take the R458 into Newmarket on Fergus. Emerald Service Station is at the north end of the town on the left-hand side if heading north.

CREDIT/DEBIT CARDS

FUEL CARDS (see key on page 6)
❾ ㉑

TRUCK FACILITIES
Truck washing facilities

DRIVER FACILITIES
Truckers' accessories

SITE COMMENTS/INFORMATION
Friendly, efficient service

All on-site facilities 07:00-21:00

F029

Enterprise Autos Ltd, Newport

**New Bridge By Pass, Crumlin, Newport
Gwent NP1 4QJ
T 01495 245713**

ON THE A467 Exit the M4 at junction 28 and take the A4072 to the roundabout with the A468 and A467. Take the A467 for 15 miles. Pass Newbridge and Enterprise Autos is on the right just before Crumlin.

CREDIT/DEBIT CARDS

FUEL CARDS (see key on page 6)
❹ ❼ ❽ ⑫ ㊱

TRUCK FACILITIES
Site long enough for wagon and drag

All on-site facilities 05:00-23:00 Mon-Sun

F030

F Howkins & Son, Lutterworth

North Kilworth, Lutterworth
Leicestershire LE17 6EP
T 01858 880208

ON THE A4304 From Junction 20 of the M1, take the A4304 towards Market Harborough. F Howkins and Son is on the right before you reach Husbands Bosworth, and near the junction with the B5414.

CREDIT/DEBIT CARDS

FUEL CARDS (see key on page 6)
4 7 12 37 38

TRUCK FACILITIES
Truck washing facilities

SITE COMMENTS/INFORMATION
Car MoT workshop

All on-site facilities 06:30-21:00 Mon-Fri, 09:00-20:00 Sat & Sun **F031**

Fairfield Service Station, Broxburn

Edinburgh Road, Broxburn
West Lothian EH52 5BQ
T 0131 3191533/01506 852567

ON THE A89 From the M9 exit at junction 1 and take the A89 towards Broxburn. Fairfield Service Station is about 1 and a half miles along on the right.

CREDIT/DEBIT CARDS

FUEL CARDS (see key on page 6)
1 2 3 10 15 44

DRIVER FACILITIES
Takeaway food

All on-site facilities 24 hours **F032**

Fleet Point Service Station, Middlesborough

Cambridge Rd, Middlesborough
Redcar and Cleveland TS3 8AG
T 01642 219300/219301

A66 A171 INTERCHANGE Take the A66 out of Middlesborough towards South Bank. Fleetpoint is situated at the roundabout with the A171 signposted towards Guisborough and the B1513.

CREDIT/DEBIT CARDS

FUEL CARDS (see key on page 6)
4 5 6

DRIVER FACILITIES
Takeaway food nearby

Toilets 06:00-22:00. All other on-site facilities 24 hours **F033**

Forfar Road Service Station, Dundee

Forfar Road, Dundee
Angus DD4 9BT
T 01382 507534 www.forfarroad.co.uk

ON THE A90 From Perth, follow A90 towards Dundee and around north side of the town. At junction with the A929 and A972 stay on the A90 as it turns left. Continue across next roundabout and Forfar Station is 200 yards on the left.

CREDIT/DEBIT CARDS

FUEL CARDS (see key on page 6)
① ③ ④ ⑫ ⑬ ⑮ ㊹

TRUCK FACILITIES
Ample room for manoeuvring

Toilets until 22:00. Other on-site facilities 24 hours | **F034**

Forge Garages, Bourton

Bourton, near Gillingham
Dorset SP8 5BD
T 01747 822409/840552

OFF THE A303 From the A303 eastbound, go past the Wincanton exit and take the exit B3081 Gillingham, and head for Bourton. Forge Garages is in the middle of the village. The A303 can be rejoined by continuing through the village.

CREDIT/DEBIT CARDS

FUEL CARDS (see key on page 6)
① ③ ④ ⑨ ⑫ ⑬ ㉧

DRIVER FACILITIES
Truckers' accessories
Post Office

All on-site facilities 07:30-19:00 Mon-Sat, 09:00-19:00 Sun | **F035**

Four Elms Service Station North, Rochester

Main Road, Chattenden, Rochester
Kent ME3 8LL
T 01634 250445

ON THE A228 Four Elms is in the village of Chattenden on the main A228 grain road, on the north-east bound carriageway.

CREDIT/DEBIT CARDS

FUEL CARDS (see key on page 6)
① ② ⑮ ㊹

All on-site facilities 06:00-21:00 | **F036**

Four Winds Service Station, Boston

East Heckington, Boston
Lincolnshire PE20 3QF
T 01205 820600

ON THE A17 Take the A17 from Sleaford to Boston. Four Winds is on the right-hand side, 600 yards beyond the turning with the B1395.

CREDIT/DEBIT CARDS

FUEL CARDS (see key on page 6)
④ ⑤ ⑥ 39

All on-site facilities 06:00-21:00 Mon-Sat, 07:00-21:00 Sun

F037

G H Lunn & Sons, Axbridge

New Road Garage, Turnpike Road, Lower
Weare, Axbridge, Somerset BS26 2JE
T 01934 732254

ON THE A38 M5 exit at junction 22 and take the A38 to Cheddar for 7 miles. G H Lunn is on the right-hand side at Lower Weare, just past the turning for Compton Bishop.

CREDIT/DEBIT CARDS

FUEL CARDS (see key on page 6)
① ⑤ ⑥ 35 36 37 39

Keyfuels only, bunker fuel 24 hours. Other on-site facilities 08:00-20:00

F038

Gillingham Service Station, Norfolk

Malthurst Ltd
Near Beccles, Norfolk NR34 0ED
T 01502 714400

A146 A143 INTERCHANGE Gillingham Service Station can be found at the Junction of the A146 Norwich to Lowestoft road and the A143 Great Yarmouth to Diss road.

CREDIT/DEBIT CARDS

FUEL CARDS (see key on page 6)
④ ⑤ ⑥ 35 36 37 39 46

All on-site facilities 24 hours

F039

Glen Service Station, Glengormley

88 Ballyclare Road, Glengormley
County Antrim BT36 8HH
T 02890 842576

ON THE B56 From the M2 A8M intersection take the A6
towards Newtownabbey for 1 mile. At the B56 turn left for
500 yards. Glen Service Station is on the left near the
Northcott Shopping Centre.

CREDIT/DEBIT CARDS

FUEL CARDS (see key on page 6)
7

SITE COMMENTS/INFORMATION
This site is next to the Northcott
Shopping Centre and within a few
metres of a park and ride bus service

All on-site facilities 07:00-23:00.

F040

Grange Farm Service Station, Northampton

Collingtree, Northampton
Northamptonshire NN4 0LY
T 01604 700498

ON THE A508 SOUTHBOUND If heading from
Northampton towards the M1 junction 15, Grange Farm is
on the southbound carriageway immediately after the exit for
the B526, a quarter of a mile from the motorway.

CREDIT/DEBIT CARDS

FUEL CARDS (see key on page 6)
1 2 3 4 5 6 13 35 36 37 44

DRIVER FACILITIES
Accommodation nearby, half a mile,
 Hilton Northampton & Innkeepers Lodge
Internet access

SITE COMMENTS/INFORMATION
Bakery on-site

Little Chef Restaurant opening times unknown. Other on-site facilities 24 hours

F041

Green Gates Service Station, Bradford

Carr Road, Greengates, Bradford
West Yorkshire BD10 0BJ
T 01274 617026

ON THE A657 Take the A658 north-eastbound out of
Bradford to the junction with the A657. Turn right onto this,
and Green Gates is 400 yards on the right.

CREDIT/DEBIT CARDS

FUEL CARDS (see key on page 6)
1 4 38 46

Toilets accessible 24 hours. Other on-site facilities accessible 07:00-22:00

F042

Green Mount Filling Station, Castlebellingham

Four Counties Oil Ltd, Greenmount, Castlebellingham, County Louth, Ireland
T 00353 (0) 429382429

ON THE N1 If heading north on the M1, take the R170 and N1 exit and head north on N1 for 2 miles and it's on the right. If heading south, take the R116 exit and head into Castlebellingham. Turn right at the N1 for 2 miles and it's on the left.

CREDIT/DEBIT CARDS

FUEL CARDS (see key on page 6)
24

TRUCK FACILITIES
Truck washing facilities

DRIVER FACILITIES
Internet access
Truckers' accessories

SITE COMMENTS/INFORMATION
Good access for LGVs

Parking and fuel bunker times unknown. All other onsite facilities 07:00-21:00   **F043**

Gulf Service Station Longdowns, Penryn

Longdowns, Penryn
Cornwall TR10 9DL
T 01209 860073

ON THE A394 Take the A394 from Helston to Falmouth. Gulf Service Station Longdowns is on the right, 100 yards before the first turning for Mabe Burnthouse village and 5 miles from the centre of Falmouth.

CREDIT/DEBIT CARDS

FUEL CARDS (see key on page 6)
1 4 12 37 45

All on-site facilities 07:00-22:00   **F044**

Harker Service Station, Carlisle

Harker, Near Carlisle
Cumbria CA6 4DT
T 01228 674274

ON THE A7 Exit junction 44 of the M6 and take the A7 north towards Longtown. Harker Service Station is about half a mile along on the left-hand side.

CREDIT/DEBIT CARDS

FUEL CARDS (see key on page 6)
1 2 3

DRIVER FACILITIES
Truckers' accessories

Toilets 24 hours. Other on-site facilities 07:30-20:00   **F045**

Haugh Head Garage, Wooler

Haugh Head, Wooler
Northumberland NE71 6QP
T 01668 281316

ON THE A697 Haugh Head Garage is on the A697 in the village of Haugh Head on the left-hand side if heading towards Morpeth and about 1 mile south of Wooler.

CREDIT/DEBIT CARDS

FUEL CARDS (see key on page 6)

1 4 15 44

TRUCK FACILITIES
Short-term coach parking (3 spaces)

DRIVER FACILITIES
Truckers' accessories

All on-site facilities 07:00-20:00 Mon-Sat, 08:00-20:00 Sun

F046

Hazelgrove Services, Yeovil

Sparkford, Yeovil
Somerset BA22 7JE
T 01935 850697

ON THE A303 Hazelgrove can be found just outside of Sparkford on the roundabout of the A303 and A359, and is easily accessible from all directions.

CREDIT/DEBIT CARDS

FUEL CARDS (see key on page 6)

4 7 37 38 40

TRUCK FACILITIES
Short-term coach parking (4 spaces, shared with LGV)

DRIVER FACILITIES
Hot drinks free with £100 fuel
Truckers' accessories
Takeaway food

SITE COMMENTS/INFORMATION
Large Spar shop
Post Office

Toilets 05:30-23:00. Post office open 09:00-13:00. Other on-site facilities 24 hours

F047

Hedworth Service Station, Jarrow

Leam Lane, Jarrow
Tyne and Wear NE32 4SL
T 0191 4898758

ON THE A194 From the end of the A194M continue on the A194 for 1 mile. Take sliproad for B1516 and Hedworth Service Station is on the left-hand side on that sliproad, just before the roundabout.

CREDIT/DEBIT CARDS

FUEL CARDS (see key on page 6)

1 46

All on-site facilities 06:00-00:00.

F048

High Noon Filling Station, Carmarthen

Whitemill, Carmarthen
Carmarthenshire SA32 7EN
T 01267 290639

ON THE A40 High Noon is on the A40 about 2 miles east of Abergwili and on the left-hand side if heading towards Llandeilo.

All on-site facilities 06:30-20:00.

CREDIT/DEBIT CARDS

FUEL CARDS (see key on page 6)
① ④ ⑬ ㊸

TRUCK FACILITIES
Short-term coach parking (3 spaces)

SITE COMMENTS/INFORMATION
Only LGV accessible garage on the A40

F049

Holborough Services, Snodland

Holborough Road, Snodland
Kent ME6 5PH
T 01634 245083

ON THE A228 From the M20, exit at junction 4 and take the A228 northbound towards Chatham. By-pass Snodland, and Holborough Services is on the left-hand side on the roundabout at the far north end of Snodland.

All on-site facilities 06:00-22:00.

CREDIT/DEBIT CARDS

FUEL CARDS (see key on page 6)
① ② ⑮ ㊹

SITE COMMENTS/INFORMATION
Train/tram/underground/metro nearby

F050

Hooley Bridge Service Station, Bury

609/621 Rochdale Old Road, Bury
Lancashire BL9 7TL
T 0161 7612890

ON THE B6222 From Rochdale take the B6222 towards Bury. Hooley Bridge Services is on the right-hand side about 1 mile away from the motorway bridge.

All on-site facilities 06:00-22:00

CREDIT/DEBIT CARDS

FUEL CARDS (see key on page 6)
① ㊻

DRIVER FACILITIES
Truckers' accessories

F051

Interchange Filling Station, Newark

Lincoln Road, Winthorpe, Newark
Nottinghamshire NG24 2DF
T 01636 705130

ON THE A46 From Grantham take the A1 northbound
around Newark, take the slip road signposted A46, turn left
at the roundabout and head for Lincoln. At the next
roundabout take the A17 towards Sleaford. Interchange
Filling Station is 100 yards along on the left.

CREDIT/DEBIT CARDS

FUEL CARDS (see key on page 6)
① ② ③

DRIVER FACILITIES
Accommodation nearby, half a mile,
    Travel Inn
Truckers' accessories

All on-site facilities 24 hours.

F052

Inverurie Service Station, Inverurie

North Street, Inverurie
Aberdeenshire AB51 4DJ
T 01467 620443

OFF THE A96 If heading south on the A96, take the first
turning into Inverurie and head towards the town centre. The
service station is on the main road and on the right-hand
side, just after the junction with the B9001.

CREDIT/DEBIT CARDS

FUEL CARDS (see key on page 6)
④ ⑦ ㊳ ㊵ ㊶

DRIVER FACILITIES
Accommodation nearby, half a mile,
    Strathburn Hotel

SITE COMMENTS/INFORMATION
Good location on main road
Showers nearby
Post Office nearby

All on-site facilities 24 hours.

F053

Jubilee Garage Ltd, Grantham

The Great North Road, Colsterworth
Grantham, Lincolnshire NG33 5JL
T 01476 860244

ON THE A1 Jubilee Garage is on the A1 at Colsterworth,
south of Grantham on the southbound carriageway, a few
yards north of the junction with the A151.

CREDIT/DEBIT CARDS

FUEL CARDS (see key on page 6)
① ② ③ ④ ⑦ ⑫ ⑬ ㊲ ㊵ ㊶

DRIVER FACILITIES
Accommodation nearby, 200 yards,
    Travelodge

All on-site facilities accessible 07:00-21:30.

F054

K P Hill Service Station, Higher Blackley

**355 Victoria Avenue, Higher Blackley
Greater Manchester M9 8WQ
T 0161 7403959**

ON THE A6104 Exit the M60 at junction 19 and follow the A576 towards Manchester city centre. After about a quarter of a mile turn left onto the A6104 Victoria Road. K P Hill Service Station is on the right-hand side after about a quarter of a mile.

CREDIT/DEBIT CARDS

FUEL CARDS (see key on page 6)
① ② ③

DRIVER FACILITIES
Phone top ups/accessories

All on-site facilities 07:00-21:00 Mon-Fri

F055

Killinick Service Station, Killinick

**Rosslare Road, Killinick
County Wexford, Ireland
T 00353 (0) 5358862**

ON THE N25 From Rosslare harbour take the N25 towards Wexford. Killinick Service Station is at Killinick on the left-hand side, 1 mile after the turning for the R740 Rosslare road.

CREDIT/DEBIT CARDS

FUEL CARDS (see key on page 6)
② ⑨ ⑭ ㉑

TRUCK FACILITIES
Short-term coach parking
Truck washing facilities

DRIVER FACILITIES
Accommodation nearby, half a mile,
Danby Lodge Hotel
Truckers' accessories

SITE COMMENTS/INFORMATION
This site is close to the port

All on-site facilities 07:00-22:00. Short term parking times unknown

F056

Kirkby Lonsdale Motors, Kirkby Lonsdale

**Kendal Road, Kirkby Lonsdale
Cumbria LA6 2HH
T 01524 271778**

ON THE A65 Kirkby Lonsdale Motors can be found on the A65. Just before the village of Kirkby Lonsdale and on the right-hand side if heading from junction 36 of the M6.

CREDIT/DEBIT CARDS

FUEL CARDS (see key on page 6)
④ ⑤ ⑥ ㊴

DRIVER FACILITIES
Truckers' accessories

All on-site facilities 07:00 19:30

F057

Knottingley Star Service Station, Knottingley

14 Pontefract Road, Knottingley
West Yorkshire WF11 0BJ
T 01977 636600

ON THE A645 Exit the M62 at junction 33 and take the A1 towards Knottingley for 800 yards. At the junction with the A645 turn right and Knottingley Star Services is 200 yards along on the right.

CREDIT/DEBIT CARDS

FUEL CARDS (see key on page 6)
① ③ ⑨

TRUCK FACILITIES
Truck dealership/workshop

DRIVER FACILITIES
Accommodation nearby, 500 yards, Travel Inn
Internet access
Truckers' accessories
Takeaway food nearby

SITE COMMENTS/INFORMATION
Very friendly staff
Train/tram/underground/metro nearby

All on-site facilities 24 hours. **F058**

Ladywood Petrol Station, Chesterfield

Chanderhill, Baslow Road, Chesterfield
Derbyshire S42 7BN
T 01246 566312

ON THE A619 Ladywood is on the A619 about 3 miles west of the centre of Chesterfield on the right-hand side if heading west and just past the turnings for Holymoorside.

CREDIT/DEBIT CARDS

FUEL CARDS (see key on page 6)
① ② ③ ④ ⑫

DRIVER FACILITIES
Hot drinks free to truckers

All on-site facilities 07:00-19:00 **F059**

Lane End Garage, Cramlington

Burradon Road, Annitsford, Cramlington
Northumberland NE23 7BD
T 0191 2500260

ON THE B1505 From the A1, take the A19 towards Wallsend. At the roundabout with the A189 and A1171, turn right onto the B1505 Front Street. Lane End Garage is 800 yards on the left-hand side before the roundabout with the B1321.

CREDIT/DEBIT CARDS

FUEL CARDS (see key on page 6)
④ ⑤ ⑥ ㊴

TRUCK FACILITIES
Truck dealership nearby

DRIVER FACILITIES
Takeaway food nearby

SITE COMMENTS/INFORMATION
Coach hire also available on-site

All on-site facilities 07:00-20:30. **F060**

Leagate Texaco Service Station, Preston

Blackpool Road, Lea, Preston
Lancashire PR4 0XB
T 01772 732321

ON THE A583 From Preston, take the A583 towards Blackpool. Leagate is on the outskirts of Preston on your left, 900 yards before the junction with the A584 and the village of Clifton.

CREDIT/DEBIT CARDS

FUEL CARDS (see key on page 6)
① ② ③ ④ ⑨

DRIVER FACILITIES
Accommodation nearby, 50 yards, Travel Inn

All on-site facilities 07:00-21:00 Mon-Fri, 09:00-20:00 Sat & Sun **F061**

Long Gardens, Shrewsbury

Dorrington, Shrewsbury
Shropshire SY5 7ER
T 01743 718275

ON THE A49 Take the A49 south from Shrewsbury. Continue for about 1 mile past the turnings for the village of Condover. Long Gardens is on the left-hand side, just before the turnings for Stapleton and about 1 mile before Dorrington.

CREDIT/DEBIT CARDS

FUEL CARDS (see key on page 6)
① ② ③ ④ ㊺

SITE COMMENTS/INFORMATION
Home made pies, pastries and cakes
Fresh fruit veg and flowers on sale

All on-site facilities 07:30-18:30 Mon-Fri, 08:00-18:30 Sat, 09:00-17:00 Sun **F062**

Longfold Motors, Longford

Strokestown Road, Longford
County Longford, Ireland
T 00353 (0) 4346055

ON THE N5 Take the N5 eastbound out of Longford. Longfold Motors is on the left-hand side, 500 yards beyond the junction with the R198.

CREDIT/DEBIT CARDS

FUEL CARDS (see key on page 6)
⑨ ㉑

DRIVER FACILITIES
Accommodation nearby, 600 yards, Longford Arms Hotel

SITE COMMENTS/INFORMATION
Easy access for LGVs
Huge forecourt

All on-site facilities 08:00-22:00. **F063**

Longton Service Station, Longton

**171 Sutherland Road, Longton
Stoke-on-Trent, Staffordshire ST4 1HZ
T 01782 333356**

OFF THE A5007 From the A50 if heading north-westbound through Stoke on Trent, take the A507 towards Longton. Follow this road right around the town's one-way system until the B5039. Turn left into this road then next right. Longton Services is half a mile on the left.

CREDIT/DEBIT CARDS

FUEL CARDS (see key on page 6)

All on-site facilities 06:00-22:00 Mon-Sat, 07:00-22:00 Sun   **F064**

Loughnanes Service Station, Birr

**Tullamore Road, Birr
County Offaly, Ireland
T 00353 (0) 50920066**

ON THE N52 Take the N52 out of Birr towards Tullamore. Loughnanes Service Station is just outside of the village on the right-hand side.

CREDIT/DEBIT CARDS

FUEL CARDS (see key on page 6)

TRUCK FACILITIES
Truck dealership nearby

DRIVER FACILITIES
Truckers' accessories

All on-site facilities 07:00-22:30.   **F065**

M32 Services, Bristol

**Silvey Oils Ltd, Newfoundland Road,
Bristol, South Gloucestershire BS2 9LU
T 0117 9550015**

ON THE A4032 From the centre of Bristol's inner ring road follow signs for the A4032 and M32. Silveys is on the north-eastbound carriageway of the A4032 just before the start of the M32.

CREDIT/DEBIT CARDS

FUEL CARDS (see key on page 6)

DRIVER FACILITIES
Accommodation nearby, half a mile, various hotels
Takeaway food

SITE COMMENTS/INFORMATION
Also note that exiting from this site should be done with great care as it can be a bit tight

Toilets 06:00-22:00. Hot food counter 07:00-14:00. Shop and fuel 24 hours   **F066**

Manor Service Station, Wakefield

Bradford Road, East Ardsley
Wakefield, West Yorkshire WF3 2HE
T 01924 872543

ON THE A650 From the M1, exit at junction 41 and take the A650 towards Morley. Manor Service Station is 400 yards on the left.

CREDIT/DEBIT CARDS

FUEL CARDS (see key on page 6)
④ ⑤ ⑥ ⑫ ㊱ ㊲ ㊴

All on-site facilities 24 hours.　　　　**F067**

Maxol Mace, Drogheda

North Road, Drogheda
County Louth, Ireland
T 00353 (0) 419845865

ON THE R132 From the M1 exit onto the N51, just north of Drogheda for 1 mile. At the roundabout take the R132 towards Drogheda for half a mile and Maxol Mace is on the right-hand side.

CREDIT/DEBIT CARDS

FUEL CARDS (see key on page 6)
⑪ ㉖

TRUCK FACILITIES
Truck washing facilities

SITE COMMENTS/INFORMATION
Friendly helpful staff

All on-site facilities 07:00-23:00　　　　**F068**

Millbrook Service Station, Oldcastle

Oldcastle, County Meath, Ireland
T 00353 (0) 498541300

ON THE R195 Take the R195 south-westbound from Virginia to Castlepollard. Millbrook Service Station is on that road, 1 mile past the junction with the R154.

CREDIT/DEBIT CARDS

FUEL CARDS (see key on page 6)
⑨ ㉑

TRUCK FACILITIES
Short-term coach parking
Truck washing facilities

DRIVER FACILITIES
Truckers' accessories

All on-site facilities 08:00-22:00. Short term parking times unknown　　　　**F069**

Morris Isaacs Garage, Llandovery

Queensway, Llandovery
Carmarthenshire SA20 0EG
T 01550 720176

ON THE A40 Take the A40 from Llangadog to Llandovery, and Morris Isaacs Garage is in the town on the left-hand side, just before the junction with the A483.

CREDIT/DEBIT CARDS

FUEL CARDS (see key on page 6)
1 **43**

DRIVER FACILITIES
Accommodation nearby, 600 yards, Castle Hotel

SITE COMMENTS/INFORMATION
Train/tram/underground/metro nearby

All on-site facilities 07:00-19:00.   **F070**

Morrisons, Rotherham

Morrisons Supermarkets Ltd
Bawtry Road, Bramley, Rotherham
South Yorkshire S66 1YZ
T 01709 709064

OFF THE A361 Exit the M18 at Junction 1 and take the A361 to Rotherham for 200 yards. Turn left at the next sliproad and Morrisons is on the right.

CREDIT/DEBIT CARDS

FUEL CARDS (see key on page 6)
1 **2** **3** **4** **12** **13** **37**

DRIVER FACILITIES
Accommodation nearby, 100 yards, Ibis, £33 per night

DRIVER FACILITIES
Phone top ups/accessories nearby
Clothing for sale nearby
Takeaway food nearby

All on-site facilities accessible 06:30-22:00 Mon-Fri, 07:00-21:00 Sat, 08:00-22:00 Sun   **F071**

Moss Hall Service Station, Blackburn

55 West Main Street, Blackburn
West Lothian EH47 7LX
T 01506 634215

ON THE A705 If heading east on the M8, exit at junction 4 and turn right onto the A801 towards Livingstone. At the T-junction with the A705 turn left towards Livingstone and Moss Hall is a few yards along on the right.

CREDIT/DEBIT CARDS

FUEL CARDS (see key on page 6)
1 **2** **3** **10** **15** **44**

TRUCK FACILITIES
Credit/debit cards accepted at auto bunker

DRIVER FACILITIES
Euro's changed/accepted

All on-site facilities accessible 24 hours   **F072**

Mulrooney's Service Station, Nenagh

Ballywilliam, Nenagh, County Tipperary Ireland
T 00353 (0) 6742881/6742520

ON THE N7 From Nenagh take the N7 towards Limerick. Mulrooney's is on the right-hand side about 3 miles from Nenagh town centre.

CREDIT/DEBIT CARDS

FUEL CARDS (see key on page 6)

DRIVER FACILITIES
Truckers' accessories

Bunker fuel 24 hours. Other on-site facilities 07:00-21:00

F073

Nantycaws Filling Station, Carmarthen

Nantycaws, Carmarthen Carmarthenshire SA32 8BG
T 01267 275955

ON THE A48 Nantycaws Filling Station is to the east of Nantycaws village and about 3 miles east of Carmarthen on the A48. It is on your left-hand side if heading towards Cross Hands.

CREDIT/DEBIT CARDS

FUEL CARDS (see key on page 6)

DRIVER FACILITIES
Truckers' accessories

SITE COMMENTS/INFORMATION
Easy access for LGVs

Toilets and standpipe 24 hours. All on-site facilities 07:00-20:00

F074

Northdown Service Station, Ashford

Maidstone Road, Charing, Ashford Kent TN27 0JS
T 01233 712375

ON THE A20 From the M20, exit at junction 8 and follow the A20 towards Harrietsham and Charing. North Down Service Station is on the right, a few hundred yards before the roundabout with the A252, and can also be accessed from junction 9 of the M20.

CREDIT/DEBIT CARDS

FUEL CARDS (see key on page 6)

SITE COMMENTS/INFORMATION
Train/tram/underground/metro nearby

All on-site facilities 06:00-21:00.

F075

Old Toll Garage, Overtown

128 Main Street, Overtown
North Lanarkshire ML2 0QP
T 01698 375052/374094

ON THE A71 From the M74 exit junction 8 and take the A71 towards Shotts. Or from the M74 junction 7 take the A72, then turn left onto the A71 for Shotts. Old Toll Garage is in the town of Overtown next to the junction with the B754 to Craigneuk.

CREDIT/DEBIT CARDS

FUEL CARDS (see key on page 6)
④⑤⑦⑧

TRUCK FACILITIES
Short-term coach parking (1 space)

DRIVER FACILITIES
Truckers' accessories

All on-site facilities 06:00-20:00. On-site short term parking times unknown   **F076**

Oliver Stanley Motors Ltd, Durrow

Cork Road, Durrow
County Laois, Ireland
T 00353 (0) 50236404

ON THE N8 Oliver Stanley Motors is on the N8 in the village of Durrow on the left-hand side if heading towards Urlingford. It is situated at the south-west end of the village.

CREDIT/DEBIT CARDS

FUEL CARDS (see key on page 6)
②⑥⑨⑪⑰⑱⑳㉑㉔㉙
Many other Irish cards accepted

SITE COMMENTS/INFORMATION
Cashback facility available for Laser Card holders

All on-site facilities 08:15-21:00 Mon-Fri, 08:15-19:00 Sat, 09:30-19:00 Sun   **F077**

Oversley Mill Services, Alcester

Alcester By-pass, Alcester
Warwickshire B49 6PQ
T 01789 400307/762684

ON THE A46 Oversley Mill Services is on the A46 at Alcester on the roundabout junction with the A435.

CREDIT/DEBIT CARDS

FUEL CARDS (see key on page 6)
①②③④⑤⑥⑫㉟㊱㊲

DRIVER FACILITIES
Accommodation nearby, 50 yards, Travelodge
Truckers' accessories

All on-site facilities 24 hours   **F078**

Paddy Mcquaid's, Emyvale

Knockafubble, Emyvale
County Monaghan, Ireland
T 00353 (0) 4788108

BETWEEN THE N2 AND R185 Take the N2 northbound from Monaghan to Emyvale. At Emyvale turn right towards Glaslough. Paddy Mcquaids is 2 miles along on the left-hand side.

CREDIT/DEBIT CARDS

FUEL CARDS (see key on page 6)
2 9 11 18 21 34

Bunker fuel 24 hours. Other on-site facilities 08:30-21:30

F079

Park Orpington Service Station, Orpington

85-87 Sevenoaks Road, Orpington
Kent BR6 9JW
T 01689 835191

ON THE A223 From the M25 exit 4, follow the A21 towards London. Take the A223 towards Orpington and Park Orpington is on the right-hand side just after you go over the railway line.

CREDIT/DEBIT CARDS

FUEL CARDS (see key on page 6)
1 4 15 44

TRUCK FACILITIES
Truck washing facilities

DRIVER FACILITIES
Truckers' accessories

All on-site facilities 24 hours

F080

Park Road Garage, Ebbw Vale

Park Road, Ebbw Vale
Gwent NP23 8UP
T 01495 302865

ON THE A4046 Park Road Garage is just north of the village of Cwm, on the A4046 a quarter of a mile north of the roundabout with Festival Drive and Queen Street. It's on the left-hand side as you head towards Ebbw Vale.

CREDIT/DEBIT CARDS

FUEL CARDS (see key on page 6)
1 4 45

All on-site facilities 07:00-22:00 Mon-Fri, 08:00-22:00 Sat-Sun

F081

Pennyland Service Station, Caithness

Scrabster Road, Thurso, Caithness
Highland KW14 7JU
T 01847 892029

ON THE A9 Follow the A9 through Thurso towards Scrabster. Pennyland is on the left-hand side as you are leaving the town.

CREDIT/DEBIT CARDS

FUEL CARDS (see key on page 6)
④ ⑦

TRUCK FACILITIES
Truck dealership/workshop

DRIVER FACILITIES
Accommodation nearby, half a mile,
  Murray House & Pentland Hotel
Phone top ups/accessories

All on-site facilities 07:00-22:00.

F082

Refinery Filling Station, South Killingholme

Humber Road, South Killingholme
North East Lincolnshire DN40 3DJ
T 01469 571564

ON THE A160 From the M180, take the A180 towards Immingham. Turn left onto the A160 to South Killingholme for 2 miles. Refinery Service Station is on the right-hand side at the east end of the village.

CREDIT/DEBIT CARDS

FUEL CARDS (see key on page 6)
① ② ③ ⑮ ㊹

DRIVER FACILITIES
Truckers' accessories

All on-site facilities 24 hours

F083

Regency Oils, Buckie

Regency Oils Ltd, 15 Marine Parade
Buckie, Aberdeenshire AB56 1UT
T 01542 832327

OFF THE A942 From the A98 Fochabers to Cullen road, take the A942 into Buckie. Continue on that road around the tight right-hand bend so that the sea is on your left. From there Regency Oils will be 200 yards on your right.

CREDIT/DEBIT CARDS

FUEL CARDS (see key on page 6)
③ ④ ⑨

All on-site facilities 08:00-20:00.

F084

Rix Garage, Scunthorpe

**Rix Ltd, Grange Lane North
Scunthorpe, North Lincolnshire DN16 1BN
T 01724 841284**

ON THE B1501 From junction 4 of the M180 take the A18 towards Scunthorpe. Continue on the A18 for 800 yards beyond the junction with the A1029. Turn right onto the B1501 Grange Lane North and Rix is 600 yards on the left.

CREDIT/DEBIT CARDS

FUEL CARDS (see key on page 6)
① ② ③ ⑩ ㉓

DRIVER FACILITIES
Truckers' accessories

Fuel bunker times unknown. All other on-site facilities 07:00-22:00   **F085**

Roundswell Services, Barnstaple

**Roundswell, Barnstaple
Devon EX31 3RZ
T 01271 328842**

ON THE A39 From Barnstaple take the A39 towards Westward Ho! Roundswell Services is on the A39 near Bickington, at the roundabout with the B3232.

CREDIT/DEBIT CARDS

FUEL CARDS (see key on page 6)
④ ⑤ ⑥ ㉟ ㊱ ㊲

DRIVER FACILITIES
Takeaway food

SITE COMMENTS/INFORMATION
Sells lottery tickets and hot food to go

All on-site facilities 24 hours   **F086**

Sandford Garage, Godshill

**Sandford, Godshill
Isle of Wight, PO38 3AL
T 01983 840303**

ON THE A3020 Take the A3020 from Newport to Shanklin. Sandford Garage is on the left-hand side in the village of Sandford, 1 mile east of Godshill.

CREDIT/DEBIT CARDS

FUEL CARDS (see key on page 6)
④ ⑤ ⑥ ⑫ ⑬ ㉟ ㊱ ㊲ ㊴

TRUCK FACILITIES
Short-term coach parking (4 spaces)
Truck washing facilities

DRIVER FACILITIES
Clothing for sale

SITE COMMENTS/INFORMATION
'The only one like it on the Isle of Wight!'

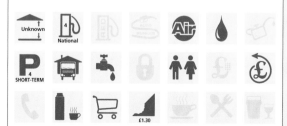

All on-site facilities 07:00-22:00. On-site short-term parking times unknown   **F087**

Shell Allestree, Derby

Duffield Road, Allestree, Derby
Derbyshire DE22 2DG
T 01332 453900

ON THE A6 Take the A6 north out of Derby. Shell Allestree is on the left-hand side, 400 yards north of the roundabout with the A38.

CREDIT/DEBIT CARDS

FUEL CARDS (see key on page 6)
④⑦⑧

All on-site facilities 24 hours   **F088**

Shell Allstop, Colchester

Langham, Colchester
Essex CO4 5NQ
T 01206 233010

ON THE A12 NORTHBOUND From Colchester, take the A12 towards Ipswich. Shell Allstop is on the left-hand side, 1 mile beyond the intersection with the A120.

CREDIT/DEBIT CARDS

FUEL CARDS (see key on page 6)
④⑧㊱

TRUCK FACILITIES
Short-term coach parking (1 space)

DRIVER FACILITIES
Hot drinks free to LGV drivers if buying fuel

SITE COMMENTS/INFORMATION
Friendly, helpful staff

All on-site facilities 07:00-23:00. On-site short term parking times unknown   **F089**

Shell Birchwood, Colchester

Dedham, Colchester
Essex CO7 6HU
T 01206 321000

ON THE A12 SOUTHBOUND Take the A12 from Ipswich towards Colchester. Shell Birchwood is about 1 mile beyond the turning for Dedham and about 1 and a half miles north of the outskirts of Colchester on the left-hand side.

CREDIT/DEBIT CARDS

FUEL CARDS (see key on page 6)
④⑧㊱

DRIVER FACILITIES
Hot drinks free to LGV drivers making other purchases

SITE COMMENTS/INFORMATION
This site is in an elevated position and is easily seen on approach

All on-site facilities 24 hours   **F090**

Shell Congleton, Congleton

**Clayton By-pass, Congleton
Cheshire CW12 1LR
T 01260 291601**

ON THE A34 Exit the M6 at junction 17 and take the A534 towards Congleton. At the junction with the A34 turn left onto it and continue on it for half a mile. Shell Congleton is on your left before the junction with the A54.

CREDIT/DEBIT CARDS

FUEL CARDS (see key on page 6)
④ ⑤ ⑦ ㊱ ㊲ ㊴ ㊵ ㊶

DRIVER FACILITIES
Accommodation nearby, half a mile, Lion and Swan
Takeaway food nearby

All on-site facilities 24 hours. **F091**

Shell Contin, Contin

**Contin, Near Strathpeffer
Highland IV14 6ES
T 01997 421948**

ON THE A835 Take the A9 north-west out of Inverness. At Tore turn left onto the A835. Shell Contin is in the middle of the village of Contin on your right-hand side, 500 yards past the turning for the A834.

CREDIT/DEBIT CARDS

FUEL CARDS (see key on page 6)
⑧

TRUCK FACILITIES
Short-term coach parking

DRIVER FACILITIES
Accommodation nearby, 100 yards, Coul House

Short term parking times unknown. All other on-site facilities 07:30-20:00 **F092**

Shell Eagle, Rochdale

**Queensway, Rochdale
Lancashire OL11 1TJ
T 01706 716960**

ON THE A664 Take the A627M into Rochdale. Turn right at the end, then left at the roundabout onto the A664. Continue for 800 yards and Shell Eagle is on the right.

CREDIT/DEBIT CARDS

FUEL CARDS (see key on page 6)
④ ⑤ ⑦ ⑧ ㊻

All on-site facilities 24 hours **F093**

Shell Grand Dale, Molton

**Main Road, Molton, Hull
East Yorkshire HU14 3HG
T 01482 635900**

ON THE A63 Shell Grand Dale is on the A63 westbound carriageway between North Ferriby and Brough. Six miles from the centre of Hull and 6 miles from the start of the M62.

CREDIT/DEBIT CARDS

FUEL CARDS (see key on page 6)
④ ⑦ ⑧ ⑫ ⑲ ㊱ ㊳ ㊴ ㊵

DRIVER FACILITIES
Truckers' accessories

All on-site facilities 24 hours

F094

Shell Old Ford Road, Bow

**445-453 Wick Lane, Bow, London,
Greater London E3 2TB
T 0208 9832500**

OFF THE A12 Take the A11 north-eastbound out of central London until the junction with the A12. Turn left onto this towards Hackney. Take the next immediate slip road and turn right across the carriageway into Wick Lane. Shell Old Ford is 50 yards on the right.

CREDIT/DEBIT CARDS

FUEL CARDS (see key on page 6)
⑧

TRUCK FACILITIES
Truck washing facilities

SITE COMMENTS/INFORMATION
Excellent customer service

Toilets accessible 06:00-23:00. All other on-site facilities 24 hours

F095

Shell Redheugh, Gateshead

**Askew Road West, Gateshead
Tyne and Wear NE8 2JX
T 0191 4903950**

OFF THE A184 From the A1M, take the A1 around Gateshead for 4 miles. Turn right at the junction with the A184 onto this road heading towards Gateshead centre. Take the sliproad signposted A189 onto the roundabout. Turn left and Shell Redheugh is on your immediate left

CREDIT/DEBIT CARDS

FUEL CARDS (see key on page 6)
④ ⑧ ㊶ ㊺

All on-site facilities 24 hours.

F096

Shell Service Station, Llanrhyshyd

Costcutters Ltd
Llanrhyshyd, Ceredigion SY23 5BT
T 01974 202903

ON THE A487 From Aberystwyth, take the A487 south for 10 miles. Shell Service Station is on the south side of the village of Llanrhyshyd on the right-hand side.

CREDIT/DEBIT CARDS

FUEL CARDS (see key on page 6)
2 4 8 12 36 39

TRUCK FACILITIES
NOT ACCESSIBLE FOR ARTICS
Truck washing facilities

DRIVER FACILITIES
Takeaway food

All on-site facilities 07:00-20:30 Mon-Sat, 08:00-20:30 Sun   **F097**

Shrewsbury Service Station, Shrewsbury

Hereford Road, Bayston Hill, Shrewsbury
Shropshire SY3 0DA
T 01743 874504

OFF THE A49 From Shrewsbury centre take the A49 south towards Hereford. Shrewsbury Services is situated on the roundabout with the A5.

CREDIT/DEBIT CARDS

FUEL CARDS (see key on page 6)
4 7 38

TRUCK FACILITIES
Short-term coach parking (6 spaces)

DRIVER FACILITIES
Accommodation nearby, 20 yards,
   Travelodge

Toilets 06:00-23:00. All other on-site facilities 24 hours   **F098**

Silverstream Service Station Ltd, Silverstream

Tamlet, Silverstream
County Monaghan, Ireland
T 00353 (0) 4785550/4785085

ON THE R213 From Casleblaney take the N2 north through Clontibret, past the junction with the R214 and turn right onto the R213. Continue for 3 miles, Silverstream is on the right, 200 yards from the border.

CREDIT/DEBIT CARDS

FUEL CARDS (see key on page 6)
2 9 11 17 18 21 24 29

TRUCK FACILITIES
Short-term coach parking (3 spaces)

DRIVER FACILITIES
Truckers' accessories

All on-site facilities 24 hours   **F099**

Six Hills Service Station, Six Hills

Fosseway, Six Hills, nr Melton Mowbray Leicestershire LE14 3PD
T 01509 880937

ON THE A46 From Leicester take the A46 towards Newark. Six Hills Service Station is on the right, 50 yards after the junction with the B676 to Burton on the Wolds.

CREDIT/DEBIT CARDS

FUEL CARDS (see key on page 6)
④ ㊲ ㊸

TRUCK FACILITIES
NOT ACCESSIBLE FOR ARTICS

DRIVER FACILITIES
Truckers' accessories

SITE COMMENTS/INFORMATION
This site offers a warm and friendly service

All on-site facilities 06:00-19:00 Mon-Fri, 07:00-19:00 Sat, 08:00-19:00 Sun

F100

Spar Texaco, Ormskirk

Alfred Jones Ltd, 242 Southport Road Ormskirk, Lancashire L39 1LZ
T 01695 580550

ON THE A570 From junction 3 of the M58, follow the A570 into Ormskirk. Stay on A570 and continue through the town towards Southport. Spar Texaco is on the right on the outskirts of Ormskirk.

CREDIT/DEBIT CARDS

FUEL CARDS (see key on page 6)
① ③ ④ ⑨

All on-site facilities 24 hours

F101

Staddlestones Nissan, Ryde

Brading Road, Ryde
PO33 1QG, Isle of Wight
T 01983 562705

ON THE A3055 Take the A3055 south out of Ryde towards Sandown. Staddlestones Nissan is on the left-hand side on the outskirts of the town, just beyond Tesco.

CREDIT/DEBIT CARDS

FUEL CARDS (see key on page 6)
④ ⑦

DRIVER FACILITIES
Takeaway food nearby

All on-site facilities 07:30-18:00

F102

Station Garage, Blyth

Front Street, Bebside, Blyth
Northumberland NE24 4JD
T 01670 352325/352419

ON THE A193 Take the A193 north-westbound out of Blyth until you reach the roundabout with the A189. Go straight across towards Bebside. Station Garage is a few yards on the left.

All on-site facilities 07:00-22:00 Mon-Fri, 07:00-21:00 Sat, 08:00-20:00 Sun

CREDIT/DEBIT CARDS

FUEL CARDS (see key on page 6)

TRUCK FACILITIES
NOT ACCESSIBLE FOR ARTICS

F103

Stat Oil Omni Park, Dublin

Stat Oil Ltd, off Swords Road
Omni Park Shopping Centre, Santry
County Dublin 9, Dublin, Ireland
T 00353 (0) 18621329/18869500

OFF THE R132 M1 towards Dublin and exit junction for R104 towards Santry. Continue for 300 yards to junction with R132. Turn left onto it for 600 yards. Turn right towards Omni Park Shopping Centre and Stat Oil is 50 yards on your right.

All on-site facilities 07:00-00:00.

CREDIT/DEBIT CARDS

FUEL CARDS (see key on page 6)

TRUCK FACILITIES
NOT ACCESSIBLE FOR ARTICS

SITE COMMENTS/INFORMATION
Clean site with good food. Friendly, helpful staff

F104

Tara Service Station, Limerick

Dock Road, Limerick
County Limerick, Ireland
T 00353 (0) 61301818/61229799/61302102

ON THE N69 From the N20 if heading north east, exit at St Patrickswell and follow the R526 towards Limerick. At Raheen Business Park roundabout turn left onto N18. Keep heading for Limerick Town centre and the Tara Service Station is 1 mile along on the left.

CREDIT/DEBIT CARDS

FUEL CARDS (see key on page 6)

DRIVER FACILITIES
Truckers' accessories

Bunker fuel 24 hours. Other on-site facilities 7:00-23:00 Mon-Fri, 07:00-22:00 Sat, 09:00-22:00 Sun

F105

Tenby Road Filling Station, Carmarthen

Llysonen Road, Carmarthen
Carmarthenshire SA33 5DT
T 01267 237854

ON THE A40 Take the A40 out of Carmarthen towards St Clears. Tenby Road Filling Station is about 2 miles out of Carmarthen town centre on the right-hand side and about 1 mile past the village of Llanllwch.

CREDIT/DEBIT CARDS

FUEL CARDS (see key on page 6)
❶ ❽

TRUCK FACILITIES
Short-term coach parking (2 spaces)

DRIVER FACILITIES
Truckers' accessories

SITE COMMENTS/INFORMATION
Easy access for LGVs

All on-site facilities 24 hours — **F106**

Texaco Service Station, Blanchardstown

Blanchardstown Corporate Park
Blanchardstown, County Dublin 15, Dublin
Ireland T 00353 (0) 18606520

OFF THE R121 Exit the M50 at junction 6 and take the N3 towards Dunshaughlin. Take the slip for the R121and turn right for Blanchardstown Industrial Park. Continue through Industrial Park to roundabout with Ballycoolin Road. Texaco Blanchardstown is on that roundabout.

CREDIT/DEBIT CARDS

FUEL CARDS (see key on page 6)
❾ ㉑

TRUCK FACILITIES
Truck washing facilities

DRIVER FACILITIES
Hot deli. food available all day

SITE COMMENTS/INFORMATION
Great service, friendly staff

All on-site facilities 06:30-23:00 — **F107**

Texaco Service Station, Newrath

Dublin Road, Newrath, Waterford
County Waterford, Ireland
T 00353 (0) 51844509

ON THE N9 Take the N9 out of Waterford towards Carlow. Texaco Service Station Waterford is on the left-hand side, 400 yards before the junction with the N24.

CREDIT/DEBIT CARDS

FUEL CARDS (see key on page 6)
❾ ㉑

TRUCK FACILITIES
Short-term coach parking (6 spaces)
Truck washing facilities

DRIVER FACILITIES
Truckers' accessories

Bunker fuel 24 hours. Other on-site facilities 07:00-21:00. Short-term parking times unknown — **F108**

The Western Gem, Mullingar

**Top Oil Ltd, Ballinalack, Mullingar
County Westmeath, Ireland
T 00353 (0) 4471160**

ON THE N4 Take the N4 north-west out of Mullingar towards Longford. The Western Gem is in the middle of the village of Ballinalack on the right-hand side.

CREDIT/DEBIT CARDS

FUEL CARDS (see key on page 6)
㉑

TRUCK FACILITIES
Short-term coach parking

All on-site facilities 07:30-00:00. Short term parking times unknown   **F109**

Tinklers Service Station, Clane

**Kilcock Road, Clane
County Kildare, Ireland
T 00353 (0) 45982949**

ON THE R403 Take the R403 out of Clane towards Dublin and Tinklers Service Station is half a mile on the left-hand side.

CREDIT/DEBIT CARDS

FUEL CARDS (see key on page 6)
⑨

TRUCK FACILITIES
Short-term coach parking (4 spaces)
Truck washing facilities

DRIVER FACILITIES
Truckers' accessories

SITE COMMENTS/INFORMATION
Friendly, helpful, efficient staff

All on-site facilities 07:00-21:00. Short term parking times unknown   **F110**

Tore Service Station, Tore

**Main Road, Tore, nr Inverness
Rosshire IV6 7RZ
T 01463 811622**

ON THE A832 From Inverness, take the A9 north-west for 7 miles. At the roundabout with the A832 and A835 turn right onto the A832 towards Munlochy. Tore Service Station is 400 yards on the left-hand side.

CREDIT/DEBIT CARDS

FUEL CARDS (see key on page 6)
①②③㊷

TRUCK FACILITIES
Short-term coach parking

DRIVER FACILITIES
Hot drinks free to LGV drivers buying fuel

All on-site facilities 06:00-22:00 Mon-Thu, 06:00-21:00 Fri, 07:00-21:00 Sat, 09:00-19:00 Sun   **F111**

Tougher Oil, Naas

**Tougher Oil Ltd, Newhall, Naas
County Kildare, Ireland
T 00353 (0) 45433143**

ON THE R445 From the M7, exit at junction 8 and take the R445 towards Newbridge for 1 and a half miles. Tougher Oil is on the left-hand side.

CREDIT/DEBIT CARDS

FUEL CARDS (see key on page 6)
⑩ ㉑

DRIVER FACILITIES
Truckers' accessories

All on-site facilities 24 hours   F112

Tower View Filling Station, Poole

**570 Ringwood Road, Parkstone
Poole, Dorset BH12 4LY
T 01202 716177**

ON THE B3068 From the A35 eastbound, continue across the roundabout signposted to Poole town centre onto the A3049. At next roundabout with the Ford Garage, take 2nd exit. At next roundabout, turn left onto B3068. Tower View is a few yards along on the left.

CREDIT/DEBIT CARDS

FUEL CARDS (see key on page 6)
④ ⑧ ㊱

All on-site facilties 06:00-22:00.   F113

Trench Lock 24-7, Telford

**Trench Lock, Telford
Shropshire TF1 6SZ
T 01952 243018**

OFF THE A442 Exit M54 junction 5 and take the A5 to the roundabout with the A442. Turn left onto the A442 for 2 miles. At the junction with the A518 turn left and Trench Lock is immediately on your right.

CREDIT/DEBIT CARDS

FUEL CARDS (see key on page 6)
① ② ④ ⑤ ⑥ ㉟ ㊱ ㊲ ㊴ ㊻

TRUCK FACILITIES
Short-term coach parking (3 spaces)

SITE COMMENTS/INFORMATION
Best LGV facilities in Telford!

All on-site facilities 24 hours. Short term on-site parking 24 hours   F114

Victoria Filling Station, Morley

Bruntcliffe Road, Morley, Leeds
West Yorkshire LS27 OJZ
T 0113 2527538

ON THE A650 Can be accessed from north or southbound carriageway of M621 or westbound carriageway of M62 at Junctions 27. Take A650 towards Wakefield for half a mile and it's on the left. Or from M62 junction 28, take A650 towards Bradford for 2 miles, it's on the right.

CREDIT/DEBIT CARDS

FUEL CARDS (see key on page 6)
① ② ③ ⑧

TRUCK FACILITIES
Truck washing facilities

DRIVER FACILITIES
Accommodation nearby, 500 yards, Old Vicarage & Innkeepers Lodge Truckers' accessories

All on-site facilities 24 hours.   **F115**

West Cross Service Station, Smethwick

166 Oldbury Road, Smethwick
West Midlands B66 1ND
T 0121 5556787

ON THE A457 From junction 1 M5 take the A4252 towards Smethwick. At the roundabout with the A457 turn right. Continue over roundabout with A4031 and West Cross is on your left.

CREDIT/DEBIT CARDS

FUEL CARDS (see key on page 6)
① ③ ④ ⑤ ⑧ ⑲ ㊻

TRUCK FACILITIES
Ample room for manoeuvring

All on-site facilities 24 hours.   **F116**

Westbank Service Station, Belfast

Nicholls Fuel Oils Ltd, Westbank Road
Cuncrue Industrial Estate
Belfast, Ulster BT3 9JL, Northern Ireland
T 02890 775863

OFF THE M2 JUNCTION 1 Exit the M2 at junction 1 and head east for the Docks onto Dargan Road. Continue for 1 mile then turn left into Westbank Road. Continue for half a mile and go past ferry terminal. Westbank Service Station is on the left.

CREDIT/DEBIT CARDS

FUEL CARDS (see key on page 6)
① ② ③ ⑨ ⑩

SITE COMMENTS/INFORMATION
This site is 600 yards from the ferry terminal

All on-site facilities 06:00-18:00. Short term on-site parking times unknown   **F117**

Whittleford Service Station, Nuneaton

Whittleford Road, Stockington, Nuneaton
Warwickshire CV10 9JD
T 02476 386327

OFF THE B4114 Take the B4114 out of Nuneaton towards Hartshill. 500 yards after the junction with the B4111, turn left down Bucks Hill. Whittleford Service Station is 900 yards on the left.

CREDIT/DEBIT CARDS

FUEL CARDS (see key on page 6)

DRIVER FACILITIES
Truckers' accessories

All on-site facilities 06:00-21:00

F118

Windmill Garage, Honiton

Offwell, Honiton
Devon EX14 9RP
T 01404 831228

ON THE A35 Take the A35 from Honiton to Axminster and Windmill Garage is on your right-hand side, about a mile and a half outside of the town of Honiton, just beyond the turning for Offwell.

CREDIT/DEBIT CARDS

FUEL CARDS (see key on page 6)

DRIVER FACILITIES
Takeaway food

SITE COMMENTS/INFORMATION
Easy access from A35 for LGVs

All on-site facilities 06:00-22:00

F119

Wrotham Heath Service Station, Wrotham Heath

London Road, Wrotham Heath
Kent TN15 7RY
T 01732 781113

ON THE A20 Exit the M26 at junction 2A and take the A20 towards Maidstone for 600 yards. Wrotham Heath Services is on the right-hand side.

CREDIT/DEBIT CARDS

FUEL CARDS (see key on page 6)

DRIVER FACILITIES
Accommodation on-site, Travel Inn
Drivers' washroom
Phone top ups/accessories
Takeaway food

All on-site facilities 24 hours

F120

A1 Diesel Ltd, Thirsk

Southways Service Station
Sinderby, Thirsk, North Yorkshire YO7 4LD
T 01845 567329

ON THE A1 From A1M northbound, A1 Diesel is on the right-hand side. Continue to next exit signposted B6267 Ainderby Quernhow. Cross the carriageway. Follow the B6267 then take A1 southbound carriageway. The site is 50 yards further on.

CREDIT/DEBIT CARDS

FUEL CARDS (see key on page 6)
① ② ③ ⑤ ⑥ ⑩ ㊴

DRIVER FACILITIES
Truckers' accessories

SITE COMMENTS/INFORMATION
Smoking allowed in shop. This site is opposite the Quernhow Transport Café

All on-site facilities 24 hours

FP121

Ashton Road Service Station, Stockport

Ashton Road, Bredbury, Stockport
Cheshire SK6 2QN
T 01614 303589

M60 JUNCTION 25 ON THE A6017 From the M60 junction 25, take the A6017 towards Denton. Ashton Road Services is about 100 yards along on the left.

CREDIT/DEBIT CARDS

FUEL CARDS (see key on page 6)
① ② ③ ④ ⑨

DRIVER FACILITIES
Truckers' accessories
Takeaway food nearby

All on-site facilities 24 hours

FP122

B & M Harland Ltd, Pickering

Malton Road Garage, Malton Road
Pickering, North Yorkshire YO18 7JL
T 01751 472673

ON THE A169 Malton Road Garage can be found on the A169 Pickering to Malton road, 200 yards south of the junction with the A170.

CREDIT/DEBIT CARDS

FUEL CARDS (see key on page 6)
④ ⑤ ⑥ ㊲ ㊴

TRUCK FACILITIES
Overnight parking in town centre nearby

DRIVER FACILITIES
Accommodation available nearby,
 500 yards, 3 hotels
Truckers' accessories

SITE COMMENTS/INFORMATION
Excellent range of quality food products
Easy access for LGVs
Post Office

All on-site facilities 06:30-22:00

FP123

Berkeley Heath Motors, Berkeley Heath

Gloucester Road, Berkeley Heath
Gloucestershire GL13 9ET
T 01453 511500

ON THE A38 Berkeley Heath is on the A38 and accessible from both junctions 13 and 14 of the M5. If heading north Berkeley Heath Motors is on the left-hand side, just after the turning for Berkeley village.

CREDIT/DEBIT CARDS

FUEL CARDS (see key on page 6)
① ② ③ ④

TRUCK FACILITIES
Overnight parking in lay-by

Toilets 24 hrs. All other on-site facilities 07:00-22:00 Mon-Sat, 08:00-21:00 Sun. Nearby parking 24 hrs in lay-by   **FP124**

Bloody Oaks Star Service Station, Tickencote

Great North Road, Tickencote
Cambridgeshire PE9 4AD
T 01780 750850

ON THE A1 Bloody Oaks is a few miles north of Stamford on the A1 northbound carriageway towards Grantham, just past the turning for the B1081.

CREDIT/DEBIT CARDS

FUEL CARDS (see key on page 6)
① ② ③ ④ ⑦ ⑩ ⑪ ⑫ ⑬ ⑭

TRUCK FACILITIES
Overnight parking in lay-by

SITE COMMENTS/INFORMATION
Lovely site, wonderful staff
Clothing for sale
Takeaway food nearby

All on-site facilities 06:00-22:00. Nearby parking 24 hours in lay-by   **FP125**

Bray Hill Service Station, Douglas

Bray Hill, Douglas IM4 4LL
Isle of Man
T 01624 621181

ON THE A2 From the ferry terminal, take the A1 north-west out of Douglas town centre towards Peel. At the junction with the A5 and A2 turn right onto the A2 towards the TT Grandstand. Bray Hill is 1 mile on the left next to the A22.

CREDIT/DEBIT CARDS

FUEL CARDS (see key on page 6)
④ ⑤ ㊻

TRUCK FACILITIES
Overnight parking at TT Grandstand Park

DRIVER FACILITIES
Accommodation available nearby, half a mile, Wellbeck Hotel & Castle Mona

All on-site facilities accessible 07:00-22:30   **FP126**

Brobot, Doncaster

Brobot Petroleum Ltd, York Road, Doncaster, South Yorkshire DN5 8LY
T 01302 390157

ON THE A638 From the centre of Doncaster, take the A630 around the north-west side of the town, then take the A19 for half a mile to the roundabout with the A638. Take the A638 for 400 yards and it's on your left opposite Morrisons.

CREDIT/DEBIT CARDS

FUEL CARDS (see key on page 6)
1 4 15 44

TRUCK FACILITIES
Coach parking available, shared with LGV
Ample room for manoeuvring

DRIVER FACILITIES
Phone top-ups/accessories
Nearby overnight parking on roadside, 4 spaces, free of charge

All on-site facilities 05:00-23:00

FP127

Casey's Auto Centre Ltd, Rosscommon

Athlone Road, Rosscommon
County Rosscommon, Ireland
T 00353 (0) 906626101

ON THE N61 Casey's Autocentre is on the roundabout junction of the N61 and N63 on the outskirts of the town of Roscommon.

CREDIT/DEBIT CARDS

FUEL CARDS (see key on page 6)
2 7 11 21 40

TRUCK FACILITIES
Overnight parking available (6 spaces)
Coach parking available (4 spaces)
Truck dealership/workshop
Ample room for manoeuvring

DRIVER FACILITIES
Drivers' washroom, rest area, quiet area
Accommodation available nearby, half a
 mile, Royal Hotel & Abbey Hotel
Takeaway food
Phone top-ups/accessories
Truckers' accessories
Train/tram/underground/metro nearby

Some facilities only 07:30-22:00. Fuel, parking, toilets, shop and other facilities 24 hours

FP128

Cheltenham Filling Station, Cheltenham

Tewkesbury Road, Cheltenham
Gloucestershire GL51 9SG
T 01242 257256

ON THE A4019 From the M5 southbound, exit at junction 10 and take the A4019 towards Cheltenham. Cheltenham Filling Station is 1 mile further on, on the left opposite Sainsburys and Gallager Retail Park.

CREDIT/DEBIT CARDS

FUEL CARDS (see key on page 6)
4 5 6 12 22 35 36 37 39 46

TRUCK FACILITIES
Overnight parking in lay-by or on roadside of nearby Retail Park

DRIVER FACILITIES
Accommodation available nearby,
 200 yards, Travel Inn
Truckers' accessories

All facilities including nearby roadside parking 24 hours

FP129

Clerkenleap Service Station, Worcester

Bath Road, Broomhall, Worcester
Worcestershire WR5 3HR
T 01905 821898

ON THE A38 Exit the M5 at junction 7 and take the A44 for 500 yards. Turn left onto the A4440 for 2 miles then left onto the A38. Clerkenleap Services is 300 yards on the right-hand side.

CREDIT/DEBIT CARDS

FUEL CARDS (see key on page 6)
5 6 12 36 37 39 46

TRUCK FACILITIES
Overnight parking in Worcester city centre 2 miles away

DRIVER FACILITIES
Internet access
Truckers' accessories
Takeaway food

All on-site facilities 06:00-23:00   **FP130**

Corby Service Station, Corby

Rockingham Road, Corby
Northamptonshire NN17 2AE
T 01536 2629044

ON THE A6116 If heading south from Uppingham on the A6003, turn left onto the A6116 towards Stanion and Brigstock. Corby Service Station is on the left at the next roundabout.

CREDIT/DEBIT CARDS

FUEL CARDS (see key on page 6)
1 4 15 44

TRUCK FACILITIES
Overnight parking in Aldi car park

DRIVER FACILITIES
Accommodation available nearby, half a mile, Hotel Elizabeth, Rockingham
Takeaway food

Nearby parking 24 hours. All on-site facilities 06:00-22:00 Mon-Fri   **FP131**

Cot House Services, Argyll

Cot House, Dunoon, Argyll
Argyll and Bute PA23 8QT
T 01369 840333

ON THE A815 Cot House Services is on the A815 between the villages of Ardbeg and Inverchapel approximately 6 miles north of Dunoon on the left-hand side if heading north.

CREDIT/DEBIT CARDS

FUEL CARDS (see key on page 6)
1 4

TRUCK FACILITIES
Overnight local parking nearby

SITE COMMENTS/INFORMATION
Regular special offers and sales, large variety of stock in shop

All on-site facilities 06:30-22:00   **FP132**

Devoys Gala, Carlow

Tullow Road, Carlow
County Carlow, Ireland
T 00353 (0) 599140400/599140705

ON THE N80 If heading from Carlow town centre to Tullow on the N80, Devoys can be found about 1 mile out of the town on the left-hand side before the R725 joins the N80.

CREDIT/DEBIT CARDS

FUEL CARDS (see key on page 6)
① ② ④ ⑨ ⑪ ⑰ ⑳ ㉑ ㉘ ㉝

TRUCK FACILITIES
Overnight LGV parking in nearby church and shopping centre
Short-term coach parking available (2 spaces)
Truck washing facilities nearby
Tyre repair/sales nearby

DRIVER FACILITIES
Takeaway food nearby

SITE COMMENTS/INFORMATION
1 mile from town centre

Nearby parking PM hours only. Nearby bunker fuel 24 hours. All on-site facilities 07:30-22:00 Mon-Sun **FP133**

Gables Service Station, Helston

Trevenen, Helston
Cornwall TR13 0NE
T 01326 572593

ON THE A394 From Helston take the A394 towards Falmouth. Gables Service Station is on the right-hand side 1 mile after the turning for Gweek.

CREDIT/DEBIT CARDS

FUEL CARDS (see key on page 6)
① ⑮ ㊹

TRUCK FACILITIES
Overnight parking next door, 2 spaces, free

DRIVER FACILITIES
Accommodation available nearby, next door, B&B £25.00
Quiet area

SITE COMMENTS/INFORMATION
Easy access for LGVs
Post Office

Nearby overnight parking 24 hours. All other on-site facilities 07:00-21:00 **FP134**

Grants Filling Station, Newtownmore

Perth Road, Newtownmore
Highland PH20 1AP
T 01540 673217

ON THE B9150 From the A9, take the B9150 into Newtonmore and Grants is on your left-hand side in the village before you reach the A86.

CREDIT/DEBIT CARDS

FUEL CARDS (see key on page 6)
① ② ④ ⑦ ㊳

TRUCK FACILITIES
Overnight parking next door at Chefs Grill

DRIVER FACILITIES
Accommodation available nearby, 500 yards, The Pines

SITE COMMENTS/INFORMATION
Large forecourt area
Train/tram/underground/metro nearby
Easy access for LGVs

Parking 24 hours at nearby Chefs Grill. All on-site facilities 07:00-22:00 Mon-Sun **FP135**

Harcombe Cross Service Station, Chudleigh

Harcombe Cross, Chudleigh
Newton Abbot, Devon TQ13 0DF
T 01626 854033

ON THE A38 From the end of the M5 continue onto the A38 towards Plymouth. Go up the steep hill and Harcombe Cross Service Station is on the south-westbound carriageway, on the downward slope.

CREDIT/DEBIT CARDS

FUEL CARDS (see key on page 6)
4 5 6 39 46

TRUCK FACILITIES
Overnight parking in lay-by

All on-site facilities 07:00-22:00

FP136

Hulland General Store, Hulland Ward

Main Road, Hulland Ward, nr Ashbourne
Derbyshire DE6 3EA
T 01335 370088

ON THE A517 Hulland General Store Ltd is in the village of Hulland Ward on the A517 on the left-hand side if heading towards Ashbourne from Belper.

CREDIT/DEBIT CARDS

FUEL CARDS (see key on page 6)
1 2 4 9 37

TRUCK FACILITIES
Overnight parking nearby
Ample room for manoeuvring

DRIVER FACILITIES
Takeaway food
Truckers' accessories
Quiet area nearby

Nearby parking 24 hours. Other on-site facilities 06:00-18:30 Mon-Sun

FP137

Jeremy's Corner Star Service Station, Bolney

London Road, Bolney
Haywards Heath, West Sussex RH17 5QD
T 01444 880100

ON THE OLD A23 If heading northbound on the A23, go past Hickstead and over the junction with the A272. Take the next sliproad to Bolney village. Turn right at the roundabout and continue for half a mile. Jeremy's is 300 yards past the pub on the right.

CREDIT/DEBIT CARDS

FUEL CARDS (see key on page 6)
1 2 3 4 5 9 15 44

TRUCK FACILITIES
Overnight parking 50 yards away

DRIVER FACILITIES
Quiet area nearby

SITE COMMENTS/INFORMATION
Very friendly site offering an excellent service to all customers

Nearby parking 24 hours. All on-site facilties 06:00-22:00

FP138

Lindisfarne Service Station, Beal

Beal, Berwick upon Tweed
Northumberland TD15 2PD
T 01289 381232

ON THE A1 SOUTHBOUND Lindisfarne is on the A1 on the right-hand side if heading north, at the junction for the road to Holy Island. Six miles south of Berwick upon Tweed.

CREDIT/DEBIT CARDS

FUEL CARDS (see key on page 6)
① ② ③ ㊺

TRUCK FACILITIES
Overnight parking in lay-by, 10 spaces

DRIVER FACILITIES
Takeaway food
Truckers' accessories

SITE COMMENTS/INFORMATION
Truckers made very welcome

Nearby parking 24 hours. All on-site facilities 06:00-23:00 Mon-Sun

FP139

Lochbroom Filling Station, Ullapool

Grave Road, Ullapool
Rosshire IV26 2SX
T 01845 612560/612298

ON THE A835 Take the A9 north-west out of Inverness. At Tore, turn left onto the A835 and continue to Ullapool. Lochbroom Filling Station is on the right-hand side just before the junction with the A893.

CREDIT/DEBIT CARDS

FUEL CARDS (see key on page 6)
① ② ⑤ ⑧

TRUCK FACILITIES
Overnight parking nearby

DRIVER FACILITIES
Accommodation available nearby, half a mile, Ceilidh Place

SITE COMMENTS/INFORMATION
Site very close to the ferry terminal

All on-site facilities 07:30-20:00

FP140

Locks Garage, Hereford

Allensmore, Hereford
Herefordshire HR2 9AS
T 01981 570206

A465 B348 INTERSECTION Locks Garage can be found on the A465 at the junction with the B4348 and on the left-hand side if heading towards Hereford.

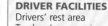

CREDIT/DEBIT CARDS

FUEL CARDS (see key on page 6)
① ② ③ ④ ⑧

TRUCK FACILITIES
Overnight parking half a mile away (6 spaces)
Coach parking (shared with LGV) available
Truck washing facilities
Ample room for manoeuvring

DRIVER FACILITIES
Drivers' rest area
Truckers' accessories
Phone top-ups/accessories
Takeaway food nearby

Nearby parking 24 hours. All on-site facilities 05:00-22:00 Mon-Sun

FP141

Long & Small Service Station, Maryport

Main Road, Flimby, Maryport
Cumbria CA15 8RB
T 01900 602742

ON THE A596 Long and Small is on the A596 on the left-hand side if heading north about 800 yards past the village of Flimby and 800 yards south of the town of Maryport.

CREDIT/DEBIT CARDS

FUEL CARDS (see key on page 6)
① ② ③ ⑨

TRUCK FACILITIES
Nearby overnight parking

DRIVER FACILITIES
Truckers' accessories

All on-site facilities 07:00-19:00 Mon-Fri

FP142

Low Row Service Station, Brampton

Low Row, Brampton
Cumbria CA8 2JE
T 01697 746344

ON THE A69 Exit the M6 at junction 44 and take the A69 eastbound. Go around Brampton and continue for 2 more miles. Low Row Service Station is on the left-hand side.

CREDIT/DEBIT CARDS

FUEL CARDS (see key on page 6)
① ② ③ ④ ⑤ ⑦ ⑫ ⑬ ㉟ ㊱ ㊲ ㊳
㊶

TRUCK FACILITIES
Nearby overnight parking

DRIVER FACILITIES
Truckers' accessories
Hot drink free with 100 litres of fuel
Takeaway food

All on-site facilities 24 hours

FP143

Lynfield Motors Ltd, Witham

London Road, Witham
Essex CM8 1ED
T 01376 536030

ON THE B1389 From Chelmsford take the A12 towards Witham. On the outskirts of Witham take the sliproad for B1389. Lynfield Motors is on the roundabout at the bottom of the sliproad.

CREDIT/DEBIT CARDS

FUEL CARDS (see key on page 6)
⑤ ⑥

TRUCK FACILITIES
Overnight parking in lay-by

SITE COMMENTS/INFORMATION
This site was the winner of the 2004 'Food to Go' award!

All on-site facilities 24 hours

FP144

Lyons of Nenagh

Limerick Road, Nenagh
County Tipperary, Ireland
T 00353 (0) 6733664/6733442
ON THE R445 From the N7 Limerick Road if heading towards Rosrea, take the first left off the N7 Nenagh bypass signposted towards the town. Follow the N52 towards the town, then take the R445, straight across at the roundabout. Lyons is half a mile along on the left.

CREDIT/DEBIT CARDS
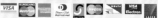
FUEL CARDS (see key on page 6)
② ④ ⑨ ⑪ ⑳ ㉑ ㊲

TRUCK FACILITIES
Nearby overnight parking
Truck washing facilities

DRIVER FACILITIES
Truckers' accessories

All on-site facilities 08:00-20:00 | **FP145**

Mellors of Challow Ltd

Faringdon Road, East Challow
Wantage, Oxfordshire OX12 9TE
T 01235 760606

ON THE A417 Take the A417 out of Wrantage towards Faringdon. Mellors of Challow is on the right-hand side, 1 mile beyond East Challow and just before the turning for West Challow.

CREDIT/DEBIT CARDS

FUEL CARDS (see key on page 6)
① ② ④ ⑦ ⑧ ⑪ ⑫ ⑬ ㊲ ㊳ ㊵ ㊶

TRUCK FACILITIES
Overnight parking on roadside within industrial estate.
Truck dealership/workshop
Windscreen repair facility
Tyre repair/sales

DRIVER FACILITIES
Drivers' washroom
Takeaway food
Truckers' accessories

All on-site facilities 07:00-19:00 | **FP146**

Parkwall Service Station, Wrexham

Mold Road, Gwersylt, Wrexham
Denbighshire LL11 4AH
T 01978 759020

ON THE A541 Take the A541 from Wrexham towards Mold. Parkwall Service Station is at Gwersylt set back from the road on the left-hand side at the start of the dual carriageway. It is also about 600 yards on from the turning for the train station.

CREDIT/DEBIT CARDS

FUEL CARDS (see key on page 6)

① ④ ⑦

TRUCK FACILITIES
NOT ACCESSIBLE FOR ARTICS
Overnight parking on road outside site

SITE COMMENTS/INFORMATION
Train/tram/underground/metro nearby

Nearby parking 24 hours. All on-site facilities 06:30-22:00 | **FP147**

Peterhead Motors, Peterhead

South Road, Peterhead
Aberdeenshire AB42 2XX
T 01779 475171

ON THE A982 If heading northbound into the town along the A982, Peterhead Motors is on the left-hand side, a few yards south of the junction with the A950.

CREDIT/DEBIT CARDS

FUEL CARDS (see key on page 6)
① ② ③ ④ ⑦

TRUCK FACILITIES
Truck washing facilities
Tank cleaning facilities
Nearby overnight parking

DRIVER FACILITIES
Truckers' accessories
Takeaway food

SITE COMMENTS/INFORMATION
Well stocked Spar Shop on-site

Toilets 06:30-22:00. Other on-site facilities 24 hours

FP148

Phoenix Filling Station, Bradford

93 Listerhills Road, Bradford
West Yorkshire BD7 3AG
T 01274 721896

ON THE B6145 Take the A641 towards City Centre. At the roundabout with Princess Way turn left Joining the A6181 and follow it around for 300 yards. At the junction with the B6145, turn left into Thornton Road, after a few 100 yards turn left into Listerhills Road.

CREDIT/DEBIT CARDS

FUEL CARDS (see key on page 6)
① ② ③ ⑨

TRUCK FACILITIES
Overnight parking, PM only next to Boots warehouse
Truck dealership/workshop nearby
Credit/debit cards accepted at auto bunker

DRIVER FACILITIES
Truckers' accessories

Nearby parking PM only. All on-site facilities 24 hours

FP149

Pierce Kavanagh Properties Ltd, Urlingford

Church View, Urlingford
County Kilkenny, Ireland
T 00353 (0) 568831213/568831234

ON THE N8 If heading north-eastbound on the N8, Pierce Kavanagh Properties is in Urlingford on the left-hand side, 200 yards before the junction with the R693.

CREDIT/DEBIT CARDS

FUEL CARDS (see key on page 6)
⑩ ㉑ ㉔

TRUCK FACILITIES
Short-term coach parking available
(10 spaces), shared with LGV
Nearby overnight parking

DRIVER FACILITIES
Truckers' accessories

Toilets 24 hours. All other on-site facilities 06:00-23:00

FP150

Q8 Bilborough Top Services, York

York/Leeds Road, Bilborough, York
North Yorkshire YO23 3PP
T 01937 832720

ON THE A64 This site can be found at Bilborough on the A64 between Leeds and York on the south-west bound carriageway, one and a half miles west of the interchange with the A1237.

Toilets 07:00-22:00. Other on-site facilities 24 hours

CREDIT/DEBIT CARDS

FUEL CARDS (see key on page 6)
1 4 10 42

TRUCK FACILITIES
Truck dealership/workshop
Nearby overnight parking

DRIVER FACILITIES
Accommodation available nearby,
400 yards, Travel Inn

FP151

Quatford Service Station, Quatford

Kidderminster Road, Quatford
nr Bridgnorth, Shropshire WV15 6QJ
T 01746 763039

ON THE A442 Take the A442 south from Bridgnorth. Quatford Service Station is on the left-hand side at the south end of the village of Quatford.

All on-site facilities 07:00-19:00. Nearby parking PM only

CREDIT/DEBIT CARDS

FUEL CARDS (see key on page 6)
1 2

TRUCK FACILITIES
Overnight parking 2 miles away, Severn Street Car Park, Bridgnorth

DRIVER FACILITIES
Takeaway food
Truckers' accessories

FP152

Roundabout Service Station, Mold

Kings Street (Heol Y Brenin), Mold
Flintshire CH7 1LB
T 01352 757232

ON THE A5119 From Wrexham take the A451 towards Mold. Continue through Mold on this road, past the roundabout with the A494 until the roundabout with the A5119. Roundabout Service Station will be right in front of you.

All on-site facilities 24 hours

CREDIT/DEBIT CARDS

FUEL CARDS (see key on page 6)
1 2 4 5 19 40 46

TRUCK FACILITIES
Overnight parking opposite site

DRIVER FACILITIES
Accommodation available nearby,
600 Yards, Bryn Awel Hotel
Takeaway food nearby

FP153

S R Tomson & Son, Tamworth

78 Glascote Road, Tamworth
Staffordshire B77 2AF
T 01827 50237/63137

ON THE B5000 From M42 junction 10 take A5 towards Tamworth until junction with the A51. Turn right on to the A51. At next major junction turn right and follow signs for Glascote. S R Tomson is on the B5000 just by McGregor School.

CREDIT/DEBIT CARDS

FUEL CARDS (see key on page 6)

TRUCK FACILITIES
Overnight parking in Castle grounds

SITE COMMENTS/INFORMATION
Excellent service

Nearby parking times unknown. All other on-site facilities 24 hours

FP154

Morrisons Filling Station, Clevedon

Morrisons Supermarkets Ltd
145 Old Church Road, Clevedon
North Somerset BS21 7TU
T 01275 875055
OFF THE M5 JUNCTION 20 Exit M5 junction 20 for Clevedon. At the next roundabout go straight ahead towards town. At the small roundabout go straight ahead then turn left at the T-junction, continue half a mile, filling station is on the right.

CREDIT/DEBIT CARDS

FUEL CARDS (see key on page 6)

TRUCK FACILITIES
Overnight parking on roadside only, 1 mile away on industrial estate

DRIVER FACILITIES
Truckers' accessories
Takeaway food nearby
Clothing for sale nearby

All on-site facilities 06:00-21:00. Nearby overnight parking PM only

FP155

Shell Crediton

Exeter Road, Crediton
Devon EX17 3BN
T 01363 778910

ON THE A377 Take the A377 out of Crediton towards Exeter. Shell Crediton is on the right-hand side, just past the train station.

CREDIT/DEBIT CARDS

FUEL CARDS (see key on page 6)

TRUCK FACILITIES
Overnight parking in train station car park, free

DRIVER FACILITIES
Truckers' accessories

SITE COMMENTS/INFORMATION
Train/tram/underground/metro nearby
Easy to find
Easy access for LGVs

All on-site facilities 06:00-23:00

FP156

Shell Lairds

New Chester Road, Birkenhead
Wirral CH43 4UX
T 0151 6660940

ON THE A41 From the M53, exit at junction 5 and take the A41 towards Birkenhead for 7 miles. Continue for 400 yards beyond the junction with the B5136 and Shell Lairds is on the right-hand side.

CREDIT/DEBIT CARDS

FUEL CARDS (see key on page 6)
8

TRUCK FACILITIES
Overnight parking on Cambell Town Road
Ample room for manoeuvring

DRIVER FACILITIES
Truckers' accessories
Takeaway food nearby

SITE COMMENTS/INFORMATION
Train/tram/underground/metro nearby

All on-site facilities 24 hours

FP157

Shell Staxton

Old Malton Road, Staxton, Scarborough
North Yorkshire YO12 6PD
T 01944 712900

ON THE A64 Shell Staxton is on the A64 south of Scarborough, just west of the roundabout with the A1039.

CREDIT/DEBIT CARDS

FUEL CARDS (see key on page 6)
8

TRUCK FACILITIES
Overnight parking 1 mile away in lay-by

SITE COMMENTS/INFORMATION
Friendly site, easy access site for LGVs

All on-site facilities and nearby parking 24 hours

FP158

Shell Swansea Bay

Fabian Way, Neath
Carmarthenshire SA11 2JU
T 01792 326900

ON THE A483 From the M4, exit at junction 42 and take the A483 towards Swansea. Turn right around at the first roundabout and Shell Swansea will be on your left. To get back to Swansea, continue to and under the M4. Turn right around at the roundabout with the A48.

CREDIT/DEBIT CARDS

FUEL CARDS (see key on page 6)
4 7 8 19 36 37 46

TRUCK FACILITIES
Overnight parking in lay-by half a mile away

SITE COMMENTS/INFORMATION
This is the only site on this road with LGV access. Staff are friendly, polite and willing to help in any situation. Staff and manager pride themselves on running a clean, well presented site

Toilets 05:00-23:00. All other on-site facilities 24 hours

FP159

Shell Wentworth Park Service Station

Maple Road, Tankersley, Barnsley
South Yorkshire S75 3DL
T 01226 350479

OFF THE A61 From junction 35 of the M1, take the A61 heading west towards Chapeltown. At the roundabout with the A616 take the 4th exit onto the industrial estate and Maple Road. Follow the road around and Shell Wentworth is on your right.

CREDIT/DEBIT CARDS

FUEL CARDS (see key on page 6)
① ② ③ ④ ⑤ ⑥ ⑧ ⑫ ⑬ ㉕ ㉟ ㊳ ㊴

TRUCK FACILITIES
Overnight parking on industrial estate road (10 spaces)
Coach parking available (5 spaces)

DRIVER FACILITIES
Accommodation available nearby,
   100 yards, Travel Inn
Truckers' accessories

Nearby parking and all on-site facilities 24 hours

FP160

Skipbridge Service Station

Green Hammerton, York
North Yorkshire YO26 8EQ
T 01423 330365

ON THE A59 From junction 47 of the A1M take the A59 towards York. Skipbridge Services is about 5 miles along on the right-hand side, past the village of Kirk Hammerton.

CREDIT/DEBIT CARDS

FUEL CARDS (see key on page 6)
⑦

TRUCK FACILITIES
Overnight parking half a mile away (15 spaces)
Coach parking available (10 spaces)
Ample room for manoeuvring
Fridge lorry area

DRIVER FACILITIES
Truckers' accessories
Takeaway food

SITE COMMENTS/INFORMATION
Train/tram/underground/metro nearby
Access for larger loads can be a little tight

Nearby parking 24 hours. Other on-site facilities 06:30-21:00

FP161

Smithaleigh Service Station

Plympton, Plymouth
Devon PL7 5AX
T 01752 893003

ON THE A38 WESTBOUND If heading east, take the sliproad for Lee Mill and Services and continue past services. Take next right and right again, re-enter carriageway and take next immediate slip. Smithaleigh is on the right. If heading west, take sliproad after Lee Mills.

CREDIT/DEBIT CARDS

FUEL CARDS (see key on page 6)

④ ⑤ ⑥

TRUCK FACILITIES
Overnight parking in lay-by

All on-site facilities 06:00-22:00

FP162

Star Kingsham

East Kingsham, Chichester
West Sussex PO19 2TH
T 01243 817100

ON THE A27 EASTBOUND Star Kingsham is on the A27 eastbound carriageway around Chichester and is located between the junction with the A286 and the junction with the B2145.

CREDIT/DEBIT CARDS

FUEL CARDS (see key on page 6)
①②③④⑨⑭

TRUCK FACILITIES
Overnight parking in lay-by prior to filling station

DRIVER FACILITIES
Accommodation available nearby, half a
  mile, Bedford Hotel
Internet access

SITE COMMENTS/INFORMATION
Train/tram/underground/metro nearby
Chirpy, friendly, customer focused staff

All on-site facilities and nearby parking 24 hours

FP163

Star Sutterton Service Station

Holbeach Road, Sutterton, Boston
Lincolnshire PE20 9LG
T 01205 462800

ON THE A17 Take the A16 from Spalding to Boston and turn right at the roundabout with the A17. Star Sutterton Service Station is 50 yards on the left.

CREDIT/DEBIT CARDS

FUEL CARDS (see key on page 6)
①②③⑨

TRUCK FACILITIES
Nearby overnight parking

DRIVER FACILITIES
Drivers' washroom
Drivers' rest area
Takeaway food nearby

SITE COMMENTS/INFORMATION
Friendly staff
Clean facilities and tidy, well stocked shop

All on-site facilities 24 hours except toilets

FP164

Steamerpoint Service Station

Barry Walker & Sons, Swaffham Road
Ickburgh, Thetford, Norfolk IP26 5HX
T 01842 878759

ON THE A1065 Take the A134 from Thetford to King's Lynn. At the junction with the A1065, turn right towards Ickburgh. Steamerpoint is 1 mile along on the right.

CREDIT/DEBIT CARDS

FUEL CARDS (see key on page 6)
①㊺

TRUCK FACILITIES
Nearby overnight parking
Short-term coach parking available

DRIVER FACILITIES
Truckers' accessories

SITE COMMENTS/INFORMATION
Easy access for LGVs

All on-site facilities 06:30-20:00

FP165

Straddle Service Station

**Clyghore, Ballyshannon
County Donegal, Ireland
T 00353 (0) 719852555**

ON THE N15 Take the N15 south from Donegal and continue on it through Ballyshannon. Straddle Service Station is on the left-hand side, 200 yards beyond the roundabout with the N3 Belleek Road.

CREDIT/DEBIT CARDS

FUEL CARDS (see key on page 6)
㉑ ㉔

TRUCK FACILITIES
Nearby overnight parking (6 spaces, free)
Short-term coach parking (5 spaces)
Truck dealership/workshop nearby

DRIVER FACILITIES
Internet access
Truckers' accessories
Euros changed/accepted

Fuel bunker 24 hours. All other on-site facilities 07:30-23:00. On-site parking times unknown   **FP166**

Suthers Star Garage

**Liverpool Road, Walmer Bridge, Preston
Lancashire PR4 5JS
T 01772 612281/616721**

OFF THE A59 Take the A59 from Ormskirk to Preston, past Tarleton and the B5247 for Leyland. Continue to Much Hoole. At the roundabout with the Fox Cub pub, take 2nd exit to Walmer Bridge and keep to the left fork. Suthers Star Garage is 200 yards on the right.

CREDIT/DEBIT CARDS

FUEL CARDS (see key on page 6)
⑤ ⑦ ⑧

TRUCK FACILITIES
Overnight parking in Longton Business Park
Tyre repair/sales

DRIVER FACILITIES
Takeaway food
Post Office nearby

SITE COMMENTS/INFORMATION
Family run business established in 1930!

All on-site facilities 07:00-22:00   **FP167**

Texaco Star Tollbar

**Gonerby Moor, Grantham
Lincolnshire NG32 2AD
T 01400 259400**

ON THE A1 SOUTHBOUND Texaco Star Tollbar is on the A1 southbound carriageway between Long Bennington and Grantham, on the left-hand side and on the corner of the turning for Marston.

CREDIT/DEBIT CARDS

FUEL CARDS (see key on page 6)
① ② ③ ④ ⑨ ⑬

TRUCK FACILITIES
Overnight parking at the Gonerby Moor roundabout A1 junction with B1174.
Credit/debit cards accepted at auto bunker

DRIVER FACILITIES
Accommodation available nearby at Gonerby Moor roundabout
Truckers' accessories

SITE COMMENTS/INFORMATION
Multi-lingual staff. Seven languages spoken! English, German, French, Spanish, Italian, Russian and Latvian

All on-site facilities 07:00-22:00   **FP168**

Thickthorn Service Station

Norwich Road, Hethersett, Norwich
Norfolk NR9 3AU
T 01603 508910

ON THE B1172 Take the A11 from Norwich to Thetford to the roundabout with the A47 and B1172. Take the B1172 towards Hethersett and Thickthorn Service Station is 200 yards on the left.

CREDIT/DEBIT CARDS

FUEL CARDS (see key on page 6)
⑧ ⑲ ㉟ ㊻

TRUCK FACILITIES
Short-term coach parking (2 spaces)
Overnight parking at Norwich cattle market

DRIVER FACILITIES
Accommodation available nearby, 10 yards, Travelodge

SITE COMMENTS/INFORMATION
This site also sells hot pasties

All on-site facilities 24 hours — **FP169**

Thomas Flynn & Sons Ltd

The Downs, Mullingar
County Westmeath, Ireland
T 00353 (0) 4476100/4476115

ON THE N4 Take the N4 out of Mullingar towards Dublin. Thomas Flynn & Sons is on the dual carriageway on the left-hand side, 1 mile after the turning for the R156 to Killucan.

CREDIT/DEBIT CARDS

FUEL CARDS (see key on page 6)
⑨ ⑳ ㉑

TRUCK FACILITIES
Short-term coach parking (7 spaces)
Nearby overnight parking (5 spaces)

DRIVER FACILITIES
Internet access
Truckers' accessories

SITE COMMENTS/INFORMATION
Low cost fuel. Excellent location

All on-site facilities 08:30-18:00. Short-term on-site and nearby overnight parking times unknown — **FP170**

Total Service Station, Ardwick

Chancellor Lane, Ardwick, Manchester
Greater Manchester M12 6JZ
T 0161 2731030

ON THE A665 Take the A75M east through Manchester to the end. Merge onto the A365 and follow signs for the A665. Turn south on the A665 towards the Longsight District. Total Service Station Ardwick is 200 yards on the left.

CREDIT/DEBIT CARDS

FUEL CARDS (see key on page 6)
④ ㊻

TRUCK FACILITIES
Overnight parking just around the corner

DRIVER FACILITIES
Truckers' accessories
Takeaway food nearby

SITE COMMENTS/INFORMATION
This site is close to all routes in and out of the city centre

All on-site facilities 24 hours — **FP171**

Viewforth Filling Station

**Kincardine Bridge Road, Falkirk
Stirlingshire FK2 8PH
T 01324 831895**

ON THE A876 Take the M9 exit 7 onto the M876 and follow it to the roundabout at the end. Continue on the A876 for 1 mile. Viewforth Services is on the left.

CREDIT/DEBIT CARDS

FUEL CARDS (see key on page 6)
① ② ③ ④ ⑤ ⑥ ⑨ ⑬ ㉟ ㊱ ㊲ ㊳

TRUCK FACILITIES
Overnight parking on lane close to the site

DRIVER FACILITIES
Takeaway food

SITE COMMENTS/INFORMATION
This site is close to all major motorways in the area

Nearby parking 24 hours. All on-site facilities 06:00-22:00

FP172

STARTING OUT

An exciting new series of novels by Wendy Glindon

Based on the author's own experiences behind the wheel, the stories centre around the enduring bond of friendship between the two main characters, vivacious lady trucker Carol Landers and her glamorous soul mate Gina, supporting each other without question, regardless of the situation, while giving the reader an insight into the lives of lady truckers on the roads of Europe where the only thing the women can ultimately rely on is their solid friendship and uncompromising trust in each other.

**Both these books are on sale at all good bookshops, Amazon on-line or direct from the author's website:
www.mothertrucker.co.uk**

DRIVING ON

Alt Border Trading Ltd

**Alt Upper, Castlefin
County Donegal, Ireland
T 00353 (0) 749146200**

ON THE R235 From Castlefin take the R235 south towards Castlederg. Alt Border Trading is 4 miles on the left-hand side, just before the border.

CREDIT/DEBIT CARDS

FUEL CARDS (see key on page 6)
⑪ ㉑ ㉔

TRUCK FACILITIES
Short-term coach parking (3 spaces)
Truck dealership/workshop

All on-site facilities 07:30-22:30 **FB173**

Asco UK, Peterhead

**Asco Oils Ltd, Upperton Yard, Damhead
Peterhead, Aberdeenshire AB42 2PF
T 01779 873014/873090**

OFF THE A90 From Ellon, take the A90 north-eastbound towards Peterhead. At the roundabout with the A982, turn left staying on the A90. Take the next small turning on the left and left again into Asco UK.

CREDIT/DEBIT CARDS

FUEL CARDS (see key on page 6)
①

TRUCK FACILITIES
Ample room for manoeuvring

Bunker fuel 24 hours. Manned by security guard **FB174**

B Brogan, Stevenson

**B Brogan Ltd, Old Quarry Road
off New Street, Stevenson, Ayrshire
KA20 3HS
T 01294 468511**

OFF THE B752 Take A78 dual carriageway west around Kilwinning. At roundabout with A738 turn left along the A78. Go past Safeway. At roundabout with A738 Townhead Street, take that road for 500 yards. Left into New Street B752 then 2nd left.

CREDIT/DEBIT CARDS

FUEL CARDS (see key on page 6)
① ② ③

TRUCK FACILITIES
Truck washing facilities
Ample room for manoeuvring
Short-term parking only with permission

DRIVER FACILITIES
Post Office nearby
Takeaway food nearby

SITE COMMENTS/INFORMATION
Fuel can be paid for in cash
Internet access coming soon to this site
Train/tram/underground/metro nearby

All on-site facilities 07:00-17:00 Mon-Fri. 08:00-12:00 Sat. **FB175**

Ballie Brothers Ltd

Linkwood Place, Linkwood Ind. Est. Elgin, Moray IV30 1HZ
T 01343 555312

OFF THE A96 Take the A96 Elgin to Lhanbryde Road, following the signs for Linkwood Industrial Estate on the outskirts of Elgin. Take the first right after turning into the estate and Ballie Brothers is on the left.

CREDIT/DEBIT CARDS

FUEL CARDS (see key on page 6)
❶❷❸

TRUCK FACILITIES
Short-term coach parking (14 spaces)
Truck washing facilities
Truck dealership/workshop
Tyre repair/sales nearby

DRIVER FACILITIES
Accommodation nearby, half a mile, Travel Inn
Takeaway food

Short-term parking and bunker fuel 24 hours. Other on-site facilities 06:30-02:00   **FB176**

Bayford & Co, Halifax

Bayford & Co Ltd, Stainland Road Greetland, Halifax, West Yorkshire HX4 8LP
T 01422 373394 www.bayford.co.uk

ON THE B6112 Bayford & Co Halifax is on the B6112 about 300 yards south of the junction with the A6026 and A609. It's on the right-hand side if heading towards Greetland.

CREDIT/DEBIT CARDS

FUEL CARDS (see key on page 6)
❶

All on-site facilities 08:00-17:15   **FB177**

Bayford & Co, Sheffield

Bayford & Co Ltd, Houghton Road North Anston Trading Est., North Anston, Sheffield, South Yorkshire S25 4JJ
T 01909 567131

OFF THE B6463 From the M1, exit at junction 31 and take the A57 to Worksop. After 1 mile turn left onto the B6463 Todwick road then take the 2nd right into Houghton Road. Bayford & Co is 200 yards along on the right.

CREDIT/DEBIT CARDS

FUEL CARDS (see key on page 6)
❶❷❸

All on-site facilities 06:00-17:15   **FB178**

Bryan J Nunn Haulage Ltd

**Transport Depot, Chapel Pond Hill
Bury St Edmunds, Suffolk IP32 7HT
T 01284 705300**

OFF THE A143 From the roundabout with the A14 and A143, take the A143 towards Diss and Great Yarmouth. Continue over the next roundabout and turn right at the next, into Hollow Road. Take the next left and Bryan J Nunn is on the right.

CREDIT/DEBIT CARDS

FUEL CARDS (see key on page 6)
① ② ③ ⑩

TRUCK FACILITIES
Truck washing facilities

Bunker fuel 24 hours

FB179

British Benzol, Bridgwater

**British Benzol Ltd, Unit 12
Wylds Road Industrial Estate
Bridgwater, Somerset TA6 4DH
T 01278 426464**

OFF THE A38 Junction 23 of M5, take A38 towards Bridgwater for about 1 and a half miles. Turn right into Wylds Road (about 800 yards before the junction with the A39) and follow the road around to the left. British Benzol is 200 yards on the left.

CREDIT/DEBIT CARDS

FUEL CARDS (see key on page 6)
①

TRUCK FACILITIES
Credit/debit cards accepted at fuel bunker
Truck dealership/workshop

DRIVER FACILITIES
Takeaway food nearby

All on-site facilities 06:00-18:00. Mon-Fri

FB180

Brobot, Atherstone

**Brobot Petroleum Ltd
30 Carlyton Road Industrial Estate
Atherstone, Warwickshire CV9 1JH
T 01827 714000**

OFF THE A5 From the M42 junction 10, take the A5 towards Nuneaton for 5 miles. By-pass Atherston to the roundabout with the B4111. Take 1st exit into Carlyton Road. Continue for 700 yards. Brobot is on the left on the left-hand bend.

CREDIT/DEBIT CARDS

FUEL CARDS (see key on page 6)
①

TRUCK FACILITIES
Ample room for manoeuvring

DRIVER FACILITIES
Accommodation nearby, half a mile, Chapel House Hotel
Takeaway food nearby

SITE COMMENTS/INFORMATION
Oil can be paid for in cash only

Oil during office hours only from 09:00-17:00. Other on-site facilities 24 hours

FB181

C H Jones Ltd Bunker Stop, Walsall

C H Jones Ltd, Queen Street
Premier Business Park, Walsall
West Midlands WS2 9PB
T 01922 615231

OFF THE A4148 From Junction 10 of the M6 take the A454 towards Walsall. After about half a mile turn right onto the A4148 towards West Bromwich. Take the next left then 2nd right and CH Jones is on the left.

CREDIT/DEBIT CARDS

FUEL CARDS (see key on page 6)
① ⑩ ⑪ ㉕ ㉗ ㉚ ㉛

DRIVER FACILITIES
Takeaway food nearby

SITE COMMENTS/INFORMATION
Train/tram/underground/metro nearby

All on-site facilities 24 hours   **FB182**

Cahir Oil Ltd

Kedra, Cahir
County Tipperary, Ireland
T 00353 (0) 5242240

ON THE N8 From Cahir take the N8 north-east towards Urlingford. Cahir Oil is on the right-hand side, 400 yards beyond the junction with the R670.

CREDIT/DEBIT CARDS
VISA · Mastercard · · ·

FUEL CARDS (see key on page 6)
② ⑪ ㉑

TRUCK FACILITIES
Truck washing facilities
Truck dealership/workshop

All on-site facilities 08:00-18:00 Mon-Fri, 08:00-13:00 Sat   **FB183**

Carlton Fuels, Liverpool

Carlton Fuels Ltd, Gores Road
Knowlsley Road Industrial Park North
Liverpool, Merseyside L33 7XS
T 0151 5466660

OFF THE A5028 From M57 junction 4, take A5208 towards Kirkby for 1 mile. At roundabout turn right on A5028. Take next slip road and follow road round into Gale Road for 250 yards. Turn left at end into Gores Road and it's 400 yards on left.

CREDIT/DEBIT CARDS

FUEL CARDS (see key on page 6)
① ② ③

TRUCK FACILITIES
Ample room for manoeuvring

DRIVER FACILITIES
Showers available

SITE COMMENTS/INFORMATION
Oil can be paid for in cash during manned times

Bunker fuel 24 hours. Other on-site facilities 07:00-19:00   **FB184**

Chandlers Oil & Gas, Grantham

**Chandlers Oil & Gas Ltd,
Warren Way, Alma Park Industrial Estate,
Grantham, Lincolnshire NG31 9SE
T 01476 576200**

OFF THE A607 Take the A607 northbound out of Grantham. Continue past Texaco garage. Turn right into Belton Lane before hospital. Take 2nd right into Harrowby Lane for 1 mile. Left into Alma Park Road for half a mile then left into Warren Way.

CREDIT/DEBIT CARDS

FUEL CARDS (see key on page 6)
❶❷❸⓫
+ Smart Cards

TRUCK FACILITIES
Ample room for manoeuvring

Bunker fuel 24 hours. Site manned from 07:30-17:30 Mon-Fri. 09:00-12:00 Sat

FB185

Chandlers Oil & Gas, Lincoln

**Chandlers Oil & Gas Ltd
Wrightsway, off Outer Circle Road
Lincoln, Lincolnshire LN2 4JY
T 01522 530505/532623**

OFF THE B1308 From Horncastle take the A158 towards Lincoln. Turn left onto the B1308 and take the next left into Wrightsway. Chandlers is on the left at the bottom of the road.

CREDIT/DEBIT CARDS

FUEL CARDS (see key on page 6)
❶❷❸

DRIVER FACILITIES
Takeaway food nearby

All on-site facilities 24 hours

FB186

Containers Birmingham Base

**C H Jones Ltd, College Road, Perry Barr
Birmingham, West Midlands B44 8DR
T 0121 5521615**

ON THE A453 Exit the M6 at junction 7 and take the A34 towards the city centre. Continue until junction with A453. Turn left onto it and go under motorway. After Texaco garage turn right into the site.

CREDIT/DEBIT CARDS

FUEL CARDS (see key on page 6)
❶❷❸

TRUCK FACILITIES
Ample room for manoeuvring

DRIVER FACILITIES
Seating area
Takeway food

Bunker fuel 24 hours. Other on-site facilities opening times unknown

FB187

Corralls, Shoreham by Sea

**CPL Petroleum Ltd, 33 Brighton Road
Shoreham by Sea, West Sussex BN43 6SA
T 01273 455511**

ON THE A259 From the A27 Shoreham by-pass take the A283 exit and head towards Shoreham town. At the roundabout with the A259 follow signs to Brighton for half a mile. Corralls is on the right just past McDonalds.

CREDIT/DEBIT CARDS

FUEL CARDS (see key on page 6)
① ② ③ ㉗

TRUCK FACILITIES
Ample room for manoeuvring

DRIVER FACILITIES
Phone top-ups/accessories
Clothing for sale
Takeaway food nearby

SITE COMMENTS/INFORMATION
Train/tram/underground/metro nearby
Lubrication oil can be paid for in cash only. This site is within half a mile of the town centre. Please note that this site no longer accepts IDS cards

Bunker fuel 24 hours. Red diesel 08:30-16:00. This site is manned from 08:30-16:00   **FB188**

CPL Petroleum, Abercarn

**CPL Petroleum Ltd, Prince of Wales Ind. Est.
Abercarn, Gwent NP11 5AR
T 01495 247400**
OFF THE A467 Take the A467 northbound through Abercarn. Look for Commercial Road on your right running parallel with the A467. Turn left into Bridge Street and follow it around to the right, continue for 400 yards, turn left into dead end road. CPL is at the end.

CREDIT/DEBIT CARDS

FUEL CARDS (see key on page 6)
① ㉗

DRIVER FACILITIES
Post Office nearby

SITE COMMENTS/INFORMATION
Artics are advised to reverse into this site

Fuel 24 hours. This site is manned from 08:30-17:00 Mon-Fri. Lubrication oil 08:30-17:00 Mon-Fri   **FB189**

CPL Petroleum, Bangor

**CPL Petroleum Ltd, Llandygai Ind. Estate,
Bangor, Gwynedd LL57 4YH
T 01248 352768**

OFF THE A5 From the A55 take the A5 towards Bangor. Go straight at the first roundabout and left at the second onto the Llandygai Industrial Estate. Follow the road to the right and go left at the T-junction. Follow round to the right and it's on the right.

CREDIT/DEBIT CARDS

FUEL CARDS (see key on page 6)
① ㉗

All on-site facilities 24 hours   **FB190**

CPL Petroleum, East Kilbride

**CPL Petroleum Ltd, 22 Hawkbank Road
College Milton North, East Kilbride
Glasgow, South Lanarkshire G74 5HA
T 01355 243692**

OFF THE A726 Take the A726 towards East Kilbride from Glasgow. Continue 1 mile past roundabout with the B766. At next roundabout, turn left onto Stewartfield Way. Right at roundabout into Castleglen Road then left at roundabout into Hawkbank Road.

CREDIT/DEBIT CARDS

FUEL CARDS (see key on page 6)
❶

TRUCK FACILITIES
Ample room for manoeuvring

DRIVER FACILITIES
Accommodation nearby, half a mile,
   Stakis East Kilbride
Takeaway food nearby
Post Office nearby

SITE COMMENTS/INFORMATION
This site is 2 miles from all town centre facilities

Fuel 24 hours. Site is manned from 08.30-17:00 Mon-Fri, when red diesel/lubrication oil are available | **FB191**

CPL Petroleum, Grimsby

**CPL Petroleum Ltd, Estate Road No 2
South Humberside Industrial Estate
Grimsby, North East Lincolnshire DN31 2TG
T 01472 350421**

OFF THE A180 From Immingham take the A180 towards Grimsby. Go past the junction with the A1136 and turn right at the next roundabout. Continue for 150 yards, CPL is on the right.

CREDIT/DEBIT CARDS

FUEL CARDS (see key on page 6)
❶ ❸ ❿ ㉗

TRUCK FACILITIES
Ample room for manoeuvring

DRIVER FACILITIES
Accommodation nearby, half a mile,
   Travel Inn

Bunker fuel 24 hours. Other on-site facilities 08:00-17:00 | **FB192**

CPL Petroleum, Inverness

**CPL Petroleum Ltd, 33 Harbour Road
Longman Industrial Estate
Inverness, Highland IV1 1UA
T 01463 238989**

OFF THE A82 From the A9 heading north, by-pass Inverness and continue past junction with the B865. Left at next round-about and take A82 towards town. Left at next roundabout then second turning on the right. CPL is at the end of the road.

CREDIT/DEBIT CARDS

FUEL CARDS (see key on page 6)
❶ ㉗

DRIVER FACILITIES
Accommodation nearby, half a mile,
   Braemore Hotel & Travel Inn
Seating area nearby
Takeaway food nearby

Red diesel 08:30-17:00. All other on-site facilities 24 hours | **FB193**

CPL Petroleum, Ripon

CPL Petroleum Ltd
Dallmires Lane Industrial Estate
Ripon, North Yorkshire HG4 1TT
T 01765 607606

OFF THE A61 From the A1 if heading south, take the A61 Ripon ring road to Harrogate. Continue across the roundabout with the B6265 and take a right at the next immediate roundabout. CPL is a couple of yards along on the right.

CREDIT/DEBIT CARDS

FUEL CARDS (see key on page 6)

All on-site facilities 08:00-17:00   FB194

CPL Petroleum, Sheffield

CPL Petroleum Ltd, Parkway Avenue
Broadoaks, Sheffield, South Yorkshire S9 3BJ
T 0114 2440537

OFF THE A57 From M1 junction 33, follow the A630 towards Sheffield. Continue onto the A57 and across the junction with the A6102. At the next exit turn right crossing the carriageway, then left at the next roundabout. CPL is 200 yards along on the right.

CREDIT/DEBIT CARDS

FUEL CARDS (see key on page 6)

TRUCK FACILITIES
Truck dealership/workshop

SITE COMMENTS/INFORMATION
Train/tram/underground/metro nearby

Toilets and bunker fuel accessible 24 hours. Truck Dealership/Workshop 08:00-18:00   FB195

CPL Petroleum, Shefford

CPL Petroleum Ltd, 139 Clifton Road
Shefford, Bedfordshire SG17 5AG
T 01462 811201

OFF THE A6001 From the A1M Junction 10, take the A507 towards Shefford. At the junction with the A6001, turn right towards Henlow. Take the next left towards Clifton. Follow this road into the village towards Shefford. CPL is on your right.

CREDIT/DEBIT CARDS

FUEL CARDS (see key on page 6)

TRUCK FACILITIES
Ample room for manoeuvring
Truck dealership/workshop

DRIVER FACILITIES
Takeaway food nearby

All on-site facilities 07:30-18:00 Mon-Fri   FB196

CPL Petroleum, Wrexham

CPL Petroleum Ltd, Bryn Lane
Wrexham Industrial Estate
Wrexham LL13 9UT
T 01978 661896

OFF THE A534 Take the A534 north eastbound out of Wrexham. At the village of Llan-y-Pwll turn right into Hugmore Lane for half a mile. At the roundabout turn left into Bryn Lane. CPL is 500 yards on the right.

CREDIT/DEBIT CARDS

FUEL CARDS (see key on page 6)

TRUCK FACILITIES
Ample room for manoeuvring

DRIVER FACILITIES
Takeaway food nearby
Post Office
Euros changed/accepted

SITE COMMENTS/INFORMATION
Fuel can be paid for in cash during opening hours

Bunker fuel 24 hours. This site is manned 09:00-17:00 Mon-Fri when toilets/lubrication oil also available **FB197**

DCI Autopoint Silverstream

Tyholland, Near Monaghan
County Monaghan, Ireland
T 00353 (0) 4788150/91788110

ON THE N12 From Monaghan, take the N12 north-eastbound towards the border. DCI Autopoint is on the right-hand side, 1 mile beyond the turning for the R185 and 1 mile before the border.

CREDIT/DEBIT CARDS

FUEL CARDS (see key on page 6)

Short-term parking times unknown. Other on-site facilities 24 hours **FB198**

Deben Transport Ltd

Oyster House, Andes Road
Nursling Industrial Estate
Southampton, Hampshire SO16 0YZ
T 02380 735566

OFF THE M271 From the M27, take the M271 towards Southampton. Exit at the next junction and turn right towards Nursling Industrial Estate. Take 2nd exit at next roundabout. Deben is 20 yards on the left.

CREDIT/DEBIT CARDS

FUEL CARDS (see key on page 6)

TRUCK FACILITIES
Truck washing facilities
Truck dealership/workshop

DRIVER FACILITIES
Accommodation nearby, half a mile,
 Holiday Inn Express

All on-site facilities 24 hours **FB199**

Dundalk Truckstop

Emo Oil Ltd, Coes Road Industrial Estate Dundalk, County Louth, Ireland
T 00353 (0) 429338977/429333833

OFF THE N52 From the M1 take the N52 around the east side of Dundalk. Continue past the roundabout with the R172 for half a mile. Turn left onto the Coes Road Ind. Est. and Dundalk Truckstop is a few yards on the left.

CREDIT/DEBIT CARDS

FUEL CARDS (see key on page 6)
(10) (11) (17) (20) (21) (28)

All on-site facilities 24 hours

FB200

F Peart & Co Ltd

Baltic Street, Hartlepool
County Durham TS25 1PW
T 01429 263331/852130

OFF THE A689 From Stockton on Tees take the A689 towards Hartlepool. Continue on this road past the junction with the B1277. Turn right at the next roundabout. Take next right after Tesco into Baltic St. F Peart is 200 yards on the left.

CREDIT/DEBIT CARDS

FUEL CARDS (see key on page 6)
(1) (3)

TRUCK FACILITIES
Ample room for manoeuvring

DRIVER FACILITIES
Takeaway food nearby
Phone top-ups/accessories nearby
Clothing for sale nearby

SITE COMMENTS/INFORMATION
Oil can be paid for in cash during office hours

All on-site facilities 06:00-22:00. This site is manned from 08:00-17:00 Mon-Fri

FB201

Ford & Slater

C H Jones Ltd, Rowley Road
Coventry, Warwickshire CV3 4PY
T 024 76302514

OFF THE A45 From junction 2 of the M6 head south west on the A46 Coventry ring road. At the roundabout with the A45 take the 2nd exit towards the airport. At the next roundabout, turn right down Rowley Road and it's on the right.

CREDIT/DEBIT CARDS

FUEL CARDS (see key on page 6)
(1) (2) (3)

DRIVER FACILITIES
Accommodation nearby, half a mile, Chace Hotel
Seating area
Takeaway food available

Bunker fuel and parking 24 hours. Other on-site facilities times unknown

FB202

Ford Fuels

Ford Fuels Ltd, Gibbs Marsh Trading Estate Stalbridge, Sturminster Newton Dorset DT10 2RU
T 01963 363014

OFF THE A30 From the A30 Sherbourne to Shaftesbury road (if heading towards Shaftesbury) go straight on at the junction with the A357. Continue for about 1 mile, turn right at signs for Gibbs Marsh, left at T-junction, and then 2nd right onto the estate.

CREDIT/DEBIT CARDS

FUEL CARDS (see key on page 6)
❶❷❸

All on-site facilities 24 hours

FB203

Four Counties Oil, Dundalk

Four Counties Oil Ltd, Newry Road Dundalk, County Louth, Ireland
T 00353 (0) 429332299/862523170

ON THE N1 Head north on the M1 to the end and the junction with the N52. Turn right, then left onto the N1. Follow this through Dundalk centre heading for Newry. Four Counties is 500 yards past the river and on the right.

CREDIT/DEBIT CARDS

FUEL CARDS (see key on page 6)
❷❻㉑㉔

TRUCK FACILITIES
Credit/debit cards accepted at fuel bunker
Truck washing facilities

All on-site facilities opening times unknown

FB204

Fuelserve, Calais

Fuelserve Ltd, Rue des Goelands Zone Industrielle Des Dunes Calais, Nord Pas De Calais 62110, France
T 0033 (0) 321971194

OFF THE E15 The Zone Industrielle Des Dunes is surrounded by the E15 to the north and east and the D119 to the south and west. Follow signs into the estate. Find the Rue des Gareness and turn onto the Rue des Oyats then onto Rue des Goelands.

CREDIT/DEBIT CARDS

FUEL CARDS (see key on page 6)
❷❸

All on-site facilities 24 hours

FB205

Fuelserve, Felixstowe

Fuelserve Ltd, Walton Ave, Felixstowe
Suffolk IP11 8HE
T 01394 674812

OFF THE A14 From Ipswich, take the A14 to Felixstowe. At the junction with the A154 turn right continuing with the A14. At the next roundabout turn right into Walton Avenue. Fuelserve is 400 yards along on the right.

CREDIT/DEBIT CARDS

FUEL CARDS (see key on page 6)
① ② ③ ⑩

TRUCK FACILITIES
Truck dealership/workshop

All on-site facilities 08:00-00:00

FB206

G E Stevens Fuels

Ruskin Buildings, 4 Oakridge Road
High Wycombe, Buckinghamshire HP11 2PE
T 01494 522782

OFF THE A40 From the M40 exit at junction 4 and take the A404 into High Wycombe. At the Roundabout with the A40 turn left onto the A40 towards West Wycombe. After 800 yards turn left into Oakridge Road. G E Stevens is 40 yards on the left.

CREDIT/DEBIT CARDS

FUEL CARDS (see key on page 6)
① ③

All on-site facilities 07:00-17:00

FB207

G R Wardle & Son Ltd

Townfoot Garage, Haltwhistle
Northumberland NE49 0EJ
T 01434 320461

ON THE OLD A69 If heading from Newcastle Upon Tyne towards Carlisle on the A69, follow the signs to Haltwhistle which direct you along the old A69. G R Wardle is about 100 yards along on the right, on the east side of the town.

CREDIT/DEBIT CARDS

FUEL CARDS (see key on page 6)
① ② ③

DRIVER FACILITIES
Accommodation nearby, 800 yards, Ashcroft Guest House

All on-site facilities 24 hours

FB208

Havant Lorry Park

**C H Jones Ltd, Southmoor Lane
Havant, Hampshire PO9 1JW
T 02392 481001**

OFF THE A27 From the A3M southbound, exit at junction 5 and go straight across the roundabout towards the A27. Turn left onto the A27 and take the next right onto Southmoor Lane. Go across the next junction and Havant is on the left.

CREDIT/DEBIT CARDS

FUEL CARDS (see key on page 6)
❶❷❸

DRIVER FACILITIES
Seating area
Takeaway food available

Bunker fuel and parking 24 hours. Café and other on-site facilities opening times unknown **FB209**

Johnstone Fuels

**Dargavel Stores, Lockerbie Road
Dumfries, Dumfries and Galloway DG1 3PG
T 01387 750747**

ON THE A709 From Dumfries take the A709 towards Lockerbie. Johnstone Fuels is on the right-hand side 1 mile beyond the junction with the A75.

CREDIT/DEBIT CARDS

FUEL CARDS (see key on page 6)
❶❷❸

All on-site facilities 24 hours **FB210**

Johnstone Oils Ltd

**Standhill, Whitburn Industrial Estate
Bathgate, West Lothian EH48 2HR
T 01506 656535**

OFF THE A7066 From the M8, exit at junction 4. Take the A801 towards Armdale and Bathgate. Continue to roundabout with A706, A7066 and B702. Turn right onto A7066 for 600 yards. Turn left and left again into Inchcross Steadings, then 3rd left. Johnstone is on right.

CREDIT/DEBIT CARDS

FUEL CARDS (see key on page 6)
❶

TRUCK FACILITIES
Ample room for manoeuvring

DRIVER FACILITIES
Takeaway food nearby

SITE COMMENTS/INFORMATION
Red diesel and lubrication oil can be paid for in cash only

All on-site facilities 08:00-17:00 Mon-Fri **FB211**

Les Woolston Haulage Ltd

1-4 Puddlers Road, Southbank
Middlesborough TS6 6TX
T 01642 430704

OFF THE A66 Take the A66 out of Middlesborough city centre towards Redcar. At the roundabout with the B1513, continue on the A66 to the next roundabout where you turn left into Normanby Road. Take next right into Puddlers Road, Les Woolston is 200 yards on right.

CREDIT/DEBIT CARDS

FUEL CARDS (see key on page 6)
① ② ③

TRUCK FACILITIES
Truck washing facilities
Truck dealership/workshop

SITE COMMENTS/INFORMATION
Train/tram/underground/metro nearby

All on-site facilities 24 hours   **FB212**

M F Oils

5 Willis Way, Fleets Industrial Estate
Poole, Dorset BH15 3SS
T 01202 676263

OFF THE A349 From the A35, A3049, A350 roundabout take the A350 directly towards Poole town centre. Turn left at the next roundabout onto A349, take the next right into Willis Way. Take next 2 available right turns then left, left, and right. MF Oils is on the left.

CREDIT/DEBIT CARDS

FUEL CARDS (see key on page 6)
① ② ③ ⑩

DRIVER FACILITIES
Accommodation nearby, half a mile,
 Travel Inn
Takeaway food nearby

All on-site facilities 09:00-17:00   **FB213**

McDonalds Oil Ltd

Top Oil Ltd, Kinsale Road
Kinsale Road Industrial Estate
Cork, County Cork, Ireland
T 00353 (0) 214316300

OFF THE N27 From the N25 that runs east to west along the south of Cork, head for the roundabout junction with the N27. At that roundabout turn northbound into Kinsale Road Industrial Estate. McDonalds Oil is 300 yards on the left-hand side.

CREDIT/DEBIT CARDS

FUEL CARDS (see key on page 6)
㉑

TRUCK FACILITIES
Truck dealership/workshop

DRIVER FACILITIES
Accommodation nearby, half a mile,
 Travelodge

All on-site facilities 24 hours   **FB214**

Morrisons HGV, Wakefield

Morrisons Supermarkets Ltd
Kenmore Road, Wakefield Industrial Estate
Carr Gate, Wakefield,
West Yorkshire WF2 0XF
T 01924 870000

M1 JUNCTION 41 OFF THE A650 Exit M1 at junction 41
and take A650. At next roundabout, turn left into Kenmore
Road and across next roundabout. Morrisons HGV on the right.

CREDIT/DEBIT CARDS

FUEL CARDS (see key on page 6)
❶❷❸

TRUCK FACILITIES
Truck washing facilities

SITE COMMENTS/INFORMATION
Train/tram/underground/metro nearby

All on-site facilities 24 hours

FB215

O J Williams

Topsham Depot, Marsh Barton Farm
Clyst St George, Exeter, Devon EX3 0QH
T 01392 876880

ON THE A376 From the M5, exit at junction 30 and take
the A376 towards Exmouth. After 2 miles turn right towards
the village of Topsham and O J Williams is 400 yards on the
left.

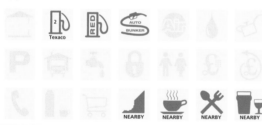

CREDIT/DEBIT CARDS

FUEL CARDS (see key on page 6)
❶❸

DRIVER FACILITIES
Accommodation nearby, 600 yards,
    Ebford House Hotel

All on-site facilities 24 hours

FB216

Oakmont Recovery

C H Jones Ltd, First Avenue, Millbrook
Southampton, Hampshire SO15 0NQ
T 02380 739990

OFF THE A33 Enter Southampton via the M271. At the
bottom of the M271 turn left onto the A33. Take next exit
before the flyover and turn right at roundabout onto First
Avenue. Take second right before the rail tracks again into
First Ave. Oakmont is on the left.

CREDIT/DEBIT CARDS

FUEL CARDS (see key on page 6)
❶❷❸

DRIVER FACILITIES
Takeaway food nearby

All on-site facilities 24 hours

FB217

Onward Refinishing Services Ltd

**Onward Business Park, Ackworth
Pontefract, West Yorkshire WF7 7BE
T 01977 614007**
OFF THE A638 From the end of the A1M, take the A638 towards South Elmsall. Past South Elmsall to Ackworth Moor Top across junction with A628 staying on A638 for half a mile. Turn right into Onward Business Park and Onward Refinishing is 20 yards ahead of you.

CREDIT/DEBIT CARDS

FUEL CARDS (see key on page 6)
① ② ③

TRUCK FACILITIES
Truck washing facilities

All on-site facilities 24 hours

FB218

P R M Commercials

**Ipswich Road, Ardleigh, Near Colchester
Essex CO7 7QL
T 01206 230165**
ON THE OLD A12 Take the A1232 northbound out of Colchester until the roundabout with the A120. Turn right onto the A120 and then immediate left onto the old A12. Continue parallel with the new A12 for 1 mile. P R M Commercials is on the right.

CREDIT/DEBIT CARDS

FUEL CARDS (see key on page 6)
⑩

TRUCK FACILITIES
Truck dealership/workshop

Bunker fuel 24 hours. Other on-site facilities 08:00-18:00

FB219

Prince Petroleum

**Broughton Lodge, Fossway,
Upper Broughton, Melton Mowbray
Leicestershire LE14 3BH
T 01664 822213**
ON THE A46 Take the A46 northbound from Leicester to Newark. Continue for 1 and a half miles after the junction with the A6006 and Prince Petroleum is on the right just past the turning for Upper Broughton.

CREDIT/DEBIT CARDS

FUEL CARDS (see key on page 6)
①

All on-site facilities 24 hours

FB220

Quay Fuels

157 Regent Road, Kirkdale, Liverpool Merseyside L5 9ZA
T 0151 2075155

ON THE A5036 From the M57 take A580 exit towards Bootle. Continue ahead at the A580 until the A59. Turn left onto this. Turn right onto A5054 Boundary Street then right at the Mersey Estuary onto A5036 Regent Road. Quay fuels is 400 yards on the right.

CREDIT/DEBIT CARDS

FUEL CARDS (see key on page 6)
①②③

TRUCK FACILITIES
Truck washing facilities

SITE COMMENTS/INFORMATION
Train/tram/underground/metro nearby

All on-site facilities 06:00-18:00

FB221

Regency Oils, Dyce

Regency Oils Ltd, Kirkhill Place Kirkhill Industrial Estate, Dyce, Aberdeen Aberdeenshire AB21 0GU
T 01542 832327

OFF THE A96 From Aberdeen take A96 to Inverurie. Continue for 2 miles beyond junction with the A947. Turn right to Kirkhill Industrial Estate. After half a mile turn right for 400 yards then left. Take next right into Kirkhill Place and it's on the left.

CREDIT/DEBIT CARDS

FUEL CARDS (see key on page 6)
①②③

DRIVER FACILITIES
Accommodation nearby, half a mile, Aberdeen Airport Thistle & Speedbird Inn

SITE COMMENTS/INFORMATION
This site is within half a mile of an airport

All on-site facilities 24 hours

FB222

Rix Derv Stop

Rix Ltd, North Quay, Montrose Angus DD10 8DS
T 01674 673562

OFF THE B9133 From the A92 heading north into Montrose, take your first right onto the B9133 Wharf Street. Keep right as the road bears right into River Street. Rix is near the bottom, on the left just before the tight left-hand bend.

CREDIT/DEBIT CARDS

FUEL CARDS (see key on page 6)
①②③㉓

TRUCK FACILITIES
Ample room for manoeuvring

DRIVER FACILITIES
Accommodation nearby, half a mile, Links Hotel

All on-site facilities 24 hours

FB223

Rix Shipping Dervstop

**Rix Ltd, King George Dock, Hull
East Riding of Yorkshire HU9 5PR
T 01482 838383**

OFF THE A1033 From the A15 bridge over the Humber heading northbound, turn right onto the A63. Stay on it into Hull and out the other side, heading towards the King George Dock. Turn right at Ferry Terminal junction, left at roundabout. Rix is on the left.

CREDIT/DEBIT CARDS

FUEL CARDS (see key on page 6)
① ② ③ ⑩ ㉓

SITE COMMENTS/INFORMATION
This site is within half a mile of the ferry terminal

All on-site facilities 24 hours

FB224

Roe Oils Ltd, Shercock

**Roe Oils Ltd, Lisdrumskeagh
Near Carrickmacross, Shercock
County Cavan, Ireland
T 00353 (0) 429669229**

ON THE R178 From Bailieborough take the R178 towards Shercock and Castleblaney. Once in Shercock follow right-hand signs to Carrickmacross on the R178. Roe Oils is 20 yards after the right turn.

CREDIT/DEBIT CARDS

FUEL CARDS (see key on page 6)
② ⑨ ⑪ ㉑

All on-site facilities 24 hours. Oil accessible 08:00-17:00 Mon-Fri

FB225

Silvey Oils, Bridgwater

**Silvey Oils Ltd, Bristol Road, Bridgwater
Somerset TA6 4BJ
T 0845 6644664/01278 431451/455763**

ON THE A38 From the M5, exit at junction 23 and follow the A38 into Bridgwater for 1 and a half miles. Silvey Oils is on the right, 800 yards before the roundabout with the A39.

CREDIT/DEBIT CARDS

FUEL CARDS (see key on page 6)
① ② ③ ⑩

Toilets 08:30-17:00 Mon-Fri. Other on-site facilities 24 hours

FB226

Silvey Oils, Pontyclun

Silvey Oils Ltd, Coed Cae Lane Ind. Estate Talbot Green, Pontyclun Mid Glamorgan CF72 9EW
T 0845 6644664

OFF THE A473 Exit M4 at junction 34 and take the A4119 towards Talbot Green. Turn left onto A473 for one mile, then turn left at roundabout towards Llanharry. Silvey Oils is 500 yards on the left.

CREDIT/DEBIT CARDS

FUEL CARDS (see key on page 6)
① ② ③ ⑩

SITE COMMENTS/INFORMATION
Train/tram/underground/metro nearby

All on-site facilities 24 hours

FB227

Silwood Depot

Team Flitwick Ltd, Riverside Estate Oliver Close, West Thurrock, Grays Essex RM20 3EE
T 01708 861122

OFF THE A126 From junction 30 of the M25 take the A13 Basildon. At the A126 turn right. Continue along the A126 to roundabout where A126 turns left. Go straight on, follow sharp right, past Truckworld, across roundabout and it's on the left.

CREDIT/DEBIT CARDS
VISA Mastercard Switch Maestro

FUEL CARDS (see key on page 6)
① ② ③ ⑨ ⑩

TRUCK FACILITIES
Credit/debit cards accepted at fuel bunker
Truck dealership/workshop
Ample room for manoeuvring

SITE COMMENTS/INFORMATION
This site is located within a few yards of Truckworld

Bunker fuel 24 hours. Other onsite facilities 08:00-17:30

FB228

Suttons Oil, Limerick

Suttons Oil Ltd, Courtbrack Avenue off Dock Road, Limerick County Limerick, Ireland
T 00353 (0) 61227333

OFF THE N69 From Cork, take N20 then R526 towards Limerick. At the Raheen Business Park roundabout, turn left onto N18, then N69 towards Limerick. After 1½ miles turn left into Courtbrack Ave after Motorzone dealership. Suttons is 150 yards on left.

CREDIT/DEBIT CARDS

FUEL CARDS (see key on page 6)
⑦ ㉑

TRUCK FACILITIES
Truck dealership/workshop

SITE COMMENTS/INFORMATION
LGVs permitted access to site in spite of Courtbrack Avenue weight limit.

All on-site facilities 08:00-12:30, 14:00-16:30

FB229

T Martin Fuels

Ballybay Road, Killyvane, Monaghan County Monaghan, Ireland
T 00353 (0) 4782279

ON THE R162 Take the R162 out of Monaghan towards Ballybay. T Martin Fuels is on the right-hand side, half a mile beyond the turning for the R188 to Rockcorry.

CREDIT/DEBIT CARDS

FUEL CARDS (see key on page 6)
21 29

TRUCK FACILITIES
Short-term coach parking (10 spaces)
Credit/debit cards accepted at fuel bunker
Truck dealership/workshop

SITE COMMENTS/INFORMATION
Easy access for LGVs

Short-term parking times unknown. All other on-site facilities 07:30-19:30 **FB230**

Top Oil, Waterford

Top Oil Ltd, Butlers Town, Holy Cross Cork Road, Waterford County Waterford, Ireland
T 00353 (0) 51871555

ON THE N25 Take the N25 out of Waterford towards Cork. Top Oil is on that road on the left, 800 yards past Waterford Industrial Estate and 300 yards before the Gaa Football Club.

CREDIT/DEBIT CARDS

FUEL CARDS (see key on page 6)
10 11 21 33

TRUCK FACILITIES
Ample room for manoeuvring

SITE COMMENTS/INFORMATION
Air only available during opening hours

Bunker fuel 24 hours. Other on-site facilities 09:00-21:00 Mon-Fri. 09:00-17:00 Sat & Sun **FB231**

Total Butler, Avonmouth

Total Butler Ltd, Royal Edward Dock Avonmouth, Bristol, South Glos. BS11 9BB
T 0117 9822524/9824711

OFF THE A4 From the M5 Junction 18, follow signs for Avonmouth docks. Straight over 2 roundabouts and through dock gates. Turn right opp Sims Metals, past Castle Cement, go over railway, then 1st left. Continue 200 yards bear right, continue 75 yards and bear right.

CREDIT/DEBIT CARDS

FUEL CARDS (see key on page 6)
1 2 3 30

DRIVER FACILITIES
Showers available

SITE COMMENTS/INFORMATION
Train/tram/underground/metro nearby

All on-site facilities 08:30-17:00 **FB232**

Total Butler, Bodmin

Total Butler Ltd, 10 Lucknow Road
Walker Lines Industrial Estate
Bodmin, Cornwall PL31 1EZ
T 01208 72551

OFF THE A30 If heading south-west on A30, take 1st Bodmin exit onto A38. Remain on A38 for 1 mile. At roundabout with the A30, turn right onto Carminow Road. 600 yards turn right into Normandy Way then right into Lucknow Road to the end.

CREDIT/DEBIT CARDS

FUEL CARDS (see key on page 6)
① ② ③ ㉕ ㉚

DRIVER FACILITIES
Showers available

All on-site facilities 09:00-17:00 Mon-Fri

FB233

Total Butler, Devizes

Total Butler Ltd, London Road
Devizes, Wiltshire SN10 2EP
T 01380 728564

ON THE A361 Take the A361 out of Devizes towards the M4. Total Butler is on the left on the outskirts of the town, just after the turning for Windsor Drive which is on the right.

CREDIT/DEBIT CARDS

FUEL CARDS (see key on page 6)
① ② ③ ㉚

All on-site and nearby facilities opening times unknown

FB234

Total Butler, Exeter

Total Butler Ltd, Marsh Green Road North
Marsh Barton Trading Est.,
Marsh Barton, Exeter, Devon EX2 8PB
T 01363 82643

OFF THE A377 Exit M5 junction 31, A30 towards Okehampton. After 1 mile take exit for A377. Continue past junction with B3123 and Sainsburys, turn right into Marsh Barton Road. Follow road round left into Marsh Green Road North and it's on the left.

CREDIT/DEBIT CARDS

FUEL CARDS (see key on page 6)
① ② ③ ㉚

DRIVER FACILITIES
Takeaway food nearby

Bunker fuel 24 hours

FB235

Total Butler, Gloucester

Total Butler Ltd, Hempstead Lane
Hempstead, Gloucester,
Gloucestershire GL2 5HU T 01452 523095

OFF THE A430 From the M5 junction 12, take the A38 then the A430 towards Gloucester town centre. Take the next left past the BP garage on your right. Take 2nd right into Secunda Way continue to roundabout. Go across into Hempstead Lane and it's on the right.

CREDIT/DEBIT CARDS

FUEL CARDS (see key on page 6)
① ② ㉕ ㉚

DRIVER FACILITIES
Takeaway food nearby

Toilets 07:00-17:00. All other on-site facilities 24 hours

FB236

Total Butler, Minehead

Total Butler Ltd, Mart Road, Minehead
Somerset TA24 5BJ
T 01643 706091

OFF THE A39 Take the A39 towards Minehead. At the first roundabout turn right onto Seaward Way towards Aquasplash and West Somerset Railway. Left at Aquasplash into Vulcan Road, left at the end into Mart Road and it's immediately on the left.

CREDIT/DEBIT CARDS

FUEL CARDS (see key on page 6)
① ② ⑩

DRIVER FACILITIES
Takeaway food nearby

All on-site facilities 08:00-17:00

FB237

Total Butler, Thirsk

Total Butler Ltd, Energy House
Thirsk Industrial Park, Thirsk
North Yorkshire YO7 3BX
T 01845 525414

OFF THE A170 Exit A1M at junction 49 and take A168 to Thirsk. After 5 miles turn left onto A170 and after 400 yards right into Thirsk Industrial Park. Take 2nd left and Total Butler is round the bend on the left.

CREDIT/DEBIT CARDS

FUEL CARDS (see key on page 6)
① ② ③ ㉚

All on-site facilities 08:00-17:00

FB238

Tougher Oil, Dublin

**Tougher Oil Ltd, J F K Drive
J F K Industrial Estate,
Bluebell, Dublin 12, County Dublin, Ireland
T 00353 (0)14569977**

OFF THE R110 From the M50, exit at junction 9 and take the R110 towards Dublin. Continue past junction with Long Mile Road and Killeen Road. Take next left and left again into J F K Drive. Follow round to the right and Tougher Oil is on the right.

Independent AUTO BUNKER

NEARBY

CREDIT/DEBIT CARDS

FUEL CARDS (see key on page 6)
10 21

All on-site facilities 24 hours

FB239

County Oil Group, Runcorn

**County Oil Group Ltd, Beca House
Ashville Way, Ashville Ind Est
Sutton Weaver, Runcorn, Cheshire WA7 3EL
T 01928 718000** www.county-oil.co.uk

OFF THE A557 M56 south-west, exit at junction 12 and take left-hand A557 towards Frodsham. After a few yards take the next right into Clifton Lane, then the 2nd left into Ashville Way. County Oil is half-way down on the right.

CREDIT/DEBIT CARDS

FUEL CARDS (see key on page 6)
❶ ❷ ❸ ❿

TRUCK FACILITIES
P free
Quiet area
Truck washing facilities
Truck dealership/workshop
Ample room for manoeuvring

DRIVER FACILITIES
Accommodation nearby, half a mile,
    Forte Posthouse
Drivers washroom

All on-site facilities 24 hours | **FPB240**

Deros Coaches

**Emo Oil Ltd, Killarney Bypass
Woodlands Industrial Estate
Killarney, County Kerry, Ireland
T 00353 (0) 643125/ 876502111**

OFF THE N22 Head north-west along the N22 towards Killarney from Cork. At the roundabout with the R876, continue ahead on the N22 Killarney Bypass. Take the next right and Deros is straight ahead at the bottom.

CREDIT/DEBIT CARDS

FUEL CARDS (see key on page 6)
⓴ ㉑

TRUCK FACILITIES
Coach parking available (20 spaces, free)
Truck washing facilities
Truck dealership/workshop
Ample room for manoeuvring

DRIVER FACILITIES
Accommodation nearby, 500 yards,
    Quality Hotel & Killarney Heights Hotels
Seating area nearby

SITE COMMENTS
Near to shopping centre and town centre facilities

All on-site facilities 24 hours | **FBP241**

Husk UK Ltd

**The Freight Terminal, Lydden Hill
Dover, Kent CT15 7JW
T 01304 831222**

OFF THE A2 From Canterbury, take the A2 towards Dover. Continue for 3 miles beyond the turning for the A260. Take the first turning across the carriageway for Ewell Minnis and Temple Ewell. Husk is immediately on your right.

CREDIT/DEBIT CARDS
VISA MasterCard Maestro

FUEL CARDS (see key on page 6)
❶ ❷ ❸ ❿

TRUCK FACILITIES
P can be paid for in cash only
Quiet area
Truck washing facilities
Truck dealership/workshop
Ample room for manoeuvring

DRIVER FACILITIES
Truckers' accessories, showers
Takeaway food, clothes shop, phone top-ups/accessories and internet nearby

SITE COMMENTS/INFORMATION
Very basic shop on-site

Parking, fuel and toilets 24 hours. Other on-site facilities and nearby shop 08:00-18:00 | **FBP242**

Maxol Direct

**Maxol Ltd, 48 Trench Road, Mallusk
Newtownabbey, County Antrim BT36 4TY
Northern Ireland
T 02890 848586**

OFF THE M2 JUNCTION 4 M2 junction 4, take A6 towards Templepatrick/Antrim for 1 mile. Take 3rd turning on left to Park Road. At the end turn left onto Mallusk Road, then next left and left again to Trench Road. Maxol is 200 yards on the left.

CREDIT/DEBIT CARDS

FUEL CARDS (see key on page 6)
⑪ ㉖

TRUCK FACILITIES
Coach parking available, shared with LGV
P free
Ample room for manoeuvring

DRIVER FACILITIES
Accommodation nearby, half a mile,
   Chimney Corner Hotel
Seating area and takeaway food nearby
Euros changed/accepted

SITE COMMENTS/INFORMATION
Parking on nearby industrial estate car park permitted from 18:00-07:00 only

All on-site facilities 24 hours. This site is manned between 09:00-17:00 Mon-Fri   **FBP243**

Oakley Fuels Ltd

**Halesfield 19, Telford
Shropshire TF7 4QT
T 01952 684600**

OFF THE A442 Take the A442 south from Telford towards Bridgnorth. Exit onto the sliproad for the A4169 towards Shifnal. At the next roundabout turn left into Halesfield 19. Continue to end of the road. Oakley Fuels is on the left.

CREDIT/DEBIT CARDS

FUEL CARDS (see key on page 6)
① ② ③ ⑩

TRUCK FACILITIES
Free overnight parking on road at end of estate
Coach parking available, shared with LGV
Quiet area
Ample room for manoeuvring
Truck dealership/workshop nearby
Windscreen repair facility nearby
Tyre repair/sales nearby

DRIVER FACILITIES
Seating area nearby
Takeaway food nearby

Bunker fuel, parking and water 24 hours. This site is manned from 08:00-17:00 Mon-Fri   **FBP244**

Pallet Yard Truckstop

**Doncaster Road, The Maltings Ind. Est.
Whitley Bridge, Goole
East Yorkshire DN14 OHH
T 01977 662881**

OFF M62 JUNCTION 34 Exit at Junction 34 M62 and follow signs for local traffic along Selby Road towards Eggborough. Go over canal bridge and turn left before level crossing, continue to end of the road. Pallet Yard Truckstop is at the dead end.

CREDIT/DEBIT CARDS

FUEL CARDS (see key on page 6)
① ② ⑩

TRUCK FACILITIES
Coach parking available, shared with LGV
P £5.00
Fridge lorry area
Ample room for manoeuvring

DRIVER FACILITIES
Seating area
Takeaway food
Showers in nearby pub

SITE COMMENTS/INFORMATION
Friendly, helpful site manager

On-site café open until 15:00. Other on-site facilities 24 hours. Nearby restaurant, bar and showers 16:00- 20:00   **FBP245**

RSL Distribution

**Fan Road, Staveley, Chesterfield
Derbyshire S43 3PT
T 01246 280177**

OFF THE A619 Exit M1 at junction 30 and head for Barlborough and Clowne. At next roundabout take the A619 to Staveley and Chesterfield. Continue for 2 miles. Turn left after railway bridge into Fan Road and RSL is round the bend on the right.

CREDIT/DEBIT CARDS

FUEL CARDS (see key on page 6)
❶ ❷

TRUCK FACILITIES
P free
Quiet area
Ample room for manoeuvring
Truck washing facilities
Truck dealership/workshop

DRIVER FACILITIES
Seating area nearby
Takeaway food nearby

All on-site facilities 07:00-18:00

FBP246

Roy Humphrey Car & Commercial

**Brome, Eye
Suffolk IP23 8AW
T 01379 870666**

ON THE A140 SOUTHBOUND Take the A14 north west out of Ipswich, then the A140 northbound towards Norwich for 10 miles. Continue half a mile past the turnings for Eye and Roy Humphrey Car and Commercial is on your right.

CREDIT/DEBIT CARDS

FUEL CARDS (see key on page 6)
❶ ❷ ❸ ❿

TRUCK FACILITIES
Coach parking available, shared with LGV
P £5.00-£10.00. Security guard
Quiet area
Fridge lorry area
Ample room for manoeuvring
Truck dealership/workshop
Windscreen repair facility
Tyre repair/sales

DRIVER FACILITIES
Phone top-ups/accessories

SITE COMMENTS/INFORMATION
A large site with Renault Trucks dealership and a part-time snack van on-site

Parking and bunker fuel 24 hours. Part time on-site snack van 07:00-16:00

FBP247

Secure Coach Parks Ltd

**Freightliner Terminal, Sir Harry Lauder Road
Portobello, Edinburgh EH15 2QA
T 0131 6691911**

OFF THE A199 Exit the M8 at junction 1 and turn right onto the A720. Continue round the city to the A1. Turn left onto the A1 towards Portobello. At the roundabout with the A199, go straight across, follow around to the left and take the first left turn into the site.

CREDIT/DEBIT CARDS

FUEL CARDS (see key on page 6)
❶ ❷ ❸

TRUCK FACILITIES
Ample room for manoeuvring
Truck washing facilities

DRIVER FACILITIES
Seating area nearby
Takeaway food nearby
Internet access nearby
Phone top-ups/accessories

SITE COMMENTS/INFORMATION
This site also has a chemical toilet drop for coaches

All on-site facilities 24 hours

FBP248

Smithy Service Station

**Carlton Fuels Ltd, Whitehurst, Chirk
Clwyd LL14 5AN
T 01691 778251/0151 5466660**

OFF THE A5 From Llangollen take the A5 eastbound towards Newbridge. Continue to the junction with the B5605 signposted Newbridge. Turn left onto the B5605 for 10 yards. Smithy Service Station is immediately on your left.

CREDIT/DEBIT CARDS

FUEL CARDS (see key on page 6)
❶❷❸

TRUCK FACILITIES
Coach parking available, shared with LGV
CCTV
Fridge lorry area
Ample room for manoeuvring
Truck dealership/workshop nearby
Tyre repair/sales

DRIVER FACILITIES
Seating area nearby
Takeaway food nearby

Bunker fuel and parking 24 hours. Lubrication oil, toilets and Red diesel 07:30-19:30 Mon-Sun **FBP249**

The Link Park

**Ex Norfolk Line Depot
Lympne Ind. Est., Lympne, Hythe
Kent CT21 4LR
T 01303 262388**

OFF THE A20 From M20 junction 11, take the A20 towards Lympne. At the junction with the A261 turn right and continue along the A20 until the B2067. Turn left onto this and The Link Park is on the left opposite the Zoo and near Spicers.

CREDIT/DEBIT CARDS

FUEL CARDS (see key on page 6)
❶❷❸❿

TRUCK FACILITIES
Nearby overnight parking not directly on road
Truck washing facilities

Nearby parking, bunker fuel and standpipe 24 hours **FBP250**

Total Butler, Barnstaple

**Total Butler Ltd, Seven Brethren Ind. Est.
Barnstaple, Devon EX31 2AS
T 01271 345977**

OFF THE B3233 Head into Barnstaple on A361. In town centre turn left onto the B3233 towards the museum. Continue past it and follow signs for North Devon Leisure Centre turning left towards Seven Brethren Estate. Follow bend to right, then left and it's on the left.

CREDIT/DEBIT CARDS

FUEL CARDS (see key on page 6)
❶❷❸㉚

TRUCK FACILITIES
Overnight parking opposite the site

DRIVER FACILITIES
Accommodation nearby, half a mile, Park Hotel & Royal and Fortesque Hotel
Seating area nearby

SITE COMMENTS/INFORMATION
Train/tram/underground/metro nearby

Fuel and standpipe 24 hours. Other on-site facilities 06:00-14:00 **FBP251**

Tougher Oil, Carlow

**Tougher Oil Ltd, Dublin Road, Carlow
County Carlow, Ireland
T 00353 (0) 599143443**

OFF THE N9 From the M9 take the N9 towards Carlow. Remain on the N9 beyond the roundabout with the N80 on the outskirts of Carlow. At the next roundabout take the N9 again then take the next immediate right onto Dublin Road. Tougher Oil is 400 yards on the right.

CREDIT/DEBIT CARDS

FUEL CARDS (see key on page 6)
⑩ ⑪ ㉑ ㉝
plus most other major Irish fuel cards

TRUCK FACILITIES
Overnight parking with permission only
Coach parking available, shared with LGV
P free
Floodlighting
Fridge lorry area
Ample room for manoeuvring

DRIVER FACILITIES
Accommodation nearby, half a mile,
  Seven Oaks Hotel
Seating area

Bunker fuel and parking 24 hours. Toilets 08:00-18:00. Restaurant from 07:00-22:00 **FBP252**

W R Kennedy

**Pennybridge Ind Est, Ballymena
County Antrim BT42 3HB
Northern Ireland
T 028 25656616/25656833**

ON THE A36 From the south end of the M2, take the A36 towards Ballymena town centre. W R Kennedy is 500 yards on the left.

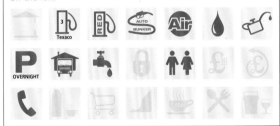

CREDIT/DEBIT CARDS

FUEL CARDS (see key on page 6)
① ② ③

TRUCK FACILITIES
Overnight parking on car park at edge of estate, plus short-term LGV parking on-site
Truck dealership/workshop

Parking, toilets and bunker fuel 24 hours. Breakdown repair centre opening times unknown **FBP253**

Watson Petroleum

**Watson Petroleum Ltd, Andes Road
Nursling Industrial Estate, Nursling
Southampton, Hampshire SO16 0AG
T 02380 737330** www.watson-petroleum.co.uk

OFF THE M271 First junction off the M271 (from north or southbound). Follow the signs for the Nursling Industrial Estate. At the estate roundabout, go straight across into Nursling Road.

CREDIT/DEBIT CARDS

FUEL CARDS (see key on page 6)
① ② ③ ⑩ ⑬

TRUCK FACILITIES
Overnight parking on roadside within estate
Coach parking available, shared with LGV
Ample room for manoeuvring

DRIVER FACILITIES
Accommodation nearby, 800 yards,
  Holiday Inn Express

SITE COMMENTS/INFORMATION
Assistance available for drivers between 08:00-18:00

Nearby parking and most on-site facilities 24 hours. Breakdown garage open 06:00-20:00 **FBP254**

Jones and Jones Transport Services

Goole Road, Moorends, Doncaster
South Yorkshire DN8 4JR
T **01405 812413**

OFF THE A614 From the M18, exit at junction 6 and take the A416 towards Rawcliffe. After 1 mile, turn right into North Common Road for 1 mile. At the T-junction turn left and Jones and Jones Transport is a few yards along on the right.

TRUCK FACILITIES
P £5.00
Quiet area
Ample room for manoeuvring
Truck dealership/workshop on site

DRIVER FACILITIES
Showers on-site (free)
Drivers' washroom
Seating area nearby
Takeaway food nearby
Phone top-ups/accessories

All on-site facilities 24 hours

L255

Locking Road Coach & Lorry Park

Francis Fox Road, Weston-super-Mare
North Somerset BS23 3
T **01934 417117/888826 NSDC ext 257**
OFF THE A371 M5, junction 21, take the A371 Weston-super-Mare towards town centre. At roundabout with the A3033, straight across, over bridge and right at next roundabout, then immediate right into the lorry park.

TRUCK FACILITIES
P £2.50
Coach parking available, shared with LGV
Quiet area
Truck dealership/workshop nearby

DRIVER FACILITIES
Accommodation half a mile away –
   Grand Atlantic & Royal Hotels
Seating area nearby
Takeaway food nearby
Phone top-ups/accessories
Laundry service nearby
Internet nearby
Clothing for sale nearby

SITE COMMENTS
Train/tram nearby

All on-site facilities 24 hours

L256

London Road Lorry Park

Upper Bognor Road, Bognor Regis
West Sussex PO22 8
T **01903 737500 Arun District Council**

ON THE A259 If heading from Littlehampton to Chichester, London Road Lorry Park is on the A259 on the left-hand side, just after the entrance to Butlins and beyond Hotham Park but just before you reach the junction with the A29.

TRUCK FACILITIES
P Free
Quiet area

DRIVER FACILITIES
Seating area nearby
Takeaway food nearby

SITE COMMENTS
Train/tram nearby

Parking 24 hours. Toilets 08:00-20:00 summer, 08:00-17:00 winter

L257

Lymington Road Coach & Lorry Park

Lymington Road, Torquay Devon TQ1 4BD
T 01803 201201/207694 Torbay DC

OFF THE A3022 Take the A3022 into the town centre. At the junction with the A379, turn left into Hele Road. Where the A379 turns sharp left, go right into Teignmouth road then next left into Lymington Road. Follow bend to the right and lorry park is on the right.

TRUCK FACILITIES
Coach parking available, shared with LGV, price unknown
Ample room for manoeuvring
Quiet area
Truck dealership/workshop on site

DRIVER FACILITIES
Shower
Accommodation half a mile away in various hotels
Seating area
Clothing for sale nearby
Takeaway food nearby

SITE COMMENTS/INFORMATION
Train/tram nearby

Parking, toilets and showers 24 hours

L258

Poole Stadium Lorry Park

Stadium Way, off Wimborne Road
Poole, Dorset BH15 2BP
T 01202 677449

OFF THE B3093 From the A350/A3049 roundabout, take the A350 into Poole town centre. Continue over 1st roundabout, left at the 2nd, over the bridge and left at next roundabout. Continue across mini roundabout and take next turning left. Lorry park is on the left.

TRUCK FACILITIES
Coach parking available, shared with LGV, price unknown
Security guard 06:00-00:00
Quiet area

DRIVER FACILITIES
Accommodation 50 yards away at the Arndale Court Hotel
Seating area nearby
Takeaway food nearby
Phone top-ups/accessories nearby
Post Office nearby
Clothing for sale nearby

SITE COMMENTS
Train/tram nearby
Very basic facilities at this site. Many more facilities in the town

All on-site facilities 24 hours

L259

Sheepen Road Lorry & Coach Park

Sheepen Road, Colchester, Essex CO1 1XQ
T 01206 282708 Colchester Borough Council

OFF THE A134 If heading from Chelmsford on the A12, take the A133 on the outskirts of Colchester. Continue over first roundabout and turn right at the next, onto the A134. At the next roundabout take last exit onto Sheepen Road. Lorry park is next to the park and ride

TRUCK FACILITIES
P Free
Coach parking available
Quiet area
Ample room for manoeuvring

DRIVER FACILITIES
Accommodation half a mile away at the George & Red Lion
Seating area nearby
Takeaway food nearby
Phone top-ups/accessories nearby
Clothing for sale nearby

Parking 24 hours. Other nearby facilities opening times greatly varied

L260

Tweed Dock Lorry Park

Tweed Dock, Berwick upon Tweed
Northumberland TD15 2AB
T 01289 307404

OFF THE A1167 From the A1, take the A698 or A1167 into Berwick upon Tweed and follow signs for Tweedmouth and then Tweed Dock. Please note that the lorry park is on the south-west bank of the river Tweed where it joins the North Sea.

TRUCK FACILITIES
P £5.00

DRIVER FACILITIES
Showers, 2 male, 1 female (charge)
Drivers' washroom
Accommodation 600 yards away at the Queens Head
Seating area nearby
Takeaway food nearby

SITE COMMENTS
This site is situated on a working dock and is very limited on spaces

All on-site facilities 16:00-07:00

L261

Westway Lorry park

Porterfield Road, Renfrew
Renfrewshire PA4 8DJ
T 0141 8866373/8867356

OFF THE A741 From the M8 junction 27 take the A741 towards Renfrew. The turning for Porterfield Road is about half a mile along on your left just before the park. Continue on Porterfield road for 400 yards. Westway Lorry Park is on your left.

TRUCK FACILITIES
P £5.00
Quiet area
Ample room for manoeuvring

DRIVER FACILITIES
Shower, 1 male (free)
Drivers' washroom
Seating area nearby
Takeaway food nearby
Accommodation nearby

All on-site facilities 24 hours

L262

3D Garages Ltd

A1 Grantshouse Services, Grantshouse
Duns, Berwickshire TD11 3RW
T 01361 850206

ON THE A1 On the A1 between Dunbar and Berwick upon Tweed. 3D Garages is located at Grantshouse opposite the junction with the A6112.

CREDIT/DEBIT CARDS

FUEL CARDS (see key on page 6)
① ② ③ ④ ⑥ ⑬ ㉟

TRUCK FACILITIES
P free
Quiet area
Ample room for manoeuvring

DRIVER FACILITIES
Drivers' washroom
Takeaway food
Phone top-ups/accessories

SITE COMMENTS/INFORMATION
Site recently refurbished
No fridge lorries overnight

Parking 24 hours. Other on-site facilities 06:00-22:00 Mon-Fri, 07:00-22:00 Sat, 07:00-21:00 Sun | **MR263**

A1 Services

North London Road, Biggleswade
Bedfordshire SG18 9BE
T 01767 601793

ON THE A1 From the A1M at Letchworth, take the A1 north towards Biggleswade. A1 Services is on the left-hand side, 300 yards before the roundabout with the A6001.

CREDIT/DEBIT CARDS

FUEL CARDS (see key on page 6)
① ② ③ ④ ⑫

TRUCK FACILITIES
P £7.00
Coach parking available (5 spaces)
Quiet area. Fridge lorry area
Ample room for manoeuvring
Truck washing facilities

DRIVER FACILITIES
Hot drinks free with 100 litres fuel
Shower (charge)
Drivers' washroom
Takeaway food
Truckers' accessories

SITE COMMENTS/INFORMATION
Friendly staff, customer focused

All on-site facilities 24 hours | **MR264**

A46 Truckstop

Gainsborough Road, Middle Rasen
Market Rasen, Lincolnshire LN8 3JU
T 01673 844994

A46 A631 INTERSECTION From Lincoln, take the A46 towards Market Rasen. At Middle Rasen turn right onto the A631 and the A46 Truckstop is 50 yards along on your right.

CREDIT/DEBIT CARDS

FUEL CARDS (see key on page 6)
① ②

TRUCK FACILITIES
P free
Quiet area
Ample room for manoeuvring

DRIVER FACILITIES
Truckers' accessories
Takeaway food nearby
Clothing for sale nearby

SITE COMMENTS/INFORMATION
Fuel can be paid for in cash

Parking, fuel and standpipe 24 hours. Other on-site facilities opening times unknown | **MR265**

Adderstone Services & Purdy lodge

W J Davidson & Son, Belford
Northumberland NE70 7JU
T **01668 213440** www.purdylodge.co.uk

ON THE A1 Adderstone Services can be found on the A1 north of Warenford at the junction with the B1341 and on the right-hand side if heading north.

CREDIT/DEBIT CARDS

FUEL CARDS (see key on page 6)
① ② ③ ④ ⑩ ⑬ ㊺

TRUCK FACILITIES
P with voucher, £10.00 (voucher = £5)
P only £5.00
Coach parking available, shared with LGV
Quiet area
Ample room for manoeuvring

DRIVER FACILITIES
Shower and drivers' washroom
Accommodation (£49.95 pn)
TV
Euros changed/accepted
Takeaway food
Truckers' accessories

On-site accommodation opening times unknown. All other on-site facilities 24 hours **MR266**

Airport Road Service Station

11 Tully Road, Nutts Corner, Crumlin
County Antrim BT29 4SW, Northern Ireland
T **02890 825706**

ON THE A26 Take the A52 westbound out of Belfast until the roundabout with the A26 and the B101. Turn right onto the A26 towards Antrim. Airport Road Service Station is 600 yards on the right.

CREDIT/DEBIT CARDS

FUEL CARDS (see key on page 6)
④ ⑦ ⑧ ㊱

TRUCK FACILITIES
P free
Coach parking available (4 spaces)
Overnight parking round back of site and in nearby lay-by

DRIVER FACILITIES
Truckers' accessories

SITE COMMENTS/INFORMATION
Lots of space for LGVs, good facilities and helpful staff

Café, 08:00-17:00 Mon-Fri, 08:00-16:00 Sat. All other on-site facilities 07:00-22:00 Mon-Sat, 09:00-22:00 Sun **MR267**

Alby Service Station

Cromer Road, Erpingham, Norwich
Norfolk NR11 7HA
T **01263 761393**

ON THE A140 Alby Service Station is on the A140 between Aylsham and Cromer. If travelling to Cromer, Alby is on the right-hand side just after the left-hand side turnings for the village of Erpingham.

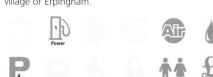

CREDIT/DEBIT CARDS

FUEL CARDS (see key on page 6)
① ② ④ ⑫ ⑬ ㊻

TRUCK FACILITIES
P £5.00
Coach parking available, shared with LGV
Ample room for manoeuvring
Quiet area

DRIVER FACILITIES
B&B accommodation nearby
Post Office
Truckers' accessories nearby

SITE COMMENTS/INFORMATION
Video/DVD rental on-site
Helpful, friendly all female staff

Parking 24 hours. Other on-site facilities 07:00-20:00 Mon-Sat, 09:00-20:00 Sun **MR268**

Ashgrove

Cairnie, Huntly
Aberdeenshire AB54 4TL
T 01466 760223

ON THE A96 Ashgrove is on the A96 at the village of Cairnie on the left-hand side. Halfway between Keith and Huntly.

CREDIT/DEBIT CARDS

FUEL CARDS (see key on page 6)
① ② ④ ⑧

TRUCK FACILITIES
Coach parking available (2 spaces)
Quiet area
Ample room for manoeuvring
Overnight parking on roadside within the complex
Truck washing facilities

DRIVER FACILITIES
Takeaway food
Phone top-ups/accessories

Fuel, shop and toilets 06:00-22:00 Mon-Sat, 08:00-22:00 Sun. Parking 24 hours
All other on-site facilities 07:00-18:30 Mon-Fri, 08:00-17:00 Sat & Sun

MR269

Ballinluig Services

Ballinluig, Pitlochry
Perth and Kinross PH9 0LG
T 01796 482212

ON THE OLD A9 Ballinluig Services can be found at Ballinluig on the A9. 20 miles north of Perth, 5 miles south of Pitlochry. Between Pitlochry and Birnam and on the right-hand side if heading north.

CREDIT/DEBIT CARDS

FUEL CARDS (see key on page 6)
① ② ③ ④ ⑤ ⑥ ⑧ ⑩ ⑬ ⑭ ㉒ ㉟
㊱ ㊲ ㊴ ㊷

TRUCK FACILITIES
P free
Coach parking available, shared with LGV
Ample room for manoeuvring
Quiet area

DRIVER FACILITIES
Showers, 1 male, 1 female (free)
Takeaway food
Phone top-ups/accessories
Truckers' accessories
Clothing for sale
Post Office nearby

Parking 24 hours. Shop and other facilities 08:00-20:30. Fuel 07:00-22:00

MR270

Ballymac Service Station

Ballymascalan, Dundalk
County Louth, Ireland
T 00353 (0) 4293713311/429371077

ON THE R173 Ballymac is about 2 miles north of Dundalk centre, on the R173 and on the left-hand side if heading away from the town. It is also about 800 yards on from the roundabout with A1 and N52.

CREDIT/DEBIT CARDS

FUEL CARDS (see key on page 6)

⑩ ㉑ ㉔

TRUCK FACILITIES
Quiet area
Truck washing facilities

DRIVER FACILITIES
Takeaway food
Phone top-ups/accessories
Truckers' accessories

All on-site facilities 24 hours

MR271

Bewicke Service Station

**Bewicke Road, Willington Quay, Wallsend
Tyne and Wear NE28 6LX**
T 01912 625809

OFF THE A187 From the A194M continue along the A194
to the A19. Turn left towards Jarrow and the Tyne Tunnel.
Once through the tunnel, follow signs for the A187
Newcastle upon Tyne. Continue for half a mile then turn right
up Bewicke Road. The site is in front of you.

CREDIT/DEBIT CARDS

FUEL CARDS (see key on page 6)
① ② ④ ㊹

TRUCK FACILITIES
P free
Quiet area
Ample room for manoeuvring

DRIVER FACILITIES
Shower (free)
Drivers' washroom

SITE COMMENTS/INFORMATION
Train/tram nearby

On-site and nearby parking not 24 hours. All other on-site facilities 24 hours | **MR272**

Blaenavon Motor Company

**Cae White, Abergavenny Road
Blaenavon, Gwent NP4 9RG**
T 01495 790235

ON THE B4246 From Abergavenny and Govilon take the
B4246 towards Blaenavon. Blaenavon Motor Company is in
the town and on your left just past the junction with the
B4248.

CREDIT/DEBIT CARDS

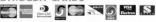

FUEL CARDS (see key on page 6)
① ② ③ ④ ⑨ ⑩ ⑫ ⑬

TRUCK FACILITIES
P free
Coach parking available, shared with LGV
Quiet area
Ample room for manoeuvring
Truck dealership/workshop nearby

DRIVER FACILITIES
B&B accommodation nearby
Takeaway food nearby

SITE COMMENTS/INFORMATION
Welsh hospitality at its best! Extremely
helpful and accommodating staff

Parking 24 hours. Other on-site facilities 06:30-22:00 | **MR273**

BP Budgens

**Witchford Road Service Station
Witchford Road, Ely,
Cambridgeshire CB6 3NN**
T 01353 669112

ON THE A142 From the A10 northbound towards Ely turn
left at the A142 Ely ring road. Staying on the A142, turn left
at the next roundabout towards Wichford and BP Budgens is
a few yards along on the right.

CREDIT/DEBIT CARDS

FUEL CARDS (see key on page 6)
⑤ ⑥

TRUCK FACILITIES
P free
Coach parking available, shared with LGV
Ample room for manoeuvring
Quiet area
Truck washing facilities

DRIVER FACILITIES
Travelodge on-site (£50 per night)
Takeaway food
Truckers' accessories

SITE COMMENTS/INFORMATION
Great food, clean friendly site with staff
who aim to please

Parking 24 hours. Travelodge opening times unknown. Other on-site facilities 06:00-23:00 | **MR274**

Bridgend Garage Ltd

**1 Main Street, Auchinleck
East Ayrshire KA18 2AB
T 01290 421224**

ON THE A76 Head south from Kilmarnock on the A76 and take the B7083 into Auchinleck village. Continue for half a mile and Bridgend Garage is on the right-hand side at the far end of the village.

CREDIT/DEBIT CARDS

FUEL CARDS (see key on page 6)
① ② ③ ④ ⑦ ⑫

TRUCK FACILITIES
P free
Coach parking available, shared with LGV
Ample room for manoeuvring
Quiet area
Truck dealership/workshop nearby

DRIVER FACILITIES
Shower
Phone top-ups/accessories
Takeaway food nearby

SITE COMMENTS/INFORMATION
Train/tram/underground/metro nearby

All on-site facilities 24 hours   **MR275**

Brobot, Derby

**Brobot Petroleum Ltd, Derby road
Egginton, Derby, Derbyshire DE65 6GY
T 01283 702565/703198**

ON THE A38 NORTHBOUND Brobot is on the northbound carriageway of the A38 between Burton upon Trent and Derby, and about half a mile before the junction with the A50.

CREDIT/DEBIT CARDS

FUEL CARDS (see key on page 6)
① ③ ④ ⑫ ⑬ ⑮ ⑯ ㊹

TRUCK FACILITIES
P free
Coach parking available, shared with LGV
Truck dealership/workshop nearby
Quiet area

DRIVER FACILITIES
Drivers' rest area

SITE COMMENTS/INFORMATION
Popular, busy site

All on-site facilities 24 hours   **MR276**

Cambridge Services

**Extra MSA Forecourts Ltd, Boxworth
Cambridge, Cambridgeshire CB3 8WU
T 01954 268900**

ON THE A14 From the M11, take the A14 towards Godmanchester. Continue past the junction for Bar Hill and take the next junction signposted for Boxworth. Cambridge Services is on that junction on the left-hand side.

CREDIT/DEBIT CARDS

FUEL CARDS (see key on page 6)
① ② ③ ⑨

TRUCK FACILITIES
P £13.00
Coach parking available (12 spaces)
Overnight security patrol
Ample room for manoeuvring
Quiet area

DRIVER FACILITIES
Showers, 3 male, 1 female (free)
Accommodation on-site (£55 per night)
Takeaway food
Truckers' accessories

SITE COMMENTS/INFORMATION
Easy access for LGVs

Parking, fuel, shop, showers and some food 24 hours   **MR277**

Centurion Services

Gloucester Road, Cirencester
Gloucestershire GL7 7RJ
T 01285 821256

ON THE A417 SOUTHBOUND If heading south, Centurion Services is located just off the southbound carriageway of the A147 Gloucester to Cirencester road, approximately 5 miles from Cirencester and just after the exits to the villages of Winstone and Elkstone.

CREDIT/DEBIT CARDS

FUEL CARDS (see key on page 6)

TRUCK FACILITIES
P £7.50
Coach parking available, shared with LGV
Ample room for manoeuvring
Overnight parking in designated spaces and on dead-end road adjacent to site

DRIVER FACILITIES
Drivers' washroom
Truckers' accessories

On-site and nearby parking 24 hours. Other on-site facilities 06:00-21:30 Mon-Sun **MR278**

Circular Services

Glasgow/Edinburgh Road, Newhouse
Near Motherwell, Strathclyde
Lanarkshire ML1 5SY
T 01698 860236

ON THE A775 From junction 6 of the M8 take the A73 heading south towards Newhouse. At the next roundabout, turn right onto the B7066 towards Belshill. Circular Services is a few yards along on the left.

CREDIT/DEBIT CARDS

FUEL CARDS (see key on page 6)

TRUCK FACILITIES
P free
Quiet area
Truck dealership/workshop nearby

DRIVER FACILITIES
Travel Inn on-site (£35 per night)
Takeaway food
Truckers' accessories

SITE COMMENTS/INFORMATION
Happy, cheerful staff. Welcoming site

Parking 24 hours. Travelodge times unknown. All other on-site facilities 05:00-16:00 **MR279**

Colsterworth Services

Travelodge Hotels Ltd, Colsterworth
Grantham, Lincolnshire NG33 5JR
T 01476 861077

ON THE A1 SOUTHBOUND If heading south from Grantham, Colsterworth services is on the A1 southbound carriageway, just beyond the roundabout with the A151.

CREDIT/DEBIT CARDS

FUEL CARDS (see key on page 6)

TRUCK FACILITIES
P with voucher, £10.00 (voucher = £6)
P only £7.00
Coach parking available (6 spaces)
Ample room for manoeuvring

DRIVER FACILITIES
Showers, 1 male, 1 female (charge)
Drivers' washroom and rest area
Travelodge on-site (£49.50 per night)
Takeaway food
Phone top-ups/accessories

Parking and fuel 24 hours. Other on-site facilities 07:00-22:00 **MR280**

Dalwhinnie Service Station

Dalwhinnie, Inverness
Highland PH19 1AF
T 01528 522311

ON THE A889 Dalwhinnie is a few miles south of Newtonmore at the A9 end of the A889 which is the road that joins the A86 to the A9.

CREDIT/DEBIT CARDS

FUEL CARDS (see key on page 6)
① ② ③ ④ ⑤ ⑥ ⑧ ⑫ ⑬

TRUCK FACILITIES
P £5.00
Coach parking available, shared with LGV
Ample room for manoeuvring

DRIVER FACILITIES
Hotel (07:30-23:00), TV, showers (free with LGV parking), drivers' washroom, and internet access
Takeaway food

SITE COMMENTS/INFORMATION
Train/tram nearby
Excellent deals for truckers using overnight and parking facilities

Parking 24 hours. Fuel/shop 07:00-20:00 Mon-Fri, 08:00-18:00 Sat, 10:00-18:00 Sun. Other facilities 07:30-23:00   **MR281**

Exelby Services North Ltd

Exelby Services Ltd, Ingleby Arncliffe
Northallerton, North Yorkshire DL6 3JT
T 01609 882280

ON THE A19 NORTHBOUND Exelby Services North is on the northbound carriageway of the A19, a few hundred yards north of the village of Ingleby Arncliffe.

CREDIT/DEBIT CARDS

FUEL CARDS (see key on page 6)
① ② ③ ⑤ ⑥ ⑩

TRUCK FACILITIES
P £2.50
Quiet area
Ample room for manoeuvring

DRIVER FACILITIES
Drivers' washroom
Drivers' rest area
Takeaway food
Phone top-ups/accessories
Truckers' accessories

Parking 24 hours. All other on-site facilities 06:00-22:00 Mon-Fri, 08:00-21:00 Sat & Sun   **MR282**

Exelby Services South Ltd & Jan's Café

Exelby Services Ltd, Ingleby Arncliffe
Northallerton, North Yorkshire DL6 3JX
T 01609 882662

ON THE A19 SOUTHBOUND Exelby Services South and Jan's Café is on the southbound carriageway of the A19, about 1 mile north of the village of Ingleby Arncliffe.

CREDIT/DEBIT CARDS

FUEL CARDS (see key on page 6)
① ③ ⑤ ⑥ ⑩

TRUCK FACILITIES
P £2.50
Quiet area
Ample room for manoeuvring

DRIVER FACILITIES
Drivers' washroom
Drivers' rest area
Takeaway food
Phone top-ups/accessories
Truckers' accessories

All on-site facilities 24 hours   **MR283**

Fishguard Harbour Garage & Restaurant

The Parade, Goodwick, Fishguard Pembrokeshire SA64 0DE
T 01348 873814

ON THE A40 From Haverfordwest, take the A40 to Fishguard. Bypass Fishguard. At the junction with the A487 turn left at the roundabout continuing on the A40 heading for the harbour. At the next roundabout take the 1st exit and the site is 500 yards on the left.

CREDIT/DEBIT CARDS

FUEL CARDS (see key on page 6)

TRUCK FACILITIES
P free if using restaurant
Coach parking available, shared with LGV
Fridge lorry area
Ample room for manoeuvring
Overnight parking next to site
Truck washing facilities
Truck dealership/workshop
DRIVER FACILITIES
Drivers' washroom. Takeaway food
Phone top-ups/accessories
SITE COMMENTS/INFORMATION
This site is within half a mile from the ferry terminal

Parking 24 hours. Fuel, showers and shop 07:00-23:00. Other on-site facilities 09:00-15:00 **MR284**

Fossway Service Station

Stragglethorpe Crossroads Radcliffe on Trent, Nottingham Nottinghamshire NG12 2JU
T 0115 9893113

ON THE A46 From Melton Mowbray, take the A606 to Nottingham. Turn right at the junction with the A46 towards Bingham. Fossway Service Station is 5 miles on the right-hand side, just past the village of Cotgrave.

CREDIT/DEBIT CARDS

FUEL CARDS (see key on page 6)

TRUCK FACILITIES
P free
Coach parking available (2 spaces)
Ample room for manoeuvring

DRIVER FACILITIES
Drivers' rest area
Truckers' accessories
Phone top-ups/accessories nearby

Parking 24 Hours. Other on-site facilities opening times unknown **MR285**

Four Winds Service Station

Bedford Road, Haynes West End, Bedford Bedfordshire MK45 3QT
T 01234 743755/742511

ON THE A6 If heading from Luton to Bedford on the A6, Four Winds is on the right-hand side about 2 miles past the intersection with the A507.

CREDIT/DEBIT CARDS

FUEL CARDS (see key on page 6)

TRUCK FACILITIES
P £7.50
Coach parking available (4 spaces)
Quiet area
Fridge lorry area
Ample room for manoeuvring

DRIVER FACILITIES
Truckers' accessories
Takeaway food nearby

All on-site facilities 07:00 19:00 Mon-Fri, 08:00-16:00 Sat & Sun. On-site parking times unknown **MR286**

Gavin Row

Ryland Road, Bunclody
County Wexford, Ireland
T 00353 (0) 5476231

ON THE N80 Gavin Row is on the N80 at the south side of the village of Bunclody. It is on your right if heading south-east.

All on-site facilities 24 hours

CREDIT/DEBIT CARDS

FUEL CARDS (see key on page 6)

TRUCK FACILITIES
P free
Coach parking available (8 spaces)
Quiet area
Ample room for manoeuvring
Truck washing facilities

DRIVER FACILITIES
Drivers' washroom
Truckers' accessories
Takeaway food, clothing, CB repairs/sales and phone top-ups/accessories nearby

SITE COMMENTS/INFORMATION
Lots of space for parking on-site

MR287

Glews Garage

Rawcliffe Road, Goole
East Yorkshire DN14 8JS
T 01405 764525

ON THE A614 From the M62, exit at junction 36 and take the A614 towards Rawcliffe. Glews garage is 50 yards on your left.

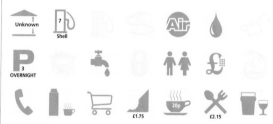

All on-site facilities 24 hours

CREDIT/DEBIT CARDS

FUEL CARDS (see key on page 6)

TRUCK FACILITIES
Coach parking available, shared with LGV

DRIVER FACILITIES
Accommodation on-site
Takeaway food
Truckers' accessories

SITE COMMENTS/INFORMATION
Clean tidy and welcoming site
Car dealership also on-site

MR288

Grantham North Services

Moto Ltd, Gonerby Moor, nr Grantham
Lincolnshire NG32 2AB
T 01476 563451 www.moto-way.com

ON THE A1 Take the A1 bypassing Grantham, and Grantham North Services is on the right-hand side at the intersection with the B1174.

All on-site facilities 24 hours

CREDIT/DEBIT CARDS

FUEL CARDS (see key on page 6)

DRIVER FACILITIES
Travelodge on-site
Takeaway food

MR289

Greenodd Service Station

Greenodd, nr Ulverston
Cumbria LA12 7RE
T 01229 861434

A5092 / A590 INTERSECTION From the A590 between Ulverston and Newby Bridge, take the A5092 towards Grizebeck. Greenodd Service Station is a few yards along on the left.

CREDIT/DEBIT CARDS

FUEL CARDS (see key on page 6)
④ ⑦ ⑧ ㉟

TRUCK FACILITIES
P free
Coach parking available, shared with LGV
Ample room for manoeuvring
Quiet area

DRIVER FACILITIES
Truckers' accessories

SITE COMMENTS/INFORMATION
Good location, most accessible LGV site for many miles

Parking 24 hours. Other on-site facilities 07:30-08:00 **MR290**

Harry Tuffin Supermarket Ltd

Church Stoke, Montgomery
Powys SY15 6AR
T 01588 620226 www.harrytuffin.co.uk

ON THE A489 From Newtown, take the A489 heading east towards Church Stoke. Harry Tuffins is on that road to the east of the village.

CREDIT/DEBIT CARDS

FUEL CARDS (see key on page 6)
③ ④ ⑨

TRUCK FACILITIES
P free
Quiet area
Ample room for manoeuvring
Truck washing facilities

DRIVER FACILITIES
Takeaway food
Post office

SITE COMMENTS/INFORMATION
Popular LGV site

Parking 24 hours. All other on-site facilities 07:00-20:00 **MR291**

Heathpark Service Station

Heathpark Way, Heathpark, Honiton
Devon EX14 1SF
T 01404 47325

ON THE A30 If heading west, exit the A30 where it is signposted Heathpark Industrial Estate. Turn left at the bottom of the sliproad and next right onto the A35. Head back towards the A30 and the service station is on the left before the A30 entrance sliproad.

CREDIT/DEBIT CARDS

FUEL CARDS (see key on page 6)
① ② ③ ⑤ ⑥ ⑧ ⑨ ㊻

TRUCK FACILITIES
P free
Coach parking available, shared with LGV
Ample room for manoeuvring
Truck washing facilities
Windscreen repair facility

DRIVER FACILITIES
Drivers' washroom
Accommodation 200 yards away at Honiton Motel
Truckers' accessories
Takeaway food nearby
Clothing for sale nearby

Parking 24 hours. Other on-site facilities 06:30-23:00 **MR292**

Hedgeley Services

**Powburn, Alnwick
Northumberland NN66 4HU
T 01665 578214**

ON THE A697 Hedgeley Services is situated on the A697 at Powburn approximately 18 miles north of Morpeth and on the right-hand side if heading north.

CREDIT/DEBIT CARDS

FUEL CARDS (see key on page 6)
① ② ③ ㊺

TRUCK FACILITIES
P free with fuel purchased
Coach parking available (6 spaces)
Quiet area
Ample room for manoeuvring
Truck washing facilities

SITE COMMENTS/INFORMATION
Popular LGV site

Parking 24 hours. Restaurant open 08:00-22:00. Other on-site facilities 06:00-22:00   **MR293**

Lalestone Service Station

**Petrol Express Ltd, Lalestone
Bridgend, South Glamorgan CF32 0LY
T 01656 662910**
ON THE A48 EASTBOUND From the M4, exit at junction 37 take the A4229 towards Pyle and North Cornelly. At the roundabout with the A48, turn right towards Lalestone. Continue for 3 miles, Lalestone Service Station is at the west end of the village on your left.

CREDIT/DEBIT CARDS

FUEL CARDS (see key on page 6)
① ③ ⑨

TRUCK FACILITIES
P free
Coach parking available (4 spaces)
Overnight parking at rear of restaurant with permission

DRIVER FACILITIES
Accommodation half a mile away at
  Great House Hotel
Truckers' accessories

SITE COMMENTS/INFORMATION
Easy access for LGVs

Parking 24 hours. Restaurant open evenings only. Other on-site facilities 06:00-09:00   **MR294**

M1 Service Area

**Drumgormal, Dungannon
County Tyrone BT71 7PG, Northern Ireland
T 02887 724541**

ON THE A4 From Belfast, take the M1 to the end. Continue along the A4 for 1 and a half miles. M1 Service Area is on your right-hand side before Granville.

CREDIT/DEBIT CARDS

FUEL CARDS (see key on page 6)
② ③ ⑤ ⑥

TRUCK FACILITIES
P free
Coach parking available (4 spaces)
Quiet area
Ample room for manoeuvring

DRIVER FACILITIES
Showers, 1 male, 1 female (free)
Drivers' washroom
Takeaway food
Phone top-ups/accessories
Truckers' accessories

Parking 24 hours. Fuel, showers and shop 06:30-22:00. Other on-site facilities 08:00-20:00   **MR295**

Merlin Service Station

**254 Bolton Road, Westhoughton
Bolton, Lancashire BL5 3EF
T 01942 793547/811122**

ON THE A6 From the M61, exit at junction 5 and take the A58 towards Westhoughton. Turn right at next roundabout onto the A6 heading for Wingates and Merlin is 600 yards on the left-hand side.

 4.2m Independent

CREDIT/DEBIT CARDS

FUEL CARDS (see key on page 6)
① ② ③

TRUCK FACILITIES
P free
Quiet area
Ample room for manoeuvring
Truck washing facilities

DRIVER FACILITIES
Takeaway food nearby

SITE COMMENTS/INFORMATION
Friendly service and car showroom on-site

Parking 24 hours. Other on-site facilities 07:00-20:30   **MR296**

Monmouth Services north-eastbound

**Dingestow, Monmouth
Monmouthshire NP25 4BG
T 01600 740444**

ON THE A40 NORTH-EASTBOUND Monmouth Services is on the A40 Abergavenny to Monmouth road on the north-eastbound carriageway, just east of the A449 Raglan interchange.

CREDIT/DEBIT CARDS

FUEL CARDS (see key on page 6)
① ④ ⑤ ⑥ 36 39 46

TRUCK FACILITIES
P with voucher, £10.00 (voucher = £6)
P only – £7.00
Coach parking available (10 spaces)
Fencing and floodlights
Quiet area
Ample room for manoeuvring

DRIVER FACILITIES
Travelodge on-site (£49.50 per night)
Shower, drivers' washroom
Clothing for sale
Takeaway food
Truckers' accessories

Parking, showers and fuel 24 hours. Takeaway open 09:00-21:00. Travelodge 06:00-22:00   **MR297**

Musselburgh Services & Little Chef

**Old Craighall, Musselburgh
East Lothian EH21 8RE
T 0131 6536070**

OFF THE A1 BY-PASS From the A1 Mussleburgh by-pass, take the exit signposted B6415 and A702 Edinburgh City by-pass. Take the B6415 towards Mussleburgh. Mussleburgh Services is 100 yards on the right.

CREDIT/DEBIT CARDS

FUEL CARDS (see key on page 6)
⑦

TRUCK FACILITIES
P with voucher, £10.00 (voucher = £6)
P only – £7.00
Coach parking available
Quiet area
Ample room for manoeuvring

DRIVER FACILITIES
Accommodation on-site (£55 per night)
Shower
Drivers' washroom
Takeaway food
Clothing for sale

Fuel, parking, shop and showers 24 hours. All other on-site facilities 07:00-22:00   **MR298**

Nolan's Service Station, Ballon

Main Street, Ballon
County Carlow, Ireland
T 00353 (0) 599159219/599159020

ON THE N80 Nolans Service Station is at Ballon on the N80. 8 miles from Carlow and on the right-hand side if heading for Bunclody.

CREDIT/DEBIT CARDS

FUEL CARDS (see key on page 6)
9 21

TRUCK FACILITIES
Ample room for manoeuvring
Overnight parking wiith permission
Truck washing facilities
Tyre repair/sales

DRIVER FACILITIES
Truckers' accessories
Takeaway food

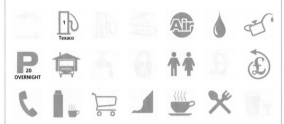

Short term parking times unknown. All other on-site facilities 06:30-22:00   **MR299**

Parkside Service Station

Trentaboy, Drumkeen, Ballybofey
County Donegal, Ireland
T 00353 (0) 749134149

ON THE N13 Take the N14 from Letterkenny towards Lifford for 1 mile, then turn right and follow the N13 southbound towards Ballybofey for 3 miles. Parkside Services is on the left-hand side.

CREDIT/DEBIT CARDS

FUEL CARDS (see key on page 6)
9 21

TRUCK FACILITIES
P free
Coach parking available (12 spaces)
Truck washing facilities
Truck dealership/workshop

DRIVER FACILITIES
Takeaway food
Truckers' accessories

SITE COMMENTS/INFORMATION
Friendly service and value for money

Parking 24 hours. All on-site facilities 07:00-22:00 Mon-Thurs, 07:00-23:00 Fri, 08:00-22:00 Sat & Sun   **MR300**

Podimore Services

Podimore, Yeovil
Somerset BA22 8JG
T 01935 841717

ON THE A303 Podimore Services is 6 miles from Yeovil on the A303 at the roundabout with the A37 and A372.

CREDIT/DEBIT CARDS

FUEL CARDS (see key on page 6)
1 10 42

TRUCK FACILITIES
P free
Coach parking available, shared with LGV
Ample room for manoeuvring
Quiet area
Truck dealership/workshop nearby

DRIVER FACILITIES
Travelodge on-site (£45 per night)
Takeaway food
Truckers' accessories

Parking, toilets, fuel and shop 24 hours   **MR301**

Rakeelan Service Station

Emo Oil Ltd, Derrylin Road, Rakeelan Ballyconnell, County Cavan, Ireland
T 00353 (0) 499526614

ON THE R205 Take the road that runs from Ballyconnell to the A509. Rakeelan Service Station is at Rakeelan on the right-hand side just before the border.

CREDIT/DEBIT CARDS

FUEL CARDS (see key on page 6)

TRUCK FACILITIES
Coach parking available (5 spaces)
Overnight parking at rear of filling station
Truck washing facilities
Truck dealership/workshop nearby

DRIVER FACILITIES
Shower
Truckers' accessories

Bunker fuel 24 hours. Other on-site facilities 07:00-22:00. Overnight parking times unknown   **MR302**

Ron Perry & Son

Elwick, Hartlepool Cleveland TS27 3HH
T 01740 644223

ON THE A19 SOUTHBOUND Take the A19 from Peterlee towards Middlesborough. Ron Perry & Son is on the southbound carriageway, 2 miles south of Elwick, 2 miles north of Wolviston, and just south of the turning for Dalton Piercy.

CREDIT/DEBIT CARDS

FUEL CARDS (see key on page 6)

DRIVER FACILITIES
Takeaway food nearby

SITE COMMENTS/INFORMATION
Excellent staff!

All on-site facilities 06:00-22:00   **MR303**

Ron Perry & Son & Café A19

Elwick, Hartlepool Cleveland TS27 3HH
T 01740 644223

ON THE A19 NORTHBOUND Take the A19 from Middlesborough towards Peterlee. Ron Perry & Son and Café A19 is on the northbound carriageway, 2 miles south of Elwick, 2 miles north of Wolviston, and just south of the turning for Dalton Piercy.

CREDIT/DEBIT CARDS

FUEL CARDS (see key on page 6)

TRUCK FACILITIES
P free
Quiet area
Ample room for manoeuvring

DRIVER FACILITIES
Takeaway food nearby

SITE COMMENTS/INFORMATION
Excellent staff!

Parking 24 hours. Other on-site facilities 06:00-22:00   **MR304**

Ross Spur Services southbound

First Motorway Services Ltd
Southbound Overcross, Ross on Wye
Herefordshire HR9 7QJ
T 01989 565027

M50 JUNCTION 4 ON THE A449 Ross Spur is located at the end of M50 on the A449 southbound carriageway towards Ross on Wye.

CREDIT/DEBIT CARDS

FUEL CARDS (see key on page 6)
5 6

TRUCK FACILITIES
P with voucher, £11.00 (voucher = £5)
P only – £8.00
Coach parking available (2 spaces)
Quiet area
Ample room for manoeuvring

DRIVER FACILITIES
Accommodation 600 yards away at
   Travel Inn
Truckers' accessories

SITE COMMENTS/INFORMATION
At time of print, on-site restaurant was closed. This site is also due for refurbishment

All on-site facilities 24 hours   **MR305**

Saltash Services

Moto Ltd, Callington Road, Carkeel
nr Saltash, Cornwall PL12 6PH
T 01752 849404 www.moto-way.com

OFF THE A388 Take the A38 from Plymouth across the Tamar Bridge towards Liskeard. At the next roundabout, turn right taking the road signposted A388 Callington. Entrance to Saltash Services is a few yards on the left at the next roundabout.

CREDIT/DEBIT CARDS

FUEL CARDS (see key on page 6)
4 7 37

TRUCK FACILITIES
Coach parking available (6 spaces)

DRIVER FACILITIES
Shower
Travelodge on-site
Takeaway food

Parking, shop and fuel 24 hours. Other on-site facilities 06:00-22:00   **MR306**

Shell Beacon

Brough
North Humberside HU15 1SA
T 01430 426110

ON THE A63 EASTBOUND Beacon services is situated beyond the end of the M62 a few 100 yards further on after it becomes the A63. This site is located on the left-hand side if heading east and is situated next to the Travelodge.

CREDIT/DEBIT CARDS

FUEL CARDS (see key on page 6)
4 8 19 36 41

TRUCK FACILITIES
P free
Coach parking available, shared with LGV
Ample room for manoeuvring
Quiet area

DRIVER FACILITIES
Hot drinks free with 100 litres of fuel
Drivers' washroom on-site
Travelodge nearby

SITE COMMENTS/INFORMATION
Friendly staff

All on-site facilities 24 hours except Little Chef Restaurant. Nearby Travelodge opening times unknown   **MR307**

Shell Ilminster

Horton Cross, Ilminster
Somerset TA19 9PT
T 01460 256000

ON THE A358 Shell Ilminster can be found where the A358 Taunton to Chard road and the A303 Ilminster to Honiton road intersect. To access this site take the Chard road from the roundabout and turn immediately right after a few yards.

CREDIT/DEBIT CARDS

FUEL CARDS (see key on page 6)
④ ⑦ ⑧ ⑲ ㊱ ㊲ ㊴ ㊵ ㊶

TRUCK FACILITIES
P free
Ample room for manoeuvring

DRIVER FACILITIES
Hot drinks free with 100 litres of fuel
Travelodge nearby (£50 per night)
Takeaway food

SITE COMMENTS/INFORMATION
Friendly helpful staff. Well stocked site

Little Chef restaurant 07:00-22:00. Other on-site facilities 24 hours

MR308

Skiach Services

Unit 4D, Evanton Industrial Estate
Evanton, Rosshire IV16 9XH
T 01349 830888

OFF THE A9 Take the A9 from Inverness to Alness, by-passing Evanton on your left. Skiach Services is on your left, just before the turning for the B9176 towards Bonar Bridge and Sittenham.

CREDIT/DEBIT CARDS

FUEL CARDS (see key on page 6)
② ③ ④ ⑦ ⑧ ⑫ ㊱ ㊳ ㊴ ㊵

TRUCK FACILITIES
P free
Coach parking available (10 spaces)
Ample room for manoeuvring

DRIVER FACILITIES
Shower, 1 male (charge)
Drivers' washroom
TV
Takeaway food
Phone top-ups/accessories

Café open until 22:00. All other on-site facilities 24 hours

MR309

Smyths Service Station

Emo Oil Ltd, Derry Road, Slane
County Meath, Ireland
T 00353 (0) 419824555

ON THE N2 Take the N2 northbound out of Slane and head for Collon. Smyths Service Station is 600 yards on the right.

CREDIT/DEBIT CARDS

FUEL CARDS (see key on page 6)
③ ⑪ ⑳ ㉑

TRUCK FACILITIES
P free
Coach parking available, shared with LGV
Overnight parking in car park
Truck washing facilities

DRIVER FACILITIES
Truckers' accessories

SITE COMMENTS/INFORMATION
Good service
Easy access for LGVs

Bunker fuel 24 hours. Other on-site facilities 06:00-22:00

MR310

Somerfield Supermarket Filling Station, Evesham

Somerfield Supermarkets Ltd
Evesham By-pass, Evesham
Worcestershire WR14 4ZP
T 01386 765270

ON THE A46 Take the A46 north around Evesham and Somerfield Supermarket Filling Station is at the roundabout with the A44.

Unknown · Somerfield · 8 OVERNIGHT · £1.50 · £2.99 · 69p · NEARBY

CREDIT/DEBIT CARDS

FUEL CARDS (see key on page 6)
4

TRUCK FACILITIES
P free
Coach parking available, shared with LGV
Ample room for manoeuvring
Quiet area

DRIVER FACILITIES
Travel Inn 200 yards away
Takeaway food
Truckers' accessories

SITE COMMENTS/INFORMATION
Friendly staff, excellent prices.
Hot food around the clock

All on-site facilities 24 hours

MR311

Stannington Services

North Road, Stannington, Morpeth
Northumberland NE61 6ED
T 01670 789386

OFF THE A1 Take the A1 from Morpeth to Newcastle upon Tyne. Continue past the junction with the A197 and the turning for the village of Clifton. Within 500 yards take the next sliproad. Stannington Services is on your left at the staggered junction.

Jet · 10 OVERNIGHT · £*

CREDIT/DEBIT CARDS

FUEL CARDS (see key on page 6)
1 15 44

TRUCK FACILITIES
P free
Quiet area
Ample room for manoeuvring

DRIVER FACILITIES
Drivers' washroom
Truckers' accessories

All on-site facilities 24 hours

MR312

Star Foston Service Station

Long street, Foston, nr Grantham
Lincolnshire NG32 2LD
T 01400 283800

ON THE A1 NORTHBOUND Star Foston is on the A1 northbound carriageway between Grantham and Long Bennington, close to the second turning for Allington if heading Northbound.

4.8m · Texaco · 4 OVERNIGHT · £2.70 · £1.10

CREDIT/DEBIT CARDS

FUEL CARDS (see key on page 6)
1 3 4 9 14

TRUCK FACILITIES
P £5.00
Quiet area
Ample room for manoeuvring

DRIVER FACILITIES
Drivers' washroom

Parking 24 hours. Other on-site facilities 06:30-22:00

MR313

Star Rainton

Rainton, Thirsk
North Yorkshire YO7 3QA
T **01765 641100**

ON THE A1 Take the A1M north past junction 49 and onto the A1. Star Rainton is half a mile on the left.

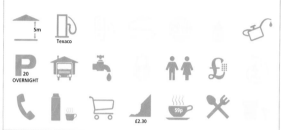

All on-site facilities 24 hours

CREDIT/DEBIT CARDS

FUEL CARDS (see key on page 6)
① ③ ⑨ ⑫

TRUCK FACILITIES
P free
Ample room for manoeuvring

DRIVER FACILITIES
Drivers' washroom and rest area
Takeaway food
Phone top-ups/accessories

SITE COMMENTS/INFORMATION
Easy access for LGVs
Only LGV site for 50 miles

MR314

Star West Wellow

Ower, Romsey
Hampshire SO51 6AS
T **02380 817100**

A36 A3090 INTERSECTION Exit the M27 at junction 2 and take the A36 towards Salisbury. Texaco Star West Wellow is 800 yards at the roundabout with the A3090.

All on-site facilities 24 hours

CREDIT/DEBIT CARDS

FUEL CARDS (see key on page 6)
① ② ③ ⑨

TRUCK FACILITIES
P free
Coach parking available, shared with LGV
Ample room for manoeuvring
Quiet area

DRIVER FACILITIES
Drivers' washroom
Premier Lodge 400 yards away
Truckers' accessories

MR315

Stracathro Service Area

Stracathro, nr Brechin
Angus DD9 7PX
T **01674 840048**

ON THE A90 By-pass Brechin on the A90 heading for Stonehaven. Two miles past the turning for the B966 you will see signs for Stracathro. Stracathro Services are just before that turning on the left.

Fuel, shop and toilets 24 hours. Other on-site facilities 06:00-21:00 Mon-Fri, 06:00-20:00 Sat, 07:00-21:00 Sun

CREDIT/DEBIT CARDS

FUEL CARDS (see key on page 6)
① ② ③ ④ ⑧ ⑫ ⑬ ㊱ ㊲ ㊳ ㊴ ㊵
㊶

TRUCK FACILITIES
P with voucher, £7.50 (voucher = £6)
Coach parking available, shared with LGV
Ample room for manoeuvring
Quiet area
Fridge lorries welcome, no separate area

DRIVER FACILITIES
Shower, 1 unisex (£1.00)
TV
Takeaway food
Truckers' accessories

MR316

Sutherlands Garage Ltd

Portree Road, Broadford IV49 9AB
Isle Of Skye
T 01471 822225

ON THE A87 Sutherlands Garage is on the A87 in the village of Broadford and on the left-hand side if heading south-east. It is also just past the junction with the B8083.

All on-site facilities 24 hours

CREDIT/DEBIT CARDS

FUEL CARDS (see key on page 6)
① ② ④ ⑦ ㊲ ㊳

TRUCK FACILITIES
P free
Coach parking available
Overnight parking at rear of forecourt
Truck washing facilities

DRIVER FACILITIES
Internet access
Laundry service
Euros changed/accepted
Takeaway food
Truckers' accessories

MR317

Swan Service Station

Worcester Road, Wychbold, Bromsgrove
West Midlands B61 7ER
T 01527 861892

ON THE A38 From M5 junction 5, take the A38 towards Bromsgrove. Continue through Wychbold and Swan Service Station is on the right before you get to Upton Warren.

Café 07:00-19:00. Other on-site facilities 24 hours

CREDIT/DEBIT CARDS

FUEL CARDS (see key on page 6)
① ② ③ ④ ⑧ ⑫ ⑬ ㊲

TRUCK FACILITIES
P £8.00
CCTV. Quiet area
Ample room for manoeuvring

DRIVER FACILITIES
Hot drinks free with 100 litres
Drivers' washroom and rest area
Premier Lodge 400 yards away
Takeaway food
Phone top-ups/accessories
Good range of truckers' accessories

SITE COMMENTS/INFORMATION
Train/tram nearby

MR318

Symonds Yat Services northbound

First Motorway Services Ltd
Symonds Yat, Whitchurch, Ross on Wye
Herefordshire HR9 6DP
T 01600 890219

ON THE A40 NORTHBOUND This site is located at Symonds Yat on the A40 northbound between Monmouth and Ross on Wye just before the junction with the A4137.

Parking 24 hours. Other on-site facilities 06:00-21:00

CREDIT/DEBIT CARDS

FUEL CARDS (see key on page 6)
① ② ③ ④ ⑤ ㊲ ㊳

TRUCK FACILITIES
P with voucher £15.00 (voucher = £7)
P only – £12.00
Coach parking available (3 spaces)
Ample room for manoeuvring
Quiet area

DRIVER FACILITIES
Shower (free), drivers' washroom
Rest area, TV
Truckers' accessories
Clothing for sale

MR319

Texaco Service Station Clones

**Monaghan Road, Clones
County Monaghan, Ireland
T 00353 (0) 4752435**

ON THE N54 Take the N54 out of Clones towards Monaghan. Texaco Service Station Clones is on the right-hand side, 100 yards past the junction with the R183.

CREDIT/DEBIT CARDS

FUEL CARDS (see key on page 6)
② ⑨ ⑪ ⑰ ⑱ ㉑

TRUCK FACILITIES
Coach parking available (5 spaces)
Overnight parking with permission only
Truck washing facilities
Truck dealership/workshop nearby

DRIVER FACILITIES
Truckers' accessories

SITE COMMENTS/INFORMATION
Friendly staff
Breakfast and hot soup on sale all day!

All on-site facilities 07:00-23:00   **MR320**

Texaco Spar Service Station, Cavan

**Dublin Road, Cavan
County Cavan, Ireland
T 00353 (0) 494332515**

ON THE N3 Take the N3 southbound around the east side of Cavan until you reach the roundabout with the N55. Turn right, continuing on the N3 for 200 yards and Texaco Spar is on the right.

CREDIT/DEBIT CARDS

FUEL CARDS (see key on page 6)
② ④ ⑤ ⑨ ⑪ ⑰ ⑱ ⑳ ㉑ ㉔ ㉜ ㉟
㊲

TRUCK FACILITIES
Coach parking available
Ample room for manoeuvring
Truck washing facilities
Truck dealership/workshop nearby

DRIVER FACILITIES
Drivers' washroom, phone top-ups/accessories
Accommodation half a mile away at
  Hotel Kilmore
Takeaway food and truckers' accessories
Post Office

SITE COMMENTS/INFORMATION
Award winning deli. counter food

All on-site facilities 05:30-00:30. Short term on-site and nearby overnight parking times unknown   **MR321**

The Filling Station

**Byrness, Newcastle upon Tyne
Tyne and Wear NE19 1TR
T 01830 520525**

ON THE A68 The Filling Station is on the south east side of the village of Byrness on the A68 Rochester to Jedburgh road, and on the left-hand side if heading towards Jedburgh.

CREDIT/DEBIT CARDS

FUEL CARDS (see key on page 6)
② ④

TRUCK FACILITIES
P with voucher – £5.00
  (voucher value – 1 meal)
Quiet area
Ample room for manoeuvring

DRIVER FACILITIES
Takeaway food
Truckers' accessories

Parking 24 hours. Other on-site facilities 08:00-07:00 in summer, 07:30-08:00 in winter   **MR322**

The Green Welly Stop

Tyndrum, Perth and Kinross FK20 8RY
T **018388 400271** www.thegreenwellystop.co.uk

ON THE A82 The Green Welly is located on the A82 between the villages of Clifton and Tyndrum on the right-hand side if heading north-west.

CREDIT/DEBIT CARDS

FUEL CARDS (see key on page 6)

TRUCK FACILITIES
P free
Coach parking available (10 spaces)
Ample room for manoeuvring
Quiet area

DRIVER FACILITIES
Takeaway food

SITE COMMENTS/INFORMATION
Train/tram nearby
Friendly, hard-working staff

Parking 24 hours. Other on-site facilities 07:00-22:00 in summer, 08:00-21:00 in winter

MR323

The Lazy Kettle Transport Café

Gledrid Service Station, Oswestry By-pass
Oswestry, Shropshire SY11 3EN
T **01691 770066**

A5/A483 INTERSECTION The Lazy Kettle is on the A483 Oswestry By-pass at the roundabout with the A5 and on the right-hand side if heading north.

CREDIT/DEBIT CARDS

FUEL CARDS (see key on page 6)

TRUCK FACILITIES
Coach parking available
Quiet area. Fridge lorry area
Ample room for manoeuvring
Truck washing facilities

DRIVER FACILITIES
Showers, 4 male, 3 female
Travelodge on-site
Drivers' washroom, rest area, internet access and phone top-ups/accessories
Truckers' accessories
Takeaway food nearby

SITE COMMENTS/INFORMATION
Plenty of room for parking, clean site

All on-site facilities 24 hours

MR324

Tullynagrow Fuelserve

Stat Oil Service Station, Tullynagrow
Creighanroe, Castleblayney to Keady Border
Castleblayney, County Monaghan, Ireland
T **00353 (0) 429751784**

ON THE R181 From the centre of Castleblaney take the R181 signposted toward Keady. Tullynagrow Fuelserve is left-hand side, half a mile from the town centre.

CREDIT/DEBIT CARDS

FUEL CARDS (see key on page 6)

TRUCK FACILITIES
P free
Coach parking available
Quiet area
Ample room for manoeuvring
Credit/debit cards accepted at auto bunker

DRIVER FACILITIES
Drivers' washroom
Glencarn Hotel on-site
Euros changed/accepted
Takeaway food and clothing for sale nearby
Phone top-ups/accessories nearby

Bunker fuel and parking 24 hours. Other on-site facilities 07:30-22:00

MR325

Wardle Services

Wardle, nr Taporley
Cheshire CW6 9JS
T 01829 260304

ON THE A51 Take the A51 from Nantwich towards Chester. Wardle Services is on the right, 3 miles beyond the junction with the A534, north west of the village of Wardle and before the village of Caveley.

CREDIT/DEBIT CARDS

FUEL CARDS (see key on page 6)

TRUCK FACILITIES
P £5.00
Coach parking available, shared with LGV
Ample room for manoeuvring
Quiet area
Truck washing facilities

DRIVER FACILITIES
Drivers' washroom
Takeaway food nearby
Clothing for sale nearby
CB sales/repairs nearby

Parking 24 hours. Other on-site facilities 07:00-19:00   **MR326**

Wardlow Mires Filling Station & Transport Café

Wardlow Mires, nr Tideswell, Buxton
Derbyshire SK17 8NY/8RU
T 01298 871445 Filling Station
T 01298 872880 Café

ON THE A623 Take the A619 westbound from Chesterfield to Baslow village. Take the A623 heading north-west Wardlow Mires Filling Station is on the right-hand side opposite the junction with the B6465.

CREDIT/DEBIT CARDS

FUEL CARDS (see key on page 6)

TRUCK FACILITIES
P with voucher – £6.00
  (voucher value – 1 meal)
Coach parking available, shared with LGV
Ample room for manoeuvring
Floodlights
Quiet area
Truck washing facilities

DRIVER FACILITIES
Shower, 1 unisex (charge)
Takeaway food

Parking 24 hours. Café/restaurant 08:00-22:00. Fuel 07:00-19:00. Shop 08:00-19:00 Mon-Fri. 09:00-18:00 Sat & Sun   **MR327**

West Cave Services

Triple 8, Brough
East Yorkshire HU15 1RZ
T 01430 422127

ON THE A63 WESTBOUND From Hull take the A63 westbound out of the city. West Cave Services is on the A63 westbound carriageway, half a mile before the M62.

CREDIT/DEBIT CARDS

FUEL CARDS (see key on page 6)

TRUCK FACILITIES
P free
Coach parking available, shared with LGV
Ample room for manoeuvring
No overnight parking for abnormal loads, access only for filling station

DRIVER FACILITIES
Travelodge 400 yards away
Truckers' accessories

SITE COMMENTS/INFORMATION
Friendly staff, good service.
Truckers' facilities due to be upgraded soon

Restaurant 07:00-22:00. Travelodge opening times unknown. Parking, shop and fuel 24 hours   **MR328**

Wynyard Park Service Area

**Coal Lane, Wolviston, Billingham
Cleveland TS22 5PZ**
T **01740 644875/644872**

A19 A689 INTERCHANGE Exit the A19 southbound at the junction with the A689 and turn right on the A689 towards Wolviston and Billingham. Turn left at the next roundabout into the service area complex. The filling station is on the left.

CREDIT/DEBIT CARDS

FUEL CARDS (see key on page 6)

TRUCK FACILITIES
P with voucher – £5.00
Coach parking available, shared with LGV
Ample room for manoeuvring

DRIVER FACILITIES
Hot drinks free with 100 litres
Holiday Inn on-site (£55 per night)
Takeaway food

SITE COMMENTS/INFORMATION
Helpful friendly staff available round the clock

Holiday Inn opening times unknown. All other on-site facilities 24 hours

MR329

Abington Services

Welcome Break Ltd, nr Abington
Biggar, South Lanarkshire ML12 6RG
T 01864 502637/502835

A74M JUNCTION 13

Unknown
Shell
OVERNIGHT

CREDIT/DEBIT CARDS

FUEL CARDS (see key on page 6)
8

DRIVER FACILITIES
Accommodation on-site, Welcome Lodge
Takeaway food

Full site details not available at time of going to press. For more information please contact site.

All on-site facilities accessible 24 hours

M330

Annandale Water Services

Roadchef Ltd
Johnstonebridge, nr Lockerbie
Dumfries and Galloway DG11 1HD
T 01576 470870

A74M JUNCTION 16

Unknown
BP
52
OVERNIGHT

CREDIT/DEBIT CARDS

FUEL CARDS (see key on page 6)
1 5 6

TRUCK FACILITIES

P *with voucher*	**P** *only*	*Voucher value*
£12.00	£9.00	£6.00

Coach parking available (12 spaces)
Quiet area. Truck dealership/workshop
Ample room for manoeuvring

DRIVER FACILITIES
Accommodation, showers, 1 m, 1 f (charge), internet access, phone top-ups/accessories, truckers' accessories
Takeaway food

SITE COMMENTS/INFORMATION
This site is in a unique scenic location with a lake

All on-site facilities accessible 24 hours

M331

Baldock Services

Extra MSA Forecourts Ltd
Radwell, Baldock, Hertfordshire SG7 5TR
T 01462 832810

A1M JUNCTION 10 Take the A507 to Baldock. Baldock services is 50 yards on the left

5.2m
Texaco
25
OVERNIGHT
£2.99
99p
£5.99

CREDIT/DEBIT CARDS

FUEL CARDS (see key on page 6)
1 2 3 4 9 37

TRUCK FACILITIES
Coach parking available (7 spaces)
P *only* £13.50
Overnight security patrol
Quiet area
Ample room for manoeuvring

DRIVER FACILITIES
Showers, 2 male, 1 female (free)
Accommodation on-site (£55 per night)
Internet access
Truckers' accessories
Takeaway food

Parking, showers, fuel and some food accessible 24 hours. Restaurant open 07:00-23:00

M332

Birch Services eastbound

Moto Ltd
Birch, Heywood
Greater Manchester OL10 2QH
T **0161 6430911** www.moto-way.com

M62 EASTBOUND BETWEEN JUNCTIONS 18 AND 19

All on-site facilities accessible 24 hours

M333

CREDIT/DEBIT CARDS

FUEL CARDS (see key on page 6)

DRIVER FACILITIES
Accommodation on-site, Travelodge
Takeaway food

Full site details not available at time of going to press. For more information please contact site.

Birch Services westbound

Moto Ltd
Birch, Heywood
Greater Manchester OL10 2RB
T **0161 6430911** www.moto-way.com

M62 WESTBOUND BETWEEN JUNCTIONS 18 AND 19

All on-site facilities accessible 24 hours

M334

CREDIT/DEBIT CARDS

FUEL CARDS (see key on page 6)

DRIVER FACILITIES
Takeaway food

Full site details not available at time of going to press. For more information please contact site.

Birchanger Services

Welcome Break Ltd
Bishops Stortford, Hertfordshire CM23 5QZ
T **01279 652364**

M11 JUNCTION 8

All on-site facilities accessible 24 hours

M335

CREDIT/DEBIT CARDS

FUEL CARDS (see key on page 6)

DRIVER FACILITIES
Accommodation on-site, Welcome Lodge
Takeaway food

Full site details not available at time of going to press. For more information please contact site.

Blackburn Services

Extra MSA Forecourts Ltd
Darwen, Blackburn, Lancashire BB3 0AT
T **01254 870360**

M65 JUNCTION 4

CREDIT/DEBIT CARDS

FUEL CARDS (see key on page 6)

TRUCK FACILITIES
P £13.50
Overnight security patrol
Quiet area
Ample room for manoeuvring

DRIVER FACILITIES
Showers, 1 male, 1 female (free)
Accommodation – Travelodge (£47 pn)
Truckers' accessories
Takeaway food

SITE COMMENTS/INFORMATION
Good LGV facilities

Parking, fuel, showers, shop and some food accessible 24 hours. Restaurant open 07:00-22:00   M336

Blyth Services

Moto Ltd
Hilltop Roundabout, Blyth
Nottinghamshire S81 8HJ
T **01909 591841** www.moto-way.com

A1M A614 INTERCHANGE On the roundabout
intersection with the A1M, A1, A164 and B6045.

CREDIT/DEBIT CARDS

FUEL CARDS (see key on page 6)

DRIVER FACILITIES
Accommodation on-site, Travelodge
Takeaway food

*Full site details not available at time of going to
press. For more information please contact site.*

All on-site facilities accessible 24 hours   M337

Bolton West Services northbound

First Motorway Services Ltd
nr Horwich, Bolton, Lancashire BL6 5UZ
T **0870 4448641**

M61 NORTHBOUND BETWEEN JUNCTIONS 6 AND 8

CREDIT/DEBIT CARDS

FUEL CARDS (see key on page 6)

TRUCK FACILITIES
P with voucher   **P** only   Voucher value
£11.00   £8.00   £5.00
Coach parking available (12 spaces)
Quiet area
Ample room for manoeuvring

DRIVER FACILITIES
Shower, 1 male (free), washroom, rest
area, TV
Accommodation – Travelodge (£55 pn)
Takeaway food
Truckers' accessories
Clothing for sale

Parking, showers, fuel and restaurant 24 hours. Shop 07:00-19:00. Travelodge opening times unknown   M338

Bolton West Services southbound

First Motorway Services Ltd
nr Horwich, Bolton, Lancashire BL6 5UZ
T **0870 4448641**

M61 SOUTHBOUND BETWEEN JUNCTIONS 6 AND 8

CREDIT/DEBIT CARDS

FUEL CARDS (see key on page 6)

TRUCK FACILITIES
P *with voucher*   **P** *only*   *Voucher value*
£11.00   £8.00   £5.00
Coach parking available (10 spaces)
Quiet area
Ample room for manoeuvring

DRIVER FACILITIES
Shower (free), washroom, rest area, TV
Accommodation on-site, Travelodge (£55 pn)
Truckers' accessories
Clothing for sale
Takeaway food nearby

Travelodge opening times unknown. All other on-site facilities accessible 24 Hours   M339

Bothwell Services southbound

Roadchef Ltd
nr Bothwell, Glasgow
South Lanarkshire G71 8BG
T **01698 854123**

M74 SOUTHBOUND BETWEEN JUNCTIONS 4 AND 5

CREDIT/DEBIT CARDS

FUEL CARDS (see key on page 6)

TRUCK FACILITIES
P *with voucher*   **P** *only*   *Voucher value*
£12.00   £10.00   £6.00
Coach parking available (10 spaces)
Ample room for manoeuvring

DRIVER FACILITIES
Shower, 1 unisex (free), TV
Internet access
Takeaway food
Truckers' accessories

Parking, fuel and Shop 24 hours. Restaurant 06:00-22:00. Showers may not be accessible 24 hours   M340

Bridgwater Services

Moto Ltd
Huntsworth Business Park, Bridgwater
Somerset TA6 6TS
T **01278 456800** www.moto-way.com

M5 JUNCTION 24 On the M5 at junction 24 on the A38.

CREDIT/DEBIT CARDS

FUEL CARDS (see key on page 6)

DRIVER FACILITIES
Takeaway food

Full site details not available at time of going to press. For more information please contact site.

All on-site facilities accessible 24 hours   M341

Burton in Kendal Services northbound

Moto Ltd
Burton West, Carnforth
Lancashire LA6 1JF
T **01524 781234** www.moto-way.com

M6 NORTHBOUND BETWEEN JUNCTIONS 35 AND 36

CREDIT/DEBIT CARDS

FUEL CARDS (see key on page 6)
⑤ ⑥

DRIVER FACILITIES
Accommodation on-site, Travelodge
Takeaway food

Full site details not available at time of going to press. For more information please contact site.

All on-site facilities accessible 24 hours

M342

Burtonwood Services eastbound

Welcome Break Ltd
Warrington
Cheshire WA5 3AX
T **01925 651656**

M62 EASTBOUND JUNCTION 8

CREDIT/DEBIT CARDS

FUEL CARDS (see key on page 6)
⑧

DRIVER FACILITIES
Takeaway food

Full site details not available at time of going to press. For more information please contact site.

All on-site facilities accessible 24 hours

M343

Burtonwood Services westbound

Welcome Break Ltd
Warrington
Cheshire WA5 3AX
T **01925 651656**

M62 WESTBOUND BETWEEN JUNCTIONS 8 AND 9

CREDIT/DEBIT CARDS

FUEL CARDS (see key on page 6)
⑧

DRIVER FACILITIES
Accommodation on-site, Welcome Lodge
Takeaway food

Full site details not available at time of going to press. For more information please contact site.

All on-site facilities accessible 24 hours

M344

Cardiff Gate Services

North Pentwyn
Cardiff, South Glamorgan CF23 8RA
T **0292 0735618**

M4 JUNCTION 30

CREDIT/DEBIT CARDS

FUEL CARDS (see key on page 6)
46

DRIVER FACILITIES
Accommodation on-site, Ibis
Takeaway food

Full site details not available at time of going to press. For more information please contact site.

All on-site facilities accessible 24 hours

M345

Cardiff West Services

Moto Ltd
Pontyclun, Cardiff
South Glamorgan CF72 8SA
T **029 20891141** www.moto-way.com

M4 JUNCTION 33

CREDIT/DEBIT CARDS

FUEL CARDS (see key on page 6)
7 38 40

DRIVER FACILITIES
Accommodation on-site, Travelodge
Takeaway food

Full site details not available at time of going to press. For more information please contact site.

All on-site facilities accessible 24 hours

M346

Charnock Richard Services northbound

Welcome Break Ltd
nr Coppul, nr Chorley,
Lancashire PR7 5LR
T **01257 791746**

M6 NORTHBOUND BETWEEN JUNCTIONS 27 AND 28

CREDIT/DEBIT CARDS

FUEL CARDS (see key on page 6)
8

DRIVER FACILITIES
Accommodation on-site, Welcome Lodge
Takeaway food

Full site details not available at time of going to press. For more information please contact site.

All on-site facilities accessible 24 hours

M347

Charnock Richard Services southbound

**Welcome Break Ltd
nr Coppul, nr Chorley,
Lancashire PR7 5LR
T 01257 791746**

M6 SOUTHBOUND BETWEEN JUNCTIONS 27 AND 28

CREDIT/DEBIT CARDS

FUEL CARDS (see key on page 6)
⑧

DRIVER FACILITIES
Accommodation on-site, Welcome Lodge
Takeaway food

*Full site details not available at time of going to
press. For more information please contact site.*

All on-site facilities accessible 24 hours

M348

Cherwell Valley Services

**Moto Ltd
Northampton Road, Bicester
Oxfordshire OX6 9RD
T 01869 346060** www.moto-way.com

M40 JUNCTION 10

CREDIT/DEBIT CARDS

FUEL CARDS (see key on page 6)
⑦ ㊳ ㊵

DRIVER FACILITIES
Accommodation on-site, Travelodge
Takeaway food
Phone top-ups/accessories
Truckers' accessories

*Full site details not available at time of going to
press. For more information please contact site.*

All on-site facilties accessible 24 hours

M349

Chester Services

**Roadchef Ltd
Hapsford
Cheshire CH2 4QZ
T 01452 623300**

M56 JUNCTION 14

CREDIT/DEBIT CARDS

FUEL CARDS (see key on page 6)
⑧

TRUCK FACILITIES
P *with voucher* **P** *only   Voucher value*
£12.00   £9.00   £6.00
Coach parking available (20 spaces)
Quiet area
Ample room for manoeuvring
Truck dealership/workshop

DRIVER FACILITIES
Accommodation on-site, Travel Inn
Showers, 1 male, 1 female (free),internet
access. Truckers' accessories
Takeaway food
Clothing for sale

All on-site facilities accessible 24 hours

M350

Chesterfield Services northbound

**Newton Wood Lane
Newton, Alfreton
Derbyshire DT56 5SZ
T 01773 594810**

M1 NORTHBOUND BETWEEN JUNCTIONS 28 AND 29

CREDIT/DEBIT CARDS

FUEL CARDS (see key on page 6)

TRUCK FACILITIES
P *with voucher*   **P** *only*   *Voucher value*
£8.00 or £12.00   £9.00   £2.00 or £6.00
Coach parking available (15 spaces)
Quiet area, fridge lorry area
Ample room for manoeuvring

DRIVER FACILITIES
Accommodation on-site (£45 pn)
Showers, 1 male, 1 female (free),
washroom, truckers' accessories
Takeaway food

SITE COMMENTS/INFORMATION
Good LGV facilities

Restaurant accessible 06:00-22:00. Some food and all other on-site facilities accessible 24 hours   **M351**

Chesterfield Services southbound

**Roadchef Ltd
Newton Wood Lane, Newton, Alfreton
Derbyshire DT56 5TZ
T 01773 594800**

M1 SOUTHBOUND BETWEEN JUNCTIONS 28 AND 29

CREDIT/DEBIT CARDS

FUEL CARDS (see key on page 6)

TRUCK FACILITIES
P *with voucher*   **P** *only*   *Voucher value*
£8.00 or £12.00   £9.00   £2.00 or £6.00
Coach parking available (15 spaces)
Quiet area, fridge lorry area
Ample room for manoeuvring

DRIVER FACILITIES
Showers, 1 male, 1 female (free),
washroom, truckers' accessories

SITE COMMENTS/INFORMATION
Good LGV facilities

Restaurant accessible 06:00-22:00. Some food and all other on-site facilities accessible 24 hours   **M352**

Chieveley Services

**Moto Ltd
Oxford Road, Thatcham, nr Newbury
Berkshire RG18 9XX
T 01635 248024** www.moto-way.com

M4 JUNCTION 13 On the M4 at junction 13, on the A34 to
Newbury.

CREDIT/DEBIT CARDS

FUEL CARDS (see key on page 6)

TRUCK FACILITIES
P *with voucher*   **P** *only*   *Voucher value*
£12.50   £10.00   £6.00
Coach parking available (15 spaces)
Ample room for manoeuvring
DRIVER FACILITIES
Accommodation nearby, Travel Inn &
  Hilton Newbury North
Showers, 1 m, 1 f (free), washroom, TV,
truckers' accessories, clothing for sale
Takeaway food
SITE COMMENTS/INFORMATION
Exit from site past filling station difficult
for wide loads

All on-site facilities accessible 24 hours   **M353**

Clacket Lane Services, eastbound

Roadchef Ltd
Westerham, nr Limpsfield
Kent TN16 2NR
T **01959 565577**

M25 EASTBOUND BETWEEN JUNCTIONS 5 AND 6
M25 anti-clockwise.

CREDIT/DEBIT CARDS

FUEL CARDS (see key on page 6)

TRUCK FACILITIES
P *with voucher*   **P** *only*   *Voucher value*
£15.00   £10.00   £7.50
Coach parking available (30 spaces)
Quiet area
Truck dealership/workshop
Ample room for manoeuvring

DRIVER FACILITIES
Accommodation on-site (£52.50 pn)
Showers, 6 male, 4 female (free),
washroom, phone top-ups/accessories
Takeaway food. Clothing for sale

On-site accommodation opening times unknown. All other on-site facilities accessible 24 hours   **M354**

Clacket Lane Services, westbound

Roadchef Ltd
Westerham, nr Limpsfield
Kent TN16 2ER
T **01959 565577**

M25 WESTBOUND BETWEEN JUNCTIONS 5 AND 6
M25 clockwise.

CREDIT/DEBIT CARDS

FUEL CARDS (see key on page 6)

TRUCK FACILITIES
P *with voucher*   **P** *only*
£15.00   £12.00
Coach parking available (32 spaces)
Quiet area. Truck dealership/workshop
Ample room for manoeuvring

DRIVER FACILITIES
Accomm. on-site, Travel Inn (£45.95 pn)
Showers, 2 m, 2 f (free), washroom, rest
area, internet access, phone top-
ups/accessories and truckers' accessories
Takeaway food. Clothing for sale

All on-site facilities accessible 24 hours   **M355**

Corley Services north-westbound

Welcome Break Ltd
Corley, Coventry
Warwickshire CV7 8NR
T **01908 299700 Head Office**

M6 NORTH-WESTBOUND BETWEEN
JUNCTIONS 3 AND 4

CREDIT/DEBIT CARDS

FUEL CARDS (see key on page 6)

DRIVER FACILITIES
Takeaway food

*Full site details not available at time of going to
press. For more information please contact site.*

All on-site facilities accessible 24 hours   **M356**

Corley Services south-eastbound

Welcome Break Ltd
Corley, Coventry
Warwickshire CV7 8NR
T **01908 299700 Head Office**

M6 SOUTH-EASTBOUND BETWEEN
JUNCTIONS 3 AND 4

CREDIT/DEBIT CARDS

FUEL CARDS (see key on page 6)
(8)

DRIVER FACILITIES
Takeaway food

Full site details not available at time of going to press. For more information please contact site.

All on-site facilities accessible 24 hours   M357

Cullompton MSA Services Ltd

Cullompton
Devon EX15 1NS
T **01884 38054**

M5 JUNCTION 28
On the M5 at junction 28. Head for Cullompton. Services are a few yards on the left.

CREDIT/DEBIT CARDS

FUEL CARDS (see key on page 6)
(1)(4)(5)(6)(37)

TRUCK FACILITIES
P £13.50
Quiet area
Ample room for manoeuvring

DRIVER FACILITIES
Takeaway food
Truckers' accessories

SITE COMMENTS/INFORMATION
This site offers exceptional high quality, value for money, food

Parking, fuel, shop and some food accessible 24 hours. Restaurant accessible 07:00-23:00   M358

Doncaster North Services

Moto Ltd
Doncaster
South Yorkshire DN8 5GS
T **01302 847700** www.moto-way.com

M18 / M180 INTERCHANGE JUNCTION 5

CREDIT/DEBIT CARDS

FUEL CARDS (see key on page 6)
(5)(6)

DRIVER FACILITIES
Accommodation on-site, Travelodge
Drivers' rest area
Takeaway food
Phone top-ups/accessories

Full site details not available at time of going to press. For more information please contact site.

All on-site facilities accessible 24 hours   M359

Donington Park Services

Disworth, Derby, Derbyshire DE74 2TN
T 01509 674951

M1 BETWEEN JUNCTIONS 23A AND 24 If heading south, exit M1 at junction 24 and take A453 towards Breedon on the Hill. Donington Park Services is at the next roundabout. If heading north, exit at junction 23A and it's on your left. From the A42 take 'other traffic' to roundabout not M1.

Unknown

BP

OVERNIGHT

CREDIT/DEBIT CARDS

FUEL CARDS (see key on page 6)
5 6

DRIVER FACILITIES
Accommodation on-site, Holiday Inn
Takeaway food

Full site details not available at time of going to press. For more information please contact site.

All on-site facilities accessible 24 hours

M360

Durham Services

Roadchef Ltd
Tursdale Road, Bowburn
County Durham DH6 5NP
T 0191 3779222

A1M JUNCTION 61
On the A1M at junction 61, Durham Services is a couple of yards along on the A688.

4.9m

Total

30
OVERNIGHT

£2.99   £1.25   £6.49   NEARBY

CREDIT/DEBIT CARDS

FUEL CARDS (see key on page 6)
1 2 4 8 46

TRUCK FACILITIES
P *with voucher*   **P** *only*   *Voucher value*
£12.00   £9.00   £6.00
Coach parking available (9 spaces)
Quiet area
Ample room for manoeuvring

DRIVER FACILITIES
Accommodation on-site, Roadchef Hotel
Showers, 1 m, 1 f (free), rest area, internet access, truckers' accessories
Takeaway food

All on-site facilities accessible 24 hours

M361

Exeter Services

Moto Ltd
Sandygate, Exeter
Devon EX2 7HF
T 01392 436266 www.moto-way.com

M5 JUNCTION 30

4.8m

Esso

OVERNIGHT

NEARBY

CREDIT/DEBIT CARDS

FUEL CARDS (see key on page 6)
7 38 40

DRIVER FACILITIES
Accommodation on-site, Travelodge
Takeaway food

SITE COMMENTS/INFORMATION
Train/tram/underground/metro nearby

Full site details not available at time of going to press. For more information please contact site.

All on-site facilities accessible 24 hours

M362

Ferrybridge Services

Moto Ltd
nr Knottingley, Wakefield
West Yorkshire WF11 0AF
T **01977 672767** www.moto-way.com

M62 JUNCTION 33

All on-site facilities accessible 24 hours

CREDIT/DEBIT CARDS

FUEL CARDS (see key on page 6)

DRIVER FACILITIES
Accommodation on-site, Travelodge
Takeaway food
Phone top-ups/accessories
Truckers' accessories

Full site details not available at time of going to press. For more information please contact site.

M363

Fleet Services north-eastbound

Welcome Break Ltd
Hartley Wintney, Basingstoke
Hampshire RG27 8PE
T **01252 628539**

M3 NORTH-EASTBOUND BETWEEN
JUNCTIONS 4A AND 5

All on-site facilities accessible 24 hours

CREDIT/DEBIT CARDS

FUEL CARDS (see key on page 6)

DRIVER FACILITIES
Takeaway food

Full site details not available at time of going to press. For more information please contact site.

M364

Fleet Services south-westbound

Welcome Break Ltd
Hartley Wintney, Basingstoke
Hampshire RG27 8BN
T **01252 627205**

M3 SOUTH-WESTBOUND BETWEEN
JUNCTIONS 4A AND 5

All on-site facilities accessible 24 hours

CREDIT/DEBIT CARDS

FUEL CARDS (see key on page 6)

DRIVER FACILITIES
Accommodation on-site, Days Inn
Takeaway food

Full site details not available at time of going to press. For more information please contact site.

M365

Frankley Services northbound

Moto Ltd
Birmingham
West Midlands B32 4AR
T **0121 5503131** www.moto-way.com

M5 NORTHBOUND BETWEEN JUNCTIONS 3 AND 4

CREDIT/DEBIT CARDS

FUEL CARDS (see key on page 6)

DRIVER FACILITIES
Drivers' rest area
Takeaway food
Truckers' accessories

Full site details not available at time of going to press. For more information please contact site.

All on-site facilities accessible 24 hours

M366

Frankley Services southbound

Moto Ltd
Birmingham
West Midlands B32 4AR
T **0121 5503131** www.moto-way.com

M5 SOUTHBOUND BETWEEN JUNCTIONS 3 AND 4

CREDIT/DEBIT CARDS

FUEL CARDS (see key on page 6)

DRIVER FACILITIES
Accommodation on-site, Travelodge
Drivers' rest area
Takeaway food
Truckers' accessories

Full site details not available at time of going to press. For more information please contact site.

All on-site facilities accessible 24 hours

M367

Gordano Services

Welcome Break Ltd
Portbury, Bristol
North Somerset BS20 7TW
T **01275 375885**

M5 JUNCTION 19

CREDIT/DEBIT CARDS

FUEL CARDS (see key on page 6)
⑧

DRIVER FACILITIES
Accommodation on-site, Welcome Lodge
Takeaway food

Full site details not available at time of going to press. For more information please contact site.

All on-site facilities accessible 24 hours

M368

Gretna Green Services

Welcome Break Ltd
Gretna
Dumfries and Galloway DG16 5HQ
T 01461 337567

A74M BETWEEN JUNCTION 21 AND THE A74

CREDIT/DEBIT CARDS

FUEL CARDS (see key on page 6)
5 6

DRIVER FACILITIES
Accommodation on-site, Welcome Lodge
Takeaway food

Full site details not available at time of going to press. For more information please contact site.

All on-site facilities accessible 24 hours | M369

Hamilton Services

Roadchef Ltd
Hamilton
Lanarkshire ML3 6JW
T 01698 282176

M74 NORTHBOUND BETWEEN JUNCTIONS 5 AND 6

CREDIT/DEBIT CARDS

FUEL CARDS (see key on page 6)
4 5 6 12 14 22 36 37 39

TRUCK FACILITIES
P *with voucher* P *only* *Voucher value*
£15.00 £12.00 £7.50
Coach parking available (12 spaces)
Quiet area
Ample room for manoeuvring

DRIVER FACILITIES
Accommodation on-site (£45 pn)
Shower, 1 unisex (free), TV, internet access, truckers' accessories, Takeaway food. Clothing for sale
Phone top-ups/accessories
Euros changed/accepted

All on-site facilities accessible 24 hours | M370

Happendon Services

Cairn Lodge Ltd
Carlisle Road, Douglas, Strathclyde ML11 0JU
T 01555 850260/851880
M74 JUNCTION 12-11 If heading northbound, exit at junction 12, at end of sliproad, turn right at the roundabout then left at the next. If heading southbound, exit at junction 11 and go straight across the roundabout. Happendon Services is about half a mile on from there.

CREDIT/DEBIT CARDS

FUEL CARDS (see key on page 6)
1 2 3 4 5 8 10 12 46

TRUCK FACILITIES
P £6.00
Coach parking available (40 spaces)
Evening security guard. Quiet area
Ample room for manoeuvring
Truck dealership/workshop nearby

DRIVER FACILITIES
Shower
Truckers' accessories. Takeaway food
Clothing for sale

SITE COMMENTS/INFORMATION
This site is soon to be refurbished

Restaurant and shop opening times unknown. All other on-site facilities accessible 24 hours | M371

Harthill Services north-eastbound

**BP Ltd
Harthill, Shotts
Lanarkshire ML7 5TT
T 01501 751791**

M8 NORTH-EASTBOUND BETWEEN
JUNCTIONS 4 AND 5

CREDIT/DEBIT CARDS

FUEL CARDS (see key on page 6)

DRIVER FACILITIES
Takeaway food

Full site details not available at time of going to press. For more information please contact site.

All on-site facilities accessible 24 hours

M372

Harthill Services south-westbound

**BP Ltd
Harthill, Shotts
Lanarkshire ML7 5TT
T 01501 751791**

M8 SOUTH-WESTBOUND BETWEEN
JUNCTIONS 4 AND 5

CREDIT/DEBIT CARDS

FUEL CARDS (see key on page 6)

DRIVER FACILITIES
Takeaway food

Full site details not available at time of going to press. For more information please contact site.

All on-site facilities accessible 24 hours

M373

Hartshead Moor Services north-eastbound

**Welcome Break Ltd
nr Clifton Brighouse
West Yorkshire HD6 4JX
T 01274 876584**

M62 NORTH-EASTBOUND BETWEEN
JUNCTIONS 25 AND 26

CREDIT/DEBIT CARDS
FUEL CARDS (see key on page 6)

DRIVER FACILITIES
Accommodation on-site, Days Inn
Takeaway food

Full site details not available at time of going to press. For more information please contact site.

All on-site facilities accessible 24 hours

M374

Hartshead Moor Services south-westbound

Welcome Break Ltd
nr Clifton Brighouse
West Yorkshire HD6 4JX
T 01274 876584

M62 SOUTH-WESTBOUND BETWEEN
JUNCTIONS 25 AND 26

CREDIT/DEBIT CARDS

FUEL CARDS (see key on page 6)
⑧

DRIVER FACILITIES
Takeaway food

Full site details not available at time of going to press. For more information please contact site.

All on-site facilities accessible 24 hours

M375

Heston Services eastbound

Moto Ltd
North Hyde Lane, Hounslow
Middlesex TW5 9NB
T 0208 5802104 www.moto-way.com

M4 EASTBOUND BETWEEN JUNCTIONS 2 AND 3

CREDIT/DEBIT CARDS

FUEL CARDS (see key on page 6)
⑤⑥

DRIVER FACILITIES
Takeaway food

Full site details not available at time of going to press. For more information please contact site.

All on-site facilities accessible 24 hours

M376

Heston Services westbound

Moto Ltd
Phoenix Way, Hounslow
Middlesex TW5 9NB
T 0208 5802104 www.moto-way.com

M4 WESTBOUND BETWEEN JUNCTIONS 2 AND 3

CREDIT/DEBIT CARDS

FUEL CARDS (see key on page 6)
⑤⑥

DRIVER FACILITIES
Accommodation on-site, Travelodge
Takeaway food

Full site details not available at time of going to press. For more information please contact site.

All on-site facilities accessible 24 hours

M377

Hilton Park Services northbound

Moto Ltd
Wolverhampton
West Midlands WV11 2AT
T **01922 701639** www.moto-way.com

M6 NORTHBOUND JUNCTION 10A

CREDIT/DEBIT CARDS

FUEL CARDS (see key on page 6)

DRIVER FACILITIES
Accommodation on-site, Travelodge
Drivers' rest area
Takeaway food
Phone top-ups/accessories
Truckers' accessories

Full site details not available at time of going to press. For more information please contact site.

All on-site facilities accessible 24 hours

M378

Hilton Park Services southbound

Moto Ltd
Wolverhampton
West Midlands WV11 2AT
T **01922 701639** www.moto-way.com

M6 SOUTHBOUND BETWEEN JUNCTIONS 10 AND 11

CREDIT/DEBIT CARDS

FUEL CARDS (see key on page 6)

DRIVER FACILITIES
Accommodation on-site, Travelodge
Drivers' rest area
Takeaway food
Phone top-ups/accessories
Truckers' accessories

Full site details not available at time of going to press. For more information please contact site.

All on-site facilities accessible 24 hours

M379

Hopwood Park Services

Welcome Break Ltd
Alvechurch, Birmingham
West Midlands B48 7AB
T **0121 4478414**

M42 JUNCTION 2

CREDIT/DEBIT CARDS

FUEL CARDS (see key on page 6)

DRIVER FACILITIES
Takeaway food

Full site details not available at time of going to press. For more information please contact site.

All on-site facilities accessible 24 hours

M380

Keele Services north-westbound

Welcome Break Ltd
Newcastle under Lyme
Staffordshire ST5 5HG
T **01782 626221**

M6 NORTH-WESTBOUND BETWEEN
JUNCTIONS 15 AND 16

CREDIT/DEBIT CARDS

FUEL CARDS (see key on page 6)
⑧

DRIVER FACILITIES
Takeaway food

SITE COMMENTS/INFORMATION
Beautiful picturesque setting

Full site details not available at time of going to press. For more information please contact site.

All on-site facilities accessible 24 hours   M381

Keele Services south-eastbound

Welcome Break Ltd
Newcastle under Lyme
Staffordshire ST5 5HG
T **01782 626221**

M6 SOUTH-EASTBOUND BETWEEN
JUNCTIONS 15 AND 16

CREDIT/DEBIT CARDS

FUEL CARDS (see key on page 6)
⑧

DRIVER FACILITIES
Takeaway food

All on-site facilities accessible 24 hours   M382

Killington Lake Services southbound

Roadchef Ltd
Killington Lake, Kendal
Cumbria LA8 0NW
T **01539 620739**

M6 SOUTHBOUND BETWEEN JUNCTIONS 37 AND 36

CREDIT/DEBIT CARDS

FUEL CARDS (see key on page 6)
④ ⑤ ⑥ ⑭ ㉒ ㊱ ㊲ ㊴ ㊶

TRUCK FACILITIES
P *with voucher*   **P** *only*   *Voucher value*
£12.00   £9.00   £6.00
Coach parking available (3 spaces)
Ample room for manoeuvring
Quiet area
Truck dealership/workshop
DRIVER FACILITIES
Accommodation (£48.95 pn), internet
access, truckers' accessories
Takeaway food. Clothing for sale
SITE COMMENTS/INFORMATION
Killington Lake is in a peaceful, picturesque
setting with friendly staff always on hand

All on-site facilities accessible 24 hours   M383

Kinross Services

Moto Ltd
nr Kinross
Perth and Kinross KY13 0NQ
T **01577 863123** www.moto-way.com

M90 AT JUNCTION 6. On the A977.

CREDIT/DEBIT CARDS

FUEL CARDS (see key on page 6)

TRUCK FACILITIES
Coach parking available (6 spaces)

DRIVER FACILITIES
Accommodation on-site, Travelodge
Shower, washroom, TV, truckers'
accessories
Takeaway food

All on-site facilities accessible 24 hours

M384

Knutsford Services northbound

Moto Ltd
Northwich Road, Knutsford
Cheshire WA16 0TL
T **01565 634167** www.moto-way.com

M6 NORTHBOUND BETWEEN JUNCTIONS 18 AND 19

CREDIT/DEBIT CARDS

FUEL CARDS (see key on page 6)

DRIVER FACILITIES
Takeaway food

Full site details not available at time of going to press. For more information please contact site.

All on-site facilities accessible 24 hours

M385

Knutsford Services southbound

Moto Ltd
Northwich Road, Knutsford
Cheshire WA16 0TL
T **01565 634167** www.moto-way.com

M6 SOUTHBOUND BETWEEN JUNCTIONS 18 AND 19

CREDIT/DEBIT CARDS

FUEL CARDS (see key on page 6)

DRIVER FACILITIES
Takeaway food

Full site details not available at time of going to press. For more information please contact site.

All on-site facilities accessible 24 hours

M386

Lancaster Services northbound

Moto Ltd
Lancaster
Lancashire LA2 9DU
T **01565 634167** www.moto-way.com

M6 NORTHBOUND BETWEEN JUNCTIONS 32 AND 33

CREDIT/DEBIT CARDS

FUEL CARDS (see key on page 6)

DRIVER FACILITIES
Accommodation on-site, Travelodge
Drivers' rest area
Takeaway food

Full site details not available at time of going to press. For more information please contact site.

All on-site facilities accessible 24 hours   **M387**

Lancaster Services southbound

Moto Ltd
Lancaster
Lancashire LA2 9DU
T **01524 791775** www.moto-way.com

M6 SOUTHBOUND BETWEEN JUNCTIONS 32 AND 33

CREDIT/DEBIT CARDS

FUEL CARDS (see key on page 6)

DRIVER FACILITIES
Accommodation on-site, Travelodge
Drivers' rest area
Takeaway food

Full site details not available at time of going to press. For more information please contact site.

All on-site facilities accessible 24 hours   **M388**

Leicester Forest East northbound

Welcome Break Ltd
Hinckley Road, Leicester
Leicestershire LE3 3GB
T **0116 2386801**

M1 NORTHBOUND BETWEEN
JUNCTIONS 21 AND 21A

CREDIT/DEBIT CARDS

FUEL CARDS (see key on page 6)

DRIVER FACILITIES
Accommodation on-site, Days Inn
Takeaway food

Full site details not available at time of going to press. For more information please contact site.

All on-site facilities accessible 24 hours   **M389**

Leicester Forest East southbound

Welcome Break Ltd
Hinckley Road, Leicester
Leicestershire LE3 3GB
T **0116 2386801**

M1 SOUTHBOUND BETWEEN
JUNCTIONS 21 AND 21A

CREDIT/DEBIT CARDS

FUEL CARDS (see key on page 6)

DRIVER FACILITIES
Accommodation on-site, Travel Inn
Takeaway food

Full site details not available at time of going to
press. For more information please contact site.

All on-site facilities accessible 24 hours — **M390**

Leigh Delamere Services eastbound

Moto Ltd
Leigh Delamere, nr Chippenham
Wiltshire SN14 6LB
T **01666 837691** www.moto-way.com

M4 EASTBOUND BETWEEN JUNCTIONS 17 AND 18

CREDIT/DEBIT CARDS

FUEL CARDS (see key on page 6)

TRUCK FACILITIES
P *with voucher* **P** *only* *Voucher value*
£14:00   £12.00   £6.00
Coach parking available (10 spaces)
Ample room for manoeuvring
Quiet area

DRIVER FACILITIES
Accommodation on-site, Travelodge
Shower, washroom, rest area, seating
area, phone top-ups/accessories,
truckers' accessories
Takeaway food. Clothing for sale

All on-site facilities accessible 24 hours — **M391**

Leigh Delamere Services westbound

Moto Ltd
Leigh Delamere, nr Chippenham
Wiltshire SN14 6LB
T **01666 837691** www.moto-way.com

M4 WESTBOUND BETWEEN JUNCTIONS 17 AND 18

CREDIT/DEBIT CARDS

FUEL CARDS (see key on page 6)

DRIVER FACILITIES
Drivers' rest area
Takeaway food
Phone top-ups/accessories
Truckers' accessories

Full site details not available at time of going to
press. For more information please contact site.

All on-site facilities accessible 24 hours — **M392**

London Gateway Services

Welcome Break Ltd
Edgware
Hertfordshire HA8 8
T 0208 9060611

M1 JUNCTION 3

All on-site facilities accessible 24 hours

CREDIT/DEBIT CARDS

FUEL CARDS (see key on page 6)
(8)

TRUCK FACILITIES

DRIVER FACILITIES
Accommodation on-site, Days Inn
Takeaway food

Full site details not available at time of going to press. For more information please contact site.

M393

Magor Services

First Motorway Services Ltd
Magor, Caldicot
Monmouthshire NP26 3YL
T 0870 9908815

M4 JUNCTION 23A

Travelodge opening times unknown. All other on-site facilities accessible 24 hours

CREDIT/DEBIT CARDS

FUEL CARDS (see key on page 6)
(4) (7) (37) (38) (40)

TRUCK FACILITIES
P *with voucher* **P** *only* *Voucher value*
£15.00   £12.00   £7.00
Coach parking available (6 spaces)
Ample room for manoeuvring
Quiet area
Truck dealership/workshop
DRIVER FACILITIES
Accomm. on-site, Travelodge £55 pn
Showers, 1 m, 1 f (free), washroom, rest
area, TV, internet access, phone top-
ups/accessories, truckers' accessories
Takeaway food
Clothing for sale

M394

Markfield Services

Welcome Break Ltd
Little Shaw Lane, Markfield
Leicestershire LE67 9PP
T 01530 244777

M1 JUNCTION 22

All on-site facilities accessible 24 hours

CREDIT/DEBIT CARDS

FUEL CARDS (see key on page 6)
(5) (6)

DRIVER FACILITIES
Accommodation on-site, Travelodge
Takeaway food

Full site details not available at time of going to press. For more information please contact site.

M395

Medway Services eastbound

Moto Ltd
Gillingham
Kent ME8 8PQ
T **01634 236900** www.moto-way.com

M2 EASTBOUND BETWEEN JUNCTIONS 14 AND 15

All on-site facilities accessible 24 hours

CREDIT/DEBIT CARDS

FUEL CARDS (see key on page 6)

DRIVER FACILITIES
Takeaway food

Full site details not available at time of going to press. For more information please contact site.

M396

Medway Services westbound

Moto Ltd
Gillingham
Kent ME8 8PQ
T **01634 236900** www.moto-way.com

M2 WESTBOUND BETWEEN JUNCTIONS 14 AND 15

All on-site facilities accessible 24 hours

CREDIT/DEBIT CARDS

FUEL CARDS (see key on page 6)

DRIVER FACILITIES
Accommodation on-site, Travelodge
Takeaway food

Full site details not available at time of going to press. For more information please contact site.

M397

Membury Services eastbound

Welcome Break Ltd
Lambourn, Hungerford
Berkshire RG17 7TZ
T **01488 71884**

M4 EASTBOUND BETWEEN JUNCTIONS 14 AND 15

All on-site facilities accessible 24 hours

CREDIT/DEBIT CARDS

FUEL CARDS (see key on page 6)

DRIVER FACILITIES
Takeaway food

Full site details not available at time of going to press. For more information please contact site.

M398

Membury Services westbound

Welcome Break Ltd
Lambourn, Hungerford
Berkshire RG17 7TZ
T **01488 71884**

M4 WESTBOUND BETWEEN JUNCTIONS 14 AND 15

CREDIT/DEBIT CARDS

FUEL CARDS (see key on page 6)

DRIVER FACILITIES
Accommodation on-site, Days Inn
Takeaway food

Full site details not available at time of going to press. For more information please contact site.

All on-site facilities accessible 24 hours

M399

Michaelwood Services northbound

Welcome Break Ltd
Lower Wick, Dursley
Gloucestershire GL11 6DD
T **01454 260631**

M5 NORTHBOUND BETWEEN JUNCTIONS 13 AND 14

CREDIT/DEBIT CARDS

FUEL CARDS (see key on page 6)

DRIVER FACILITIES
Takeaway food

Full site details not available at time of going to press. For more information please contact site.

All on-site facilities accessible 24 hours

M400

Michaelwood Services southbound

Welcome Break Ltd
Lower Wick, Dursley
Gloucestershire GL11 6DD
T **01454 260631**

M5 SOUTHBOUND BETWEEN JUNCTIONS 13 AND 14

CREDIT/DEBIT CARDS

FUEL CARDS (see key on page 6)

DRIVER FACILITIES
Takeaway food

Full site details not available at time of going to press. For more information please contact site.

All on-site facilities accessible 24 hours

M401

Newport Pagnell Services northbound

Welcome Break Ltd
Newport Pagnell
Bedfordshire MK16 8DS
T **01908 217722**

M1 NORTHBOUND BETWEEN JUNCTIONS 14 AND 15

CREDIT/DEBIT CARDS

FUEL CARDS (see key on page 6)
⑧

DRIVER FACILITIES
Accommodation on-site, Welcome Lodge
Takeaway food

Full site details not available at time of going to press. For more information please contact site.

All on-site facilities accessible 24 hours

M402

Newport Pagnell Services southbound

Welcome Break Ltd
Newport Pagnell
Bedfordshire MK16 8DS
T **01908 217722**

M1 SOUTHBOUND BETWEEN JUNCTIONS 14 AND 15

CREDIT/DEBIT CARDS

FUEL CARDS (see key on page 6)
⑧

DRIVER FACILITIES
Takeaway food

Full site details not available at time of going to press. For more information please contact site.

All on-site facilities accessible 24 hours

M403

Northampton Services northbound

Roadchef Ltd
Northampton
Northamptonshire NN4 9QY
T **01604 831888**

M1 NORTHBOUND JUNCTION 15A

CREDIT/DEBIT CARDS

FUEL CARDS (see key on page 6)
⑤⑥

TRUCK FACILITIES
P with voucher   **P** only   Voucher value
£15.00   £12.00   £7.00
Coach parking available (10 spaces)
Ample room for manoeuvring
Quiet area
Truck washing facilities
DRIVER FACILITIES
Showers, 2 m, 2 f (charge), washroom,
internet access, seating area, phone top-
ups/accessories, truckers' accessories
Takeaway food. Clothing for sale
SITE COMMENTS/INFORMATION
New building with modern facilities

All on-site facilities accessible 24 hours

M404

Northampton Services southbound

Roadchef Ltd
Northampton
Northamptonshire NN4 9QS
T **01604 831888**

M1 SOUTHBOUND JUNCTION 15A

5.2m
BP

20
OVERNIGHT

NEARBY

All on-site facilities accessible 24 hours

CREDIT/DEBIT CARDS

FUEL CARDS (see key on page 6)
⑤ ⑥

TRUCK FACILITIES
P *with voucher* **P** *only* *Voucher value*
£15.00   £12.00 £7.00
Coach parking available (10 spaces)
Ample room for manoeuvring
Quiet area
Truck washing facilities
DRIVER FACILITIES
Showers, 2 m, 2 f (charge), washroom,
internet access, seating area, phone top-
ups/accessories, truckers' accessories
Takeaway food. Clothing for sale
SITE COMMENTS/INFORMATION
New building with modern facilities

M405

Norton Canes Services

Roadchef Ltd
Betty's Lane, Norton Canes, Cannock
Staffordshire WS11 9UX
T **01543 272540**

NEW M6 TOLL MOTORWAY BETWEEN TOLL 6 AND
TOLL 7. Can be accessed from east or westbound or from
the A5

Unknown
BP

51
OVERNIGHT

£3.49   £1.79   £6.99   NEARBY

All on-site facilities accessible 24 hours

CREDIT/DEBIT CARDS

FUEL CARDS (see key on page 6)
⑤ ⑥

TRUCK FACILITIES
P *with voucher* **P** *only* *Voucher value*
£12.00   £9.00   £6.00
Coach parking available (28 spaces)
Ample room for manoeuvring
Quiet area
DRIVER FACILITIES
Accommodation on-site (£49.50 pn)
Showers, 3 m, 1 f (free), washroom,
internet access, phone top-ups/accessories,
truckers' accessories
Takeaway food. Clothing for sale
SITE COMMENTS/INFORMATION
New site. Only service area on M6 toll

M406

Oxford Services

Welcome Break Ltd
Thame Road, Waterstock, Oxford
Oxfordshire OX33 1LJ
T **01865 876372**

M40 JUNCTION 8

Unknown
BP

54
OVERNIGHT

CREDIT/DEBIT CARDS

FUEL CARDS (see key on page 6)
④ ⑤ ⑥ 36 37 39 40

TRUCK FACILITIES
P *with voucher* **P** *only*
£14.00   £12.00
Coach parking available (13 spaces)

DRIVER FACILITIES
Accommodation on-site, Days Inn
Showers, 3 m, 1 f (free)
Phone top-ups/accessories
Truckers' accessories
Takeaway food
Euros changed/accepted
CB sales/repairs

M407

Pease Pottage Services

Moto Ltd
Pease Pottage, nr Crawley
East Sussex RH11 9YA
T **01293 535756** www.moto-way.com

M23 JUNCTION 11

CREDIT/DEBIT CARDS

FUEL CARDS (see key on page 6)

DRIVER FACILITIES
Takeaway food

Full site details not available at time of going to press. For more information please contact site.

All on-site facilities accessible 24 hours · M408

Peterborough Services

Extra MSA Forecourts Ltd
Great North Road, Haddon, Peterborough
Cambridgeshire PE7 3UQ
T **01733 362950**

A1M JUNCTION 17. Take A605 towards Warmington. Peterborough Services is 100 yards on the left.

CREDIT/DEBIT CARDS

FUEL CARDS (see key on page 6)
① ② ③ ④ ⑨

TRUCK FACILITIES
P £13.50
Coach parking available (19 spaces)
Overnight security patrol
Quiet area
Ample room for manoeuvring

DRIVER FACILITIES
Accommodation on-site (£55 pn)
Showers, 2 m, 1 f (free), internet access, truckers' accessories. Takeaway food

SITE COMMENTS/INFORMATION
Good LGV facilities

Parking, showers, shop, fuel and some food accessible 24 hours. Other on-site facilities 07:00-23.00 · M409

Pont Abraham Services

Roadchef Ltd
Llanedi, nr Pontardulais
Carmarthenshire SA4 0FU
T 01792 884663

M4 JUNCTION 49 ON THE A48 At the end of the M4 at the roundabout with the A48 and A483

CREDIT/DEBIT CARDS

FUEL CARDS (see key on page 6)
④ ⑤ ⑥ ⑭ ㉗ ㊳

TRUCK FACILITIES
P *with voucher*   **P** *only*   *Voucher value*
£12.00   £9.00   £6.00
Coach parking available (6 spaces)
Quiet area
Ample room for manoeuvring

DRIVER FACILITIES
Internet access, phone top-ups/accessories
Takeaway food
Clothing for sale

SITE COMMENTS/INFORMATION
Friendly staff and excellent service

All on-site facilities accessible 24 hours · M410

Reading Services eastbound

Moto Ltd
Burghfield, Reading
Berkshire RG30 3UQ
T **01189 566966** www.moto-way.com

M4 EASTBOUND BETWEEN JUNCTIONS 11 AND 12

CREDIT/DEBIT CARDS

FUEL CARDS (see key on page 6)
5 6

DRIVER FACILITIES
Accommodation on-site, Travelodge
Shower
Phone top-ups/accessories
Truckers' accessories
Takeaway food

Full site details not available at time of going to press. For more information please contact site.

All on-site facilities accessible 24 hours   **M411**

Reading Services westbound

Moto Ltd
Burghfield, Reading
Berkshire RG30 3UQ
T **01189 566966** www.moto-way.com

M4 WESTBOUND BETWEEN JUNCTIONS 11 AND 12

CREDIT/DEBIT CARDS

FUEL CARDS (see key on page 6)
5 6

DRIVER FACILITIES
Accommodation on-site, Travelodge
Shower, phone top-ups/accessories
Truckers' accessories
Takeaway food

Full site details not available at time of going to press. For more information please contact site.

All on-site facilities accessible 24 hours   **M412**

Rownhams Services north-eastbound

Roadchef Ltd
Rownhams, Southampton
Hampshire SO16 8AP
T **02380 734480**

M27 NORTH-EASTBOUND BETWEEN
JUNCTIONS 3 AND 4

CREDIT/DEBIT CARDS

FUEL CARDS (see key on page 6)
7 38 40

TRUCK FACILITIES
P *with voucher*   **P** *only*
£12.00   £9.00
Coach parking available (22 spaces)
Quiet area
Ample room for manoeuvring

DRIVER FACILITIES
Accommodation on-site (£48.95 pn)
Washroom, TV, internet access
Phone top-ups/accessories
Truckers' accessories
Takeaway food

All on-site facilities accessible 24 hours   **M413**

Rownhams Services south-westbound

Roadchef Ltd
Rownhams, Southampton
Hampshire SO16 8AP
T **02380 734480**

M27 SOUTH-WESTBOUND BETWEEN
JUNCTIONS 3 AND 4

CREDIT/DEBIT CARDS

FUEL CARDS (see key on page 6)

TRUCK FACILITIES
P *with voucher*   **P** *only*
£12.00   £9.00
Coach parking available (22 spaces)
Quiet area
Ample room for manoeuvring

DRIVER FACILITIES
Accommodation on-site (£48.95 pn)
Washroom, TV, internet access
Phone top-ups/accessories,
Truckers' accessories
Takeaway food

All on-site facilities accessible 24 hours

M414

Sandbach Services northbound

Roadchef Ltd
Sandbach
Cheshire CW11 2FZ
T **01270 767134**

M6 NORTHBOUND BETWEEN JUNCTIONS 16 AND 17

CREDIT/DEBIT CARDS

FUEL CARDS (see key on page 6)

TRUCK FACILITIES
P *with voucher*   **P** *only*   *Voucher value*
£20.00   £15.00   £7.50
Coach parking spaces available
Quiet area
Ample room for manoeuvring
Truck dealership/workshop

DRIVER FACILITIES
Showers, 1 m, 1 f (charge)
TV
Truckers' accessories
Takeaway food
Clothing for sale

All on-site facilities accessible 24 hours

M415

Sandbach Services southbound

Roadchef Ltd
Sandbach
Cheshire CW11 2FZ
T **01270 767134**

M6 SOUTHBOUND BETWEEN JUNCTIONS 16 AND 17

CREDIT/DEBIT CARDS

FUEL CARDS (see key on page 6)

TRUCK FACILITIES
P *with voucher*   **P** *only*   *Voucher value*
£20.00   £15.00   £7.50
Coach parking spaces available
Quiet area
Ample room for manoeuvring
Truck dealership/workshop

DRIVER FACILITIES
Showers, 1 m, 1 f (charge)
TV
Truckers' accessories
Takeaway food
Clothing for sale

All on-site facilities accessible 24 hours

M416

Sarn Park Services

Welcome Break Ltd
Bridgend
South Glamorgan CF32 9RW
☎ 01656 768521

M4 JUNCTION 36

All on-site facilities accessible 24 hours

CREDIT/DEBIT CARDS

FUEL CARDS (see key on page 6)

DRIVER FACILITIES
Accommodation on-site, Welcome Lodge
Takeaway food
Clothing for sale nearby

Full site details not available at time of going to press. For more information please contact site.

M417

Sedgemoor Services northbound

Welcome Break Ltd
Rooksbridge, Axbridge
Somerset BS24 0JL
☎ 01934 750659

M5 NORTHBOUND BETWEEN JUNCTIONS 21 AND 22

All on-site facilities accessible 24 hours

CREDIT/DEBIT CARDS

FUEL CARDS (see key on page 6)

DRIVER FACILITIES
Accommodation on-site, Welcome Lodge
Takeaway food

Full site details not available at time of going to press. For more information please contact site.

M418

Sedgemoor Services southbound

Roadchef Ltd
Rooksbridge, Axbridge
Somerset BS26 2UF
☎ 01934 750888

M5 SOUTHBOUND BETWEEN JUNCTIONS 21 AND 22

All on-site facilities accessible 24 hours

CREDIT/DEBIT CARDS

FUEL CARDS (see key on page 6)

TRUCK FACILITIES
P *with voucher* **P** *only* *Voucher value*
£12.00   £9.00   £6.00
Coach parking available (12 spaces)
Ample room for manoeuvring
Quiet area. Truck dealership/workshop

DRIVER FACILITIES
Shower, 1 male (free), washroom
Truckers' accessories. Takeaway food
Clothing for sale
Internet access, phone top-ups/accessories
and CB sales/repairs nearby

M419

Severn View Services

Moto Ltd
Aust, Bristol
South Gloucestershire BS35 4BH
T **01454 632855** www.moto-way.com

M48 AT JUNCTION 1 on the English side of the old Severn Bridge.

CREDIT/DEBIT CARDS

FUEL CARDS (see key on page 6)

DRIVER FACILITIES
Accommodation on-site, Welcome Lodge
Takeaway food

Full site details not available at time of going to press. For more information please contact site.

All on-site facilities accessible 24 hours

M420

Southwaite Services northbound

Moto Ltd
Southwaite, nr Carlisle
Cumbria CA4 0NT
T **01697 473476** www.moto-way.com

M6 NORTHBOUND BETWEEN JUNCTIONS 41 AND 42

CREDIT/DEBIT CARDS

FUEL CARDS (see key on page 6)

DRIVER FACILITIES
Takeaway food
Phone top-ups/accessories
Truckers' accessories

Full site details not available at time of going to press. For more information please contact site.

All on-site facilities accessible 24 hours

M421

Southwaite Services southbound

Moto Ltd
Southwaite, nr Carlisle
Cumbria CA4 0NT
T **01697 473476** www.moto-way.com

M6 SOUTHBOUND BETWEEN JUNCTIONS 41 AND 42

CREDIT/DEBIT CARDS

FUEL CARDS (see key on page 6)

DRIVER FACILITIES
Accommodation on-site, Travelodge
Takeaway food
Phone top-ups/accessories
Truckers' accessories

Full site details not available at time of going to press. For more information please contact site.

All on-site facilities accessible 24 hours

M422

Stafford Services Northbound

Moto Ltd
Stone
Staffordshire ST15 0EU
T **01785 811188** www.moto-way.com

M6 NORTHBOUND BETWEEN JUNCTIONS 14 AND 15

CREDIT/DEBIT CARDS

FUEL CARDS (see key on page 6)
⑤ ⑥

DRIVER FACILITIES
Accommodation on-site, Travelodge
Takeaway food

Full site details not available at time of going to press. For more information please contact site.

All on-site facilities accessible 24 hours   **M423**

Stafford Services southbound

Roadchef Ltd
Stone
Staffordshire ST15 0EU
T **01785 826300**

M6 SOUTHBOUND BETWEEN JUNCTIONS 14 AND 15

CREDIT/DEBIT CARDS

FUEL CARDS (see key on page 6)
⑦ ㉘ ㊵

TRUCK FACILITIES
P with voucher   **P** only   Voucher value
£12.00   £9.00   £6.00
Coach parking available (15 spaces)
Ample room for manoeuvring
Quiet area

DRIVER FACILITIES
Accommodation on-site (£46.95 pn)
Showers, 1 m, 1 f (free), washroom,
Internet access, phone top-ups/accessories,
truckers' accessories. Dog walking area
and kids play area. Takeaway food
Clothing for sale

All on-site facilities accessible 24 hours   **M424**

Stirling Services

Moto Ltd
Pirnhall interchange, Stirling
Stirlingshire FK7 8EU
T **01786 813614** www.moto-way.com

M9 M80 INTERCHANGE Exit at junction 9 from either the M9 or the M80 and Stirling Services is on the roundabout at the bottom of either sliproad.

CREDIT/DEBIT CARDS

FUEL CARDS (see key on page 6)
④ ⑦ ㉘ ㊵

TRUCK FACILITIES
Coach parking available (6 spaces)

DRIVER FACILITIES
Accommodation on-site, Travelodge
Shower, 1 male (free)
TV
Takeaway food
Post Office

Full site details not available at time of going to press. For more information please contact site.

All on-site facilities accessible 24 hours   **M425**

Strensham Motorway Services northbound

Roadchef Ltd
Strensham, Worcester
Worcestershire WR8 0BZ
T 01684 293004

M5 NORTHBOUND BETWEEN JUNCTIONS 7 AND 8

All on-site facilities accessible 24 hours

CREDIT/DEBIT CARDS

FUEL CARDS (see key on page 6)

TRUCK FACILITIES
P with voucher   **P** only   Voucher value
£15.00   £12.00   £7.50
Coach parking available (15 spaces)
Ample room for manoeuvring
Quiet area. Truck dealership/workshop
DRIVER FACILITIES
Accommodation on-site, Premier Travel
   Inn (£47.95 and £45.95)
Showers, 1 m, 2 f (free), washroom
Phone top-ups/accessories, truckers'
accessories. Takeaway food. Clothing for
sale. Meal vouchers for drivers purchasing
fuel and coach driver discounts

M426

Strensham Motorway Services southbound

Roadchef Ltd
Strensham, Worcester
Worcestershire WR8 9LJ
T 01684 290577

M5 SOUTHBOUND BETWEEN JUNCTIONS 7 AND 8

Shop 07:00-23:00. Takeaway 10:00-22:00. Costa Coffee 07:00-21:00 All other on-site facilities 24 hours

CREDIT/DEBIT CARDS

FUEL CARDS (see key on page 6)

TRUCK FACILITIES
P with voucher   **P** only   Voucher value
£15.00   £12.00   £7.50
Coach parking available (20 spaces)
Ample room for manoeuvring
Quiet area. Truck washing facilities
Truck dealership/workshop

DRIVER FACILITIES
Accommodation on-site (£44.50 pn)
Showers, 2 m, 1 f (free)
Phone top-ups/accessories, truckers'
accessories. Takeaway food
Clothing for sale

M427

Swansea Services

Moto Ltd
Penllergar, Swansea
Carmarthenshire SA4 1GT
T 01792 896222 www.moto-way.com

M4 JUNCTION 47

All on-site facilities accessible 24 hours

CREDIT/DEBIT CARDS

FUEL CARDS (see key on page 6)

DRIVER FACILITIES
Accommodation on-site, Travelodge
Takeaway food

*Full site details not available at time of going to
press. For more information please contact site.*

M428

Tamworth Services

Moto Ltd
Green Lane, Wilnecote, Tamworth
Staffordshire B77 5PS
T **01827 260120** www.moto-way.com

M42 JUNCTION 10

CREDIT/DEBIT CARDS

FUEL CARDS (see key on page 6)

DRIVER FACILITIES
Shower
Takeaway food
Phone top-ups/accessories

Full site details not available at time of going to press. For more information please contact site.

All on-site facilities accessible 24 hours

M429

Taunton Deane Services northbound

Roadchef Ltd
Taunton
Somerset TA3 7PF
T **01823 271111**

M5 NORTHBOUND BETWEEN JUNCTIONS 25 AND 26

CREDIT/DEBIT CARDS

FUEL CARDS (see key on page 6)

TRUCK FACILITIES
P *with voucher* **P** *only*   *Voucher value*
£12.00   £9.00   £6.00
Coach parking available (30 spaces)
Ample room for manoeuvring
Quiet area

DRIVER FACILITIES
Accommodation on-site (£47.95 pn)
Takeaway food
Phone top-ups/accessories
Truckers' accessories
Clothing for sale

All on-site facilities accessible 24 hours

M430

Taunton Deane Services southbound

Roadchef Ltd
Taunton
Somerset TA3 7PF
T **01823 271111**

M5 SOUTHBOUND BETWEEN JUNCTIONS 25 AND 26

CREDIT/DEBIT CARDS

FUEL CARDS (see key on page 6)

TRUCK FACILITIES
P *with voucher* **P** *only*   *Voucher value*
£12.00   £9.00   £6.00
Coach parking available (30 spaces)
Ample room for manoeuvring
Quiet area

DRIVER FACILITIES
Accommodation on-site (£47.95 pn)
Takeaway food
Phone top-ups/accessories
Truckers' accessories
Clothing for sale

All on-site facilities accessible 24 hours

M431

Tebay Services northbound

Westmorland Ltd
nr Orton, Cumbria CA10 3
T **01539 624505/624360/ 624511**

M6 NORTHBOUND BETWEEN JUNCTIONS 38 AND 39

Unknown

BP

P

OVERNIGHT

All on-site facilities accessible 24 hours

CREDIT/DEBIT CARDS

FUEL CARDS (see key on page 6)
3 **5**

DRIVER FACILITIES
Accommodation on-site, Westmorland Hotel
Takeaway food

Full site details not available at time of going to press. For more information please contact site.

M432

Tebay Services southbound

Westmorland Ltd
nr Orton, Cumbria CA10 3
T **01539 624505/624360/ 624511**

M6 SOUTHBOUND BETWEEN JUNCTIONS 38 AND 39

Unknown

BP

P

OVERNIGHT

All on-site facilities accessible 24 hours

CREDIT/DEBIT CARDS

FUEL CARDS (see key on page 6)
3 **5**

DRIVER FACILITIES
Takeaway food

Full site details not available at time of going to press. For more information please contact site.

M433

Thurrock Services

Moto Ltd, Arterial Road, West Thurrock,
Grays, Essex RM16 3BG T **01708 865487**
www.moto-way.com

M25 BETWEEN JUNCTIONS 30 AND 31 From the M25 clockwise, exit at junction 30. Keep to left and turn left at roundabout onto A1306 then left at next roundabout into services. From M25 anti-clockwise, exit at junction 31 and turn right onto A1306 then left at next roundabout into services.

Unknown

Esso

P

OVERNIGHT

All on-site facilities accessible 24 hours

CREDIT/DEBIT CARDS

FUEL CARDS (see key on page 6)
7 **38** **40**

DRIVER FACILITIES
Shower
Accommodation on-site, Travelodge
Takeaway food

Full site details not available at time of going to press. For more information please contact site.

M434

Toddington Services northbound

Moto Ltd
Toddington, Dunstable
Bedfordshire LU5 6HR
T **01525 878423** www.moto-way.com

M1 NORTHBOUND BETWEEN JUNCTIONS 11 AND 12

CREDIT/DEBIT CARDS

FUEL CARDS (see key on page 6)

DRIVER FACILITIES
Takeaway food
Phone top-ups/accessories
Truckers' accessories

Full site details not available at time of going to press. For more information please contact site.

All on-site facilities accessible 24 hours   M435

Toddington Services southbound

Moto Ltd
Toddington, Dunstable
Bedfordshire LU5 6HR
T **01525 878422** www.moto-way.com

M1 SOUTHBOUND BETWEEN JUNCTIONS 11 AND 12

CREDIT/DEBIT CARDS

FUEL CARDS (see key on page 6)

DRIVER FACILITIES
Accommodation on-site, Travelodge
Takeaway food
Phone top-ups/accessories
Truckers' accessories

Full site details not available at time of going to press. For more information please contact site.

All on-site facilities accessible 24 hours   M436

Trowell Services northbound

Moto Ltd
Trowell, Ilkeston
Nottinghamshire NG9 3PL
T **0115 9320291** www.moto-way.com

M1 NORTHBOUND BETWEEN JUNCTIONS 25 AND 26

CREDIT/DEBIT CARDS

FUEL CARDS (see key on page 6)

TRUCK FACILITIES
P *with voucher*   **P** *only*   *Voucher value*
£12.00   £10.00   £6.00
Coach parking available (30 spaces)
CCTV. Quiet area
Fridge lorry area, shared with LGV

DRIVER FACILITIES
Accommodation on-site, Travelodge
Showers, washroom, rest area, TV,
phone top-ups/accessories, truckers'
accessories
Takeaway food

All on-site facilities accessible 24 hours   M437

Trowell Services southbound

Moto Ltd
Trowell, Ilkeston
Nottinghamshire NG9 3PL
T 0115 9320291 www.moto-way.com

M1 SOUTHBOUND BETWEEN JUNCTIONS 25 AND 26

All on-site facilities accessible 24 hours

CREDIT/DEBIT CARDS

FUEL CARDS (see key on page 6)

TRUCK FACILITIES
P with voucher **P** only Voucher value
£12.00 £10.00 £6.00
Coach parking spaces available
CCTV. Quiet area
Fridge lorry area, shared with LGV

DRIVER FACILITIES
Accommodation on-site, Travelodge
Showers, washroom, rest area, TV,
phone top-ups/accessories, truckers'
accessories
Takeaway food

M438

Warwick Services north-westbound

Welcome Break Ltd
Ashore
Warwickshire CV35 0AA
T 01926 651681

M40 NORTH-WESTBOUND BETWEEN
JUNCTIONS 12 AND 13

All on-site facilities accessible 24 hours

CREDIT/DEBIT CARDS

FUEL CARDS (see key on page 6)

DRIVER FACILITIES
Accommodation on-site, Days Inn
Takeaway food

Full site details not available at time of going to
press. For more information please contact site.

M439

Warwick Services south-eastbound

Welcome Break Ltd
Ashore
Warwickshire CV35 0AA
T 01926 651681

M40 SOUTH-EASTBOUND BETWEEN
JUNCTIONS 12 AND 13

All on-site facilities accessible 24 hours

CREDIT/DEBIT CARDS

FUEL CARDS (see key on page 6)

DRIVER FACILITIES
Accommodation on-site, Welcome Lodge
Takeaway food

Full site details not available at time of going to
press. For more information please contact site.

M440

Washington Services northbound

Moto Ltd
Portobello, Birtley, Durham
County Durham DH3 2SJ
T **0191 4103436** www.moto-way.com

A1M NORTHBOUND JUNCTION 64

Unknown | Esso

P 32 OVERNIGHT

NEARBY

CREDIT/DEBIT CARDS

FUEL CARDS (see key on page 6)
④ ⑦ ㉚ ㉙ ㊵ ㊶

TRUCK FACILITIES
Coach parking available (3 spaces)

DRIVER FACILITIES
Accommodation on-site, Travelodge
Phone top-ups/accessories
Truckers' accessories
Takeaway food
Shower, washroom and rest area nearby

All on-site facilities accessible 24 hours

M441

Washington Services southbound

Moto Ltd
Portobello, Birtley, Durham
County Durham DH3 2SJ
T **0191 4103436** www.moto-way.com

A1M SOUTHBOUND JUNCTION 64

Unknown | Esso

P 32 OVERNIGHT

CREDIT/DEBIT CARDS

FUEL CARDS (see key on page 6)
④ ⑦ ㉚ ㉙ ㊵ ㊶

TRUCK FACILITIES
Coach parking available (3 spaces)

DRIVER FACILITIES
Accommodation on-site, Travelodge
Shower, rest area, TV
Phone top-ups/accessories
Truckers' accessories
Takeaway food

All on-site facilities accessible 24 hours

M442

Watford Gap Services northbound

Roadchef Ltd
Watford, nr Northampton
Northamptonshire NN6 7UZ
T **01327 879001**

M1 NORTHBOUND BETWEEN JUNCTIONS 16 AND 17

5.2m | BP

P 20 OVERNIGHT

£1.89 £3.79 £6.99

CREDIT/DEBIT CARDS

FUEL CARDS (see key on page 6)
① ⑤ ⑥ ⑭ ㉒ ㊵

TRUCK FACILITIES
P *with voucher*　**P** *only*　*Voucher value*
£15.00　　　　£12.00　£7.50
Coach parking available (10 spaces)
Ample room for manoeuvring

DRIVER FACILITIES
Accommodation on-site
Showers, 2 m, 2 f (free), washroom
Phone top-ups/accessories
Truckers' accessories
Takeaway food
Clothing for sale

All on-site facilities accessible 24 hours

M443

Watford Gap Services southbound

Roadchef Ltd
Watford, nr Northampton
Northamptonshire NN6 7UZ
T **01327 879001**

M1 SOUTHBOUND BETWEEN JUNCTIONS 16 AND 17

All on-site facilities accessible 24 hours

M444

CREDIT/DEBIT CARDS

FUEL CARDS (see key on page 6)

TRUCK FACILITIES
P *with voucher*   **P** *only*   *Voucher value*
£15.00   £12.00   £7.50
Coach parking available (10 spaces)
Ample room for manoeuvring

DRIVER FACILITIES
Accommodation on-site
Showers, 2 m, 2 f (free), washroom,
phone top-ups/accessories, truckers'
accessories, takeaway food
Clothing for sale

Winchester Services northbound

Roadchef Ltd
Shroner Wood, Martyr Worthy
nr Winchester, Hampshire SO21 1PP
T **01962 792500/792510**

M3 NORTHBOUND BETWEEN JUNCTIONS 8 AND 9

All on-site facilities accessible 24 hours

M445

CREDIT/DEBIT CARDS

FUEL CARDS (see key on page 6)

TRUCK FACILITIES
P *with voucher*   **P** *only*   *Voucher value*
£12.00   £9.00   £4.00
Coach parking available (12 spaces)
Ample room for manoeuvring
Quiet area

DRIVER FACILITIES
Washroom, phone top-ups/accessories,
truckers' accessories, takeaway food

SITE COMMENTS/INFORMATION
Value for money food with great
facilities for LGV drivers

Winchester Services southbound

Roadchef Ltd
Shroner Wood, Martyr Worthy
nr Winchester, Hampshire SO21 1PP
T **01962 792510/792500**

M3 SOUTHBOUND BETWEEN JUNCTIONS 8 AND 9

All on-site facilities accessible 24 hours

M446

CREDIT/DEBIT CARDS

FUEL CARDS (see key on page 6)

TRUCK FACILITIES
P *with voucher*   **P** *only*   *Voucher value*
£12.00   £9.00   £4.00
Coach parking available (12 spaces)
Ample room for manoeuvring
Quiet area

DRIVER FACILITIES
Accommodation on-site (£45 pn)
Washroom, phone top-ups/accessories,
truckers' accessories, takeaway food

SITE COMMENTS/INFORMATION
Good LGV facilities

Woodall Services northbound

Welcome Break Ltd
nr Killamarsh, nr Sheffield
South Yorkshire S26 7XR
T **0114 2486434**

M1 NORTHBOUND BETWEEN JUNCTIONS 30 AND 31

CREDIT/DEBIT CARDS

FUEL CARDS (see key on page 6)
⑧

DRIVER FACILITIES
Takeaway food

Unknown
Shell

P
OVERNIGHT

Full site details not available at time of going to press. For more information please contact site.

All on-site facilities accessible 24 hours   **M447**

Woodall Services southbound

Welcome Break Ltd
nr Killamarsh, nr Sheffield
South Yorkshire S26 7XR
T **0114 2486434**

M1 SOUTHBOUND BETWEEN JUNCTIONS 30 AND 31

CREDIT/DEBIT CARDS

FUEL CARDS (see key on page 6)
⑧

DRIVER FACILITIES
Accommodation on-site, Days Inn
Takeaway food

Unknown
Shell

P
OVERNIGHT

Full site details not available at time of going to press. For more information please contact site.

All on-site facilities accessible 24 hours   **M448**

Woolley Edge Services northbound

Moto Ltd
West Bretton, Wakefield
West Yorkshire WF4 4LQ
T **01924 830371** www.moto-way.com

M1 NORTHBOUND BETWEEN JUNCTIONS 38 AND 39

CREDIT/DEBIT CARDS

FUEL CARDS (see key on page 6)
⑦ 38 40

DRIVER FACILITIES
Takeaway food
Phone top-ups/accessories

Unknown
Esso

P
OVERNIGHT

Full site details not available at time of going to press. For more information please contact site.

All on-site facilities accessible 24 hours   **M449**

Woolley Edge Services southbound

Moto Ltd
West Bretton, Wakefield
West Yorkshire WF4 4LQ
T **01924 830371** www.moto-way.com

M1 SOUTHBOUND BETWEEN JUNCTIONS 38 AND 39

CREDIT/DEBIT CARDS

FUEL CARDS (see key on page 6)

DRIVER FACILITIES
Accommodation on-site, Travelodge
Takeaway food
Phone top-ups/accessories

Unknown
Esso

P
OVERNIGHT

Full site details not available at time of going to press. For more information please contact site.

All on-site facilities accessible 24 hours   M450

LADY TRUCKERS CLUB

Benefits of Membership

- Quarterly newsletter containing useful information for lady truckers and truckers in general.
- Free monthly copy of *Truckstop News*.
- 24 hour Advice/Help line for members in any part of the UK or abroad.
- Discounted entries to Truck shows and events throughout the UK.

For annual membership, please send your name, address, postcode, phone numbers, e-mail, date of birth and driver number, along with a cheque for £15 (made payable to Lady Truckers Club) and a copy of your LGV/PCV licence to:

Danneke Neale, 7 Sinclair Court, Scarborough, Yorks YO12 7DS
Tel: 01723 351425   Mob: 07791 601307
email: dneale7@aol.com
www.ladytruckersclub.co.uk

Anglia Motel

Washway Road, Fleet, nr Holbeach, Spalding, Lincolnshire PE12 8LT
T 01406 422766

ON THE A17 From Kings Lynn take the A17 towards Sleaford. By-pass the village Fleet Hargate and continue for 1 mile. Anglia Motel is on the left-hand side 800 yards past the turning for the B1515.

CREDIT/DEBIT CARDS

FUEL CARDS (see key on page 6)

TRUCK FACILITIES
P free
Coach parking available (20 spaces)
Ample room for manoeuvring
Quiet area

DRIVER FACILITIES
Accommodation £34.50 pn
Showers, 2 m, 2 f (charge), washroom, rest area, TV
Takeaway food

Parking and nearby fuel 24 hours. Showers 07:00-23:00 Mon-Sun. Other on-site facilities 07:00-21:00 Mon-Sun **P451**

Chris's Café & Motel

Wycombe Road, Studley Green Stokenchurch, Buckinghamshire HP14 3XB
T 01494 482121

ON THE A40 From M40 junction 5, take the A40 through Stokenchurch and continue for 1 mile from the outskirts. Chris's Café is on the left. From M40 junction 4, take the A4010 to the A40. Turn left onto A40 and continue for 2 miles. Chris's Café is on the right.

CREDIT/DEBIT CARDS

FUEL CARDS (see key on page 6)

TRUCK FACILITIES
P with voucher £9.00
Quiet area
Ample room for manoeuvring

DRIVER FACILITIES
Accommodation £20 B&B and evening meal
Shower, 1 m (charge), washroom, rest area, TV
Takeaway food

SITE COMMENTS/INFORMATION
Home cooked food and pleasant atmosphere. Cheques accepted

Parking and showers 24 hours. Other on-site facilities 06:00-19:00 Mon-Thu, 06:00-14:00 Fri, 06:30-12:00 Sat **P452**

Crawford Arms Hotel

11 Carlisle Road, Crawford South Lanarkshire ML2 6TP
T 01864 502267

OFF THE A702 Come off the A74M at junction 14 and follow signs for Crawford village. The Crawford Arms is located in the middle of the village on your left, just past the turning for Belstane Avenue.

CREDIT/DEBIT CARDS

FUEL CARDS (see key on page 6)

TRUCK FACILITIES
P with voucher £10.00 Voucher value £4.00
Quiet area
CCTV
Ample room for manoeuvring

DRIVER FACILITIES
Accommodation £25 B&B and evening meal
Showers, 2 m, 1 f (free), washroom, TV

SITE COMMENTS/INFORMATION
Good home cooked food
Easy access to motorway

Parking and nearby fuel 24 Hours. Other on-site facilities 06:00-01:00 Mon-Fri, 08:00-01:00 Sat & Sun **P453**

Halfway House Public House

1 Watling Street, Kilsby, nr Rugby
Warwickshire CV23 8YE
T 01788 822888

ON THE A5 From the M1 exit 18, take the A5 towards Hinckley. Turn left at the next roundabout onto the A428, across next roundabout then left again at the next onto the A5 towards Kilsby. Halfway House is 400 yards along on the right.

CREDIT/DEBIT CARDS

FUEL CARDS (see key on page 6)

TRUCK FACILITIES
Coach parking available
Quiet area

DRIVER FACILITIES
Accommodation £17.50 pn
Tea/coffee free with breakfast
Washroom
TV
Takeaway food
Clothing for sale nearby

SITE COMMENTS/INFORMATION
Home made food in traditional pub. Warm, friendly atmosphere. Only £2.10 for a pint!

Parking and nearby fuel 24 hours. Other on-site facilities 07:00-23:00 **P454**

Red Lion Pub

Weedon Road, Northampton
Northamptonshire NN7 4DE
T 01604 831914

ON THE A45 From the M1 exit at junction 16 and take the A45 towards Nottingham for 600 yards. The Red Lion Pub will be on your right.

CREDIT/DEBIT CARDS

FUEL CARDS (see key on page 6)

TRUCK FACILITIES
P *with voucher* £10.00
Voucher value 2 x £2.50
Quiet area
Ample room for manoeuvring

DRIVER FACILITIES
Showers, 3 m, 1 f (free), washroom, TV
Takeaway food

SITE COMMENTS/INFORMATION
This site is set around a 300-year-old traditional pub. Food is cooked to order on site by friendly, helpful staff

Parking accessible 24 hours. All other on-site facilities accessible 06:00-21:30 Mon-Fri **P455**

Redbeck Café (recently renamed Chris's Diner)

Boothferry Road, Boothferry Bridge
Howden, nr Goole East Yorkshire DN14 7
T 01430 430409

ON THE A1228 Take the M62 eastbound towards Hull and exit at junction 37 onto the A614. At the next roundabout, turn left towards Howden continue for 1 mile then turn right onto the A1228 Boothferry Road. Redbeck Café is immediately on your right.

CREDIT/DEBIT CARDS

FUEL CARDS (for nearby fuel)

TRUCK FACILITIES
P *with voucher* £7.00 *Voucher value* £2.00
Quiet area
Ample room for manoeuvring

DRIVER FACILITIES
Accommodation £12.00
Showers, 4 m (free), washroom, rest area, TV, phone top-ups/accessories
Truckers' accessories
Takeaway food

Parking 24 hours. Showers 07:00-23:00. Other on-site facilities 09:00-22:00 Tue-Fri, 17:30-22:00 Sat & Sun **P456**

Routemaster Motel & Truckstop

Walton Avenue, Felixstowe
Suffolk IP11 3HE
T 01394 674111

OFF THE A14 Head for Felixstowe on the A14. At the roundabout with the A154 turn right continuing with the A14. At the next roundabout take the last exit into Walton Avenue. Routemaster is 400 yards on the left.

CREDIT/DEBIT CARDS

FUEL CARDS (see key on page 6)

TRUCK FACILITIES
P £5.00
Ample room for manoeuvring
Quiet area

DRIVER FACILITIES
Accommodation £16.00 pp
Bathrooms (8), washroom, rest area
TV

Parking accessible 24 hours. Other on-site facilities accessible 07:30-21:00 Mon-Tues, 06:30-21:00 Fri **P457**

The Albion Inn & Truckstop

14 Bath Road, Ashcott, Bridgwater
Somerset TA7 9QT
T 01458 210281

ON THE A39 From junction 23 of the M5, head towards Glastonbury on the A39. The Albion Inn is on your right, 8 and a half miles from the motorway, just after the turning for Pedwell and just before you get into the village of Ashcott.

CREDIT/DEBIT CARDS

FUEL CARDS (see key on page 6)

TRUCK FACILITIES
P £5.00
Coach parking available (2 spaces)
Quiet area
Ample room for manoeuvring
Fridge lorry area (Switch off at 22:00)

DRIVER FACILITIES
Accommodation £20 pn
Showers, 1 m, 1 f (charge), washroom, rest area, TV, truckers' accessories
Takeaway food
Post Office nearby

SITE COMMENTS/INFORMATION
Small, friendly site where drivers receive a warm welcome and personal attention

Showers and parking 24 hours. Other on-site facilities 07:00-20:00 Mon-Thur, 07:00-15:00 Fri **P458**

The Fox Inn

Great North Road, Colsterworth
Grantham, Lincolnshire NG33 5LN
T 01572 767697

ON THE A1 The Fox Inn can be found on the A1 southbound carriageway about 2 miles south of Colsterworth and the junction with the A151. Both north and southbound carriageways are easily accessible upon exit from this site.

CREDIT/DEBIT CARDS

FUEL CARDS (see key on page 6)

TRUCK FACILITIES
P with voucher £7.50
Voucher value £5.00 off meal
Coach parking available, shared with LGV
Ample room for manoeuvring

DRIVER FACILITIES
Accommodation £39.95 pn
Shower, unisex (free), washroom, TV

Parking and showers 24 hours **P459**

The Gandon Inn

Emo, Portlaoise
County Laois, Ireland
T 00353 (0) 50226622

ON THE N7 From the N7, take exit signposted Mountmellick and Portarlington. The Gandon Inn is a few yards on your left.

CREDIT/DEBIT CARDS

FUEL CARDS (see key on page 6)
❷ ❼ ㉑

TRUCK FACILITIES
P free
Coach parking available (2 spaces)
Ample room for manoeuvring
Quiet area
Truck dealership/workshop nearby

DRIVER FACILITIES
Accommodation €45.00 B&B
Shower, rest area, TV, internet access
Phone top-ups/accessories
Takeaway food. CB repairs/sales nearby

SITE COMMENTS/INFORMATION
This site is very close to the motorway
with good access for LGVs

Showers, parking and bunker fuel accessible 24 hours. Other on-site facilities accessible 07:00-23:00   **P460**

The Meadows Inn

Derby Cattle Market Lorry Park
Chequers Road, West Meadows Ind. Estate
Derby, Derbyshire DE21 6
T 01332 361344

ON THE A52 From the A601 Derby Inner Ring Road, take the A52 towards Nottingham. Continue past the roundabout with the A61, and Derby Cattle Market is 400 yards on the right.

CREDIT/DEBIT CARDS

FUEL CARDS (see key on page 6)

TRUCK FACILITIES
P £5.00 night/£3.00 day
Coach parking available (20 spaces)
Quiet area
Ample room for manoeuvring

DRIVER FACILITIES
Showers, 3 m (free), washroom, TV
Takeaway food

SITE COMMENTS/INFORMATION
Home cooked food served in
comfortable air-conditioned pub

Parking 24 hours. All other on-site facilities 10:00-14:30, 16:30-23:30. Nearby fuel 24 hours   **P461**

Big Mike's Breakfast Bar

**Near M4 Junction 49, Cross Hands
Carmarthenshire SA40 0**

ON THE A483 From the end of the M4, take the A483
towards Ammanford and continue for half a mile. Big Mike's
is in a lay-by on the left.

CREDIT/DEBIT CARDS

FUEL CARDS (see key on page 6)

TRUCK FACILITIES
Parking in lay-by set close to road

DRIVER FACILITIES
Seating area
Takeaway food

Parking accessible 24 hours. Other on-site facilities accessible 06:30-15:00 **S462**

Bistro Café

**Nottingham Road, Sedgebrook
nr Grantham, Lincolnshire NG32 2EP
T 01949 842164**

ON THE A52 If heading from Grantham to Nottingham on
the A52, the Bistro Café is on your right-hand side at the
village of Sedgebrook.

CREDIT/DEBIT CARDS

FUEL CARDS (see key on page 6)

TRUCK FACILITIES
P free
Parking in lay-by set close to road
Coach parking available, shared with LGV
Truck dealership/workshop nearby

DRIVER FACILITIES
Takeaway food

Parking 24 hours. Other on-site facilities 06:30-16:00 Mon-Fri, 06:30-13:00 Sat & Sun **S463**

Dinky's Dinah's

**Welshpool Road, Ford, nr Shrewsbury
Shropshire SY59 9
T 01743 850070**

ON THE A458 Dinky's Dinah's is a static portacabin café
situated on the A458 Shrewsbury to Welshpool road in a
large lay-by in the village of Ford. It's located on the left-hand
side if heading towards Shrewsbury after Butt Lane on the
left and before the BP garage.

CREDIT/DEBIT CARDS

FUEL CARDS (for nearby fuel)
⑤

TRUCK FACILITIES
P free
Parking in lay-by set back from road
Coach parking available (6 spaces)
Ample room for manoeuvring

DRIVER FACILITIES
Seating area
Truckers' accessories
Takeaway food. Clothing for sale

SITE COMMENTS/INFORMATION
Excellent service around the clock

All on-site facilities accessible 24 hours. Nearby fuel not accessible 24 hours **S464**

Heather's Kaf

Oswestry By-pass, Sweeney, nr Morda Oswestry, Shropshire SY10 8

ON THE A483 If heading south towards Welshpool, by-pass Oswestry on the A483. Go past the roundabout with the A5 and Heather's Kaf is 1 mile on your right-hand side.

CREDIT/DEBIT CARDS

FUEL CARDS (see key on page 6)

TRUCK FACILITIES
P *free*, in lay-by set close to road
Truck dealership/workshop nearby
Tyre repair/sales nearby

DRIVER FACILITIES
Seating area
Takeaway food

SITE COMMENTS/INFORMATION
Clean and tidy site with smiley, friendly staff

Parking, fuel and nearby shop accessible 24 hours. Other on-site facilities accessible 07:30-16:00

S465

Penrith Country Cuisine

Penrith, Cumbria CA11 8

ON THE A66 EASTBOUND From the M6, exit at junction 40 and take the A66 Eastbound. Penrith Country Cuisine is in 100 yards in a big lay-by on your left. To get back to the M6, continue east for 400 yards and turn around at the roundabout.

CREDIT/DEBIT CARDS

FUEL CARDS (see key on page 6)

TRUCK FACILITIES
Parking in large lay-by
Coach parking available, shared with LGV
Ample room for manoeuvring
Truck dealership/workshop nearby

DRIVER FACILITIES
Breakfast price includes tea or coffee
Accommodation nearby, 500 yards, North Lakes Shire Inns Hotel
Takeaway food. CB sales/repairs nearby

SITE COMMENTS/INFORMATION
This site has very quick and easy access from, and back, to the M6

Parking 24 hours in lay-by. All other on-site facilities 07:30-14:30 Mon-Fri, 08:30-14:00 Sat

S466

Val's Diner

Telford/Donnington Roundabout Redhill, Telford, Shropshire TF2 9PA

ON THE A5 From M54 Junction 4 take the B5060 towards Oakengates. At the roundabout with the A5, turn left towards Cannock. Val's Diner is half a mile along on the right-hand side in a lay-by.

CREDIT/DEBIT CARDS

FUEL CARDS (see key on page 6)

TRUCK FACILITIES
P free
Parking in large lay-by set back from road
Truck washing facilities nearby

DRIVER FACILITIES
Accommodation nearby, Oaks at Redhill Hotel
Showers, 1 m, 1 f (free to customers)
Washroom, seating area
Takeaway food

SITE COMMENTS/INFORMATION
Home cooked food, friendly staff and a lovely cuppa. Nearby town centre facilities 1 mile away

Parking and showers accessible 24 hours. Other on-site facilities accessible 04:00-14:00

S467

Wyn's Catering

Pen Top, Llanllwini
Carmarthenshire SA39 9

ON THE A485 Wyn's is on the A485 Carmarthen to Lampeter road between New Inn and Llanllwini. It is situated on the left-hand side if heading north, at the top of the hill in a big lay-by.

CREDIT/DEBIT CARDS

FUEL CARDS (see key on page 6)

TRUCK FACILITIES
P free
Parking in lay-by set back from road.
Coach parking available (5 spaces)
Ample room for manoeuvring

SITE COMMENTS/INFORMATION
Good quality and good value food
Site run by a female trucker!
Flasks made up by staff on request

Parking accessible 24 hours. Other on-site facilities accessible 08:00-14:00

S468

Boss Hogs Transport Café

**London Road, Copdock, Ipswich
Suffolk IP8 3JW
T 01473 730797**

OFF THE A12 If heading from Colchester to Ipswich, take the exit signposted to Copdock onto the London road. Boss Hogs is 400 yards along on the right.

CREDIT/DEBIT CARDS

FUEL CARDS (see key on page 6)

DRIVER FACILITIES
Drivers' washroom

On-site facilities opening times unknown

TC469

Langrick Station Café

**Main Road, Langrick, Boston
Lincolnshire PE22 7AH
T 01205 820023**

ON THE B1192 The Langrick Station Café can be found on the right-hand side of the B1192 if heading north between Brothertoft and New York, north-west of Boston.

CREDIT/DEBIT CARDS

FUEL CARDS (see key on page 6)

TRUCK FACILITIES
P free
Short-term coach parking available, shared with LGV
Quiet area
Ample room for manoeuvring

DRIVER FACILITIES
Seating area
Takeaway food

All on-site facilities accessible 06:30-18:00 Mon- Fri, 06:30-12:00 Sat

TC470

Michaels Café

**London Road, Polhill, Halstead
Sevenoaks, Kent TN14 7AA
T 01959 534284**

ON THE A224 Exit the M25 at junction 4 and take the A224 towards Dunton Green. Continue for 1 mile and Michaels is on the left.

CREDIT/DEBIT CARDS

FUEL CARDS (see key on page 6)

DRIVER FACILITIES
Accommodation on-site, £22.95 pn
Seating area

On-site facilities accessible 07:00-15:00 Mon-Fri, 08:00-15:00 Sat

TC471

Sue's Pitstop

(formerly the Redwood Café)
Ledston Luck Enterprise Park
Kippax, Leeds, West Yorkshire LS25 7BD
T 0113 2863307

OFF THE A656 From A1M southbound take A1 then A63 towards Garforth and Kippax for 1 mile. Left at roundabout onto A656 for half a mile then left into Ledston Luck Enterprise Park. Follow the road around 2 left bends and it's on the left.

CREDIT/DEBIT CARDS

FUEL CARDS (see key on page 6)

TRUCK FACILITIES
P free
Short-term coach parking available
Ample room for manoeuvring
Truck dealership/workshop nearby

DRIVER FACILITIES
Drivers' washroom
Seating area
Takeaway food

All on-site facilities accessible. 07:00-15:00 Mon-Fri, 07:00-11:00 Sat

TC472

The Pantry Café

Willoughby, between Daventry and Rugby
Warwickshire CV23 8BL
T 01788 890262

ON THE A45 If heading from Daventry to Rugby on the A45, The Pantry Café is on the left-hand side in the middle of the village of Willoughby.

CREDIT/DEBIT CARDS

FUEL CARDS (see key on page 6)

TRUCK FACILITIES
Short-term coach parking nearby
Ample room for manoeuvring

DRIVER FACILITIES
Takeaway food

All on-site facilities opening times unknown

TC473

Venture Café

London Road, Addington, West Malling
Kent ME19 5PL
T 01732 842020

ON THE A20 Exit the M26 at junction 2A and take the A20 towards Maidstone. Venture Café is situated 1 mile on the right-hand side between the villages Wrotham Heath and Addington.

CREDIT/DEBIT CARDS

FUEL CARDS (see key on page 6)

TRUCK FACILITIES
Ample room for manoeuvring

DRIVER FACILITIES
Accommodation nearby, half a
    mile, Travel Inn
Seating area
Takeaway food

All on-site facilities accessible 07:00-00:00. Short-term parking times unknown

TC474

A1 Stadium Diner

Bourne Road, Colsterworth, Grantham Lincolnshire NG33 5JN
T 01476 860916

ON THE A151 From the A1 north or southbound, take the A151 at the roundabout towards Bourne and A1 Stadium Diner is 500 yards on the left-hand side.

CREDIT/DEBIT CARDS

FUEL CARDS (see key on page 6)
① ② ③ ⑩

TRUCK FACILITIES
P *with voucher* **P** *only* *Voucher value*
£8.00   £6.00   £2.00
Coach parking available (10 spaces)
Quiet area on-site. Fridge lorry area
Ample room for manoeuvring

DRIVER FACILITIES
Accommodation nearby, Travelodge
Showers, 5 m, 1 f (charge), washroom,
TV, truckers' accessories, CB repairs/sales
Takeaway food. Clothing for sale

SITE COMMENTS/INFORMATION
Good, fresh, cooked to order food

Parking, bunker fuel and showers accessible 24 hours. Other on-site facilities accessible 06:00-21:30   **T475**

Ashford International Truckstop

(formerly known as Eurotunnel)
GSE Waterbrook Ltd, Waterbrook Avenue
Sevington, nr Ashford, Kent TN24 0LH
T 01233 502919
M20 JUNCTION 10 ON THE A2070 From M20, junction 10, follow signs to Lorry park. Take A2070 towards Orlestone onto Bad Munstereifel Road. Continue for a quarter of a mile and Waterbrook Avenue is on the left at the next roundabout.

CREDIT/DEBIT CARDS

FUEL CARDS (see key on page 6)
① ② ③ ④ ⑩ ㊲ ㊻

TRUCK FACILITIES
P *with voucher* £12.50, *voucher* = £2.50
P free for 2 hours for patrons only
Coach parking. Fridge lorry/quiet area
Truck washing facilities. Tyre repair/sales
DRIVER FACILITIES
Accommodation on-site, single £19.95
Showers (free), rest area, TV, internet, Euros
changed/accepted, phone top-ups/
accessories, clothing for sale, truckers'
accessories, CB repairs/sales, takeaway food
SITE COMMENTS/INFORMATION
Euronettes and maps on sale. HM Customs
clearance facilities. Livestock not permitted

All on-site facilities accessible 24 hours   **T476**

Barton Park Services

Moto Ltd, A1 Great North Road
Barton, nr Richmond
North Yorkshire DL10 6NA
T 01325 377777

OFF THE A1 Exit A1M at junction 56 and head towards Barton. Barton Park Services is immediately on your right.

CREDIT/DEBIT CARDS

FUEL CARDS (see key on page 6)
① ② ③ ⑤ ⑥ ⑩

TRUCK FACILITIES
P *with voucher* £6.50
Voucher value £1.50
Ample room for manoeuvring

DRIVER FACILITIES
Showers – 3 m (charge), washroom, rest
area, TV, phone top-ups/accessories,
clothing for sale, truckers' accessories

Shop, parking, fuel and some food accessible 24 hours. Other facilities accessible 06:00-23:00   **T477**

Birmingham Truckstop

The Wharf, Wharf Road, Tyseley
Birmingham, West Midlands B11 2DA
T 0121 6282339

ON THE B1416 From the M42, exit at junction 6 and take the A45 towards Birmingham. At the junction with the A4040, turn left towards Tyseley. After 900 yards turn right onto B4146 Wharfdale Road. Continue into Wharf Road. Truckstop is on your left.

CREDIT/DEBIT CARDS

FUEL CARDS (see key on page 6)

TRUCK FACILITIES
P £5.00
Coach parking. Fridge lorry area
Ample room for manoeuvring
Truck dealership/workshop

DRIVER FACILITIES
Accommodation on-site, £15.00 pppn
Showers – 3 m (free), washroom, rest area, TV, phone top-ups/accessories

SITE COMMENTS/INFORMATION
Train/tram nearby
Home cooked and prepared food is of the highest quality at very affordable prices

Parking and showers accessible 24 hours. Restaurant accessible 06:00-21:00 Mon-Fri. 06:00-12:00 Sat   **T478**

Brough Lorry Park

Grand Prix Services, Main Street
Brough, Cumbria CA17 4AY
T 01768 341328

ON THE B6276 The village of Brough is off the A66 at the junction with the A685. If heading from Penrith on the A66 exit for Brough onto the B6276 and the Lorry Park is 400 yards along on your left.

CREDIT/DEBIT CARDS

FUEL CARDS (see key on page 6)

TRUCK FACILITIES
Coach parking shared with LGV
CCTV. Quiet area on-site. Fridge lorry area
Ample room for manoeuvring
Truck dealership/workshop nearby

DRIVER FACILITIES
Showers – 3 unisex (free), washroom, TV
Takeaway food
Post Office nearby

SITE COMMENTS/INFORMATION
On-site fuel can be purchased for cash only

Parking 24 hours. All other on-site facilities 06:15-22:00 Mon-Fri. Nearby cashpoint machine until 20:00   **T479**

Clondalkin Truck & Trailer Park

Cloverhill Road
Clondalkin Commercial Park, Clondalkin
Dublin 22, County Dublin, Ireland
T 00353 (0) 14572161/14572173/14578400

OFF THE R113 M50 junction 9, take N7 to junction with the R113, turn right onto Fonthill Road South. Right at next two roundabouts staying on the R113 New Nangor Road, then take next left, 2nd right and Clondalkin Park is 4th turning on left.

CREDIT/DEBIT CARDS

FUEL CARDS (see key on page 6)
(9) (21)

TRUCK FACILITIES
P €17.00
Coach parking (15 spaces)
Fridge lorry area
Ample room for manoeuvring
Truck dealership/workshop

DRIVER FACILITIES
Showers – 1 m, 1 f (free), washroom, TV
Takeaway, internet access and clothing for sale nearby

SITE COMMENTS/INFORMATION
Train/tram/underground/metro nearby

All on-site facilities accessible 24 Hours   **T480**

Corby Truckstop

C H Jones Ltd, 14 Pilot Road
Phoenix Park Way Ind. Est., Corby
Northamptonshire NN17 5YH
T 01536 203533
OFF THE A6086 From Kettering, take the A43 north-east bound towards Stamford. At the junction with the A6116 turn left towards Corby centre. Across next roundabout onto the A6086, right at the next 2 roundabouts and it's on the right.

CREDIT/DEBIT CARDS

FUEL CARDS (see key on page 6)
① ②

TRUCK FACILITIES
P £6.50
Coach parking available, shared with LGV
Ample room for manoeuvring

DRIVER FACILITIES
Washroom, showers
Truckers' accessories
Takeaway food

Bunker fuel, showers and parking accessible 24 hours. Other on-site facilities times unknown **T481**

Crawley Crossing Bunker Stop

C H Jones Ltd, Bedford Road
Husbourne Crawley, Bedfordshire MK43 0UT
T 01908 281084

OFF THE A507 From the M1, exit at junction 13 and head south on the A507 towards Woburn. Crawley Crossing is half a mile along on the right.

CREDIT/DEBIT CARDS

FUEL CARDS (see key on page 6)
① ② ③ ⑩

TRUCK FACILITIES
P with voucher £6.00
Voucher value £1.00
Coach parking available, shared with LGV
Quiet area. Fridge lorry area
Ample room for manoeuvring

DRIVER FACILITIES
Shower – 1 unisex (free), washroom, TV
Euros changed/accepted
Truckers' accessories, CB repairs/sales
Takeaway food
SITE COMMENTS/INFORMATION
This site is number 180 in the keyfuels book

Truckers' shop 08:30-17:00 Mon-Thurs, 08:00-15:00 Fri. Café 07:00-22:00 Mon-Thurs, 07:00-08:00 Fri
Bunker fuel, showers and other on-site facilities 24 hours **T482**

Davidsons Junction 40 Ltd

Ullswater Rd, Penrith
Cumbria CA11 7JH
T 01768 867101

ON THE A592 From the M6 junction 40, follow the A592 towards Penrith. Davidsons is half a mile along on the left just past the park.

CREDIT/DEBIT CARDS

FUEL CARDS (see key on page 6)
① ② ③

TRUCK FACILITIES
P £7.00 with free coffee
Coach parking available (6 spaces)
Quiet area
Ample room for manoeuvring
Truck washing facilities
Truck dealership/workshop

DRIVER FACILITIES
Accommodation nearby, half a mile
Showers – 3 m, free if parking,
washroom, rest area, truckers' accessories
Takeaway food and clothing for sale nearby

All on-site facilities accessible 24 hours **T483**

Europa Truckstop

**Wellburn Interchange, Lesmahagow
Strathclyde ML11 0HY
T 01555 894889** www.europatruckstop.com

AT THE M74 JUNCTION 10 If heading south, exit at
junction 9 and take B7086 to Kirkmuirhill for 600 yards. Turn
right onto B7078 for 2 miles. Turn right at roundabout with
Junction 10, go under motorway and Europa is ahead of you
at the next roundabout.

CREDIT/DEBIT CARDS

FUEL CARDS (see key on page 6)
① ② ③ ④ ⑥ ⑩–㉝ inclusive

TRUCK FACILITIES
P *with voucher* £8.00, *Voucher* = £2.00
Coach parking available (50 spaces)
Ample room for manoeuvring
Quiet area. Fridge lorry area
Truck washing facilities

DRIVER FACILITIES
Accommodation on-site, £15 single
Showers (free), rest area, TV, internet,
Euros changed/accepted, phone top-
ups/accessories, clothing for sale,
truckers' accessories, CB repairs/sales
Takeaway food

All on-site facilities accessible 24 hours   **T484**

Golden Fleece

**Exelby Services Ltd, Carleton, Carlisle
Cumbria CA4 0AN
T 01228 542766**

M6 JUNCTION 42 ON THE A6 From the M6 exit at
junction 42 and take the A6 towards Penrith. Golden Fleece
is a couple of yards along on the left-hand side.

CREDIT/DEBIT CARDS

FUEL CARDS (see key on page 6)
① ② ③ ⑤ ⑥ ⑩

TRUCK FACILITIES
Quiet area
Ample room for manoeuvring

DRIVER FACILITIES
Showers – 1 m, 1 f (charge), washroom,
clothing for sale, truckers' accessories

Parking and fuel accessible 24 hours. Other on-site facilities opening times unknown   **T485**

Grahams Transport Stop

**Taunton Road, North Petherton
Bridgwater, Somerset TA6 6PR
T 01278 663052/663076**

ON THE A38 From the M5 junction 24 follow signs for A38
North Petherton and Taunton. Grahams/Woods is about 500
yards from the M5 roundabout on your left-hand side.

CREDIT/DEBIT CARDS

FUEL CARDS (see key on page 6)
① ② ③ ⑩

TRUCK FACILITIES
P £5.00
Ample room for manoeuvring
Quiet area

DRIVER FACILITIES
Showers – 2 unisex (charge), washroom,
TV, truckers' accessories
Takeaway food available

SITE COMMENTS/INFORMATION
Good home cooked food, good value
for money, friendly atmosphere, family
run business

Parking and bunker fuel 24 hours. Other on-site facilities 06:00-20:00 Mon-Thurs, 06:30-17:00 Fri, 07:00-23:00 Sat **T486**

Heatherghyll Truckstop

Carlisle Road, Crawford
South Lanarkshire ML12 6
T 01864 502641

OFF THE A702 If heading north, exit the A74M at junction 14 and follow the A702. Turn right at the roundabout near the entrance slip road for the A74M and Heatherghyll is on the left. If heading south, Exit A74 at junction 14, go across roundabout and it's on the left

CREDIT/DEBIT CARDS

FUEL CARDS (see key on page 6)

TRUCK FACILITIES
P *with voucher* £9.00 **P** *only* £5.00
Coach parking (2 spaces)
Ample room for manoeuvring
Truck dealership/workshop

DRIVER FACILITIES
Showers – 2 m, 1 f, washroom, rest area, TV, internet access
Phone top-ups/accessories
Takeaway food

SITE COMMENTS/INFORMATION
Excellent site

Parking and nearby fuel accessible 24 hours. Other on-site facilities accessible 06:00-23:00   **T487**

Heywood Distribution Park

Estate Office, Pilsworth Road, Heywood
Lancashire OL10 2TT
T 01706 368645
www.heywooddistributionpark.com

OFF THE A58 From the M66, exit at junction 3 and head towards Heywood. At the T-junction turn right and follow the road left as it bears left into Pilsworth Road. Heywood Distribution Park is within 1 mile.

CREDIT/DEBIT CARDS

FUEL CARDS (see key on page 6)

TRUCK FACILITIES
P £7.50
Coach parking (20 spaces)
24 hour guards with dogs
Secure fencing, CCTV and floodlighting
Quiet area. Fridge lorry area
Ample room for manoeuvring
Truck washing facilities
Tyre repair/sales nearby

DRIVER FACILITIES
Accommodation nearby,
   see Birch Motorway Services Eastbound
Washroom, rest area, TV. Takeaway nearby

SITE COMMENTS/INFORMATION
Police Secured Car Park Award

Parking and showers 06:00-00:00. Some facilities open 08:00-14:00. Other on-site facilities times vary   **T488**

J G B Altens Lorry Park

Units 1 and 2 Hareness Road
Altens Industrial Estate, Aberdeen
Aberdeenshire AB12 3LE
T 01224 876674

OFF THE A956 From Stonehaven take the A90 to Aberdeen. After Marywell take the A956 towards Nigg and Torry. At the junction signposted for the B9077 and the A90, turn right into Hareness Road and Altens Lorry Park is 100 yards on the right.

CREDIT/DEBIT CARDS

FUEL CARDS (see key on page 6)

TRUCK FACILITIES
Quiet area on-site. Fridge lorry area
Ample room for manoeuvring
Truck dealership/workshop

DRIVER FACILITIES
Accommodation nearby, half a mile,
   Thistle Aberdeen Altens
Showers (free), washroom, rest area,
phone top-ups/accessories, truckers'
accessories, takeaway food
Post Office nearby

All on-site facilities accessible 24 hours   **T489**

Junction 23 Truckstop

**Ashby Road, East Shepshed, Leicester
Leicestershire LE12 9BS
T 01509 507480/507479**

ON THE A512 From the M1, exit at junction 23 and head west on the A512 towards Ashby de la Zouch. Junction 23 Truckstop is 200 yards on the right.

CREDIT/DEBIT CARDS

FUEL CARDS (see key on page 6)
① ② ③ ④ ⑩

TRUCK FACILITIES
P with voucher £9.00
Voucher value – £2.50
CCTV, security guard. Quiet area
Ample room for manoeuvring
Truck washing facilities

DRIVER FACILITIES
Showers – m & f (free), washroom, TV
Truckers' accessories
Takeaway food available

Parking, bunker fuel, shop and showers 24 hours. Other on-site facilities 06:00-21:30 Mon-Fri, 06:00-11:00 Sat **T490**

Junction 29 Truckstop

**Hardwick View Road
Holmewood Industrial Estate, Holmewood
Chesterfield, Derbyshire S42 5SA
T 01246 856536**

OFF THE A6175 From junction 29 of the M1 take the A6175 towards Holmewood for 1 mile. At the next roundabout turn left into Holmewood Industrial Estate. Follow the road around and Junction 29 Truckstop is on the right.

CREDIT/DEBIT CARDS

FUEL CARDS (see key on page 6)
① ② ③ ⑩ ㉚

TRUCK FACILITIES
P with voucher £9.50
Voucher value – £2.20
Coach parking shared with LGV
Quiet area on-site. Fridge lorry area
Ample room for manoeuvring

DRIVER FACILITIES
Showers – 6 m, 1 f (free with parking), washroom, rest area, TV, phone top-ups/accessories, clothing for sale, truckers' accessories, CB repairs/sales, takeaway food

All on-site facilities accessible 24 hours **T491**

Lee Mills Truckstop & Transport Café

**Lee Mills Bridge, Lee Mills, Ivybridge
Devon PL21 9EE
T 01752 202167**

OFF THE A38 Signposted from the A38. If heading south, 1 mile beyond Ivybridge and if heading north, 1 and a half miles from the outskirts of Plymouth.

CREDIT/DEBIT CARDS

FUEL CARDS (see key on page 6)
① ② ③ ④ ⑨ ⑫ ⑮ ⑰ ⑱ ㉕ ㉗ ㉘
㉛ ㊲ ㊹

TRUCK FACILITIES
P £6.00
Coach parking available, shared with LGV
Quiet area
Ample room for manoeuvring
Truck dealership/workshop nearby
Credit/debit cards accepted at bunker

DRIVER FACILITIES
Showers – 3 unisex. washroom, TV, phone top-ups/accessories, clothing for sale, truckers' accessories, takeaway food
Post Office nearby

Parking and bunker fuel 24 hours. Other on-site facilities 06:30-19:30 Mon-Fri, 07:00-17:30 Sat **T492**

Londonderry Lodge Truckstop & Exelby Services Ltd

Londonderry, Northallerton
North Yorkshire DL7 9ND/B
T 01677 422143/422185

ON THE OLD A1 If heading north on A1 take the exit before the A684 signposted for Exelby and Leeming and turn across the carriageway. Londonderry Lodge and Exelby Services will be in front of you to the right.

CREDIT/DEBIT CARDS

FUEL CARDS (see key on page 6)
① ② ③ ④ ⑤ ⑥ ⑩ ㊱ ㊲

TRUCK FACILITIES
P £3.50 and £3.70
Ample room for manoeuvring
Quiet area
Truck dealership/workshop

DRIVER FACILITIES
Accommodation on-site, £18:00 pn
Showers – 1 m, 1 f (free), washroom, rest area, TV, truckers' accessories
Takeaway food

SITE COMMENTS/INFORMATION
Although 2 separate companies, they are next door to each other

Showers 05:00-00:00 weekdays. Bunker fuel 24 hrs between 09:00 Sun and 18:00 Sat. All other facilities 24 hrs   **T493**

Muirpark Truckstop & Garage

Falkirk Road, Bannockburn
Stirlingshire FK7 8AL

ON THE A9 From junction 9 of the M9 or junction 9 of the M80, take the A91 towards Bannockburn. At the roundabout with the A9, turn right onto the A9 towards Falkirk. Muirpark is a few yards along on the left-hand side.

CREDIT/DEBIT CARDS

FUEL CARDS (see key on page 6)
① ② ③ ④ ⑨

TRUCK FACILITIES
P free
Quiet area
Ample room for manoeuvring

DRIVER FACILITIES
Showers – 3 m, 1 f (£1.00), washroom, rest area, TV, takeaway food
Clothing and CB sales/repairs nearby

SITE COMMENTS/INFORMATION
Family run business, home cooked food, friendly service and helpful staff

Parking and fuel 24 hours. Other on-site facilities 07:00-22:00 Mon-Thurs, 07:00-14:00 Fri   **T494**

NT Truckstop, Alconbury

(Previously BP Nightowl), Rusts Lane
Alconbury, nr Huntingdon
Cambridgeshire PE28 4DJ
T 01480 454476 53

OFF THE A1M JUNCTION 13 From A14 northbound, exit where it merges to A1M, the site is on the left on sliproad. From A1 heading north, exit where it merges to A1M, right at next roundabout, left at the 2nd, right at the 3rd. Truckstop is on left.

CREDIT/DEBIT CARDS

FUEL CARDS (see key on page 6)
① ② ③

TRUCK FACILITIES

	P with voucher	P only	Voucher value
	£13.00	£10.00	£3.00

CCTV, anticlimb fencing, security guards
Ample room for manoeuvring
Quiet area. Fridge lorry area
Truck washing facilities

DRIVER FACILITIES
Accommodation on-site, £19 and £25 pn
Showers – 8 unisex (£3.00), washroom, rest area, TV, clothing shop, truckers' accessories, CB repairs/sales
Takeaway food

Bunker fuel, parking and shop 24 hours. Restaurant 05:00-23:00 Mon-Fri, 06:00-12:00 Sat
Bar 06:00-23:00 Mon-Fri. All other on-site facilities 24 hours Mon-Fri, 12:00-17:00, Sat & Sun   **T495**

NT Truckstop, Carlisle

(Previously BP Nightowl), Parkhouse Road Kingstown Industrial Estate, Carlisle Cumbria CA3 0JR
T 01228 534192

OFF THE A7 From junction 44 of the M6, take the A7 towards Kingstown. Take the next right across the carriageway and follow signs for the industrial estate. You will see the Truckstop on your right.

CREDIT/DEBIT CARDS

FUEL CARDS (see key on page 6)
❶❷❸

TRUCK FACILITIES
P *with voucher* **P** *only* *Voucher value*
£13.00 £10.00 £3.00
CCTV, anticlimb fencing, security guards
Ample room for manoeuvring
Quiet area. Fridge lorry area

DRIVER FACILITIES
Accommodation on-site, £17.99-£34.99 pn
Showers – 6 m, 6 f (free), washroom, rest area, TV, clothing shop, truckers' accessories, CB repairs/sales
Takeaway food

Bunker fuel accessible 24 hours. Restaurant 06:00-23:00 Mon, 05:00-23:00 Tue-Fri, 05:00-12:00 Sat, 05:00-22:00 Sun. Bar 06:00-23:00 Mon, Tue, Thurs, Fri. 12:00-23:00 Wed. All other on-site facilities accessible 24 hours **T496**

NT Truckstop, Newcastle

(Previously BP Nightowl), Portobello Road Birtley, nr Newcastle upon Tyne County Durham DH3 2SN
T 01914 920940

OFF THE A1231 From the A1 and A1M in either direction or the A194M Washington exit, take the exit signposted A1231 and B1288 and follow it towards Birtley. The Truckstop is a little further along on that road at the roundabout with the B1288.

CREDIT/DEBIT CARDS

FUEL CARDS (see key on page 6)
❶❷❸

TRUCK FACILITIES
P *with voucher* **P** *only* *Voucher value*
£13.00 £10.00 £3.00
CCTV, anticlimb fencing, security guards
Ample room for manoeuvring
Quiet area. Fridge lorry area
DRIVER FACILITIES
Accommodation on-site, £14.99 & £25.50
Showers – 6 m, 6 f (free), washroom, rest area, TV, clothing for sale, truckers' accessories, CB repairs/sales
Takeaway food

Bunker fuel 24 hours. Restaurant 05:00-23:00 Mon-Fri, 06:00-12:00 Sat. Shop accessible 24 hours Mon-Sat, closes 12:00 Sat. Bar 06:00-23:00 Mon-Fri. Fuel and all other facilities 24 hours **T497**

NT Truckstop, Rugby

(Previously BP Nightowl), Watling Street Clifton upon Dunsmore, Rugby Warwickshire CV23 0AE
T 01788 535115

ON THE A5 Exit at junction 18 of the M1 onto the A428 towards Rugby then take the A5 towards Hinckley. The Truckstop is about 3 miles along on the right-hand side.

CREDIT/DEBIT CARDS

FUEL CARDS (see key on page 6)
❶❷❸

TRUCK FACILITIES
P *with voucher* **P** *only* *Voucher value*
£13.00 £10.00 £3.00
CCTV, anticlimb fencing, security guards
Ample room for manoeuvring
Quiet area. Fridge lorry area

DRIVER FACILITIES
Showers – 8 unisex (£2.00), washroom, rest area, TV, laundry service, clothing for sale, truckers' accessories, CB repairs/sales
Takeaway food

Bunker fuel 24 hours. Restaurant 24 hours from 15:00 Sun-13:00 Sat. Shop 06:00-23:00 Mon-Fri, 06:00-14:00 Sat, 15:00-22:00 Sun. Bar 06:00-23:00 Mon-Fri, 19:00-22:30 Sun. All other on-site facilities accessible 24 hours **T498**

NT Truckstop, Wolverhampton

(Previously BP Nightowl), Cannock Road Hilton Industrial Estate, Featherstone Wolverhampton, West Midlands WV10 7HP
T 01902 307535

OFF THE A460 From the M54 junction 1 head south towards Wolverhampton on the Cannock road. Turn left at the first roundabout into the Hilton Industrial Estate and NT Truckstop is on your right.

CREDIT/DEBIT CARDS

FUEL CARDS (see key on page 6)
❶❷❸

TRUCK FACILITIES
P with voucher   **P** only   Voucher value
£13.00   £10.00   £3.00
CCTV, anticlimb fencing, security guards
Ample room for manoeuvring
Quiet area. Fridge lorry area

DRIVER FACILITIES
Showers – 10 unisex (£2.00), washroom, rest area, TV, clothing for sale, truckers' accessories, CB repairs/sales
Takeaway food

Restaurant open 05:00-23:00 Tues, Wed, Thurs, 06:00-23:00 Mon and Sat, 15:00-20:00 Sun. Shop open 24 hours from 07:00 Sun-12:00 Sat. Bar open 05:00-23:00 Mon-Fri, 15:00-22:00 Sun. All other on-site facilities 24 hours **T499**

Nunney Catch Café & Truckstop

Ford Fuels Ltd, Nunney Road, Nunney Catch nr Frome, Somerset BA11 4NZ
T 01373 836331

ON THE A361 Take the A361 from Shepton Mallet towards Frome. Nunney Catch Café is on your left at the roundabout with the A359, 3 miles before the town of Frome.

CREDIT/DEBIT CARDS

FUEL CARDS (see key on page 6)
❶❷❸❿

TRUCK FACILITIES
P £1.00
Coach parking available, shared with LGV
Floodlighting, CCTV. Quiet area
Ample room for manoeuvring
Truck dealership/workshop nearby
Tyre repair/sales nearby
Windscreen repair nearby

DRIVER FACILITIES
Showers, washroom, TV, takeaway food

SITE COMMENTS/INFORMATION
Parking is free if paying to draw cash

Parking and bunker fuel 24 hours. All other on-site facilities 07:00-19:30 Mon-Thur, 07:00-16:30 Fri, 07:30-13:00 Sat **T500**

Penrith Truckstop

Penrith Ind. Est., Penrith Cumbria CA11 9EH
T 01768 866995

M6 JUNCTION 40 OFF A592 Signposted from junction 40 of the M6. Take A592 into Ullswater Road then left into Hawsater Road. Penrith Truckstop will be on your right.

CREDIT/DEBIT CARDS

FUEL CARDS (see key on page 6)
❶❷❸

TRUCK FACILITIES
P with voucher £10.00
Voucher value – £2.00 and free shower
Quiet area. Fridge lorry area
Ample room for manoeuvring
Truck dealership/workshop on-site

DRIVER FACILITIES
Accommodation on-site, single £17.99
Showers (free to overnight patrons), rest area, TV, internet, phone top-ups/accessories, clothing for sale, truckers' accessories, CB repairs/sales
Takeaway food. Train/tram nearby

Parking and fuel 24 hours. All other facilities 24 hours from between 06:00 Mon-13:00 Sat, 12:00-22:00 Sun **T501**

Poplar 2000 Services & Truckstop

Cliff Lane, Lymm
Cheshire WA13 0SP
T 01925 757777

OFF THE A50 From junction 20 M6 northbound or junction 9 M56 in either direction exit onto the sliproad and turn right at 3 consecutive roundabouts. From junction 20 M6 southbound, exit onto sliproad, across 1st roundabout and right at the next.

CREDIT/DEBIT CARDS

FUEL CARDS (see key on page 6)
① ② ③ ⑤ ⑥ ⑩

TRUCK FACILITIES
P £8.00
Coach parking (13 spaces)
Quiet area. Fridge lorry area
Ample room for manoeuvring
Credit/debit cards at auto bunker
Truck washing facilities
Truck dealership/workshop

DRIVER FACILITIES
Accommodation on-site, Travelodge
Showers (charge), rest area, TV, phone
top-ups/accessories, clothing for sale,
truckers' accessories, CB repairs/sales
Takeaway food

Travelodge opening times unknown. All other on-site facilities accessible 24 hours

T502

Portsmouth Truckstop & Lorry Park

C H Jones Ltd, Walton road
Railway Triangle Ind. Est., Farlington
Portsmouth, Hampshire PO6 1UJ
T 023 92376000

OFF THE A2030 From M27, head eastbound onto the A27 towards A3M and Chichester. Take the next exit, turn left onto A2030. Take the next immediate left. At the end of the road go left then next right. Truckstop is on the right before bridge.

CREDIT/DEBIT CARDS

FUEL CARDS (see key on page 6)
① ② ③ ④⑥

TRUCK FACILITIES
P *with voucher*   **P** *only*   *Voucher value*
£11.00   £8.00   £4.00
Coach parking available (10 spaces)
Quiet area. Fridge lorry area
Ample room for manoeuvring
Truck dealership/workshop

DRIVER FACILITIES
Accommodation on-site, £14.00 pn
Showers (free), rest area, TV, laundry
service, internet, phone top-
ups/accessories, clothing for sale,
truckers' accessories, takeaway food

All on-site facilities accessible 24 hours

T503

Roll Inn Motel & Truckstop

10 Tan House Lane, Widnes
Cheshire WA8 0RR
T 0151 4246355

OFF THE A562 Exit the M62 at junction 7 and take the A557 towards Widnes for 2 miles. At the junction with the A562, turn left into it for 400 yards. At the next roundabout turn right into Tan House Lane and then immediately left. Roll Inn is on your left.

CREDIT/DEBIT CARDS

FUEL CARDS (see key on page 6)
① ② ③ ④

TRUCK FACILITIES
P *with voucher*   **P** *only*   *Voucher value*
£11.00   £6.00   £5.00
Ample room for manoeuvring
Quiet area
Truck washing facilities
Truck dealership/workshop

DRIVER FACILITIES
Accommodation on-site, £20 pn
Showers (free), washroom, rest area, TV,
phone top-ups/accessories

All on-site facilities accessible 24 hours

T504

Route 46

Formerly Vale Truckstop, Cheltenham Road Ashton Under Hill, nr Evesham Worcestershire WR11 7QP
T 01386 881321

ON THE A46 From junction 9 of the M5, take the A46 towards Evesham. Continue for 3 miles after the junction with the A435. Route 46 is on the right-hand side, opposite the turning for Ashton Under Hill village.

CREDIT/DEBIT CARDS

FUEL CARDS (see key on page 6)
③⑧

TRUCK FACILITIES
P with voucher £12.00. Free meal
Coach parking available (10 spaces)
Night time security guard. Quiet area
Ample room for manoeuvring

DRIVER FACILITIES
Accommodation on-site £18.00
Showers (free if parking overnight), rest area, TV, takeaway food

SITE COMMENTS/INFORMATION
This site has been open for 25 years and offers a great mixed grill in the restaurant

Parking, adjoining shop and fuel 24 hours. Other on-site facilities 24 hours from 06:00 Mon-20:00 Fri **T505**

Silvey's Truckstop

Silvey Oils Ltd, Oakleigh Acres Draycott Cerne, Chippenham Wiltshire SN15 5LH
T 01249 750645

M4 JUNCTION 17 ON THE B4122 From the M4, exit at junction 17 and take the B4122 towards Sutton Benger. Silvey's Truckstop is about half a mile on the right-hand side.

CREDIT/DEBIT CARDS

FUEL CARDS (see key on page 6)
①②③⑩㉛

TRUCK FACILITIES
P with voucher   P only   Voucher value
£12.00   £9.00   £3.50
Ample room for manoeuvring
Quiet area. Fridge lorry area
Truck washing facilities
Truck dealership/workshop

DRIVER FACILITIES
Showers – 6 m, 1 f (charge), washroom, rest area, TV, phone top-ups/accessories, clothing for sale, truckers' accessories
Takeaway food

SITE COMMENTS/INFORMATION
Wide selection of foods available

Parking and fuel 24 hours. Showers 24 hours between 06:00 Mon and 11:00 Sat. Restaurant 06:00 and 23:00 **T506**

South Mimms Services & Truckstop

Welcome Break Ltd Old St Albans Road, South Mimms Hertfordshire EN6 3NE
T 01707 649998

M25 JUNCTION 23

CREDIT/DEBIT CARDS

FUEL CARDS (see key on page 6)
①②③⑤⑥⑩

DRIVER FACILITIES
Accommodation on-site
 3 hotels, all within 600 yards
Showers, washroom
Takeaway food

All on-site facilities accessible 24 hours **T507**

Swindon Truckstop

**Oxford Road, Stratton St Margaret
Swindon, Wiltshire SN3 4ER
T 01793 824812**
www.swindontruckstop.co.uk

ON THE A420 From M4 junction 15 continue along the A419 for several miles. Take A420 towards Oxford. Turn right at the next roundabout, continue past Sainsburys onto the service access road into Swindon Truckstop's lorry park.

CREDIT/DEBIT CARDS

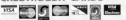

FUEL CARDS (see key on page 6)

① ② ③ ④ ⑩ ⑫ ⑬ ⑮ ㉕ ㉗ ㉘ ㉜ ㉝ ㊷

TRUCK FACILITIES
P *with voucher* £8.50, *Voucher* = £1.00
Coach parking. Quiet area
Fridge lorry area – electric hook-ups avail.
Ample room for manoeuvring
Truck dealership/workshop, tyre repair/sales and windscreen repair nearby
DRIVER FACILITIES
Accommodation nearby, 600 yards, Madison Inn
Showers (charge), TV, truckers' accessories, takeaway food
Phone top-ups/accessories nearby

Parking 24 hours. Other on-site facilities 06:00-22:00 Mon-Fri, 06:00-12:00 Sat **T508**

T Baden Hardstaff

**South Notts Truckstop, Hillside
Gotham Road, Kingston on Soar
Nottingham, Nottinghamshire NG11 0DF
T 01159 831234**

OFF THE A453 From M1 junction 24, take A453 towards Nottingham. Continue for 3 miles then turn right towards West Leake and Gotham. Continue for half a mile then turn right towards Kingston on Soar. Truckstop is 200 yards on the left.

CREDIT/DEBIT CARDS

FUEL CARDS (see key on page 6)
①

TRUCK FACILITIES
P £6.00
Ample room for manoeuvring
Quiet area. Fridge lorry area
Truck washing facilities

DRIVER FACILITIES
Showers – 6 m, 1 f (free), washroom

Parking accessible 24 hours. Other on-site facilities accessible 08:00-18:00 **T509**

Tebay Truckstop

**M6 Diesel Services Ltd & Westmorland Ltd
Tebay, Penrith, Cumbria CA10 3SS
T 015396 24336/624511**

M6 JUNCTION 38 OFF THE A685 Exit junction 38 of the M6 and take the A685 towards Kirkby Stephen. Turn left at the next roundabout onto the B6260 and Tebay Truckstop is on the right.

CREDIT/DEBIT CARDS

FUEL CARDS (see key on page 6)
① ② ③ ④ ⑩ ⑬

TRUCK FACILITIES
P *with voucher* £5.00
P *only* – 2 hours £1.00, £3.50 overnight
Voucher value £1.50
Ample room for manoeuvring
Quiet area
Truck washing facilities
DRIVER FACILITIES
Hot drinks free to truckers
Showers – 3 m, 1 f (free), TV
Truckers' accessories
SITE COMMENTS/INFORMATION
Newly refurbished site

Café accessible 07:00-23:00. All other on-site facilities accessible 24 hours **T510**

The Avon Lodge Truckstop

Third Way, Avonmouth, Bristol
South Gloucestershire BS11 9YP
T 0117 9827706

M5 JUNCTION 18 OFF THE A4 From Junction 18 of the M5 keep to the far right-hand lane off the sliproad, following signs to Avonmouth and industrial estates. At the roundabout turn right onto Avonmouth Way, then next left onto Third Way. The Truckstop is round the bend on the left.

CREDIT/DEBIT CARDS

FUEL CARDS (see key on page 6)
① ② ③ ⑤ ⑥ ⑩

TRUCK FACILITIES
P *with voucher* £12.00
Voucher value £2.50
Quiet area. Ample room for manoeuvring
Truck washing facilities
Truck dealership/workshop
Tyre repair/sales nearby

DRIVER FACILITIES
Accommodation on-site, £12 pn
Showers (free if parking), rest area, TV, phone top-ups/accessories, clothing for sale, truckers' accessories, CB repairs/sales
Takeaway food. Train/tram nearby

Bunker fuel 24 hours. Parking 07:00-21:30 Mon, 06:00-21:30, 06:00-21:30 Tues-Fri, 06:00-23:30 Sat, closed Sun **T511**
Café 07:00-20:00 Mon, 06:00-20:00 Tues-Fri, 06:00-11:00 Sat

The Burnside

36 Hirst Road, Harthill
Lanarkshire WL7 5TN
T 01501 751430

ON THE B7066 Exit the M8 at junction 5 and take the B7075 towards Shotts and Stane. After 200 yards turn left onto the B7066 towards Harthill. The Burnside is 800 yards on the right.

CREDIT/DEBIT CARDS
VISA · MasterCard · AmEx · DELTA

FUEL CARDS (see key on page 6)

TRUCK FACILITIES
P *with voucher* £9.00
Voucher value 2 course meal
Ample room for manoeuvring
Coach parking available (10 spaces)
Quiet area

DRIVER FACILITIES
Showers – 4 m, 1 f (charge), washroom, rest area, TV, internet access
Takeaway food

Parking accessible 24 hours. Other on-site facilities accessible 05:30-01:00 **T512**

The Last Drop

Tayside Truckstop, Smeaton Road
West Gourdie Ind. Est., Dundee
Angus DD2 4UT

OFF THE A90 From Perth, take the A90 to Dundee and around the north side of the town. Turn left into Myrekirk Road at the roundabout signposted to Gourdie Industrial Estate. Continue to the end of the road then turn right and right again and it's on your right.

CREDIT/DEBIT CARDS

FUEL CARDS (see key on page 6)
① ② ③

TRUCK FACILITIES
P up to 2 hours free. Overnight £8
Coach parking (4 spaces). CCTV
Ample room for manoeuvring
Quiet area. Fridge lorry area
Truck washing facilities
Truck dealership/workshop

DRIVER FACILITIES
Accomm. nearby, half a mile, Travelodge
Showers – 3 unisex (free), washroom, rest area, TV, Euros changed/accepted
Takeaway food

Parking & bunker fuel 24 hours. Bar 12:00-23:00 Mon-Thu, 12:00-00:00 Fri, 11:00-00:00 Sat, 12:30-23:00 Sun **T513**
Restaurant 07:30-20:45 Mon, 06:30-20:45 Tue-Fri, 07:30-23:45 Sat. Other on-site facilities accessible 06:30-21:00

The Stockyard

Hellaby Industrial Estate, Hellaby
South Yorkshire S66 8HN
T 01709 730083/700200

M18 JUNCTION 1 OFF THE A631 Exit the M18 at
junction 1 and take the A631 towards Maltby for 200 yards.
At next roundabout turn left into Denby Way. Follow road
around and The Stockyard is on the left.

CREDIT/DEBIT CARDS

FUEL CARDS (see key on page 6)

TRUCK FACILITIES
P *with voucher* £7.00, *voucher* = £1.50
Quiet area. Fridge lorry area
Ample room for manoeuvring
Truck dealership/workshop
DRIVER FACILITIES
Accommodation nearby, half a mile,
   Campanile & Hellaby Hall
Showers (free), rest area, TV, clothing for
sale, truckers' accessories, takeaway food
SITE COMMENTS/INFORMATION
At the time of going to print, this site
did not provide fuel however this is soon
to be introduced along with security
features and a re-surfaced lorry park

Parking accessible 24 hours. Other on-site facilities accessible 05:00-23:00 **T514**

Truckhaven

Carnforth Truckstop, Scotland Road
Warton, Carnforth, Lancashire LA5 9RQ
T 01524 736699

ON THE A6 From the M6 junction 35, join the A601M
towards Carnforth and Morcambe. At the first roundabout
turn left onto the A6. Continue for 200 yards and Truckhaven
is on your right.

CREDIT/DEBIT CARDS

FUEL CARDS (see key on page 6)
① ② ④ ⑦ ⑭ ㉛ ㊳

TRUCK FACILITIES
P *with voucher* £8.00 inc. eve. meal
Voucher value £1.50
Ample room for manoeuvring
24 hour patrols, CCTV. Quiet area

DRIVER FACILITIES
Accomm. on-site, £17.50 single,
   £22.50 twin
Showers – 8 m, 2 f (free), washroom,
rest area, TV, truckers' accessories
Takeaway food

Fuel, parking and showers 24 hours. Other on-site facilities closed between 23:00 Fri and 7:00 Sat, 23:00 Sat and 05:00 Sun **T515**

Truckworld

Team Flitwick Ltd, Oliver Road
West Thurrock, Grays, Essex RM20 3ED
T 01708 860040

OFF THE A126 If heading south, exit M25 at junction 30, if
heading north exit at 31. Take the A1306 to Lakeside
Shopping. Turn right at next roundabout onto B186, across 3
roundabouts. At 4th, take A126. Across next roundabout,
then sharp right. Truckworld on right.

CREDIT/DEBIT CARDS

FUEL CARDS (see key on page 6)
① ② ③ ⑩

TRUCK FACILITIES
P *with voucher* £10.00, *voucher* = £2.50
Coach parking shared with LGV
Fencing, floodlights, CCTV and 24 hour
guarding
Quiet area. Fridge lorry area
Ample room for manoeuvring
Truck washing facilities, tyre repair/sales
DRIVER FACILITIES
Accomm. on-site, £20 single, £44 double
Showers, rest area, TV, laundry service,
Euros changed/accepted, truckers'
accessories, CB repairs/sales, takeaway food

Restaurant 06:00 23:00. Showers, parking and bunker fuel 24 hours. Other on-site facilities unknown **T516**

Watling Street Café & Filling Station

**Watling Street, Flamstead, St Albans
Hertfordshire AL3 8HA
T 01582 840215/840270**

ON THE A5 From the M1, exit at junction 9 and take the A5 towards Dunstable. Watling Street Café is 500 yards on the right-hand side.

CREDIT/DEBIT CARDS

FUEL CARDS (see key on page 6)
❶❷❸❿

TRUCK FACILITIES
P *with voucher* P *only* *Voucher value*
£8.00   £4.00   £4.00
Coach parking. Quiet area. Fridge lorry area
Ample room for manoeuvring
Credit/debit cards at auto bunker
Truck washing facilities
Truck dealership/workshop

DRIVER FACILITIES
Accommodation on-site, £8 pn
Showers (free), rest area, TV, CB repairs/sales
Takeaway food

SITE COMMENTS/INFORMATION
This site is close to the M1

Bunker fuel, parking and toilets 24 hours. Other on-site facilities accessible 06:00-21:00. Shop times unknown **T517**

Yorkies Café & Fuelserve, Risby

**Old Newmarket Road, Risby
nr Bury St Edmunds, Suffolk IP28 6QU/RU
T 01284 811772/01473 46679**

ON THE A14 Take the A14 westbound out of Bury St Edmunds for 4 miles. 1 mile after the junction with the B1106, take the sliproad for Risby. Cross the carriageway, and turn left at the T-junction then right. Yorkies and Fuelserve are on the left.

CREDIT/DEBIT CARDS

FUEL CARDS (see key on page 6)
❶❷❸

TRUCK FACILITIES
P *with voucher* £8.50
Voucher value 1 meal
Quiet area
Credit/debit cards at auto bunker

DRIVER FACILITIES
Shower – 1 m (charge), washroom, rest area, TV, clothing for sale, truckers' accessories

Bunker fuel and Parking 24 hours. Other on-site facilities 07:00-22:00 Mon-Thu, 07:00-20:00 Fri **T518**

A35 Café

Top of Town Car Park, Bridport Road Dorchester, Dorset DT1 1XT
T 01305 269199
ON THE B3150 From the A37 and A35 Dorchester Ring Road, take the B3150 into the town. Remain on the B3150 for 500 more yards after the junction with the B3144. The Military Keep is on your left and Top of Town Car Park is on the same side just past it.

CREDIT/DEBIT CARDS

FUEL CARDS (see key on page 6)

TRUCK FACILITIES
P £2.50 overnight, £1.00 for 1 hour
Coach parking available, shared with LGV
Ample room for manoeuvring
Quiet area. Truck dealership/workshop
Tyre repair/sales, truckwash and windscreen repair nearby
DRIVER FACILITIES
Accommodation nearby
Truckers' accessories. Takeaway food
Post Office, phone top-ups/accessories and clothing for sale nearby
SITE COMMENTS/INFORMATION
Town centre location

Parking and nearby fuel accessible 24 hours. Café accessible 06:45-19:00. Other on-site times may vary **TT519**

Ace Café, London

Ace Corner, Old North Circular Road Stonebridge, London NW10 7UD
T 0208 9611000 www.ace-cafe-london.com
OFF THE A406 The Ace Café is on Ace Corner which is the junction of Beresford Avenue and the Old North Circular Road. This runs parallel with the New North Circular Road (A406.) The Ace Café is in the section between the A404 Harrow Road and the A40.

CREDIT/DEBIT CARDS

FUEL CARDS (for nearby fuel)
7

TRUCK FACILITIES
Coach parking available, shared with LGV
Quiet area
Truck dealership/workshop, tyre repair/sales, truckwash and windscreen repair nearby
DRIVER FACILITIES
Accommodation nearby, Holiday Inn
Rest area, TV, internet access, Euros changed/accepted, clothing for sale, Takeaway food
Phone top-ups/accessories nearby
SITE COMMENTS
Train/tram nearby
World famous biker café. See website

Most on-site facilities 07:00-23:00. Parking not accessible 24 hours. Fuel accessible 24 hours nearby **TT520**

Airport Café

Main Road, Sellindge, nr Lymne Kent TN25 6DA
8 01303 813185

ON THE A20 If heading west along the M20 exit at junction 11 and take the A20 to Sellindge. Continue for 2 and a half miles and Airport Café is on the right about 1 mile before the village of Sellindge.

CREDIT/DEBIT CARDS

FUEL CARDS (see key on page 6)

TRUCK FACILITIES
Coach parking available, shared with LGV
Ample room for manoeuvring
Quiet area

Parking accessible 24 hours. All other on-site facilities accessible 08:00-15:00 Mon-Fri, 08:00-12:00 Sat **TT521**

Barny's Café De Chauffeur

Melton Ross Road, Barnetby le Wold Brigg, North East Lincolnshire DN38 6LB
T 01652 688931/880966

ON THE A18 Come off junction 5 of the M180 interchange before it becomes the A180. Follow signs for the A18 and Humberside airport. Barney's is located 400 yards along on the right.

CREDIT/DEBIT CARDS

FUEL CARDS (see key on page 6)

TRUCK FACILITIES
P *with voucher*   P *only*   *Voucher value*
£6.50   £5.50   £1.50
Coach parking (4 spaces). Quiet area
Fridge lorry area, swich off by 22:00
Ample room for manoeuvring
Truck dealership/workshop nearby
Tyre repair/sales nearby
DRIVER FACILITIES
Accommodation nearby, B&B, in village
Showers (charge), rest area, TV, internet,
Euros changed/accepted, truckers'
accessories, CB repairs/sales, takeaway food
SITE COMMENTS/INFORMATION
Home cooked food and air conditioning

Parking, nearby fuel and shop 24 hours. Other on-site facilities 06:00-21:00 Mon-Fri, 06:00-14:00 Sat, 07:00-17:00 Sun **TT522**

Billie Jeans Café

The Nant, Pentre Halkyn, Holywell Flintshire CH8 8BD
T 01352 781118/712144

ON THE A55 If heading towards Chester on the A55, take the sliproad signposted for Pentre Halkyn and turn right at the T-junction. Billie Jeans Café is on the left-hand side of the re-entry sliproad, just before you go back onto the A5.

CREDIT/DEBIT CARDS

FUEL CARDS (see key on page 6)

TRUCK FACILITIES
P *with voucher*   P *only*   *Voucher value*
£6.50   £3.00   1 meal
Ample room for manoeuvring
Quiet area. Floodlighting
Truck dealership/workshop

DRIVER FACILITIES
Accommodation nearby, half a mile
Takeaway food

Toilets and parking 24 hours. Other on-site facilities 07:30-17:00 Mon-Thur, 07:30-15:30 Fri, 07:30-12:00 Sat **TT523**

Burnzie's Transport Café

10a Skipton Road, Steeton, Keighley West Yorkshire BD20 6NR
T 01535 656120

ON THE B6265 From the A629 take the A6068 towards Colne. Continue for 400 yards then take the B6265 Skipton road. Continue for 2 miles and Burnzie's is on that road in the middle of Steeton on the left-hand side.

CREDIT/DEBIT CARDS

FUEL CARDS (see key on page 6)

TRUCK FACILITIES
P *with voucher*   P *only*   *Voucher value*
£5.00   £2.00   £3.00
Coach parking available, shared with LGV
Ample room for manoeuvring
Quiet area
Truck dealership/workshop
DRIVER FACILITIES
Clothing shop
Takeaway food

SITE COMMENTS/INFORMATION
Train/tram nearby
Good quality food and value for money

Parking accessible 24 hours. Other on-site facilities accessible 07:00-15:00 **TT524**

By Pass Café

**Great North Road, Cromwell Halt
Newark, Nottinghamshire NG23 6JF
T 01636 822321**

ON THE A1 If heading north from Newark on the A1, the By Pass Café is on the left just after the turnings for Cromwell and just before you get to Carlton on Trent.

CREDIT/DEBIT CARDS

FUEL CARDS (see key on page 6)

TRUCK FACILITIES
P free
Quiet area
Truck dealership/workshop

DRIVER FACILITIES
Showers – m & f (free), washroom, TV, clothing for sale

SITE COMMENTS/INFORMATION
All meals made from fresh produce

Parking accessible 24 hours. All other on-site facilities accessible 06:00-20:00 Mon-Sun

TT525

Caenby Corner Café

**Caenby Corner, Glentham, Market Rasen
Lincolnshire LN8 3AR
T 01673 878388**

ON THE A15 From Lincoln, take the A15 north towards the M180. Caenby Corner Café is near Glentham on the left-hand side at the junction with the A631.

CREDIT/DEBIT CARDS

FUEL CARDS (see key on page 6)

TRUCK FACILITIES
P free. Quiet area
Ample room for manoeuvring

DRIVER FACILITIES
Washroom, rest area
Takeaway food
Phone top-ups/accessories nearby

SITE COMMENTS/INFORMATION
Easy access for LGVs. This site is soon due for major redevelopment, to include Hotel, bar, filling station, restaurant and new parking area

Parking and nearby filling station accessible 24 hours. Other on-site facilities accessible 06:30-22:00

TT526

Café Royal

**Tannery Road, off West Street, Bridport
Dorset DT6 1QX
T 01308 422012**

OFF THE A35 From Charmouth on the A35, take the B3162 towards Bridport and Tannery Road is about 1 mile along on the left. Or from Beaminster on the A3066, turn right at the junction with the A35 onto the B3162. Tannery Road is 600 yards on the left.

CREDIT/DEBIT CARDS

FUEL CARDS (see key on page 6)

TRUCK FACILITIES
Coach parking available (15 spaces)
Ample room for manoeuvring
Quiet area

DRIVER FACILITIES
Washroom, TV
Phone top-ups/accessories nearby

SITE COMMENTS/INFORMATION
Situated in the bus station complex, very close to the town centre. Play area for kids and pool table on site. Nearby seaside walks

Parking accessibility times unknown. All other on-site facilities accessible 07:00-23:00

TT527

Carlton Transport Café

Arterial Road, Wickford
Essex SS12 9HZ
T 01268 727313

ON THE A127 From the A13, take the A130 towards Battlesbridge. After 1 mile turn left onto the A127 towards Basildon. Carlton Transport Café is 1 mile along on the right.

CREDIT/DEBIT CARDS

FUEL CARDS (see key on page 6)

TRUCK FACILITIES
Coach parking available
Ample room for manoeuvring
Overnight parking nearby

DRIVER FACILITIES
Washroom
Takeaway food

All on-site facilities accessible 08:00-13:00 — **TT528**

Cartgate Diner

Cartgate Service Area
Cartgate roundabout, Tintinhull
nr Yeovil, Somerset BA22 8

ON THE A303 If heading from Ilminster to Yeovil on the A303, Cartgate Service Area is on the left-hand side at the roundabout with the A3088.

CREDIT/DEBIT CARDS

FUEL CARDS (see key on page 6)

TRUCK FACILITIES
P free
Coach parking. Quiet area. Fridge lorry area
Ample room for manoeuvring

DRIVER FACILITIES
Shower – 1 unisex (charge), washroom, TV, truckers' accessories
Takeaway food

SITE COMMENTS/INFORMATION
Site run by truck owners. Provides huge portions of food for the hungriest of men! Discounts and loyalty cards available. Recently refurbished site

All on-site facilities accessible 24 hours — **TT529**

Cedar Transport Café

Harelawside, Grantshouse, Duns
Berwickshire TD11 3RP
T 01361 850371

OFF THE A1 From Dunbar, take the A1 to Berwick upon Tweed. Continue for 200 yards past the turning for the A6112 and take the next left into a 'crescent'. The Cedar Café will be on your left-hand side.

CREDIT/DEBIT CARDS

FUEL CARDS (see key on page 6)

TRUCK FACILITIES
P free
Coach parking available (6 spaces)
Quiet area
Ample room for manoeuvring

DRIVER FACILITIES
Showers – 1 m, 1 f (charge), washroom, TV
Takeaway food

SITE COMMENTS/INFORMATION
Varied menu. Winner of *Commercial Motor*'s best truckstop and best breakfast awards

08:00-20:00 Sun-Fri, 08:00-17:00 Sat. Parking accessible 24 hours — **TT530**

Frankie's Café

Bridge Road, Sutton Bridge, Spalding Lincolnshire PE12 9SH
T 01406 350180

ON THE OLD A17 From Kings Lynn, take A17 west for 10 miles. At Sutton Bridge take B1359 into the village. Frankie's is 1 mile on the right-hand side. From Holbeach take the A17, turn left at roundabout with A1101 for half mile then right at T-junction, continue for 2 miles.

CREDIT/DEBIT CARDS

FUEL CARDS (for nearby fuel)

TRUCK FACILITIES
Lorry park situated across road
P free. Coach parking
Ample room for manoeuvring
Quiet area nearby

DRIVER FACILITIES
Accommodation on-site, £20 B&B
Showers – 1 unisex (charge)
Takeaway food

SITE COMMENTS/INFORMATION
Traditional transport café, operational for 50 years. Family run, all home made food from fresh produce

Parking and nearby filling station with shop and toilets 24 hours. Other on-site facilities 06:00-15:00 **TT531**

George's Diner

361 North Woolwich Road, Silvertown London, Greater London E16 2BS
T 0207 4762379

OFF THE A1011 From the A13 at Newham, take the A1011 towards Royal Victoria Dock. Continue until the roundabout with the A112. Take the second exit and George's Diner is on the left.

CREDIT/DEBIT CARDS

FUEL CARDS (see key on page 6)

TRUCK FACILITIES
P £5.00
Ample room for manoeuvring

DRIVER FACILITIES
Accommodation nearby, half a mile, Sunborn Yacht
Showers – 1 m, 1 f (free), washroom
Takeaway food

SITE COMMENTS/INFORMATION
Train/tram nearby
This site is 6 miles from the centre of London

Parking and shop times unknown. Other on-site facilities 06:00-19:00. Nearby fuel 24 hours **TT532**

Glan-Yr-Afon Restaurant

Glan-Yr-Afon, nr Corwen Gwynedd LL21 0HA
T 01490 460420

ON THE A494 From the A5 heading east, go through the village of Corwen, continue for a few miles before turning left onto the A494 towards Bala. Glan-Yr-Afon Café is a few miles along on the right next to the Texaco garage.

CREDIT/DEBIT CARDS

FUEL CARDS (see key on page 6)

TRUCK FACILITIES
P £5.00-£10.00
Coach parking (5 spaces) shared with LGV
Quiet area

DRIVER FACILITIES
Accommodation nearby
Rest area
Takeaway food
Clothing for sale nearby

SITE COMMENTS/INFORMATION
Lovely friendly atmosphere and customer focused staff

On-site and nearby parking 24 hours. Other on-site facilities 08:00-20:00 Mon-Sun **TT533**

Greasy Joe's Café

**Kings Meadow Lorry Park
Old Swindon Road, Cirencester
Gloucestershire GL7 1
T 01285 640275**

OFF THE A419 From Swindon take the A419 towards Cirencester. At the McDonald's roundabout on the outskirts of the town turn left and Greasy Joe's is on your right.

CREDIT/DEBIT CARDS

FUEL CARDS (see key on page 6)

TRUCK FACILITIES
Ample room for manoeuvring
Truck dealership/workshop
Tyre repair/sales nearby

DRIVER FACILITIES
Accommodation on-site, £6 pn
Shower – 1 unisex (free), washroom, TV
Phone top-ups/accessories
Clothing for sale
Takeaway food

Parking, nearby fuel and shop accessible 24 hours. Other on-site facilities accessible 06:00-18:00   **TT534**

Harbour Café

**21 Harbour Quay, Wick, Caithness
Highland KW1 5EP
T 01955 602433**

ON THE A99 From the A882 follow signs for Wick town centre. Turn left at the junction with the A99 into Cliff Road, continue for a few yards. Turn right into River Street and follow it around along Martha Terrace, then sharp left into Harbour Quay.

CREDIT/DEBIT CARDS

FUEL CARDS (see key on page 6)

TRUCK FACILITIES
Lorry park opposite at harbour front
P free. Coach parking
Ample room for manoeuvring
Truck dealership/workshop nearby

DRIVER FACILITIES
Accommodation on-site, £17.00 room only, £22.00 B&B
Takeaway food
Clothing for sale nearby

SITE COMMENTS/INFORMATION
Train/tram nearby
Close to town centre facilities

Nearby parking accessible 24 hours at harbour front. Other on-site facilities accessible 07:00-22:00   **TT535**

Harbour Restaurant

**Shore Road, Perth Harbour, Perth
Perth and Kinross PH2 8BD
T 01738 625788**

OFF THE A912 If heading south, exit at junction 9 of M90 and re-enter the carriageway heading north. Exit at junction 10 onto the A192 towards Perth. In three quarters of a mile turn right into Friarton Road. Harbour Restaurant is half a mile on the right.

CREDIT/DEBIT CARDS

FUEL CARDS (see key on page 6)

TRUCK FACILITIES
P free. Quiet area
Ample room for manoeuvring

DRIVER FACILITIES
Accommodation on-site, £25.00 B&B
Shower – 1 m, (charge), washroom

SITE COMMENTS/INFORMATION
Please note that there is considerably more parking available around this site in the evening and throughout the night than is available during the day. Phone for more details

Parking 24 hours. All other on-site facilities 06:30-18:00 Mon-Thurs, 06:30-16:00 Fri, 08:00-13:00 Sat
Nearby shop and fuel 24 hours   **TT536**

Hillside Café

**Codford Road, Codford, Warminster
Wiltshire BA12 0JZ
T 01985 850712**

ON THE A36 The Hillside Café can be found on the right-hand side of the A36 Salisbury to Bath road just after the village of Codford and 3 miles beyond the junction with the A303 if heading north.

CREDIT/DEBIT CARDS

FUEL CARDS (for nearby fuel)

TRUCK FACILITIES
P *only* £7.00
Ample room for manoeuvring
Quiet area
Truck dealership/workshop nearby

DRIVER FACILITIES
Washroom, rest area
Takeaway food

SITE COMMENTS/INFORMATION
Clean and friendly site. Home cooked food

Parking 24 hours. Nearby fuels 05:00-20:00. Other on-site facilities 06:00-19:00 Mon-Thurs, 06:00-17:00 Fri, 06:00-11:45 Sat   **TT537**

Horse Shoe Café

**Abernyte Road, Inchture, Tayside
Perth and Kinross PH14 9
T 01828 686283**

ON THE A90 If heading to Dundee from Perth, exit at the Inchture interchange and turn left onto the B953 towards Abernyte and the Horse Shoe Café is about half a mile along on the left.

CREDIT/DEBIT CARDS

FUEL CARDS (see key on page 6)

TRUCK FACILITIES
P free
Ample room for manoeuvring
Quiet area
Truck dealership/workshop

DRIVER FACILITIES
Washroom
Takeaway food

SITE COMMENTS/INFORMATION
Plans to build shower block and more parking spaces underway
Refurbishment planned soon

Parking and nearby fuel accessible 24 hours. Other on-site facilities accessible 07:30-21:00   **TT538**

Jacks Hill Café

**Watling Street, Towcester
Northamptonshire NN12 8ET
T 01327 851350/350522**

ON THE A5 From M1 turn left at junction 15A onto the A43 towards Oxford. Continue until roundabout with the A5. Turn right onto the A5 towards Weedon and Jacks Hill Café is on the left-hand side.

CREDIT/DEBIT CARDS

FUEL CARDS (see key on page 6)

TRUCK FACILITIES
P *with voucher* £5.00
Coach parking (ring in advance)
Ample room for manoeuvring
Quiet area

DRIVER FACILITIES
Accomm. on-site £10 pn, incl. parking
Showers – (charge), washroom, rest area,
TV, Euros changed/accepted, clothing for sale, truckers' accessories, CB repairs/sales,
Takeaway food

SITE COMMENTS/INFORMATION
Air conditioned café

Showers, toilets and parking 24 hours. Café 06:00- 21:30 Mon-Fri, 06:00-14:00 Sat, 07:00-14:30 Sun.
TV room and bar 18:00-23:00 Mon-Thurs   **TT539**

Johns Cross Café

Robertsbridge, Battle
East Sussex TN32 5JH
T 01580 881911

ON THE A21 From Hastings take the A21 northbound towards Royal Tunbridge Wells. Continue for 1 mile beyond the junction with the A2100 and Johns Cross Café is on your left, 600 yards before Poppinghole Lane on your right.

CREDIT/DEBIT CARDS

FUEL CARDS (see key on page 6)

TRUCK FACILITIES
P with voucher £8.00
Voucher value £3.00
Coach parking by prior arrangement, shared with LGV
Ample room for manoeuvring
Quiet area

DRIVER FACILITIES
TV
Takeaway food

Parking and payphone 24 hours. All other on-site facilities 07:00-17:00 Mon-Sun | **TT540**

Let's Eat Café

Tarporley Road, Lower Whitley
Warrington, Cheshire WA4 4EZ
T 01928 717322

ON THE A49 From the M56, exit at junction 10 and take the A49 south towards Whitchurch. Let's Eat Café is 3 miles further on the right-hand side, 800 yards before the junction with the A533.

CREDIT/DEBIT CARDS

FUEL CARDS (see key on page 6)

TRUCK FACILITIES
P with voucher   P only   Voucher value
£10.00   £6.00   £4.00
Coach parking (10 spaces)
Quiet area
Ample room for manoeuvring

DRIVER FACILITIES
Showers – 2 m, 2 f (free), TV
Phone top-ups/accessories
Takeaway food

SITE COMMENTS/INFORMATION
Clean friendly, newly refurbished café seating 50

Parking 24 hours. Other on-site facilities 07:00-19:00 Mon-Thurs, 07:00-15:00 Fri, 08:00-13:00 Sat & Sun | **TT541**

Limes Café

Old Rufford Road, Bilsthorpe
nr Mansfield, Nottinghamshire NG22 8
T 01623 411254

ON THE A614 From Ollerton, take the A614 south towards Nottingham. Limes Café is 3 miles on the right-hand side, close to the village of Bilsthorpe and about 1 and a half miles before the roundabout with the A617.

CREDIT/DEBIT CARDS

FUEL CARDS (see key on page 6)

TRUCK FACILITIES
P free
Ample room for manoeuvring
Quiet area

DRIVER FACILITIES
Accommodation on-site, £15 pn
Washroom
Takeaway food

SITE COMMENTS/INFORMATION
This site has been established for more than 50 years providing home cooked food using fresh produce

Parking facilities accessible 24 hours. Other on-site facilities accessible 07:00-18:00 | **TT542**

Lincoln Farm Café

**Kenilworth Road, Hampton in Arden
West Midlands B92 0LS
T 01675 442301/442769**

ON THE A452 From M42 exit at junction 6, take A45
towards Coventry then take A452 Kenilworth Road towards
Kenilworth, across junction with B4102 and Lincoln Farm
Café is about 2 miles further on the right-hand side.

CREDIT/DEBIT CARDS

FUEL CARDS (see key on page 6)

TRUCK FACILITIES
P *with voucher* £8.50 *Voucher value* £3.50
Ample room for manoeuvring
Quiet area. Night attendant

DRIVER FACILITIES
Accommodation on-site, £15 pn B&B
Showers – 7 unisex (free to overnight
visitors), rest area, TV, Euros
changed/accepted, truckers' accessories
Takeaway food

SITE COMMENTS/INFORMATION
Good value, home cooked food and
drinks. Friendly staff and atmosphere

Parking 24 hours. Nearby fuel and other on-site facilities 06:00-24:00 Monday, 04:00-24:00 Tues-Fri   **TT543**

Little Bistro

**Burneston, Bedale
North Yorkshire DL8 2JJ
T 01845 567990**

ON THE A1 SOUTHBOUND Little Bistro is set back from
the road on the A1 southbound carriageway, 4 miles south of
Leeming Bar, 1 mile after the turning for Gatenby but before
the turning for Pickhill.

CREDIT/DEBIT CARDS

FUEL CARDS (see key on page 6)

TRUCK FACILITIES
P *with voucher*   P *only*   *Voucher value*
£6.00   free   £6.00
Coach parking (10 spaces)
Ample room for manoeuvring

DRIVER FACILITIES
Showers – 3 m, 3 f (free), washroom,
rest area, TV, clothing shop, truckers'
accessories, takeaway food

SITE COMMENTS/INFORMATION
All food freshly cooked. Friendly staff,
quick service and high standards. Good
atmosphere and a pleasant environment

Parking accessible 24 hours. Other on-site facilities accessible 07:00-21:00   **TT544**

Lynn's Raven Café

**Prees Heath, Whitchurch
Shropshire SY13 2AF
T 01948 665691**

ON THE A41 A49 INTERSECTION If coming from
Whitchurch, take the A41 south to the roundabout with the
A49. Take the 3rd exit off the roundabout and follow the
road as it bends to the right. Lynn's Raven Café is 100 yards
on your left.

CREDIT/DEBIT CARDS

FUEL CARDS (see key on page 6)

TRUCK FACILITIES
Coach parking shared with LGV
Ample room for manoeuvring
Quiet area. Floodlighting

DRIVER FACILITIES
Accommodation next door, Raven Pub
Showers – unisex, washroom, rest area, TV,
internet access, Euros changed/accepted
Takeaway food

SITE COMMENTS/INFORMATION
Sunday carvery 12:00-14:00, snooker
table, all day breakfasts available
Café being refurbished

Parking 24 hours. Other on-site facilities 07:00-20:00 Mon, 06:00-20:00 Tues, Wed, & Thurs,
06:00-19:00 Fri, 07:00-15:00 Sat & Sun   **TT545**

Markham Moor Truckstop

**Milton Road, Markham Moor, Retford
Nottinghamshire DN22 0QU
T 01777 838921**

ON THE A1 A638 INTERCHANGE From Newark take the
A1 northbound for 15 miles. At the roundabout with the
A638 take the turning for Milton. Markham Moor Truckstop
is within 20 yards on the right-hand side.

CREDIT/DEBIT CARDS

FUEL CARDS (for nearby fuel)

TRUCK FACILITIES
P *with voucher* £10.00
Voucher value £2.00 plus shower
Coach parking available, shared with LGV
Ample room for manoeuvring
Fridge lorry area
DRIVER FACILITIES
Accomm. nearby, 50 yards, Travelodge
Showers – 3 m, 1 f (£2.00), washroom,
rest area, TV, phone top-ups/accessories
SITE COMMENTS/INFORMATION
This site has a very clean, large spacious
restaurant serving home-made
farmhouse food

Parking 24 hours. Restaurant 06:00-22:00 Mon, 05:30-22:00 Tues-Fri, 06:00-10:00 Sat. Showers 06:00-22:00 Mon-Sat **TT546**

Nell's Café & Truckstop

**Watling Street, Gravesend East
Gravesend, Kent DA12 5PU
T 01474 362457**
ON THE A2 From the A2 if heading eastbound. Continue
past the A227 exit, the Premier Lodge and Manor Hotel and
take the Gravesend East exit immediately afterwards into
Valley Drive. Follow the sliproad round and take the very next
right. Nell's is in front of you.

CREDIT/DEBIT CARDS

FUEL CARDS (see key on page 6)

TRUCK FACILITIES
P free
Coach parking available (10 spaces)
Ample room for manoeuvring
Quiet area nearby
DRIVER FACILITIES
Accommodation nearby, half a mile,
Manor Hotel & Premier Lodge
Showers – 2 m, (free), washroom, TV,
truckers' accessories, takeaway food
SITE COMMENTS/INFORMATION
Excellent location, easy to find site,
home cooked food

Nearby and on-site parking and fuel 24 hours. Other on-site facilities 0:630-20:00 **TT547**

New Oak Moor Transport Café

**304 Lichfield Road, Barton under Needwood,
nr Burton on Trent, Staffordshire DE13 8ED
T 01283 712712**

ON THE A38 From Lichfield take the A38 towards Burton
on Trent. Continue for three quarters of a mile past the
turning for Barton under Needwood, and New Oak Moor
Transport Café is on your left.

CREDIT/DEBIT CARDS

FUEL CARDS (see key on page 6)

TRUCK FACILITIES
P *only* free to customers only
Coach parking, by prior arrangement,
shared with LGV
Ample room for manoeuvring

DRIVER FACILITIES
Accomm. nearby, half a mile, Travelodge
Showers – 2 unisex, TV
Euros changed/accepted
Takeaway food

SITE COMMENTS/INFORMATION
This site is due for refurbishment,
internet access coming soon

Parking 24 hours. Other on-site facilities 06:00-20:00 Mon-Thurs, 06:00-18:00 Fri, 07:00-12:00 Sat **TT548**

Newport Truckstop

**C H Jones Ltd, Lynwood Garage
Langstone, Newport, Gwent NP18 2LX
T 01633 411155**

M4 JUNCTION 24 ON THE A48 Exit the M4 at junction 24 and take the A48 towards Chepstow. Newport Truckstop is on the A48 within 300 yards on the right-hand side.

CREDIT/DEBIT CARDS

FUEL CARDS (see key on page 6)
① ② ③ ㊻

TRUCK FACILITIES
Ample room for manoeuvring
Quiet area

DRIVER FACILITIES
Accommodation nearby, half a mile,
Hilton, Travel Inn & Holiday Inn
Rest area
Takeaway food

Parking, bunker fuel and toilets accessible 24 hours. Other on-site times unknown **TT549**

Nocton Heath Truckstop & Country kitchen

**Sleaford Road, Nocton Heath, Lincoln
Lincolnshire LN4 2AR
T 01522 811299**

ON THE A15 If heading along the A15 from Sleaford to Lincoln, Nocton Heath is on the right just after the turning for the B1202 and before the turning for the B1178.

CREDIT/DEBIT CARDS

FUEL CARDS (see key on page 6)

TRUCK FACILITIES
P *with voucher £6.50*
Voucher value £6.50
Coach parking (3 spaces). Quiet area
Ample room for manoeuvring
Truck dealership/workshop

DRIVER FACILITIES
Showers – 1 m, 1 f (charge), washroom,
rest area, TV
Takeaway food

SITE COMMENTS/INFORMATION
Meals prepared using fresh local produce. Recent refurbishment

Parking 24 hours. Restaurant weekends only. Café and all other on-site facilities 06:00-22:00 Mon-Fri,
06:00-17:00 Sat, 09:00-15:00 Sun **TT550**

Norfolk Dumpling

**Harford Livestock Market, Hall Road
Norwich, Norfolk NR4 6DW
T 01603 451392**

OFF THE A140 From the A47 Norwich southern by-pass, take the A140 to Norwich town. Turn right into Hall Road and follow the signs for the Livestock Market and Lorry Park.

CREDIT/DEBIT CARDS

FUEL CARDS (see key on page 6)

TRUCK FACILITIES
P £5.00. Coach parking (5 spaces)
Ample room for manoeuvring
Quiet area. Fridge lorry area
Truck dealership/workshop
DRIVER FACILITIES
Accommodation nearby, Holiday Inn
Showers – 1 m, 1 f (free), washroom, TV
Takeaway food
SITE COMMENTS/INFORMATION
Well lit lorry park. Firm hard standing
Only 1 mile from town centre

Parking accessible 24 hours. Other on-site facilities accessible 06:00-00:00 **TT551**

Oakdene Café

**London Road, Wrotham, Sevenoaks
Kent TN15 7RR
T 01732 884873**

ON THE A20 From M20, exit at junction 2 and follow A20 towards M26 and Wrotham Heath. Oakdene is on the left 200 yards from M26. From M26, exit at junction 2A and take A20 towards Wrotham. Oakdene is 200 yards on the right.

CREDIT/DEBIT CARDS

FUEL CARDS (for nearby fuel)
 46

TRUCK FACILITIES
P £5.00
Ample room for manoeuvring
Quiet area

DRIVER FACILITIES
Accomm. nearby, half a mile, Travel Inn
Washroom, phone top-ups/accessories
Takeaway food

SITE COMMENTS/INFORMATION
This site provides hot, fresh cooked food

Parking, nearby fuel and shop 24 hours. Other on-site facilities 06:00-06:30 Mon-Fri, 06:00-17:00 Sat & Sun **TT552**

PJ's Transport Café

**Sudbury Services, Lichfield Road
Sudbury, Ashbourne, Derbyshire DE6 5GX
T 01283 820669**

ON THE A515 From A50 Stoke to Derby road, turn off onto the A515 towards Lichfield. PJ's is on this road past a river and railway crossing and can be found at the back of the Texaco garage on your left.

CREDIT/DEBIT CARDS

FUEL CARDS (see key on page 6)
3 4 9 37

TRUCK FACILITIES
P *with voucher* £8.00 Inc. eve. meal
Ample room for manoeuvring
Quiet area

DRIVER FACILITIES
Accommodation nearby, Boars Head
Showers – 2 m, 1 f (free), washroom,
rest area, TV, truckers' accessories
Takeaway food

SITE COMMENTS/INFORMATION
Home cooked food at value for money prices

Parking 24 hours. Fuel 06:00-22:00. Other facilities 07:00-22:00 Mon-Thurs, 07:00-20:00 Fri **TT553**

Quernhow Transport Café & Caravan Site

**And CB Truck & Accessories.
Baldersby, Thirsk, North Yorkshire YO7 4LG
T 01845 567221**

ON THE A1 NORTHBOUND From Harrogate take the A1M towards Darlington. Continue past Ripon onto the A1 for 5 miles. Quernhow Transport Café is on the left-hand side 3 miles after the junction with the A61, and 400 yards before the junction with the B6267.

CREDIT/DEBIT CARDS

FUEL CARDS (see key on page 6)

TRUCK FACILITIES
P *with voucher* £6.50 P *only* £6.00
Voucher value – shower and breakfast
Coach parking (10 spaces). Quiet area
Ample room for manoeuvring

DRIVER FACILITIES
Accommodation on-site, £39.95 en-suite
   room, B&B and evening meal
Showers – 6 m, 6 f, washroom, TV,
laundry service, Euros changed/accepted,
phone top-ups/accessories, clothing for
sale, truckers' accessories, CB
repairs/sales, takeaway food

SITE COMMENTS/INFORMATION
This site is opposite A1 Diesel Ltd. Credit
and debit card facility coming soon

All on-site facilities accessible 24 hours. For nearby fuel times see A1 Diesel Ltd **TT554**

The Red Lodge Inn

70 Turnpike Road, Red Lodge
nr Bury St Edmunds, Suffolk IP28 8LB
T 01638 750529

ON THE OLD A11 (B1085) From the A14 Newmarket by-pass, take the A11 towards Norwich. After 1 mile take the B1085 towards Red Lodge village. The transport café is in the middle of the village on your left.

CREDIT/DEBIT CARDS

FUEL CARDS (see key on page 6)

TRUCK FACILITIES
P £6.50
Coach parking available, shared with LGV
Ample room for manoeuvring
Quiet area. Floodlighting

DRIVER FACILITIES
Shower – 2 unisex, washroom, rest area, TV, internet access
Takeaway food

SITE COMMENTS/INFORMATION
Sandwich price quoted is for a mega sandwich with all the trimmings

All on-site facilities 10:30-22:30 Mon-Sat, 10:30-12:00 Sun. Food available to 21:30 **TT555**

Robo's Café and Diner

London Road South, Pycombe
Sussex BN45 7FJ
T 01273 844055

ON THE A23 Take the A23 south towards Brighton. Continue for half a mile past the junction with the A273 and Robo's is accessed via a lay-by on your left.

CREDIT/DEBIT CARDS

FUEL CARDS (see key on page 6)

TRUCK FACILITIES
Overnight **P** in access lay-by for LGVs
P free
Coach parking available, shared with LGV
Ample room for manoeuvring
Truck dealership/workshop nearby

DRIVER FACILITIES
Takeaway food

SITE COMMENTS/INFORMATION
Lorry parking in entrance lay-by only, cars can use car park next to café. Trucks please park considerately as this is also an access road. This site will accept payment by cheque

Parking and nearby shop and fuel 24 hours. All other on-site facilities 05:45-15:00 Mon-Fri, 05:45-12:00 Sat **TT556**

Roman Café

Bridge End Road, Ropsley, Grantham
Lincolnshire NG31 6
T 01476 576477

ON THE A52 Take the A52 out of Grantham towards Boston. Roman Café is on the right-hand side, 4 miles past the junction with the B6403 and a few hundred yards after the last turning for Ropsley.

CREDIT/DEBIT CARDS

FUEL CARDS (see key on page 6)

TRUCK FACILITIES
P free
Coach parking available, shared with LGV
Ample room for manoeuvring

DRIVER FACILITIES
Takeaway food

SITE COMMENTS/INFORMATION
Friendly staff. Nice atmosphere to relax in after a long drive

Parking 24 hours. Nearby fuel 07:30-16:30. Other on-site facilities in winter 08:00-15:00. In summer 07:30-16:30 **TT557**

Rookery Café & Truckstop

Great North Road, Welham Green
Hatfield, Hertfordshire AL9 5SF

ON THE A1000 From the A1M, exit at junction 12 and take the A1001 east and onto the A1000. Rookery Café and Truckstop is on the right-hand side just after the roundabout turning for Welham Green

CREDIT/DEBIT CARDS

FUEL CARDS (see key on page 6)

TRUCK FACILITIES
P *with voucher* £10.00
Coach parking (10 spaces). Quiet area
Ample room for manoeuvring

DRIVER FACILITIES
Showers - 2 M (free), washroom, rest area, TV, takeaway food
Internet access, phone top-ups/ accessories and clothing for sale nearby

SITE COMMENTS/INFORMATION
Train/tram nearby

Parking 24 hours. All other on-site facilities 06:00-14:00, 17:00-21:00. Nearby fuel 24 hours

TT558

Scoffalot Café

186 Hessle Road, Hull
East Riding of Yorkshire HU3 3AD
T 01482 323289

OFF THE A63 From the M62, take the A63 into Hull. Continue past the junction with the A1166 for 1 mile. At next roundabout (a weird shaped one) take the 2nd exit onto Hessle Road. Scoffalot is 50 yards opposite the Total garage.

CREDIT/DEBIT CARDS

FUEL CARDS (for nearby fuel)
㊻

TRUCK FACILITIES
Overnight parking on the road and in nearby garage car park. **P** free
Coach parking available, shared with LGV
Ample room for manoeuvring
Tyre repair/sales, tank cleaning, windscreen repair and quiet area nearby
DRIVER FACILITIES
Washroom, takeaway food
Laundry, phone top-ups/accessories, truckers' accessories, Post Office and Euros accepted/changed nearby
SITE COMMENTS/INFORMATION
Close to Leisure Land. Roast dinner every day. Abnormal loads park on road only

All on-site facilities 06:30-14:00 Mon-Sun

TT559

Silver Ball Café

London Road, Reed, nr Royston
Hertfordshire SG8 8BD
T 01763 848200

ON THE A10 Take the A10 from Royston towards Buntingford for 3 miles. Silver Ball Café is on the right at Reed, just past the turning for Therfield.

CREDIT/DEBIT CARDS

FUEL CARDS (see key on page 6)

TRUCK FACILITIES
P *with voucher*   **P** *only*   *Voucher value*
£9.00   £5.00   £4.50
Coach parking (10 spaces). Quiet area
Ample room for manoeuvring

DRIVER FACILITIES
Accommodation on-site
Showers – m (charge), washroom, TV
Takeaway food

SITE COMMENTS/INFORMATION
Site easily accessible for LGVs

Parking and showers 24 hours. Other on-site facilities 06:00-22:00

TT560

Six Hills Café

**669 The Foss Way, Thrussington
Leicester, Leicestershire LE7 4TF
T 01664 424129**

ON THE A46 From Leicester take the A46 north-eastbound towards Bingham. Six Hills Café is on the right-hand side, 600 yards after the turnings for Seagrave and Thrussington.

CREDIT/DEBIT CARDS

FUEL CARDS (see key on page 6)

TRUCK FACILITIES
P £2.00
Ample room for manoeuvring
Quiet area

DRIVER FACILITIES
Accommodation nearby, 500 yds,
  Travelodge
Takeaway food

SITE COMMENTS/INFORMATION
Filling station next door to café

Parking 24 hours. Nearby fuel and shop 06:30-22:00. All other on-site facilities 07:00-16:00 Mon-Fri, 07:30-12:00 Sat **TT561**

Smokey Joe's Café & Truckstop

**Blackwater, nr Scorrier, Redruth
Cornwall TR16 5BJ
T 01209 821810/822279**

OFF THE A30 A3047 INTERSECTION If heading south-west on A30, take 3rd exit for Blackwater at the A390 roundabout. Go through Blackwater for 1 mile. Smokey Joe's is on right. If heading north-east on A30, take the A3047 exit, turn right at roundabout. Continue 1mile and it's on the left

CREDIT/DEBIT CARDS

FUEL CARDS (see key on page 6)

TRUCK FACILITIES
P *with voucher* £8.50 P *only* £4.00
Voucher value – shower, meal and
  bottomless tea or coffee
Coach parking available, shared with LGV
Ample room for manoeuvring
Quiet area. Floodlighting
Truck dealership/workshop nearby
DRIVER FACILITIES
Shower – 1 unisex, washroom, TV
Takeaway food
Post Office and CB repairs/sales nearby
SITE COMMENTS/INFORMATION
Last orders for food 1 hour before closing

07:00-22:00 Mon-Thur, 07:00-20:00 Fri, 08:00-20:00 Sat, 10:00-20:00 Sun **TT562**

Square Deal Café

**Bath Road, Knowle Hill, Reading
Berkshire RG10 9YL
T 01628 822426/823393**

ON THE A4 Take the A4 from Maidenhead to Reading. Square Deal Café is on your left-hand side in the middle of Knowle Hill village, just before the Castle Royal Golf Club.

CREDIT/DEBIT CARDS

FUEL CARDS (see key on page 6)

TRUCK FACILITIES
Nearby overnight parking on request
  only
Ample room for manoeuvring
Quiet area nearby

DRIVER FACILITIES
Accommodation nearby, half a mile,
  Bird In Hand Hotel

All on-site facilities opening times unknown **TT563**

Standeford Farm Café

176 Stafford Road, Standeford Wolverhampton, West Midlands WV10 7BN
T 01902 790389

ON THE A449 From junction 12 of the M6 follow the A5 towards Telford, turn left onto the A449 heading towards Wolverhampton. Or from Junction 2 of the M54, turn right towards Stafford. Standeford Farm Café is on the A449 in the village of Standeford.

CREDIT/DEBIT CARDS

FUEL CARDS (see key on page 6)

TRUCK FACILITIES
P *with voucher*   **P** *only*   *Voucher value*
£10.00   £5.00   £4.25
Ample room for manoeuvring
Coach parking. Quiet area

DRIVER FACILITIES
Showers – 2 m, 1 f (free), washroom, rest area, TV
Takeaway food

Parking 24 hours. Other on-site facilities 05:30-20:00   **TT564**

Stibbington Diner

2 Old Great North Road, Stibbington Peterborough, Cambridgeshire PE8 6LR
T 01780 782891

OFF THE A1 SOUTHBOUND Take the A1 south from Stamford and continue for 1 and a half miles beyond the junction with the A47. Stibbington Diner is on your left just before the railway line and 1 and a half miles before the turning for the village of Water Newton.

CREDIT/DEBIT CARDS

FUEL CARDS (see key on page 6)

TRUCK FACILITIES
P £5.00
Coach parking available, shared with LGV
Ample room for manoeuvring
Quiet area. Floodlighting
Fridge lorry area

DRIVER FACILITIES
Showers – 4 m, 1 f, washroom
Takeaway food

SITE COMMENTS/INFORMATION
Fridge lorries must switch off after 21:00

All on-site facilities open 24 hours from Mon-Sat at 14:00, 08:00-22:00 Sun   **TT565**

Super Sausage Café

Watling Street, Potterspury, nr Towcester Northamptonshire NN12 7QX
T 01908 542964

ON THE A5 If heading from Milton Keynes to Towcester on the A5, Super Sausage is on the left-hand side in the middle of the village of Potterspury.

CREDIT/DEBIT CARDS

FUEL CARDS (see key on page 6)

TRUCK FACILITIES
P free
Quiet area
Ample room for manoeuvring

DRIVER FACILITIES
Washroom, rest area, clothing for sale
Takeaway food

SITE COMMENTS/INFORMATION
Large choice of meals to suit all diets and tastes. Fast efficient service from friendly staff

Parking 24 hours. Other on-site facilities 07:00-18:00 Mon-Fri, 08:00-16:00 Sat & Sun   **TT566**

Super Sausage Café & Truckstop

**St Andrews Road, Northampton
Northamptonshire NN1 2SD
T 01604 636099**

ON THE A5059 Take the A508 northbound into city centre.
At the junction with the A5123 turn left onto this road and
across next roundabout. At junction with A45, continue
ahead onto the A5095 towards Market Harborough. Super
Sausage is a quarter of a mile on left.

CREDIT/DEBIT CARDS

FUEL CARDS (see key on page 6)

TRUCK FACILITIES
P *with voucher*   P *only*   *Voucher value*
£6.00   £5.00   £1.00
Coach parking (22 spaces). Quiet area
Ample room for manoeuvring

DRIVER FACILITIES
Accommodation on-site £7 pn
Showers – 2 m (free), washroom, rest area, TV,
Internet access, takeaway food, phone
top-ups/accessories, clothing nearby

SITE COMMENTS/INFORMATION
Situated in Northampton, close to town
centre facilities. Train/tram nearby

Parking 24 hours. Other on-site facilities 06:00-21:00 Mon-Thurs, 06:00-19:30 Fri, 06:00-15:00 Sat   **TT567**

The Bungalow Café

**45 London Road, Marks Tey, Colchester
Essex CO6 1EB
T 01206 210242**

ON THE B1408 From the A12 take the B1408 towards
Colchester for half a mile. The Bungalow Café is on the right-
hand side.

CREDIT/DEBIT CARDS

FUEL CARDS (see key on page 6)

TRUCK FACILITIES
P £2.50
Quiet area

DRIVER FACILITIES
Accommodation nearby, half a mile,
 Marks Tey Hotel
Takeaway food nearby

Parking 24 hours. Toilets 06:00-16:00 Mon-Fri. Nearby shop and filling station 06:00-15:00.
Other on-site facilities 06:00-17:00 Mon-Fri   **TT568**

The Cabin Café

**Crawley Road, Faygate, Horsham
West Sussex RH12 4SE
T 01293 851575**

ON THE A264 From the M23, exit at junction 11 (Pease
Pottage) and take the A264 towards Horsham. Straight
across first roundabout, left at the second and The Cabin is a
mile further on the right.

CREDIT/DEBIT CARDS

FUEL CARDS (see key on page 6)

TRUCK FACILITIES
P *with voucher* £10.00
Ample room for manoeuvring

DRIVER FACILITIES
Shower – 1 unisex (charge), washroom,
rest area, TV, clothing for sale

SITE COMMENTS/INFORMATION
Train/tram nearby

Parking 24 hours. Other on-site facilities 06:00-19:00 Mon-Thurs, 06:00-13:00 Fri, 07:00-12:00 Sat   **TT569**

The Chef's Grill Diner

**Perth Road, Newtonmore, nr Inverness
Highland PH20 1BB
T 01540 673702**

OFF THE A9 ON THE B9150 From Perth, take the A9 towards Inverness. Take the B9150 into Newtonmore and The Chef's Grill Diner is 1 mile on your left before you reach the A86.

CREDIT/DEBIT CARDS

FUEL CARDS (see key on page 6)
TRUCK FACILITIES
Nearby **p** on local roads.
P with voucher £8.00 **P** only £8.00
Voucher value – 1 meal
Coach parking shared with LGV
Quiet area. Fridge lorry area
Fridges must switched off by 23:00
Ample room for manoeuvring
Truck dealership/workshop nearby
DRIVER FACILITIES
Accommodation nearby, various hotels
Shower – 1 unisex, TV, laundry service, truckers' accessories, takeaway food
SITE COMMENTS/INFORMATION
Staff will arrange accommodation for you and deliver you to the hotel personally

Parking 24 hours. Restaurant and other facilities 06:30-22:00 Mon-Fri. 06:30-20:00 Sat. 08:00-20:00 Sun. Bar until Midnight Sun, Mon, Tues & Wed and until 01:00 Thurs **TT570**

The Famous Midway Truckstop

**Pree's Heath, Whitchurch
Shropshire SY13 3JT
T 01948 663160**

ON THE A41 This site is located on the Midway roundabout at the junction of the A41 and the A49, 4 miles south of Whitchurch.

CREDIT/DEBIT CARDS

FUEL CARDS (see key on page 6)

TRUCK FACILITIES
Lorry park situated across road
P 30p for 2 hours, £4.00 overnight
Ample room for manoeuvring
Quiet area nearby
Truck dealership/workshop nearby
DRIVER FACILITIES
Showers (free), rest area, TV, internet, truckers' accessories, takeaway food
SITE COMMENTS/INFORMATION
This site has won many awards and TV appearances and boasts free library access and a variety of special deals

Nearby parking 24 hours. Other on-site facilities 05:45-20:00 Mon-Fri, 05:45-18:00 Sat, 07:30-14:00 Sun **TT571**

The Highwayman Café

**Malton Road, Stockton on Forest
York, North Yorkshire YO32 9TL**

ON THE A64 The Highwayman Café is situated on the A64 York to Scarborough road just outside of York and north-east of the Hapgrove roundabout junction with the A1237.

CREDIT/DEBIT CARDS

FUEL CARDS (see key on page 6)

TRUCK FACILITIES
P free
Coach parking (20 spaces). Quiet area
Ample room for manoeuvring
Truck dealership/workshop nearby

DRIVER FACILITIES
Accommodation nearby, Holiday Inn
Rest area, phone top-ups/accessories
Takeaway food

SITE COMMENTS/INFORMATION
Clean, well maintained site

All on-site facilities 07:00-16:30 Mon-Fri, 07:00-15:30 Sat, 08:00-15:00 Sun **TT572**

The Hollies Transport Café

**Watling Street, Hatherton, Cannock
Staffordshire WS11 1SB
T 01543 503435**

ON THE A5 From the M6, exit at junction 12 and take the A5 towards Cannock. The Hollies is 1 mile along on the left-hand side.

CREDIT/DEBIT CARDS

FUEL CARDS (see key on page 6)

TRUCK FACILITIES
P with voucher £5 Voucher value – 50p
Ample room for manoeuvring

DRIVER FACILITIES
Accommodation on-site, £10 room only
Showers – 1 m, 1 f (charge), washroom,
TV, truckers' accessories
Takeaway food

All on-site facilities accessible 24 hours   **TT573**

The Lazy Trout Café

**Marshbrook, nr Church Stretton
Shropshire SY6 6RG
T 01694 781282**

ON THE A49 Take the A49 from Ludlow to Shrewsbury. The Lazy Trout is on the left-hand side, half a mile north of Marshbrook and 1 mile south of Little Stretton.

CREDIT/DEBIT CARDS

FUEL CARDS (see key on page 6)

TRUCK FACILITIES
P free. Quiet area
Ample room for manoeuvring
Truck dealership/workshop nearby

SITE COMMENTS/INFORMATION
Believed to be the oldest truckstop in the country and world renowned (Corgi have even made a model of it!). Set in beautiful countryside. Proprietors considering 24 hour, 7 days a week opening in the near future

Parking 24 hours. All other on-site facilities 07:00-16:00   **TT574**

The Merrychest Café

**Watling Street, Bean, nr Dartford
Kent DA2 8AH
T 01474 832371**

ON THE A296 From the M25, exit at junction 2 and take the A2 towards Gravesend. After 1 and a half miles take the B225 towards Bluewater Shopping Centre then take the A296 sliproad heading eastbound back onto the A2. The Merrychest is on that sliproad on the right.

CREDIT/DEBIT CARDS

FUEL CARDS (see key on page 6)

TRUCK FACILITIES
P free
Ample room for manoeuvring
Quiet area

DRIVER FACILITIES
Rest area, phone top-ups/accessories

SITE COMMENTS/INFORMATION
Friendly, family run business

Parking 24 hours. Other on-site facilities 06:30-17:00 Mon-Fri, 06:30-12:00 Sat   **TT575**

The Ranch Café

Newark Lorry Park, Great North Road Newark, Nottinghamshire NG24 1BN
T 01636 611198
OFF THE B6326 From Leicester, take the A46 towards Newark and around the west side of the town. At the roundabout with the A617 and A616 take the B6326 towards the town. At the B6166, turn right and The Ranch Café is on your right.

CREDIT/DEBIT CARDS

FUEL CARDS (see key on page 6)

TRUCK FACILITIES
P *with voucher*   **P** *only*   *Voucher value*
£9.00   £6.50   £2.50
Coach parking shared with LGV
Ample room for manoeuvring
Quiet area. Floodlighting
DRIVER FACILITIES
Accommodation nearby, half a mile,
   South Parade Hotel
Showers – 4 m, 1 f (free if paying to park), washroom, truckers' accessories
Takeaway food
SITE COMMENTS/INFORMATION
Train/tram nearby

Parking 24 hours. Other on-site facilities 06:00-21:00. Nearby fuel accessible 24 hours   **TT576**

The Salt Box Café

Hatton, nr Derby
Derbyshire DE65 5PT
T 01283 813189
ON THE A511 If heading east along the A50, exit at junction 6 onto the A511 for 1 mile. The Salt Box is on the right after the junction with the A516. If heading west, exit the A50 at junction 5 onto the A516 for 2 miles and The Salt Box is on the left

CREDIT/DEBIT CARDS

FUEL CARDS (for nearby fuel)

TRUCK FACILITIES
P *with voucher £7.50 Voucher value £2.50*
Coach parking (5 spaces)
Quiet area. Fridge lorry area
Ample room for manoeuvring
Truck dealership/workshop nearby
DRIVER FACILITIES
Showers – 3 m (charge), washroom, rest area, TV, takeaway food
Post Office, internet access, phone top-ups/accessories nearby
SITE COMMENTS/INFORMATION
Train/tram nearby

Parking 24 hours. Nearby fuel and shop 07:00-23:00. Other on-site facilities 07:00-19:00 Mon-Fri, 07:00-14:00 Sat   **TT577**

Tollgate Snack Bar

Y Bwthyn, Glyndyfrwdy, nr Corwen
Denbighshire LL21 9HW
T 01490 430398

ON THE A5 If heading east towards Llangollen on the A5 from Betwys-y-coed continue through the villages of Corwen and Glyndyfrwdy. Tollgate Snack Bar is on the left-hand side, half a mile east of the centre of the village of Glyndyfrwdy.

CREDIT/DEBIT CARDS

FUEL CARDS (see key on page 6)

TRUCK FACILITIES
Overnight parking in 3 lay-bys
P free. Quiet area nearby
Ample room for manoeuvring

DRIVER FACILITIES
Washroom
Takeaway food

SITE COMMENTS/INFORMATION
Site housed in a purpose built stone and slate building, with outstanding views of the Welsh mountains

Parking accessible 24 hours. Other on-site facilities accessible 08:00-16:00 Mon-Sun   **TT578**

Travellers Rest Truckstop

Wallneuk Road, Paisley, nr Glasgow
Renfrewshire PA3 4BT
T 0141 5872448
OFF THE A741 From the M8, exit at junction 27 and take
the A741 towards Paisley town centre for 1 mile. Opposite
the right-hand turning for the A726, take the left turning
into Wallneuk Road signposted for the Superbowl, and
Travellers Rest is opposite the Superbowl.

CREDIT/DEBIT CARDS

FUEL CARDS (see key on page 6)

TRUCK FACILITIES
P *with voucher* £10.00
Voucher value – 3 course meal
Coach parking (40 spaces). Quiet area
Ample room for manoeuvring
Fencing and CCTV. Truckwash nearby
Truck dealership/workshop nearby
DRIVER FACILITIES
Accommodation nearby, half a mile,
  Watermill Hotel
Showers – 2 m, washroom, TV
Takeaway food. CB sales/repairs nearby
SITE COMMENTS/INFORMATION
Train/tram nearby. Walking distance of
town centre

Parking 24 hours. Other on-site facilities 06:20-23:00 Mon-Fri, 06:20-02:00 Sat & Sun **TT579**

Treacy's

The Heath, Portlaoise
County Lois, Ireland
T 00353 (0) 50246539

OFF THE N7 From the M7 take the R422 exit towards
Portarlington. Go through the first roundabout take the 2nd
exit at the next roundabout and it's 1 mile on the right-hand
side.

CREDIT/DEBIT CARDS

FUEL CARDS (see key on page 6)

TRUCK FACILITIES
P free
Coach parking (2 spaces). Quiet area
Ample room for manoeuvring
Truck dealership/workshop nearby

DRIVER FACILITIES
Accommodation nearby
Showers, washroom, TV
CB sales/repairs nearby

SITE COMMENTS/INFORMATION
Family run site, close to the motorway

Parking 24 hours. Bar from 07:00-12:00. Nearby fuel 07:00-23:00. All other on-site facilities 07:00-22:00 **TT580**

Truckers Rest

Watling Street, Four Crosses, Cannock
Staffordshire WS11 1SF
T 01543 469183
ON THE A5 From junction 12 of the M6 take the A5
towards Cannock. The Truckers Rest is about 2 miles along
on the right. From junction 11 take the A460 towards
Cannock, turn left at the junction with the A5 and the
Truckers Rest is within a mile on your left.

CREDIT/DEBIT CARDS

FUEL CARDS (see key on page 6)

TRUCK FACILITIES
P £5.00
Coach parking (10 spaces). Quiet area
Ample room for manoeuvring

DRIVER FACILITIES
Accommodation nearby, 400 yards,
  Roman Way Hotel & Travel Inn
Showers (£1.00), washroom, TV
Takeaway food

SITE COMMENTS/INFORMATION
Excellent food and service

All on-site facilities accessible 24 hours **TT581**

Windy Ridge Eating House

Torpoint Road, Trerulefoot, Saltash
Cornwall PL12 5BJ
T 01752 841344

OFF THE A38 This site is situated on the A374 Torpoint Road close to the roundabout with the main A38 Liskeard to Plymouth road.

CREDIT/DEBIT CARDS

FUEL CARDS (see key on page 6)

TRUCK FACILITIES
P *with voucher £7 Voucher value – £3*
Coach parking (20 spaces)
Ample room for manoeuvring

DRIVER FACILITIES
Shower – 1 unisex (£1.00), washroom, rest area, TV, internet access, truckers' accessories.
Takeaway food

SITE COMMENTS/INFORMATION
This site boasts excellent breakfasts

Nearby fuel and on-site parking 24 hours. Other on-site facilities 06:15-21:30. Nearby shop 24 hours **TT582**

Woodside Café

Knayton, Thirsk
North Yorkshire YO7 4AQ
T 01845 537459

ON THE A19 SOUTHBOUND Take the A19 from Middlesborough to Thirsk. Woodside Café is on the left-hand side 1 mile after the turning for the village of Borrowby and 1 mile before North Kilvington.

CREDIT/DEBIT CARDS

FUEL CARDS (see key on page 6)

TRUCK FACILITIES
P £2.00
Ample room for manoeuvring
Quiet area

DRIVER FACILITIES
Showers – 1 m (free if buying meal), TV

Parking 24 hours. Other on-site facilities 06:00-20:00 Mon-Thurs, 06:30-18:00 Fri **TT583**

Woodview Café & Garage

Thornhaugh, Peterborough
Cambrigeshire PE8 6HA
T 01780 783410/01733 772030

ON THE A1 NORTHBOUND From the A1M, take the A1 towards Stamford. Woodview Café and Garage is on the left-hand side just past the village of Thornhaugh and about 1 mile north of the junction with the A47.

CREDIT/DEBIT CARDS

FUEL CARDS (see key on page 6)

TRUCK FACILITIES
P *with voucher* P *only* *Voucher value*
£6.00   £4.00   £2.00
Ample room for manoeuvring
Truck dealership/workshop

DRIVER FACILITIES
Washroom, TV
Takeaway food

Toilets, parking, shop and fuel 24 hours. Other on-site facilities 07:00-20:00 Mon-Thurs, 07:00-17:00 Fri, 07:00-13:00 Sat **TT584**

Woody's Truckstop

12 Henderson Road, Longman Ind. Est. Inverness, Invernesshire IV1 1SN
T 01463 715815/239162

OFF THE A82 Take the A9 along the east side of Inverness. At the roundabout with A82, turn towards town along Longman Road. At the next roundabout turn around heading back out of the town, take next left. Woody's is 400 yards on the right.

CREDIT/DEBIT CARDS

FUEL CARDS (see key on page 6)

TRUCK FACILITIES
P £5.00. Quiet area
Coach parking available, shared with LGV
Ample room for manoeuvring
CCTV, security guard
Fridge lorry area at bottom of lorry park
Truck dealership/workshop nearby
Tyre repair/sales, truckwash and windscreen repairs nearby

DRIVER FACILITIES
Showers – 2 m, 1 f, washroom, TV
Euros changed/accepted Takeaway food
CB sales/repairs nearby

Parking 24 hours. All other on-site facilities 05:45-21:00 Mon-Fri, 05:45-18:00 Sat, 08:00-14:00 Sun **TT585**

Woolley's Café

Coast Road, Tan-Lan, Ffynnongroyw nr Holywell, Flintshire CH8 9UU
T 01745 560483

ON THE A458 Take the A548 from Prestatyn to Flint for 3 miles. Wooley's Café is on the left-hand side just before the village of Ffynnongroyw.

CREDIT/DEBIT CARDS

FUEL CARDS (see key on page 6)

TRUCK FACILITIES
P £2.50
Ample room for manoeuvring
Quiet area

SITE COMMENTS/INFORMATION
This site is close to a car wash and garden centre

Parking 24 hours. All on-site facilities 08:00-17:00 **TT586**

Necton Diner

Norwich Road, Necton Norfolk PE37 8QQ
T 01760 724180

ON THE A47 From Swaffham take the A47 towards Norwich. Necton diner is about 3 miles from Swaffham at the village of Necton and on the right-hand side if heading towards Norwich.

CREDIT/DEBIT CARDS

FUEL CARDS (see key on page 6)

TRUCK FACILITIES
P *with voucher* £10.00
Voucher value £5.20
Fridge lorry area
Ample room for manoeuvring

DRIVER FACILITIES
Shower – 1 m (charge), washroom, TV
Takeaway food

Parking and nearby fuel 24 hours. Other on-site facilities 07:00-19:30 **TT587**

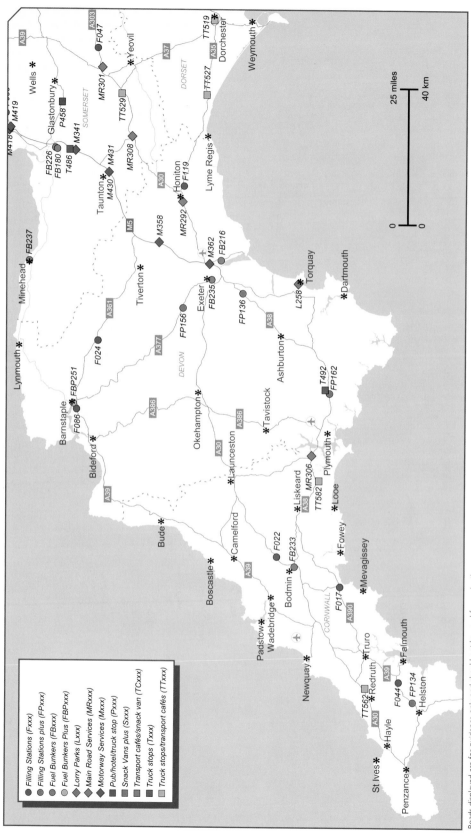

Legend:
- ● Filling Stations (Fxxx)
- ● Filling Stations plus (FPxxx)
- ● Fuel Bunkers (FBxxx)
- ● Fuel Bunkers Plus (FBPxxx)
- ◆ Lorry Parks (Lxxx)
- ◆ Main Road Services (MRxxx)
- ◆ Motorway Services (Mxxx)
- ■ Pub/hotel/truck stop (Pxxx)
- ■ Snack Vans plus (Sxxx)
- ■ Transport cafés/snack van (TCxxx)
- ■ Truck stops (Txxx)
- ■ Truck stops/transport cafés (TTxxx)

Roads displayed are for guidance only and should not be used for navigation

25 miles
40 km

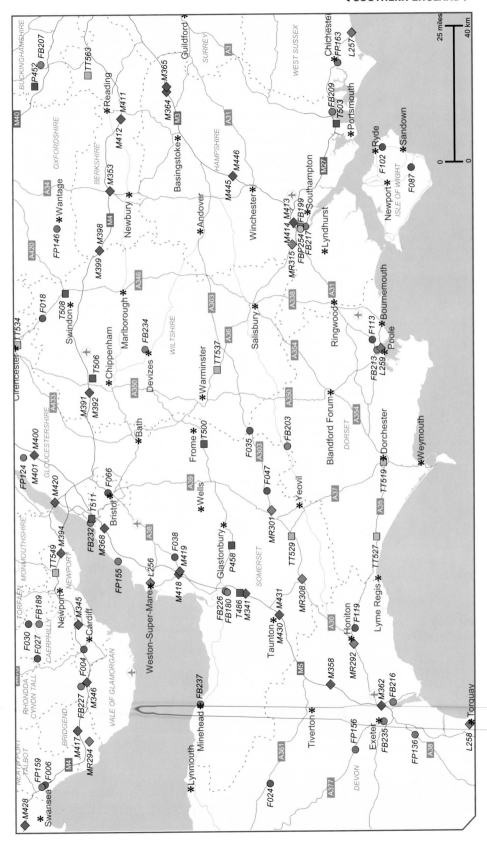

Legend:

- Filling Stations (Fxxx)
- Filling Stations plus (FPxxx)
- Fuel Bunkers (FBxxx)
- Fuel Bunkers Plus (FBPxxx)
- Lorry Parks (Lxxx)
- Main Road Services (MRxxx)
- Motorway Services (Mxxx)
- Pub/hotel/truck stop (Pxxx)
- Snack Vans plus (Sxxx)
- Transport cafés/snack van (TCxxx)
- Truck stops (Txxx)
- Truck stops/transport cafés (TTxxx)

Scale: 0 — 25 miles / 0 — 40 km

Calais 7 Miles FB205

Harwich, FB219, F003, Colchester, L260, TT568, A12, FP144, TT528, A13, A127, M434, TT547, F036, TT516, FB228, T532, T157.5, Chelmsford, M335, M11, Harlow, Hatfield, TT558, T507, M393, A406, F095, London, A205, F080, TC471, Southend-on-Sea, St Albans, A1(M), TT520, M376, Watford, A41, M1, T517, Luton, M436, M435, Leighton Buzzard, Hemel Hempstead, A413, FB207, A404, Aylesbury, A41, M40, M407, Oxford, P452, TT563, Reading, M411, M412, M353, Wantage, FP146, M4, M398, M399, A34, M349, A44, A346, Newbury, Andover, A303, Winchester, M445, M446, M364, M365, M3, Basingstoke, A31, MR315, M414, M413, FBP254, FB199, FB217, Southampton, Lyndhurst, T508, Ryde, Portsmouth, FB209, Chichester, FP163, L257, A272, A3, Guildford, A24, TT569, FP138, M408, Crawley, M23, M355, M354, Brighton, A27, A22, A26, A21, Tunbridge Wells, TT552, F120, TC474, F050, M397, M396, M2, Maidstone, M20, F075, A2, A229, Eastbourne, TT540, A259, Hastings, Brighton, A188, TT556, FB188, Ramsgate, Canterbury, F007, FBP242, A299, Dover, Folkestone, A28, Ashford, TT521, FBP250, T476

Roads displayed are for guidance only and should not be used for navigation

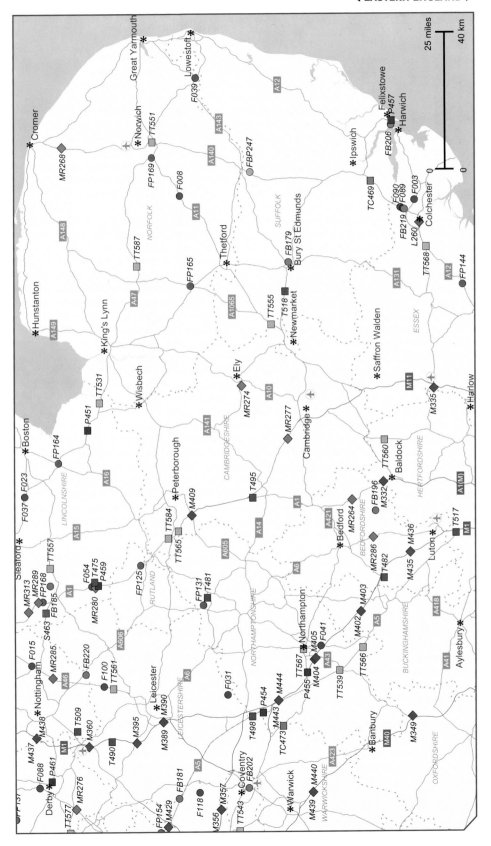

Wisbech

Ely
MR274

Saffron Walden

Harlow
M335
M11

P451
TT531

Huntingdon
MR277

Cambridge
TT560

Baldock
M332
FB196

M25
M393

Peterborough
M409
TT565
TT584
Stamford
A47
A1
CAMBRIDGESHIRE
A14
A1

Bedford
MR264
Newport Pagnell
M286
Ampthill
T482
Bletchley
M436
M435

Hatfield
TT558
T507

St Albans
T517
M1

Watford

LINCOLNSHIRE
A15
F054
T475
P459
MR280
P125
FP125
RUTLAND
A606
A1

FP131
T481
Corby

M403
M402
Towcester
M349

Leighton Buzzard

Luton
Hemel Hempstead
A41

Aylesbury
M407
P452
FB207

FB220
F100
TT561
LEICESTERSHIRE
A47
A6

Leicester
M390
M389
A5
M395

Lutterworth
F031
Rugby
T498
P454
M444
M443
TC473

Northampton
TT567
M405
F041
P455
M404
TT539
TT566
A5

Buckingham
M349

Banbury

Oxford

A423
A44
OXFORDSHIRE
A40
A420
A44

T509
MR276
T490
M360
A38
A444

FP154
M429
F118
FB181

Coventry
M357
TT543
FB202
M356
Warwick
M440
M439
A46
WARWICKSHIRE
A29

Evesham
F078
MR311
T505
A44

Cheltenham
FP129
Cirencester
TT534
MR278
F018
A433
GLOUCESTERSHIRE
A40

TT548
FB187
Birmingham
M406
M378
F001
FB182
M379
F116
M5
M366
M380
M318
Alcester
Worcester
FP130
A38
M426
M427
Gloucester
FB236
M400
M401
FP124

TT581
TT573
TT564
M54
T499
Wolverhampton
A442
A456
WORCESTERSHIRE
A449
A4103
M50

Shrewsbury
S467
FBP244
F114
FP152
SHROPSHIRE
A49

Leominster
A44
HEREFORDSHIRE

Hereford
FP141
A4112

Ross-on-Wye
MR305
Whitchurch
MR319
MR297
MONMOUTHSHIRE

Oswestry
S465
S464
F098
F062
TT574
MR291

F030
FB189
MR273

STAFFORDSHIRE
M6
WEST MIDLANDS
M42
BUCKINGHAMSHIRE
M40
HERTFORDSHIRE
A1(M)
BEDFORDSHIRE

Roads displayed are for guidance only and should not be used for navigation

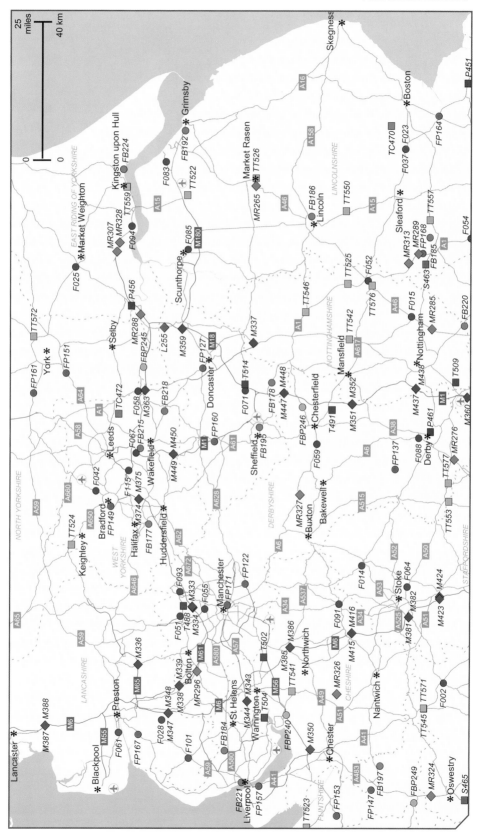

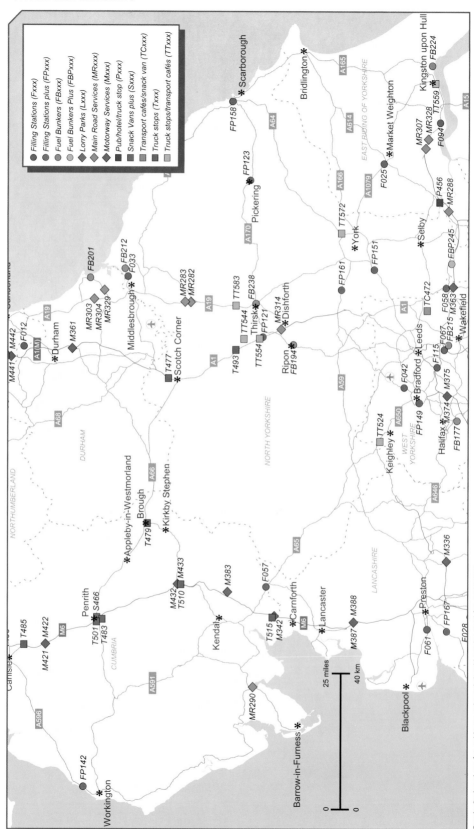

Legend:
- Filling Stations (Fxxx)
- Filling Stations plus (FPxxx)
- Fuel Bunkers (FBxxx)
- Fuel Bunkers Plus (FBPxxx)
- Lorry Parks (Lxxx)
- Main Road Services (MRxxx)
- Motorway Services (Mxxx)
- Pub/hotel/truck stop (Pxxx)
- Snack Vans plus (Sxxx)
- Transport cafés/snack van (TCxxx)
- Truck stops (Txxx)
- Truck stops/transport cafés (TTxxx)

Roads displayed are for guidance only and should not be used for navigation

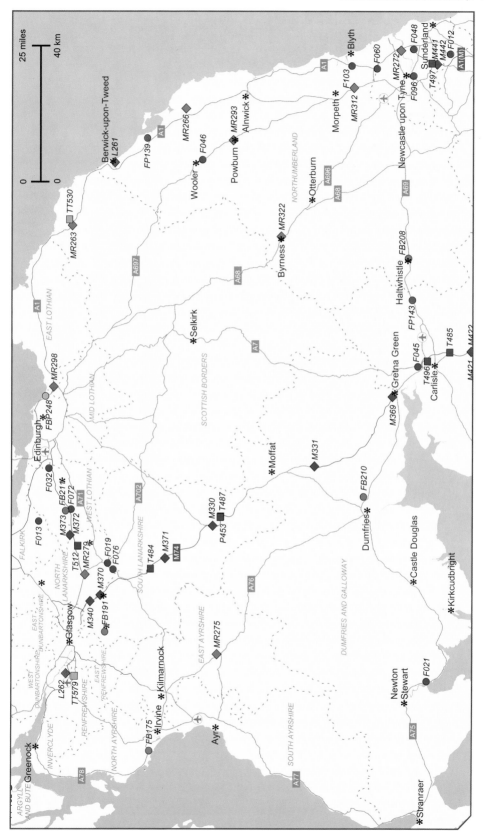

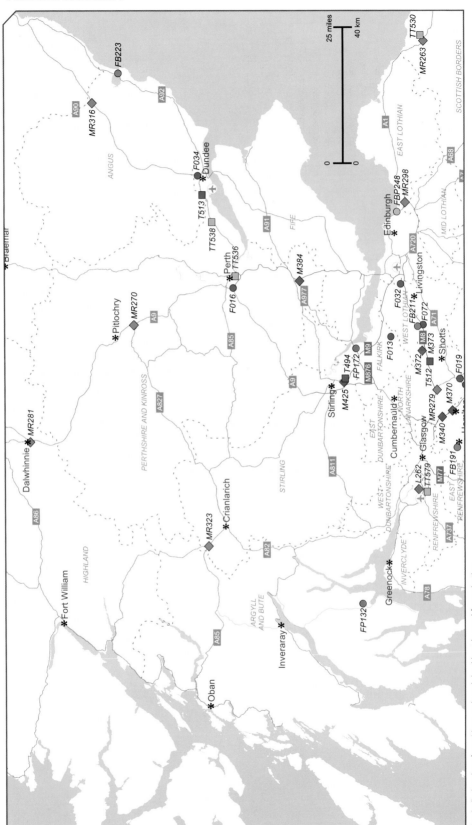

Roads displayed are for guidance only and should not be used for navigation

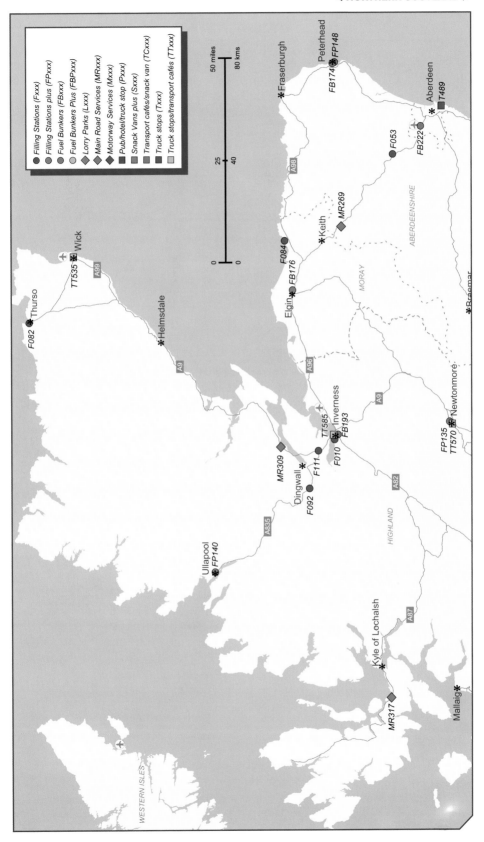

Filling Stations (Fxxx)
Filling Stations plus (FPxxx)
Fuel Bunkers (FBxxx)
Fuel Bunkers Plus (FBPxxx)
Lorry Parks (Lxxx)
Main Road Services (MRxxx)
Motorway Services (Mxxx)
Pub/hotel/truck stop (Pxxx)
Snack Vans plus (Sxxx)
Transport cafés/snack van (TCxxx)
Truck stops (Txxx)
Truck stops/transport cafés (TTxxx)

FB184
FB221
Liverpool
FP157
M344
M343
T504
FBP240

Holyhead ✱

Prestatyn✱ ☐ TT586

ANGLESEY
Colwyn Bay✱
Bangor
✱ FB190

A55
☐ TT523
FLINTSHIRE

M350
✱ Chester
MR32

Caernarfon✱

ABERCONWY
& COLWYN
DENBIGHSHIRE

FP153 ●

CHESHIR

A487

A5
A494

FP147 ●
● FB197

A483

GWYNEDD

TT533 ☐ TT578 ☐

FBP249
TT545
TT571

Porthmadog✱

Bala✱
MR324 ◆

● S465

A4

Dolgellau✱

A458

S464
● F098
● F062

Shrewsb
✱

SHROPSHIRE

A470

MR291 ◆
TT57

Aberystwyth✱

✱Llangurig

POWYS

A487

● F097

CEREDIGION

Llandrindod Wells✱

A44

Leominster✱

A49

✱Cardigan

MR284
◆✱Fishguard

● S468

CARMARTHENSHIRE

F070 ✱Llandovery

A483

A438

HEREFORDSHIRE

FP141

A40

● F009
✱Brecon

Haverfordwest✱

A40

Carmarthen
F106 ✱
F074 ✱
● F049

A48
S462 ☐

A477

✱Pembroke

M410 ◆

M428 ◆

BLAENAU
GWENT

MONMOUTHSHIRE

MR319 ◆

F081 ●
MR273 ◆
MR2◆

NEATH PORT
TALBOT
RHONDDA
CYNON TAFF

F030 ●

FP159
F006

Swansea✱

F027 ●
● FB189

M42

CAERPHILLY

TT549

BRIDGEND

A470

Newport✱

M394

M4

M417 ◆
MR294 ◆

FB227 ☐
M346 ◆

F004 ◆
✱Cardiff

M345 ◆

T5
FB232 ☐
F0

M368 ●

FP155 ●

Brist

VALE OF GLAMORGAN

Weston-Super-Mare✱ L256 ◆

A38

M418 ◆
● F038

0
25
50 miles

0
40
80 kms

Roads displayed are for guidance for guidance only and should not be used for navigation

● Filling Stations (Fxxx)
● Filling Stations plus (FPxxx)
● Fuel Bunkers (FBxxx)
● Fuel Bunkers Plus (FBPxxx)
◆ Lorry Parks (Lxxx)
◆ Main Road Services (MRxxx)

◆ Motorway Services (Mxxx)
■ Pub/hotel/truck stop (Pxxx)
■ Snack Vans plus (Sxxx)
☐ Transport cafés/snack van (TCxxx)
■ Truck stops (Txxx)
☐ Truck stops/transport cafés (TTxxx)

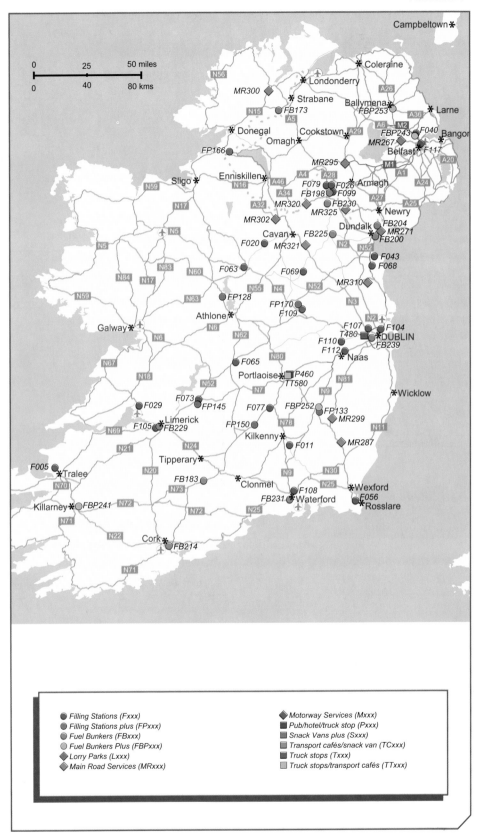

Campbeltown ✳

✳ Coleraine

0 25 50 miles
0 40 80 kms

N56

MR300 ◆

✳ Londonderry
✳ Strabane
FB173 ●

Ballymena ✳
FBP253

✳ Larne

N15

A5

A26

A36

✳ Donegal
Omagh ✳

Cookstown ✳

A29

A6 M2
FBP243
MR267 ◆

F040 ●
✳ Bangor

FP166 ●

MR295 ◆

Belfast ✳ ● F117

A20

M1

Sligo ✳

Enniskillen ✳

A4 A28

A1

N59

N16

A46

F079 ● F026 ●
FB198 ● F099 ●

✳ Armagh

A24

N17

A34

A32 MR320 ◆

FB230 ●

A27

N5

MR302 ◆

MR325 ◆

✳ Newry
FB204 ●

A25

N5

Cavan ✳

FB225 ●

Dundalk ✳
MR271 ◆
FB200 ●

N83

N60

F020 ●

MR321 ◆

N2

N52

N84

N17

F063 ●

F069 ●

F043 ●
F068 ●

N59

N55

N4

MR310 ◆

N63

FP128 ●

N52

N3

Athlone ✳

FP170 ●
F109 ●

N2

Galway ✳

N6

F107 ● F104 ●
T480 ■
F110 ●
F112 ●

✳ DUBLIN
FB239 ●

N67

N6

F065 ●

N80

✳ Naas

N18

N52

Portlaoise ✳ ■ P460
TT580

N81

N7

✳ Wicklow

F029 ●
F073 ●
FP145 ●

N9

Limerick ✳
F105 ● FB229 ●

F077 ●

FBP252 ●
FP133 ●
MR299 ◆

N69

FP150 ●

N78

N11

N21

N24

Kilkenny ✳

F011 ●

MR287 ◆

Tipperary ✳

N20

FB183 ●

N30

F005 ●
✳ Tralee

N73

Clonmel ✳

N25

✳ Wexford
F056 ●

N70

N9

F108 ●
FB231 ● Waterford ✳

✳ Rosslare

Killarney ✳ ● FBP241

N72

N26

N71

N22

Cork ✳
● FB214

N71

● Filling Stations (Fxxx)
● Filling Stations plus (FPxxx)
● Fuel Bunkers (FBxxx)
● Fuel Bunkers Plus (FBPxxx)
◆ Lorry Parks (Lxxx)
◆ Main Road Services (MRxxx)

◆ Motorway Services (Mxxx)
■ Pub/hotel/truck stop (Pxxx)
■ Snack Vans plus (Sxxx)
■ Transport cafés/snack van (TCxxx)
■ Truck stops (Txxx)
□ Truck stops/transport cafés (TTxxx)

Acknowledgements

The publishers would like to thank the following people for their help and support with this publication:

Helen Richmond and Rob Last from Future Publishing (*Trucking* magazine).

Chris Love, Andy Kelly and Sarah Tennent from Scania UK.

AUTHOR ACKNOWLEDGEMENTS

- Sanjiv Patel (I.T. financial and emotional support)
- Jean Melbourne (for everything)
- Paddy Searle (for his fantastic jokes and proof reading skills)
- Mr & Mrs Patel (for feeding me and fixing my errant computer)
- Colin Turner (for his help in dire need)
- Colin Barge at VBG (for his help with the section on coupling/uncoupling a rigid and drawbar trailer)
- Wendy Glindon (for keeping me laughing and providing many useful listings.)
- Simon Harrison (for bringing life to my terrible sketches)
- John Kilpatrick, Mark Finch and Mark Neilson at Pertemps Bristol, Walsall and everywhere!
- Drivers On Call, Parcelforce and Manpower (for keeping me in gainful employment)
- Pro-active, Wolverhampton (for making sense of the working time directive)
- Kevin Smith (for advice on additional qualifications)
- Arthur at Catalyst (for many listings and advice)
- Marie at St Johns Ambulance HQ (for permission to use first aid information)
- Poundland, James Irlam, HW Plastics, Parcelforce British Bakeries, Apetito, and the drivers and truck manufactures at Truckfest South West 2005 (for letting me take pictures of their lorries, and equipment.)
- All my translators Katie, Janka, Jean and Stephane Allier and Peter Sinai.
- Ian, Tony and all at Parcelforce Coventry for their various contributions.
- Croner's Road Transport Operation (for help with regards to driving hours regulations)
- Richard Thackham and Volvo Trucks for additional photography
- Ben for modelling
- All at Haynes Publishing (for their patience and hard work!)
- All sites who took the time and made the effort in order to be included in this publication and every person (you know who you are) who has helped me in some way to make this book a reality.

I thank you from the bottom of my steel toe-cap boots!

Author:	Lisa Marie Melbourne
Project Manager:	Louise McIntyre
Data development and page build:	James Robertson
Design:	Lee Parsons
Illustrations:	Matthew Marke
Copy editor:	Ian Heath
Maps:	Customised Mapping

TROWBRIDGE
LEARNING CENTRE